Green planet blues

J   D1627181

"As a professor   ...out Conca
and Dabelko's *Green Planet Blues*. This edition builds gracefully from the must-
read classics of the 1970s to today's need-to-know issues—such as globalization,
the WTO, and the role of local and global civil society. Using a political economy
lens to bring to   ve assembled
a spectacular v

DATE DUE

Brodart Co.   Cat. # 55 137 001   Printed in USA

"This is the bes   environmental politics. The   ces that capture all of the k   ng field. The
fourth edition   ditors' finely
honed skills in

       Scho   *ne*

"The fourth ed   ew of global
environmental   it. This up-
to-date revised   interested in
environmental   tudents and
teachers in this

       —*As*   *it,*

"*Green Planet E*   *ental politics*
reader. It prese   thinking on
critical issues i   , justice, security, and sust   e, and it remains an invalu   vironmental
politics. It is no   trong representation of voi   ally minded
students everyw

—*Jon Barnett, Associate Professor, University of Melbourne*

"In this updated edition of their classic textbook, Conca and Dabelko have produced a volume that stimulates and challenges. The diverse views represented in the volume challenge orthodox thinking, making for stimulating reading and class discussion. Where other volumes often present a consolidated view of the dominant thinking (or at least the dominant view in the U.S.), this volume provides readers with a much broader view of the perspectives of individuals and institutions shaping the dynamic of global environmental politics. The fourth edition reflects recent trends and new knowledge, notably in globalization and peacebuilding as well as more broadly. It is essential reading to understanding the dynamics shaping international environmental law and institutions now and in the foreseeable future."

—*Carl Bruch, Senior Attorney and*
Codirector of International Programs, Environmental Law Institute

GREEN PLANET BLUES

A project of the Harrison Program on
The Future Global Agenda, University of Maryland

GREEN
PLANET
BLUES

FOUR DECADES OF
GLOBAL ENVIRONMENTAL POLITICS

Fourth Edition

KEN CONCA AND
GEOFFREY D. DABELKO, EDITORS

**WESTVIEW
PRESS**
A Member of the Perseus Books Group

Westview Press books are available at special discounts for bulk purchases in the United States by corporations, institutions, and other organizations. For more information, please contact the Special Markets Department at the Perseus Books Group, 2300 Chestnut Street, Suite 200, Philadelphia, PA 19103, or call (800) 810-4145, ext. 5000, or e-mail special.markets@perseusbooks.com.

Library of Congress Cataloging-in-Publication Data

Green planet blues : four decades of global environmental politics / Ken Conca And Geoffrey D. Dabelko, editors. — 4th ed.
    p. cm.
  Includes bibliographical references and index.
  ISBN 978-0-8133-4411-9 (alk. paper)
  1. Environmental policy—Political aspects. 2. Sustainable development. 3. Green movement.
I. Conca, Ken. II. Dabelko, Geoffrey D.
  HC79.E5G6916 2010
  363.7—dc22

                                                                    2009038745

10 9 8 7 6 5 4 3 2 1

CONTENTS

PART THREE
INSTITUTIONS OF GLOBAL
ENVIRONMENTAL GOVERNANCE 117

PART FOUR
THE SUSTAINABILITY DEBATE 199

PART FIVE
FROM ECOLOGICAL CONFLICT
TO ENVIRONMENTAL SECURITY? 247

PART SIX
ECOLOGICAL JUSTICE 307

PREFACE

This book originated as a project of the University of Maryland's Harrison Program on the Future Global Agenda. We are grateful to Horace Harrison for making the program possible, to then-director Dennis Pirages for supporting the idea, and to Michael Alberty for his help as coeditor on the first edition. We also appreciate the support of the Woodrow Wilson International Center for Scholars and its Environmental Change and Security Program. For their help, advice, and support as we prepared this and previous editions, we thank Liliana Andonova, Jon Barnett, Michele Betsill, Steve Catalano, Beth Chalecki, Elizabeth DeSombre, Shannon Green, Peter Jacques, Sara Kamins, Elisabeth Malzahn, Kay Mariea, John M. Meyer, Ronald Mitchell, Adil Najam, Kate O'Neill, Rodger Payne, Rodrigo Pinto, Dennis Pirages, Kurt Rakouskas, Armin Rosencranz, Antoinette Smith, Jennifer Swearingen, Marietta Urban, Stacy VanDeveer, Toby Wahl, Greg White, and Sarah Wilton. We are also grateful to several anonymous respondents to the student and faculty surveys we distributed to collect feedback on previous editions.

As with past editions, we have updated the text to take account of several new developments. In this fourth edition we have added new material on the environment and globalization; transnational activist networks; the United Nations and institutional reform of global environmental governance; the "greening" of bilateral development assistance; trade and the environment; the ecological footprint of high-consuming society; environment, conflict, and peacebuilding; environment, poverty, and social justice; and the links between climate change and human rights. In doing so, we have had to say goodbye to some staples of earlier editions, which feels much like parting with old friends. Readers are encouraged to refer to older editions of the book for material that remains insightful and useful. As always, we have tried to remain true to the book's original goals of discussing cross-cutting issues of power and authority, juxtaposing different environmental paradigms, and presenting a diversity of voices.

At the end of the introduction to each part, we have included a list of questions that we have found useful in stimulating critical thought, discussion, and learning. We have also added substantially to the book's open-access Web site at www.bsos.umd.edu/harrison. There, readers will find background information on the authors and organizations represented in this book, suggested additional readings and resources, critical-thinking exercises, steps that readers may take if they wish to get involved in campaigns for the planet and its people, and links to a wide array of useful sites and resources.

Because some of the selections presented in this volume are excerpts from longer works, a brief explanation of our editing philosophy is in order. In those cases where space limitations precluded reprinting an entire essay, our goal has been to edit in such a way as to emphasize the underlying ideas and concepts. In many cases, this has meant leaving out complex elaborations, trenchant asides, or supporting examples. We have preserved the original notes corresponding to the material reproduced here but left out notes corresponding to passages of text not included. For one essay (Lélé) containing a large number of in-line citations in the original, we have preserved the factual citations but removed several of the more general references to enhance readability and conserve space. Readers seeking further background, greater detail, or additional references should consult the original material.

See www.bsos.umd.edu/harrison for supporting material.

INTRODUCTION: FOUR DECADES OF GLOBAL ENVIRONMENTAL POLITICS

KEN CONCA AND
GEOFFREY D. DABELKO

Think globally, act locally. Spaceship Earth. The common heritage of humanity. Pollution does not respect national borders. The Earth is one, but the world is not. We have not inherited the Earth from our parents; we have borrowed it from our children. The global commons.

Each of these well-known phrases invokes similar themes: the interconnectedness of the global environment; the close ties between environmental quality and human well-being; and the common fate that these realities impose upon all of the planet's occupants, present and future. We live, as we have for some time, in an era of global environmental politics.

Pollution, ecosystem destruction, and natural resource depletion are not new problems. Many regions and localities were grappling with these issues long before the industrial revolution or even the emergence of the modern system of nation-states. And just as environmental problems have a long-standing history, so do the political struggles that inevitably accompany those problems. Thus, severe shortages of wood led to conservation efforts in Babylonia during the time of Hammurabi.[1] Measures to protect wetlands in recognition of their importance as sources of fish, game, and fuel have been traced to the sixth century AD in the Huang-Huai-Hai Plain of northeastern China.[2] Air-quality crises in London during the early stages of the industrial revolution led to the formation of smoke-abatement societies advocating legislative action.[3] One can easily imagine the political controversies that must have engulfed each of these episodes, given that these measures protecting environmental quality or altering access to natural resources would have offended powerful interests.

Today, the dramas of environmental politics are increasingly played out on a global stage. It is generally agreed that human transformation of the environment is a global-scale problem.[4] In some cases this is because the system under stress is globally interconnected in a physical sense, as in the case of the Earth's climate, the oceans, or the atmosphere's protective ozone layer. In other cases, accumulated local events produce consequences of global significance, as in the depletion of the world's fisheries or the reduction of the planet's biological diversity.

People increasingly speak of global environmental problems. But what do we mean when we speak of global environmental politics? To answer this question, consider what people see when they look at a forest. Some see a stock of timber to be exploited for economic gain. Others see a complex ecological system that holds the soil in place, stabilizes the local water cycle, moderates the local climate, and fosters biological diversity. Still others see the forest as a home for people and other living things, a site to engage in cultural practices, or perhaps an ancestral burial ground. Finally, some see the forest as a powerful cultural symbol on broader scales: The forest as a dynamic living system reflects the potential harmony between humanity and nature and provides a link between the past and the future. Playing out the differences in these visions of the forest—whether that means trying to reconcile them, seeking a delicate balance among them, or fighting to make one preeminent—is the stuff of politics, by any definition of the term.

We live in a world that is at once fragmented by the political division into sovereign states and reassembled by pervasive flows of people, goods, money, ideas, images, and technology across borders. In such a world, conflicting visions of the forest take on international significance. Some see in the forest an important source of international economic power, giving those who control it influence in international markets and a reliable source of foreign exchange. Others see it as a powerful symbol of global interdependence: The forest reflects the global consequences of local acts in that its destruction may alter the global climate or deplete the global stock of biological diversity. Still others see a very different sort of international symbol: The forest represents national sovereignty in that it confirms a nation's right to do as it sees fit within its territory. Such rights may seem luxuries that a crowded planet cannot afford. But this is not often the view of people who feel their sovereign rights immediately threatened—particularly if those rights were won in a struggle for independence that forged their very nation.

Often these competing visions reflect different interests held by individuals, groups, and perhaps even entire nations. They are also a product, however, of the structures that govern world politics. The institution of national sovereignty, the division of labor in the capitalist world economy, the rise of transnational networks of environmentalists, the predominance of powerful beliefs about the links between consumption and "progress"—all of these underlying features of contemporary world politics shape what people see when they look at the forest.

Competing visions, values, and interests often lead to conflict. Actors disagree about the nature of the problem, the effectiveness or fairness of proposed solutions, and the appropriate location of responsibility. Thus, studying global environmental politics means understanding the conflicts of interest that surround environmental issues—but also asking how interests, values, and visions related to the environment are shaped.

The study of global environmental politics also involves the search for cooperative solutions to ecological dilemmas. The idea that global environmental problems require "international cooperation" is widely accepted, but the appropriate scope and content of such cooperation are hotly contested. Does international cooperation mean formal, treaty-based agreements among governments? Does it mean a broader "global bargain" between North and South, linking a number of issues in a single package? Or does it refer to a still broader process of global dialogue not limited to governments, in which different societies move toward a global convergence of values? Does an increasingly global network of environmental organizations represent an effective new form of international cooperation, or is it simply one more way in which the strong impose their will upon the weak? Is the goal of international cooperation to create an increasingly dense web of transnational linkages, one that binds nations to a common future and a common commitment to environmental protection? Or should we be agreeing instead to begin delinking an ever more tightly coupled, "globalizing" world system, so that various localities and regions have more flexibility to pursue responses appropriate to their unique circumstances?

Finally, an important dimension of the study of global environmental politics is connecting the patterns of international conflict and cooperation we see over the environment to some of the larger changes under way in world politics. If studying the structure of world politics gives us insight into the character of global environmental problems, the reverse is also true. It is no surprise that as the world has tumbled into the twenty-first century, environmental problems have emerged as a critical theme in the study of international relations and world politics. At a time when much conventional wisdom in international relations is being challenged, studying the politics of the global environment may also give us greater insight into the emerging patterns of world politics as a whole.

From Stockholm to
Johannesburg—and Beyond

Three global summit meetings—the 1972 UN Conference on the Human Environment, held in Stockholm, Sweden; the 1992 UN Conference on Environment and Development, held in Rio de Janeiro, Brazil (known popularly as the Earth Summit); and the 2002 World Summit on Sustainable Development, held in Johannesburg, South Africa—provide useful benchmarks for the evolution of global environmental politics.[5] The contrasts among these three events reflect many underlying changes in the world during the intervening three decades.

One important shift is that of international political context. The first global environmental summit, in Stockholm, occurred in the shadow of the Cold War. The governments of Eastern Europe and the Soviet Union boycotted the conference after a dispute over the representation of a then-divided Germany. Two decades later, the Rio summit took place in the relatively optimistic afterglow of the end of the Cold War, amid a general sense of new opportunities for global cooperation. A decade later in Johannesburg, much of that optimism had faded in the light of globalization controversies; increasingly muscular American unilateralism; the gritty reality of enduring global political, economic, and cultural conflicts; and the shocking events of September 11, 2001.

A second clear change from Stockholm 1972 to Johannesburg 2002 was the emergence of global public awareness and concern. The Stockholm conference took place in the wake of the first Earth Day (1970) and at a time of rising popular concern in the United States and Europe about environmental problems, particularly air and water pollution. Many of the participants at Stockholm—particularly those from the North—framed environmental problems as the by-products of an affluent, industrialized lifestyle. The implication was that the poorer regions of the world did not suffer as much from environmental problems as did the wealthy, nor (it was said) did they exhibit the same level of concern about such problems. By the time of the Rio conference, however, the notion that there is both a "pollution of affluence" *and* a "pollution of poverty" had gained much broader acceptance. As the environmental causes of poverty became clearer, what many of those suffering from poverty have presumably known all along became more generally understood: Environmental concerns were not the exclusive property of affluent people or industrialized countries, hence Rio's linkage between environment and development. By the time of the Johannesburg summit, known in UN circles as "Rio plus ten," development issues had become central to the discussion—so much so that some environmental advocates felt the environmental agenda was being largely ignored, and referred to the event ruefully as "Rio minus ten."

A third important trend over these decades was the tremendous growth in the scientific understanding of environmental problems. Stockholm focused attention principally on relatively narrowly defined problems of air and water pollution, whereas Rio embraced a far broader and more complex agenda. This shift reflected in part a changing scientific paradigm—one that views the Earth as a single integrated system with complex links among the large-scale ecological systems of land, oceans, atmosphere, and biosphere.[6] The discussion at Rio, especially Agenda 21, an ambitious eight-hundred-page blueprint for sustainable development in the twenty-first century, also reflected scientists' greater capacity to measure, monitor, and model complex processes of environmental change.[7] Yet the growth of scientific knowledge is never immune to political context; as delegates gathered in Johannesburg just one year after the destruction of the World Trade Center on 9/11, the continued commitment of governments to open information flows and exchange of environmental data could not be taken for granted in light of fears about "environmental terrorism."

Governments and other actors gathering to discuss global environmental problems themselves underwent notable changes in the decades since the Stockholm conference. Almost none of the governments gathered in Stockholm had any form of national environmental bureaucracy; two decades later in Rio, virtually all did. In many cases, these agencies enabled governments to take advantage of the growth of environmental knowledge so as to analyze more effectively the causes and consequences of environmental problems. In some cases, these agencies had evolved into advocates for various environmental protection programs, producing more complex internal debates within national delegations. By the time of the Johannesburg summit in 2002, environmental considerations had also been mainstreamed in the rhetoric and policy guidelines—if not always the practice—of intergovernmental organizations, such as the World Bank, the International Monetary Fund, and the World Trade Organization, and the development assistance practices of donor countries (see Part Three of this volume).

Nongovernmental organizations also underwent substantial change. During the Stockholm conference, 134 NGOs, virtually all from the industrialized world, were officially accredited participants. Two decades later, more than 1,400 NGOs were officially participating in the Rio summit, with about one-third of these groups from the global South—and countless more unofficial participants.[8] Over time, international networking and coalition building among environmental groups have become much more common.[9]

A final measure of the changes from Stockholm to Johannesburg is the growth in the number of international environmental treaties, agreements, and cooperative accords. By some estimates there are now more than 1,000 international environmental agreements in place. Many of these are relatively narrow in scope: agreements between two neighboring countries on specific environmental problems or regional agreements involving small numbers of countries and narrow agendas. But the list also includes several major international accords adopted since the Stockholm conference, including agreements on ocean pollution, acid rain, preservation of the ozone layer, the international trade in endangered species, and environmental protection in Antarctica. The designers of international accords at Rio had a much broader set of examples upon which to draw than did their predecessors at Stockholm; as a result, they also had at least a crude understanding of what makes various approaches to international environmental cooperation effective.[10] Between Rio and Johannesburg, some important new international agreements were reached, such as the Cartagena Protocol on Biosafety and the Stockholm Convention on Persistent Organic Pollutants. By the time of the Johannesburg summit, however, the tenuous compromise of the 1997 Kyoto Protocol to the Framework Convention on Climate Change had come unraveled with the U.S. decision to withdraw from the agreement, casting a pall over the prospects for ambitious multilateral environmental diplomacy.

It is equally important to stress what has not changed in the nearly four decades since the 1972 Stockholm conference. Many of the stumbling blocks to effective global response seen at Stockholm were also in full evidence at the subsequent gatherings, and remain with us today. These include the tremendous mistrust and suspicion governing relations between North and South in world politics; the tenacious embrace of traditional conceptions of national sovereignty by governments, even as they acknowledge the need for coordinated global responses to problems that do not respect borders; and the tensions between the long-term vision necessary for ecologically sane planning and the short-term concern for economic growth and political stability that preoccupies most governments.

Perhaps the most important continuity is that global environmental change has continued at an alarming rate. Between 1970 and 2000, global commercial energy consumption, a major source of environmental impacts, roughly doubled; other global indicators of human impact on the environment, including food production, water use, overall economic activity, and population, increased in roughly similar proportions. To be sure, these very crude indicators of human stress on environmental systems can mask as much as they reveal. They say nothing about how underlying activities actually affect the environment, about who or what may be responsible, or who suffers the consequences most directly and immediately. But they do indicate the scale of the problem and the enormity of the challenge of reorienting fundamental practices that drive growth, production, consumption, and environmental transformation in the current world system.

This mixed picture of continuity and change raises an obvious question: Compared to where things stood at the Stockholm conference, where do we stand as we look to the future? Many environmental advocates were dismayed with the 2002 Johannesburg summit. Whereas Rio had produced multilateral treaties on climate and biodiversity and the ambitious goals embodied in Agenda 21, Johannesburg focused instead on the lag in implementing these commitments; although many welcomed the focus on implementation, the meeting produced little in the way of tangible products or specific targets and timetables for action.

Does the period since Stockholm tell an optimistic story of global society moving to meet the challenges of ecological interdependence, or do those years chronicle an unwillingness or inability to grapple with the root causes of the problem? Perhaps both are true. Growing knowledge and awareness, organizational adjustments, and occasional substantive breakthroughs over the past four decades may reveal important possibilities for change, learning, and effective global cooperation. At the same time, enduring divisions and the far less optimistic tenor of Johannesburg when compared to Rio served to underscore the depth of the political challenge posed by global environmental problems.

Conflicting Views of the Environmental Problematique

Growing scientific understanding and shared levels of public concern do not automatically translate into a shared understanding of the social causes of environmental problems. One of the first challenges facing students of global environmental politics is to sort out a potentially bewildering debate on the causes of pollution and environmental degradation. Some of this uncertainty lies in the realm of science. The physical, chemical, and biological mechanisms involved in processes such as climate change, desertification, and deforestation are sometimes quite poorly understood by leading experts, to say nothing of citizens, policymakers, or interest groups. For example, the global interaction of oceans, atmosphere, land, and biosphere has only recently become a central concern of such disciplines as oceanography, atmospheric science, and terrestrial ecology, causing a growing number of scholars to rethink traditional disciplinary boundaries in these fields. Although knowledge is expanding rapidly on many fronts, scientific uncertainty remains substantial in the face of the complex processes of environmental change.

These aspects of technical complexity are matched by similar controversies, debates, and uncertainties surrounding the social dimensions of environmental change. In explaining why human populations have had such a substantial impact on planetary ecosystems, different analysts invoke factors as diverse as values, technology, culture, ideology, public policy, demographic change, and the social structures of class, race, or gender. Some observers elevate one or a few of these factors to the role of central cause, treating the others as mere symptoms. Others have sought to develop more complex models that stress the interaction of these various forces and processes.

Many see the problem as essentially one of values—in particular, the value that modern societies attach to consumption. Alan Durning has asserted that

> the soaring consumption lines that track the rise of the consumer society are, from another perspective, surging indicators of environmental harm. The consumer society's exploitation of resources threatens to exhaust, poison, or unalterably disfigure forests, soils, water, and air. We, its members, are responsible for a disproportionate share of all the global environmental challenges facing humanity.[11]

Our consumer culture translates wants into needs, stresses material-intensive forms of social gratification, and overwhelms older, more ecologically sustainable traditions that stand in its way. As consumerism spreads through increasingly sophisticated advertising, pop culture, and the global media, more and more regions of the planet adopt the aspirations of the consumer society.[12]

Technology is another commonly cited culprit. Barry Commoner, a key figure in raising public awareness about environmental problems in the United States in the 1960s and 1970s through such widely read books as *Making Peace with the Planet* and *The Closing Circle*, used the simple example of the production of beer bottles in the United States to illustrate the technological dimension.[13] Writing in the mid-1970s, Commoner investigated the impact of three factors commonly cited as causes of environmental problems—population growth, rising levels of consumption per capita, and technological change. He found that the number of beer bottles produced in America increased by a dramatic 593 percent from 1950 to 1967, even though the population grew by only 30 percent and beer consumption by only 5 percent per capita. Clearly, a technological change—the replacement of reusable beer kegs and returnable bottles with single-use, throwaway bottles—led to the bulk of the increase, and hence, to the bulk of the environmental impact in terms of energy use, trash, and so on. Commoner argued that similar technological changes at work across most of the key sectors of modern society were at the heart of the environmental crisis. The surge in popularity of sport-utility vehicles in the United States and elsewhere in the 1990s provides a more recent example of this process.

Some observers argue that prevailing technologies and values are expressions of underlying power dynamics in society. For example, "social ecologists" such as Murray Bookchin—though not necessarily disagreeing with Durning's assessment of the consumer society or Commoner's cautions about technology—have stressed the importance of social inequality. Bookchin warned against attributing environmental problems to such vague and impersonal formulations as "values," "technology," and "humanity." Such reasoning "serves to deflect our attention from the role society plays in producing ecological breakdown."[14] According to Bookchin,

> a mythic "Humanity" is created—irrespective of whether we are talking about oppressed ethnic minorities, women, Third World people, or people in the First World—in which everyone is brought into complicity with powerful corporate elites in producing environmental dislocations. In this way, the social roots of ecological problems are shrewdly obscured. A new kind of biological "original sin" is created in which a vague group of animals called "Humanity" is turned into a destructive force that threatens the survival of the living world.[15]

According to Bookchin, the key to understanding lies instead in seeing how social inequality feeds environmental degradation and resource overexploitation. In this view, societies constructed upon hierarchies of race, class, and gender are fundamentally based on exploitation and thus have an inherent tendency to seek domination over nature rather than a means of living in harmony with it, just as they promote the domination of some people by others.[16]

Vandana Shiva, who has written extensively about forestry issues in postcolonial India, provides a model aimed at linking diverse causal forces such as technology, values, and social structure.[17] For Shiva, history is key: Technological and demographic change, hierarchical patterns of social structure, and consumption-oriented values are co-evolutionary products of Indian society's dominant historical experience—the political, economic, and social transformations brought about by more than a century of British colonial rule. Thus, in her view, "causes" of environmental degradation in India as diverse as the industrial revolution, the capitalist world economy, and the destructive power of modern science and technology are "the philosophical, technological, and economic components of the same process."[18]

Sorting out this diverse array of claims about social causes of environmental change requires carefully detailed, historical study of the ways in which economic, social, and political institutions in society co-evolve over time.[19] Many of the selections in this volume present models of the causes of environmental problems, at varying levels of detail and complexity. It will become apparent to the reader that these various causal claims are based on very different understandings of the sources of power, interest, authority, and legitimacy in society. Sorting out such diverse claims does not guarantee that effective policies and institutions will be designed. Actors may agree on the causes of a problem but still disagree on the appropriate responses; they may see their interests affected differently or hold different views about the fairness or effectiveness of a particular response. But grappling with the complex array of causes does seem to be a necessary preliminary step if appropriate responses are to be crafted. Perhaps just as important, examining the diversity of claims also helps us to understand the equally diverse beliefs about history, justice, and responsibility that various actors bring to the debate.

Global Environmental Politics:
Power, Ideas, and Voices

The material in this book has been selected with three goals in mind. One goal has been to pay particular attention to underlying questions of power, interest, authority, and legitimacy that shape global environmental debates. The challenge of the global environment is often framed as a largely technical and administrative task of promoting policy coordination among governments. Clearly, rational policies and effective intergovernmental cooperation will be a crucial part of any meaningful response to the challenge. But a narrow focus on governments, treaties, and public policies can blur our understanding of some of the deeper components of the problematique. The environmental problems facing the global community raise deeper questions of governmental authority, of the relationship between the state and society, and of processes of economic and cultural globalization that challenge state sovereignty and the autonomy of local communities.

Second, we have tried to emphasize the *ideas* that have most powerfully shaped the evolving debate over the global environment. By assembling under one cover some of the most influential voices in the debate, we hope to provide a firsthand sense of how ideas have shaped action, while at the same time stressing the obstacles to changing the world through new ideas alone. Thus we examine some of the most powerful paradigms that prevailed at the time of the Stockholm conference and the controversies engendered by those views. We also explore the powerful and controversial new paradigms that have emerged, in the years since the Stockholm conference, around themes of sustainability, environmental security, and ecological justice. Comparing these sets of ideas over time reveals how people's thinking has changed as it highlights enduring themes.

Our third goal has been to present a broad range of voices in what is and must be a *global* debate. This goal might appear to conflict with our previously stated intention of presenting the most powerful and influential ideas: One might be tempted by a sense of urgency to try to narrow the debate to what the most powerful voices consider feasible or desirable (much as some governments have tried to woo a reluctant United States to participate in the global climate regime). In our view, any such narrowing of the debate on the grounds of political expediency would be deeply troubling on moral grounds, given the stakes involved for people, their livelihoods, their health, and all forms of life on the planet. It also strikes us as potentially disastrous—not expedient at all—given the current lack of global consensus on so many fundamental issues. The poor and powerless might lack the ability to shape the ecological future they desire, but they might well have the power to veto proposed "solutions" that ignore their needs and interests. Although universal agreement is a utopia difficult even to imagine, durable responses to global environmental problems can be achieved only through a broad social consensus. Thus we have chosen essays for this book with the intent of including perspectives from the South as well as the North, and with voices that are rural as well as urban, female as well as male, and critical of existing institutions as well as broadly comfortable working within them.

The book's organization is meant to serve these goals. We begin in Part One with a discussion of the dominant paradigms and controversies that shaped debate at the time of the Stockholm conference and during the conference itself. The views and debates that prevailed in that era provide a useful reference point for measuring what has changed since then. Part One focuses in particular on three provocative and influential ideas of that era: first, the notion that there are inherent "limits to growth" on a planet of finite natural resources and limited ecological resilience; second, the claim that where nature is concerned, self-interested individual behavior often adds up to a collective "tragedy of the commons"; and third, the idea that environmental threats increasingly demand controlling, perhaps even authoritarian, responses.

In Part Two we examine how the structure of the international system shapes the types of problems we face and the types of solutions we can imagine. The discussion focuses on the roles of national sovereignty, transnational capitalism, and the myriad manifestations of "globalization" in shaping political and economic institutions, patterns of environmental harm, and the possibilities for political responses. Part Two also examines environmentalism as a global social movement, investigating whether we might be seeing the emergence of different forms of political authority that challenge these dominant aspects of system structure.

Part Three examines the challenges of international cooperation and institutional reform. Here we provide the reader with a tour of several of the most important sites in which global environmental governance occurs: through multilateral environmental agreements among governments, in the institutionalized practices of international trade and development assistance, in the organizational structure of the United Nations, in more fluid and emergent approaches such as so-called multistakeholder initiatives, and in modern understandings of science and its limits.

The volume concludes with three powerful and controversial paradigms that have crystallized and given form to the debates in the period since the Stockholm conference: sustainability (Part Four), environmental security (Part Five), and ecological justice (Part Six). For some observers, these three paradigms are complementary and potentially harmonious facets of a single vision for the planet and its people. Others see tensions and contradictions inherent in the simultaneous pursuit of development, security, and justice in world affairs. Convergent or not, they are likely to remain the conceptual building blocks for environmental initiatives of the future.

In compiling this material, we have deliberately avoided organizing the book around a conventional list of environmental "issue areas" (climate change, deforestation, toxics, acid rain, and so on) or generic types of environmental problems, such as transboundary pollution flows or problems of the global commons. To be sure, these are useful ways to organize one's thinking about complex, multidimensional problems. However, by focusing on crosscutting themes of power, authority, and responsibility, we hope this book will provide a useful complement to these other approaches, which are already well represented in the literature.

Notes

1. John Perlin, *A Forest Journey: The Role of Wood in the Development of Civilization* (Cambridge, MA: Harvard University Press, 1991), p. 46.

2. Zoo Daqing and Zhang Peiyuan, "The Huang-Huai-Hai Plain," in B. L. Turner II, William C. Clark, Robert W. Kates, John F. Richards, Jessica T. Mathews, and William B. Meyer, eds., *The Earth as Transformed by Human Action* (New York: Cambridge University Press, 1990).

3. Peter Brimblecombe, *The Big Smoke: A History of Air Pollution in London since Medieval Times* (London: Methuen, 1987).

4. United Nations Environment Programme, *Global Environmental Outlook 4* (Nairobi: UNEP, 2007). See also Turner et al., *The Earth as Transformed by Human Action.*

5. For an overview of the Stockholm conference, see Lynton Caldwell, *International Environmental Policy*, 3rd ed. (Durham, NC: Duke University Press, 1996). On Rio, see Peter M. Haas, Marc A. Levy, and Edward A. Parson, "Appraising the Earth Summit: How Should We Judge UNCED's Success?" *Environment* 34, no. 8 (1992): 6–11 and 26–33; Michael Grubb, Matthias Koch, Abby Munson, Francis Sullivan, and Koy Thomson, *The Earth Summit Agreements: A Guide and Assessment* (London: Earthscan Publications, 1993); Pratap Chatterjee and Matthias Finger, *The Earth Brokers: Power, Politics and World Development* (London: Routledge, 1994). On Johannesburg, see James Gustav Speth, "Perspective on the Johannesburg Summit," *Environment* 45, no. 1 (January/February 2003): 24–29.

6. For a statement of this new vision around the time of the Rio Earth Summit, see U.S. National Academy of Sciences, *One Earth, One Future: Our Changing Global Environment* (Washington, DC: National Academy Press, 1990), especially pp. 15–19.

7. On the growth of scientific knowledge about the environment from Stockholm to Rio, see Mostafa K. Tolba, Osama A. El-Kholy, E. El-Hinnawi, M. W. Holdgate, D. F. McMichael, and R. E. Munn, *The World Environment, 1972–1992: Two Decades of Challenge* (London: Chapman & Hall, 1992), chapter 20.

8. Haas, Levy, and Parson, "Appraising the Earth Summit."

9. On international coalitions and networking, see the contribution of Kothari in Part Two; see also Margaret Keck and Katherine Sikkink, *Activists Beyond Borders: Advocacy Networks and International Politics* (New York: Cornell University Press, 1998); Sanjeev Khagram, James V. Riker, and Kathryn Sikkink, eds., *Restructuring World Politics: Transnational Social Movements, Networks and Norms* (Minneapolis: University of Minnesota Press, 2002); and Sanjeev Khagram, *Dams and Development: Transnational Struggles for Water and Power* (Ithaca, NY: Cornell University Press, 2004).

10. On the effectiveness of international environmental regimes, see Oran R. Young, ed., *The Effectiveness of International Environmental Regimes* (Cambridge, MA: MIT Press, 1999); Edward L. Miles, Arild Underdal, Steiner Andresen, Jørgen Wettestad, and Jon Birger Skjærseth, *Environmental Regime Effectiveness: Confronting Theory with Evidence* (Cambridge, MA: MIT Press, 2001).

11. Alan Durning, *How Much Is Enough? The Consumer Society and the Future of the Earth* (New York: W. W. Norton, 1992), p. 23.

12. See Thomas Princen, Michael Maniates, and Ken Conca, *Confronting Consumption* (Cambridge, MA: MIT Press, 2002).

13. Barry Commoner, *Making Peace with the Planet*, 5th ed. (New York: New Press, 1992), pp. 148–150.

14. Murray Bookchin, *Remaking Society: Pathways to a Green Future* (Boston: South End Press, 1990), p. 9.

15. Ibid., pp. 9–10.

16. This theme is central to much of the literature on ecological justice; see Part Six of this book.

17. Vandana Shiva, "People's Ecology: The Chipko Movement," in Saul Mendlovitz and R. B. J. Walker, eds., *Towards a Just World Peace* (London: Butterworths, 1987). See also Vandana Shiva, *Ecology and the Politics of Survival: Conflicts over Natural Resources in India* (Newbury Park, CA: Sage, 1991); and Ramachandra Guha, *The Unquiet Woods: Ecological Change and Peasant Resistance in the Himalayas* (Berkeley: University of California Press, 1989).

18. Shiva, "People's Ecology," p. 262.

19. On the concept of co-evolution see Richard B. Norgaard, "Sociosystem and Ecosystem Coevolution in the Amazon," *Journal of Environmental Economics and Management* 8 (1981): 238–254.

PART ONE

THE DEBATE AT STOCKHOLM

As discussed in the introductory chapter, the 1972 UN Conference on the Human Environment, held in Stockholm, was a seminal event in the history of global environmental politics. Many important international agreements had already been concluded by the time of the Stockholm conference, including a treaty governing Antarctica (1959), a partial nuclear-test-ban treaty (1963), a treaty governing the exploration and use of outer space (1967), and several international agreements on ocean-related matters such as whaling, the use of marine resources, and pollution. But the Stockholm conference was the first broadly international effort to evaluate and discuss the environment in systematic, comprehensive terms, and it helped establish the trajectory of future efforts—the complex array of diplomatic initiatives and debates, attempts at transnational institution building, and global movements for social change that unfolded during the decades that followed.

Although the Stockholm conference took place almost four decades ago, many of its central debates are still current. These include several key questions revisited later in this book: Is global pollution mainly a problem of poverty or a problem of affluence? What is the balance of responsibility between the North and the South in global environmental degradation? Does the institution of national sovereignty help or hinder the effort to construct international responses to environmental problems? An understanding of the dominant ideas and controversies at the Stockholm conference provides an important historical perspective on the debates and disputes that dominate contemporary global environmental politics.[1]

In this section we introduce some of the ideas that shaped debate during the Stockholm era. We pay particular attention to three powerful and controversial claims from that era: the idea that there are inherent "limits to growth" facing the international economy, the world's population, and global consumption; the idea that self-interested individual behavior toward the environment adds up to a collective "tragedy of the commons"; and the claim that the environmental crisis demands a firm, authoritarian state to deal with the problems facing a "scarcity society."

Although thinking about the environment has evolved considerably in the years since the Stockholm conference, these themes are not just of historical interest. They have strongly influenced the nature of scientific and social-scientific inquiry since the conference, with many analysts and activists working to either prove or disprove the existence of limits to growth, a tragedy of the commons, or a political basis for ecological authoritarianism. These ideas also have shaped the political strategies pursued by governments, corporations, environmentalists, and other actors seeking to promote or hinder various forms of international environmental cooperation.

For the industrialized countries of the North, the Stockholm conference was a response to mounting public anxiety over the environmental consequences of industrial society. By the early 1970s, concerns over problems as diverse as air and water pollution, wilderness preservation, toxic chemicals, urban congestion, nuclear radiation, and rising prices for natural-resource commodities began to fuse into the notion that the world was rapidly approaching natural limits to growth in human activity. The best-selling book *The Limits to Growth* did much to galvanize public fears. Using a technique known as systems modeling, the authors tried to predict the consequences of unlimited growth in human numbers and consumption. As the passage presented here indicates, they concluded that the convergence of several trends—accelerating industrialization, rapid population growth, widespread malnutrition, depletion of nonrenewable resources, and a deteriorating environment—was moving the world rapidly toward overall limits on global growth. To avoid a potentially catastrophic collapse of the world's economic and social systems, it would be necessary to implement planned restraints on growth in population and in resource consumption.

Critics of *The Limits to Growth* argued that the book overstated the urgency of the problem, overlooked the possibility of substituting less-scarce inputs, and underestimated the possibility for technological solutions.[2] (These arguments foreshadowed the emergence in the 1980s of the concept of "sustainable development," which argues that some forms of economic growth can be compatible with natural limits; see Part Four.) The book's central claims were highly controversial, and most Northern governments were reluctant to fully endorse or embrace its findings. But the fears articulated in *The Limits to Growth* found widespread popular support in industrial societies, where they converged with the arguments of the growing coalition of environmental organizations.

Not surprisingly, the idea of limits to growth, and the controversy surrounding it, was received quite differently in the South. Among the less-industrialized countries, the idea of limits to growth evoked not only intellectual skepticism but also political suspicions. These suspicions were expressed eloquently in a 1972 essay by João Augusto de Araujo Castro, at that time Brazilian ambassador to the United States and an influential voice in North-South diplomacy. The South has never been monolithic in its views on problems of development and the environment. But as Castro made clear, many in the South linked the North's environmental concerns to the broader pattern of North-South relations. Thus, there was widespread agreement among Third World governments at the Stockholm conference that the North was responsible for the global environmental crisis; that the North, having reaped the fruits of industrialization, now sought to close the door on the South; that the environmental problems of poverty differed fundamentally from those of affluence; and that solutions crafted with the North's problems in mind would be ineffective, or worse, if imposed on the South.

The South's unity at the Stockholm conference made it clear that a global response to environmental problems would require linking the environmental debate to the development concerns of the South and to a broader dialogue about the political and economic "rules of the game" in the international system. The message was clear: If such connections were not drawn, the South would not participate.

Just as the idea of limits to growth dominated the debate over the consequences of environmental problems, the debate over causes crystallized around the powerful and controversial idea of the "tragedy of the commons." This view was popularized by biologist Garrett Hardin in a now-famous essay that appeared in the influential scholarly journal *Science* in 1968. According to Hardin, the "tragedy" occurred when self-interested actors enjoyed open access to, or un-limited use of, natural resources or environmental systems. Because consumers could benefit fully from additional exploitation while bearing only a small part of the "costs" of that exploitation (for ex-ample, environmental degradation)—costs shared with all other users—the overwhelming tendency would be toward greater ex-ploitation of the resource. Each actor would pursue this logical indi-vidual behavior until the result for the system as a whole was the destruction or degradation of the resource in question. Individual logic would produce collective disaster—hence the notion of tragedy. Using the example of overgrazing on the town commons of medieval England (hence the tragedy of the *commons*), Hardin suggested that the same combination of self-interest and open access that had caused this earlier catastrophe was at the root of current problems of pollution and overpopulation. The solutions offered by Hardin were either to replace open access with enforceable private property rights, so that individual users would reap the full costs as well as the full benefits of their actions, or to impose governmental restrictions on access.

Hardin's model came to be enormously influential in shaping thinking about global environmental problems, particularly for such so-called global commons as the oceans and atmosphere, which do not fall under the domain of any single government. One reason for its influence is the model's simple elegance: The tragedy of the commons combines a recognizable human motive (self-interest) with a recognizable set of social rules (those allowing open access to natural resources and the environment) to produce a result that most would recognize as undesirable (rapid depletion or destruction of the resource in question).

Yet Hardin's model is, at heart, just a metaphor: The English commons is invoked as a simplified representation of the complex social rules, customs, goals, and behavioral incentives that shape how people interact with the environment individually and collectively. Whether such a "tragedy" actually lies at the center of global environmental problems depends on whether this abstraction is in fact an accurate representation of human behavior and social institutions. Even if the tragedy seems plausible conceptually, how widely does it apply as a description of the real world?

Susan J. Buck argues that despite its widespread acceptance, Hardin's tragedy does not even describe accurately the situation of the commons in medieval England on which the metaphor is based. According to Buck, access to the town commons was never unrestrained but rather was governed by a complex set of community rules that ensured sustainable use. The commons system was destroyed not by population growth and self-interested individual behavior, as Hardin asserted, but by changing political and economic conditions in Britain, which gave powerful actors the incentive and ability to privatize the commons and to overwhelm community-based systems of property rights. Thus, rather than representing a tragedy, the endurance of the commons system, in some cases for several hundred years, shows that there may be possibilities other than the stark choice Hardin poses between purely private property and purely open access.

In the decades since Hardin's essay was published, scholars have produced a large body of empirical evidence addressing the question of whether Hardin's tragedy actually exists.[3] Research has focused on a wide range of natural-resource and environmental systems—often referred to as "common-pool resources"—that are potentially subject to the "tragedy," including fisheries, wildlife populations, surface water, groundwater, rangelands, and forests. Much of this work has found that Hardin's formulation, though sometimes applicable, is by no means universal. Whether a "tragedy" of overconsumption ensues depends on the type of social rules governing these natural resources or environmental systems. The enforceable private property rights Hardin advocated are just one such set of rules, and not necessarily the most appropriate for all situations. Elinor Ostrom's influential book *Governing the Commons*, published in 1990, provided both theory and evidence that self-organizing, sustainable management of shared resources is possible under certain conditions.[4] Ostrom, who won the 2009 Nobel Prize in ecomomics, and her colleagues have argued that common-pool resources are more likely to be governed sustainably if governing rules and institutions follow certain design principles.

> Given the large variation in common-pool resources, their patterns of use, and their users, researchers agree that no single institutional design can be devised that will work in all of the many different common-pool resource situations. Researchers also agree, however, that we can discuss a set of general principles that increase performance of an institutional design:
>
> 1. Rules are devised and managed by resource users.
> 2. Compliance with rules is easy to monitor.
> 3. Rules are enforceable.
> 4. Sanctions are graduated.
> 5. Adjudication is available at low cost.
> 6. Monitors and other officials are accountable to users.
> 7. Institutions to regulate a given common-pool resource may need to be devised at multiple levels.
> 8. Procedures exist for revising rules.[5]

The work of Buck, Ostrom, and others is of critical importance in the effort to craft international responses to environmental problems. If Hardin's tragedy does apply to the global commons, it will be exceedingly difficult to craft effective international responses to global environmental problems. This is so because both of Hardin's preferred solutions, privatizing the commons or subjecting it to the control of a powerful central authority, are infeasible in the current international system. If these are the only choices, the tragedy seems likely to proceed apace. However, if systems of collective management can be shown to have been effective on the local or regional level, it may also be possible to design such systems to operate on the international level.[6] Under these circumstances there could still be a tragedy of the commons, but it would result from our lack of skill and effectiveness in designing fair and efficient international responses rather than from some ironclad logic of nature.

What would be the political consequences of the limits to growth and the tragedy of the commons? Hardin provided a provocative answer to this question when he spoke of the need for strong rules limiting access to the commons. For Hardin, "The social arrangements that produce responsibility are arrangements that create coercion."

This idea was also further developed by William Ophuls in his 1977 book, *Ecology and the Politics of Scarcity*.[7] According to Ophuls, a new era of scarcity would be marked by an authoritarian political response, just as scarcity in the past had been the trigger for various forms of violence, oppression, and war. The "scarcity society" Ophuls described would perceive "the necessity for political control" in order to avoid "ecological self-destruction." The result he foresaw was a political future "much less libertarian and much more authoritarian, much less individualistic and much more communalistic than our present." Ophuls did see an alternative to this grim scenario, which he labeled a "democracy of restraint." In this scenario, it would be possible to forge an ecologically rational future without coercive authority, provided that human gratification could be decoupled from material consumption. But a democracy of restraint would demand a prompt response to environmental problems and a broad social consensus on the importance of taking action—circumstances that Ophuls deemed unlikely.

In Part Six, on the question of ecological justice, we present very different interpretations of the links between freedom, democracy, justice, and the environment. But the questions Ophuls raised about the ability of today's governments to respond effectively and in a timely fashion, and the attention he drew to the close link between control of nature and control of people, remain critical themes in environmental politics.

Despite their critics, and despite changes in our understanding in the decades since the Stockholm conference, the concepts of "limits to growth" and "the tragedy of the commons" remain powerfully influential in global environmental politics. Not only did they help shape the pathway from Stockholm; they are also readily seen in contemporary controversies. The dispute about growth limits has reemerged in current debates over the environmental consequences of international trade (see Part Three) and the prospects for sustainability (see Part Four). Similarly, those skeptical about the prospects for effective international cooperation invoke both the logic of self-interested behavior and the commons-like features of global environmental systems—just as Hardin did more than forty years ago. And the increasingly widespread fear that environmental degradation threatens national and international security raises for some the specter of authoritarian solutions (see Part Five on environmental change and violent conflict). The evolution of global environmental politics cannot be understood without examining the history of these ideas; weighing their claims carefully and critically is as important today as it was in the Stockholm era.

Thinking Critically

1. How well have the essays by Meadows, Castro, and Hardin, which were all written between 1968 and 1972, withstood the test of time? Do they still provide an adequate framework for understanding and addressing global environmental problems? What aspects of their essays seem anachronistic? What aspects ring true today? Imagine what a dialogue among these thinkers would be like if they were to meet today and discuss the durability of one another's claims.

2. Contrast Castro's claims about the environment and development with the essays on sustainability in Part Four. Do either the advocates or the critics of the sustainability paradigm frame the problem in the same way as Castro?

3. Does the criticism of Hardin presented in Buck's essay invalidate his central claim about the tragedy of the commons? In other words, can Hardin still be right about the larger problem even if he misread the history of the English commons, and even if exceptions to his pessimistic scenario can be found? What do you think Hardin would say to his critics?

4. If Buck, Ostrom, and others are correct to argue that sustainable governance of the commons is feasible on a local scale, can we imagine similar forms of governance on a larger scale? What are the limits of scale for these forms of governance, and at what scale are these limits likely to be encountered?

5. Consider Ostrom's list above of design principles for sustainable management of common-pool resources. Would it be difficult politically or administratively to incorporate these principles into international environmental agreements on a regional or global commons? Which would likely be the sticking points in international negotiations, and why?

6. Contrast Hardin's arguments about the need for strong command-and-control governance with the essays on ecological justice in Part Six. Is the concentration of power in the hands of the state part of the problem or part of the solution? In an era in which many governments face profound skepticism and frequent crises of authority, are people likely to look to the state for solutions to the problems of the "scarcity society"?

Notes

1. Lynton Caldwell, *International Environmental Policy*, 3rd ed. (Durham, NC: Duke University Press, 1996).

2. Several of these criticisms are summarized in W. D. Nordhaus, "World Dynamics: Measurement without Data," *Economic Journal* 83, no. 332 (December 1973): 1156–1183.

See also Julian Simon and Herman Kahn, *The Resourceful Earth* (Oxford: Basil Blackwell, 1984).

3. Much of this research is summarized in Nives Dolšak and Elinor Ostrom, *The Commons in the New Millennium: Challenges and Adaptation* (Cambridge, MA: MIT Press, 2003). See also David Feeny, Fikret Berkes, Bonnie J. McCay, and James M. Acheson, "The Tragedy of the Commons: Twenty-Two Years Later," *Human Ecology* 18, no. 1 (1990): 1–19.

4. See Elinor Ostrom, *Governing the Commons: The Evolution of Institutions for Collective Action* (London: Cambridge University Press, 1990).

5. Nives Dolšak and Elinor Ostrom, "The Challenges of the Commons," in Dolšak and Ostrom, *The Commons in the New Millennium*, p. 22.

6. See Robert O. Keohane and Elinor Ostrom, eds., *Local Commons and Global Interdependence* (London: Sage, 1995).

7. William Ophuls, *Ecology and the Politics of Scarcity* (San Francisco: W. H. Freeman, 1977). An updated version of this argument was presented around the time of the 1992 Rio Earth Summit in A. Stephen Boyan and William Ophuls, *Ecology and the Politics of Scarcity Revisited* (San Francisco: W. H. Freeman, 1992).

1

THE LIMITS TO GROWTH

DONELLA H. MEADOWS, DENNIS L. MEADOWS, JØRGEN RANDERS, AND WILLIAM W. BEHRENS III[*]

Problems and Models

Every person approaches his problems . . . with the help of models. A model is simply an ordered set of assumptions about a complex system. It is an attempt to understand some aspect of the infinitely varied world by selecting from perceptions and past experience a set of general observations applicable to the problem at hand. . . .

Decisionmakers at every level unconsciously use mental models to choose among policies that will shape our future world. These mental models are, of necessity, very simple when compared with the reality from which they are abstracted. The human brain, remarkable as it is, can only keep track of a limited number of the complicated, simultaneous interactions that determine the nature of the real world.

We, too, have used a model. Ours is a formal, written model of the world.[†] It constitutes a preliminary attempt to improve our mental models of long-term, global problems by combining the large amount of information that is already in human minds and in written records with the new information-processing tools

---

[*] Excerpted from Donella H. Meadows, Dennis L. Meadows, Jørgen Randers, and William W. Behrens III, *The Limits to Growth* (Washington, DC: Potomac Associates, 1972). Reprinted with permission.

[†] The prototype model on which we have based our work was designed by Professor Jay W. Forrester of the Massachusetts Institute of Technology. A description of that model has been published in his book *World Dynamics* (Cambridge, Mass: Wright-Allen Press, 1971).

that mankind's increasing knowledge has produced—the scientific method, systems analysis, and the modern computer.

Our world model was built specifically to investigate five major trends of global concern—accelerating industrialization, rapid population growth, widespread malnutrition, depletion of nonrenewable resources, and a deteriorating environment. These trends are all interconnected in many ways, and their development is measured in decades or centuries, rather than in months or years. With the model we are seeking to understand the causes of these trends, their interrelationships, and their implications as much as one hundred years in the future.

The model we have constructed is, like every other model, imperfect, oversimplified, and unfinished. We are well aware of its shortcomings, but we believe that it is the most useful model now available for dealing with problems far out on the space-time graph. To our knowledge it is the only formal model in existence that is truly global in scope, that has a time horizon longer than thirty years, and that includes important variables such as population, food production, and pollution, not as independent entities, but as dynamically interacting elements, as they are in the real world. . . .

In spite of the preliminary state of our work, we believe it is important to publish the model and our findings now. Decisions are being made every day, in every part of the world, that will affect the physical, economic, and social conditions of the world system for decades to come. These decisions cannot wait for perfect models and total understanding. They will be made on the basis of some model, mental or written, in any case. . . .

Our conclusions are:

1. If the present growth trends in world population, industrialization, pollution, food production, and resource depletion continue unchanged, the limits to growth on this planet will be reached sometime within the next one hundred years. The most probable result will be a rather sudden and uncontrollable decline in both population and industrial capacity.
2. It is possible to alter these growth trends and to establish a condition of ecological and economic stability that is sustainable far into the future. The state of global equilibrium could be designed so that the basic material needs of each person on earth are satisfied and each person has an equal opportunity to realize his individual human potential.
3. If the world's people decide to strive for this second outcome rather than the first, the sooner they begin working to attain it, the greater will be their chances of success.

These conclusions are so far-reaching and raise so many questions for further study that we are quite frankly overwhelmed by the enormity of the job that must be done. We hope that this book will serve to interest other people . . . to raise the space and time horizons of their concerns and to join us in understanding and preparing for a period of great transition—the transition from growth to global equilibrium. . . .

A Finite World

We have mentioned many difficult trade-offs . . . in the production of food, in the consumption of resources, and in the generation and clean-up of pollution. By now it should be clear that all of these trade-offs arise from one simple fact—the earth is finite. The closer any human activity comes to the limit of the earth's ability to support that activity, the more apparent and unresolvable the trade-offs become. When there is plenty of unused arable land, there can be more people and also more food per person. When all the land is already used, the trade-off between more people or more food per person becomes a choice between absolutes.

In general, modern society has not learned to recognize and deal with these trade-offs. The apparent goal of the present world system is to produce more people with more (food, material goods, clean air, and water) for each person. . . . We have noted that if society continues to strive for that goal, it will eventually reach one of many earthly limitations. . . . It is not possible to foretell exactly which limitation will occur first or what the consequences will be, because there are many conceivable, unpredictable human responses to such a situation. It is possible, however, to investigate what conditions and what changes in the world system might lead society to collision with or accommodation to the limits to growth in a finite world. . . .

Technology and the Limits to Growth

Although the history of human effort contains numerous incidents of mankind's failure to live within physical limits, it is success in overcoming limits that forms the cultural tradition of many dominant people in today's world. Over the past three hundred years, mankind has compiled an impressive record of pushing back the apparent limits to population and economic growth by a series of spectacular technological advances. Since the recent history of a large part of human society has been so continuously successful, it is quite natural that many people expect technological breakthroughs to go on raising physical ceilings indefinitely. These people speak about the future with resounding technological optimism. . . . The hopes of the technological optimists center on the ability of technology to remove or extend the limits to growth of population and capital. We have shown that in the world model the application of technology to apparent problems of resource depletion or pollution or food shortage has no impact on the essential problem, which is exponential growth in a finite and complex system. Our attempts to use even the most optimistic estimates of the benefits of technology in the model did not prevent the ultimate decline of population and industry, and in fact did not in any case postpone the collapse beyond the year 2200. . . .

Applying technology to the natural pressures that the environment exerts against any growth process has been so successful in the past that a whole culture has evolved around the principle of fighting against limits rather than learning to live with them. . . . But the relationship between the earth's limits and man's activities is changing. The exponential growth curves are adding millions of people and billions of tons of pollutants to the ecosystem each year. Even the ocean, which once appeared virtually inexhaustible, is losing species after species of its commercially useful animals. . . .

There may be much disagreement with the statement that population and capital growth must stop soon. But virtually no one will argue that material growth on this planet can go on forever. . . . Man can still choose his limits and stop when he pleases by weakening some of the strong pressures that cause capital and population growth, or by instituting counterpressures, or both. Such counterpressures will probably not be entirely pleasant. They will certainly involve profound changes in the social and economic structures that have been deeply impressed into human culture by centuries of growth. The alternative is to wait until the price of technology becomes more than society can pay, or until the side effects of technology suppress growth themselves, or until problems arise that have no technical solutions. At any of those points the choice of limits will be gone. Growth will be stopped by pressures that are not of human choosing, and that, as the world model suggests, may be very much worse than those which society might choose for itself.

. . . Technological optimism is the most common and the most dangerous reaction to our findings from the world model. Technology can relieve the symptoms of a problem without affecting the underlying causes. Faith in technology as the ultimate solution to all problems can thus divert our attention from the most fundamental problem—the problem of growth in a finite system—and prevent us from taking effective action to solve it. . . .

The Transition from Growth to Global Equilibrium

We can say very little at this point about the practical, day-by-day steps that might be taken to reach a desirable, sustainable state of global equilibrium. Neither the world model nor our own thoughts have been developed in sufficient detail to understand all the implications of the transition from growth to equilibrium. Before any part of the world's society embarks deliberately on such a transition, there must be much more discussion, more extensive analysis, and many new ideas contributed by many different people. . . .

Although we underline the need for more study and discussion of these difficult questions, we end on a note of urgency. We hope that intensive study and debate will proceed simultaneously with an ongoing program of action. The details are not yet specified, but the general direction for action is obvious. Enough is known already to analyze many proposed policies in terms of their tendencies to promote or to regulate growth.[1] . . . Efforts are weak at the moment, but they could be strengthened very quickly if the goal of equilibrium were recognized as desirable and important by any sizable part of human society. . . .

Taking no action to solve these problems is equivalent to taking strong action. Every day of continued exponential growth brings the world system closer to the ultimate limits to that growth. A decision to do nothing is a decision to increase the risk of collapse. We cannot say with certainty how much longer mankind can postpone initiating deliberate control of his growth before he will have lost the chance for control. We suspect on the basis of present knowledge of the physical constraints of the planet that the growth phase cannot continue for another one hundred years. Again, because of the delays in the system, if the global society waits until those constraints are unmistakably apparent, it will have waited too long.

If there is cause for deep concern, there is also cause for hope. Deliberately limiting growth would be difficult, but not impossible. The way to proceed is clear, and the necessary steps, although they are new ones for human society, are well within human capabilities. Man possesses, for a small moment in his history, the most powerful combination of knowledge, tools, and resources the world has ever known. He has all that is physically necessary to create a totally new form of human society—one that would be built to last for generations. The two missing ingredients are a realistic, long-term goal that can guide mankind to the equilibrium society and the human will to achieve that goal. Without such a goal and a commitment to it, short-term concerns will generate the exponential growth that drives the world system toward the limits of the earth and ultimate collapse. With that goal and that commitment mankind would be ready now to begin a controlled, orderly transition from growth to global equilibrium.

Note

1. See, for example, "Fellow Americans Keep Out!" *Forbes*, June 15, 1971, p. 22, and *The Ecologist*, January 1972.

2

ENVIRONMENT AND DEVELOPMENT: THE CASE OF THE DEVELOPING COUNTRIES

JOÃO AUGUSTO DE ARAUJO CASTRO*

Introduction

Interest in the field of ecology, which is centered in the developed countries, has recently increased due to the sudden discovery of a possible imbalance between man and earth. Resulting from the population explosion and the misuse of existing and newly developed technologies, this potential imbalance could bring about an environmental crisis menacing the future of mankind. In several countries the emergence of an interest in ecological problems has not been confined to the realm of the scientific community. It has aroused public concern which has expressed itself, although sometimes vaguely, in such initiatives as Earth Week, celebrated in the United States in April 1970, and the mushrooming of a specialized literature.

As would be expected, the methods envisaged to resolve on a world basis the so-called environmental crisis were inspired by the realities of a fraction of that very same world: the family of the developed countries. Furthermore, the bulk of the solutions in hand, mainly of a technical nature, seek primarily to make healthier the consequences of the Industrial Revolution without necessarily providing a tool for a further distribution of its benefits among states.

This study seeks to introduce some neglected aspects of the interests of developing countries into discussions about a world ecological policy. The working

* Kay, David A., and Eugene B. Skolnikoff, eds., *World Eco-Crisis: International Organizations in Response.* © 1972 by the Board of Regents of the University of Wisconsin System. Reprinted by permission of the University of Wisconsin Press.

hypothesis is that the implementation of any worldwide environmental policy based on the realities of the developed countries tends to perpetuate the existing gap in socioeconomic development between developed and developing countries and so promote the freezing of the present international order. . . .

Developed Countries

Although there does not yet exist a systematic body of doctrine, the new ecological policy of the developed countries contains several elements that have already stimulated important developments in academic thought, as indicated by the growing literature on the matter, and attitudes of governments and private sectors in these countries, mainly in their relations with the developing countries.

A short historical digression may help in analyzing the rationale of this ecological policy. As a localized phenomenon in the countries of the Northern Hemisphere, the Industrial Revolution of the eighteenth century was not brought about by one single factor. It was not, for instance, the result of inventions or the coming into operation of new machines. As in the case of other major movements in history, it was the result of the interplay of many factors, some obscure in themselves, whose combined effort laid down the foundations of a new industrial system. Growing organically, cell by cell, new patterns of industrial organization were soon translated into the establishment of a new international order. Around the group of countries enjoying the benefits of the Industrial Revolution there existed an increasing family of countries, trying, mostly unsuccessfully, to modernize their own means of production.

This new international order and the relatively uneven distribution of political power among states, based on the use and monopoly of advanced technologies, may be considered one of the most enduring effects of the Industrial Revolution. And since then, as a normal corollary of the new order, the technologically advanced countries have been endeavoring to maintain their political and economic position in the world while the technologically less endowed countries have been seeking to alter, through development, this global status quo.

This permanent struggle between the two groups of countries persists in the present days and it is unlikely that it will cease in the near future. For this to happen one would have to assume a perfectly homogeneous world community whose conflicts would have been eliminated through a perfect satisfaction, on a homogeneous basis, of all human needs. This condition is most likely to be found only in the realms of utopia. . . .

According to a helpful image taken from academic and governmental sources in the developed countries our planet could be visualized as a "spaceship earth," where life could only be sustained, nay simply possible, through maintenance of a delicate equilibrium between the needs of the passengers and the ability of the craft to respond to those needs. Undisturbed until recently, this equilibrium would now be menaced by an excess of population and the consequences of the use of both previously existing and newly developed technologies. Elaborating the same image, "spaceship earth" would be divided into two classes of passengers, the first coincident with the technologically advanced countries and the second representative of the technologically less endowed countries, which would necessarily have to trade off positions with a view to maintaining the equilibrium of the vessel. . . .

In order to maintain the equilibrium of the vessel the problems created by population explosion and the use of both previously existing and new technologies should, in the view of developed countries, now be dealt with globally, irrespective of the unequal distribution, on a world scale, of the benefits and related destructive effects on the environment engendered by the Industrial Revolution. Germane to such a global ecological policy is the need for world planning for development which, to be successful, might purposely aim at freezing the present relative positions of the two classes inside the vessel.

Provided that the first class already enjoys low average rates of population growth and is unlikely to opt for a slower rate of industrial growth for the sole purpose of guaranteeing a purer atmosphere or cleaner water, the new ecology-saving policy would be more successful if applied in the areas where the environmental crisis has not yet appeared, even in its least acute forms. Actually, these areas would mainly comprise the territory of the second class. Thus: the second class should be taught to employ the most effective and expeditious birth control methods and to follow an orderly pollution-reducing process of industrialization. In the case of industrialization, the mainstream of socioeconomic development, the lesson must be even harsher: The second class must organize production in accordance with environment-saving techniques already tested by the first class or be doomed to socioeconomic stagnation. . . .

Nowadays some ecologists do not hesitate to say that the developing countries can never hope to achieve the consumption patterns of the developed countries. Some seemingly appalling calculations are offered as proof of this. To raise the living standards of the world's existing population to American levels the annual production of iron would have to increase 75 times, that of copper 100 times, that of lead 200 times, and that of tin 250 times. Were a country such as India to make use of fertilizers at the per capita level of the Netherlands, it would consume one-half of the world's total output of fertilizers. Clearly, the parity of the developing countries with the developed ones is no longer compatible with the existing stocks of natural resources. Again, according to those wise men, the increasing expectations in developing countries, which are sometimes associated with something approaching a revolution, are nothing more than expectations of elites and therefore must be curbed. Most of the population of these countries, it is claimed, do not have an ambition to reach Western standards and do not even know that "such a thing as development is on the agenda."

Now, the alleged exhaustion of natural resources is accompanied, in general, by forecasts of the fateful coming of formidable ecological hecatombs. The continuing progress of developed countries would require an economic lebensraum in the Southern Hemisphere. In the name of the survival of mankind developing countries should continue in a state of underdevelopment because if the evils of industrialization were to reach them, life on the planet would be placed in jeopardy. . . .

Very few reasonable people underwrite these fanciful ideas. Yet, it cannot be denied that the environment in developed countries is threatened and that it should be preserved. The difficulty in dealing with environmental problems nowadays is that they have become a myth. . . . From an uttermost neglect of ecological problems public opinion in the United States has swung to an outright "geolatry." The environment has been rediscovered and Mother Earth now has a week dedicated to her in the calendar. Schoolchildren crusade to clean up the streets; college students organize huge demonstrations; uncivilized industries that dump their wastes in the air, in the water, or on the ground are denounced as public enemies.

. . . The simplistic concepts that ecology is disturbed because there are "too many people" or because they "consume too much" must be discarded as nothing more than fallacies. There is abundant evidence that the earth is capable of supporting a considerably greater population at much higher levels of consumption. The simple fact that in half a century mankind found it possible to wage four major wars, with a terrible waste of wealth, is a clear indication that we are not after all so short of resources although we may be short of common sense. . . .

Environmental problems not only pose a new and compelling argument for disarmament and peace but also call attention to the question of efficiency in the organization of production. It is widely known, but seldom remembered when the availability of natural resources is discussed, that in developed countries billions of dollars are spent every year to purchase so-called farm surpluses. Millions of tons of agricultural products have been regularly stored or destroyed to keep prices up in the world markets. . . .These figures and these facts evidently do not agree with the superficial statements which have been made about the irreparable strain being put on natural resources.

Pollution of the air and water and related damages to the environment are loosely attributed, in general, to faulty technologies, but few have bothered to assess objectively the exact proportions of the problem. According to experts at the Organisation for Economic Co-operation and Development (OECD) safeguarding the environment in the United States would require annual expenditures of . . . less than 2 percent of the American GNP [Gross National Product]. Clearly, there is no real cause for most of the fuzzy agitation about the environment. Put in their proper perspective, environmental problems are little more than a question of the reexamination of national priorities. . . .

When discussing the environment some ecologists and other wise men, as often happens in many other instances, try haphazardly to superimpose peculiar situations prevailing in developed countries onto the realities of the developing countries. . . . If the peculiarities of developing countries are taken into account, it will not be difficult to recognize that, in broad terms, they are still at a prepollution stage or, in other words, have not yet been given the chance to become polluted. . . . The 24 countries of Latin America, the least underdeveloped region in the developing world, have less than one-tenth of the total number of motor vehicles in the United States. Only a few ecologists and other wise men would say that Latin Americans should rather have fewer cars and cleaner air.

There is a pollution of affluence and a pollution of poverty. It is imperative to distinguish between the two lest some pollution be prevented at the cost of much economic development. Were it not for the dangers arising from the confusion between the two kinds of pollution, there would be no need for calling attention to the precarious housing conditions, poor health, and low sanitary standards not to mention starvation in developing countries. The linear transposition of ecological problems of the developed countries to the context of the developing ones disregards the existence of such distressing social conditions. Wherever these conditions prevail, the assertion that income means less pollution is nonsense. It is obvious, or should be, that the so-called pollution of poverty can only be corrected through higher incomes, or more precisely, through economic development.

The most sensible ecologists are of the opinion that the pollution levels can be attributed not so much to population or affluence as to modern technologies. In the United States the economy would have grown enough, in the absence of technological change, to give the increased population about the same per capita amounts of goods and services today as in 1946. The ecological crisis has resulted mainly from the sweeping progress in technologies. Modern technologies have multiplied the impact of growth on the environment and, consequently, generated most of the existing pollution. Those who haphazardly transpose developed countries' situations to the milieu of an underdeveloped country repeatedly warn the latter against the dangers of modern technologies and rapid industrialization. "Don't let happen to your cities what happened to New York; keep your beautiful landscapes." It is ironic that developed countries, which create and sell modern technologies, should caution developing countries against utilizing them. Is this done to justify the secondhand technologies that sometimes accompany foreign direct investments?

Developing Countries

A somewhat apathetic attitude on the part of the developing countries regarding the environmental issue does not imply negation of the relevance of the matter and the need for true international cooperation to solve the problem it poses for the survival of mankind. This apathetic attitude, however, clearly is derived from the developing countries' socioeconomic experience which differs, to a large extent, from that of the developed countries. Consequently, one has to bear in mind that, not having enjoyed the opportunity to experience their own Industrial Revolution, the developing countries have not been stimulated to think about the environmental crisis as posed in the present days. The phenomenon of urbanization in the Southern Hemisphere, even in the countries experiencing a considerable degree of progress, may raise questions about poor living standards in some areas but has not thus far led to industrial congestion.

As indicated in the elements of the ecological policy of the developed countries, the equilibrium of "spaceship earth" would depend on the enforcement of measures bearing on population and on the use of the previously existing and new technologies chiefly in the second class of the vessel or, in other words, in the territory of the developing countries. Even if applied to their full extent, those measures would not result at some foreseeable date in a single-class carrying vessel, preferably closer to the first steerage. This ecological policy, which aims primarily at the equilibrium of the vessel, could better succeed if the relative positions of the classes were maintained, for the emergence of one single class would presuppose a considerable change in the living standards of the first class, something that may not be attained in the light of present global socioeconomic realities. . . .

On the question of the preservation of the environment the passengers' survival would call for the enforcement of a drastic decision, globally applied, to maintain a "green area reserve" which would have to coincide mainly with the territories of the developing countries. This step would safeguard, against complete exhaustion, the natural elements (soil, atmosphere, and water) still available on the planet just to provide some sort of counteraction to the spoilage of the same natural elements used up in the countries where the benefits of the Industrial Revolution were massively concentrated.

Besides the ethical question raised by this policy, as expressed in the ostensive imbalance between responsibility for the damage and obligation for repair, the developing countries, in abiding by its prescriptions, would make a commitment to conservatism rather than to conservation. Furthermore, the possibility of a widespread application of developed countries' ecological policy, theoretically conceived to secure the equilibrium of "spaceship earth," may risk transforming the Southern Hemisphere countries into the last healthy weekend areas for the inhabitants of a planet already saturated with the environment created by the Industrial Revolution. As a token of compensation the Southern Hemisphere countries could claim to have resurrected, and adequately preserved, the environmental milieu for the living and the survival of Rousseau's "happy savage." In expressing their concern over the environmental crisis the developing countries cannot accept, without further refinement, the ecological policy devised by the developed countries whose socioeconomic structure was deeply influenced by the unique phenomenon of the Industrial Revolution.

The first step toward the refinement of that policy may be the rejection of the principle that the ecology issue, taken on a global basis, can be dealt with exclusively through a technical approach, as suggested by the developed countries.

Given the implications for the international order, including the freezing of the status quo, any environment-saving policy must necessarily be imbued with a solid and well-informed political approach. This would provide an opportunity for the developing countries, by preserving their national identities, to join safely in the effort of the international community to preserve the equilibrium of "spaceship earth."

As a normal corollary of the political approach, ecological policy should not depart from the broader framework of socioeconomic development. In this regard a second step of refinement would require a corresponding universal commitment to development if the task of preserving the environment is to be shared by the world community. . . .

Evidently, no country wants any pollution at all. But each country must evolve its own development plans, exploit its own resources as it thinks suitable, and define its own environmental standards. The idea of having such priorities and standards imposed on individual countries or groups of countries, on either a multilateral or a bilateral basis, is very hard to accept.

That is why it is disturbing to see the International Bank for Reconstruction and Development (IBRD) set up its own ecological policy. Repercussions on the environment, defined according to IBRD ecologists, have become an important factor in determining whether financial assistance by that institution should be granted for an industrial project in developing countries. It seems reasonable that the preservation of the environment should not exclude the preservation of national sovereignty. Ecological policies should rather be inserted into the framework of national development.

It is perhaps time for the developing countries to present their own views on the framing of an environmental policy in spite of the fact that the developed countries have not yet ended their own controversial debate or furnished definite and convincing data on the issue. In adopting a position the developing countries recognize the existence of environmental problems in the world and the possibility of finding solutions through both national efforts and international cooperation.

The first point to be touched on concerns the question of national sovereignty. In this regard any ecological policy, globally applied, must not be an instrument to suppress wholly or in part the legitimate right of any country to decide about its own affairs. In reality this point would simply seek to guarantee on an operational level the full exercise of the principle of juridical equality of states as expressed, for instance, in the Charter of the United Nations. . . . Sovereignty, in this context, should not be taken as an excuse for isolationism and consequently for escapism in relation to international efforts geared to solving environmental problems. For the developing countries it is crucial to consider, in the light of their own interests, nationally defined, the whole range of alternative solutions devised or implemented in the developed countries. Naturally, it is assumed that all countries can act responsibly and that none is going to deliberately favor policies that may endanger the equilibrium of "spaceship earth."

Closely linked to the problem of sovereignty, the question of national priorities calls for an understanding of the distinction between the developmental characteristics of developed and developing countries. As has been previously pointed out in this article, while the ecological issue came to the forefront of public concern as a by-product of postindustrial stages of development, it is not yet strikingly apparent in the majority of the developing countries. And different realities, of course, should be differently treated or, at least, given the fittest solutions.

In the developing countries the major concern is an urgent need to accelerate socioeconomic development, and a meaningful ecological policy must not hamper the attainment of that goal in the most expeditious way.... In this context the developing countries, while rejecting the implementation of any ecological policy which bears in itself elements of socioeconomic stagnation, could only share a common responsibility for the preservation of the environment if it was accompanied and paralleled by a corresponding common responsibility for development....

Conclusion

This study has probed very briefly some aspects of an ecological policy in the light of the interests of the developing countries.... Emphasis has been laid on the undesirability of transposing, uncritically, into the realities of the developing countries the solutions already envisaged by the developed countries to eliminate or reduce the so-called environmental crisis to the extent that those solutions may embody elements of socioeconomic stagnation.... Finally, a preliminary and broad picture of a position of the developing countries has stressed the relation between preservation of environment and the urgent need to speed up socioeconomic development and the desirability of a common world effort to tackle both these aspects simultaneously. This common effort, however, should not preclude or trespass on national interest as a departing point for the setting up of concepts and operational guidelines of an ecological policy for the developing countries.

In conclusion, a discussion of any meaningful ecological policy for both developed and developing countries ... would better reflect a broad socioeconomic concern, as tentatively suggested in this article, rather than confine itself to a strictly scientific approach. Man's conceptual environment, and nothing else, will certainly prevail in shaping the future of mankind, for the preservation of the environment presupposes a human being to live in it and a human mind to conceive a better life for man on this planet. From the point of view of man—and we have no other standpoint—Man, Pascal's "roseau pensant," is still more relevant than Nature.

3

THE TRAGEDY OF
THE COMMONS

GARRETT HARDIN[*]

Tragedy of Freedom in a Commons

... The tragedy of the commons develops in this way. Picture a pasture open to all. It is to be expected that each herdsman will try to keep as many cattle as possible on the commons. Such an arrangement may work reasonably satisfactorily for centuries because tribal wars, poaching, and disease keep the numbers of both man and beast well below the carrying capacity of the land. Finally, however, comes the day of reckoning, that is, the day when the long-desired goal of social stability becomes a reality. At this point, the inherent logic of the commons remorselessly generates tragedy.

As a rational being, each herdsman seeks to maximize his gain. Explicitly or implicitly, more or less consciously, he asks, "What is the utility to me of adding one more animal to my herd?" This utility has one negative and one positive component.

1. The positive component is a function of the increment of one animal. Since the herdsman receives all the proceeds from the sale of the additional animal, the positive utility is nearly +1.
2. The negative component is a function of the additional overgrazing created by one more animal. Since, however, the effects of overgrazing are

---

* Excerpted from Garrett Hardin, "The Tragedy of the Commons," *Science* 162 (December 13, 1968): 1243-1248. Copyright (c) 1968 American Association for the Advancement of Science. Reprinted with permission from AAAS.

shared by all the herdsmen, the negative utility for any particular deci-sionmaking herdsman is only a fraction of –1.

Adding together the component partial utilities, the rational herdsman con-cludes that the only sensible course for him to pursue is to add another animal to his herd. And another; and another. . . . But this is the conclusion reached by each and every rational herdsman sharing a commons. Therein is the tragedy. Each man is locked into a system that compels him to increase his herd without limit—in a world that is limited. Ruin is the destination toward which all men rush, each pursuing his own best interest in a society that believes in the freedom of the commons. Freedom in a commons brings ruin to all.

Some would say that this is a platitude. Would that it were! In a sense, it was learned thousands of years ago, but natural selection favors the forces of psycho-logical denial.[1] The individual benefits as an individual from his ability to deny the truth even though society as a whole, of which he is a part, suffers. Educa-tion can counteract the natural tendency to do the wrong thing, but the inex-orable succession of generations requires that the basis for this knowledge be constantly refreshed. . . .

In an approximate way, the logic of the commons has been understood for a long time, perhaps since the discovery of agriculture or the invention of private property in real estate. But it is understood mostly only in special cases which are not sufficiently generalized. Even at this late date, cattlemen leasing national land on the western ranges demonstrate no more than an ambivalent understanding, in constantly pressuring federal authorities to increase the head count to the point where overgrazing produces erosion and weed dominance. Likewise, the oceans of the world continue to suffer from the survival of the philosophy of the commons. Maritime nations still respond automatically to the shibboleth of the "freedom of the seas." Professing to believe in the "inexhaustible resources of the oceans," they bring species after species of fish and whales closer to extinction.[2]

The National Parks present another instance of the working out of the tragedy of the commons. At present, they are open to all, without limit. The parks them-selves are limited in extent—there is only one Yosemite Valley—whereas the pop-ulation seems to grow without limit. The values that visitors seek in the parks are steadily eroded. Plainly, we must soon cease to treat the parks as commons or they will be of no value to anyone.

What shall we do? We have several options. We might sell them off as private property. We might keep them as public property, but allocate the right to enter them. The allocation might be on the basis of wealth, by the use of an auction sys-tem. It might be on the basis of merit, as defined by some agreed-upon standards. It might be by lottery. Or it might be on a first-come, first-served basis, adminis-tered to long queues. These, I think, are all the reasonable possibilities. They are all objectionable. But we must choose—or acquiesce in the destruction of the commons that we call our National Parks.

Pollution

In a reverse way, the tragedy of the commons reappears in problems of pollution. Here it is not a question of taking something out of the commons, but of putting something in—sewage, or chemical, radioactive, and heat wastes into water; noxious and dangerous fumes into the air; and distracting and unpleasant advertising signs into the line of sight. The calculations of utility are much the same as before. The rational man finds that his share of the cost of the wastes he discharges into the commons is less than the cost of purifying his wastes before releasing them. Since this is true for everyone, we are locked into a system of "fouling our own nest," so long as we behave only as independent, rational, free-enterprisers.

The tragedy of the commons as a food basket is averted by private property, or something formally like it. But the air and waters surrounding us cannot readily be fenced, and so the tragedy of the commons as a cesspool must be prevented by different means, by coercive laws or taxing devices that make it cheaper for the polluter to treat his pollutants than to discharge them untreated. We have not progressed as far with the solution of this problem as we have with the first. Indeed, our particular concept of private property, which deters us from exhausting the positive resources of the earth, favors pollution. The owner of a factory on the bank of a stream—whose property extends to the middle of the stream—often has difficulty seeing why it is not his natural right to muddy the waters flowing past his door. The law, always behind the times, requires elaborate stitching and fitting to adapt it to this newly perceived aspect of the commons.

The pollution problem is a consequence of population. It did not much matter how a lonely American frontiersman disposed of his waste. "Flowing water purifies itself every 10 miles," my grandfather used to say, and the myth was near enough to the truth when he was a boy, for there were not too many people. But as population became denser, the natural chemical and biological recycling processes became overloaded, calling for a redefinition of property rights.

How to Legislate Temperance?

Analysis of the pollution problem as a function of population density uncovers a not generally recognized principle of morality, namely: the morality of an act is a function of the state of the system at the time it is performed.[3] Using the commons as a cesspool does not harm the general public under frontier conditions, because there is no public; the same behavior in a metropolis is unbearable. A hundred and fifty years ago a plainsman could kill an American bison, cut out only the tongue for his dinner, and discard the rest of the animal. He was not in any important sense being wasteful. Today, with only a few thousand bison left, we would be appalled at such behavior. . . .

That morality is system-sensitive escaped the attention of most codifiers of ethics in the past. "Thou shalt not . . ." is the form of traditional ethical directives which make no allowance for particular circumstances. The laws of our society follow the pattern of ancient ethics, and therefore are poorly suited to governing a complex, crowded, changeable world. Our epicyclic solution is to augment statutory law with administrative law. Since it is practically impossible to spell out all the conditions under which it is safe to burn trash in the backyard or to run an automobile without smog control, by law we delegate the details to bureaus. The result is administrative law, which is rightly feared for an ancient reason—Quis custodiet ipsos custodes?—"Who shall watch the watchers themselves?" John Adams said that we must have "a government of laws and not men." Bureau administrators, trying to evaluate the morality of acts in the total system, are singularly liable to corruption, producing a government by men, not laws.

Prohibition is easy to legislate (though not necessarily to enforce); but how do we legislate temperance? Experience indicates that it can be accomplished best through the mediation of administrative law. We limit possibilities unnecessarily if we suppose that the sentiment of Quis custodiet denies us the use of administrative law. We should rather retain the phrase as a perpetual reminder of fearful dangers we cannot avoid. The great challenge facing us now is to invent the corrective feedbacks that are needed to keep custodians honest. We must find ways to legitimate the needed authority of both the custodians and the corrective feedbacks.

Freedom to Breed Is Intolerable

The tragedy of the commons is involved in population problems in another way. In a world governed solely by the principle of "dog eat dog"—if indeed there ever was such a world—how many children a family had would not be a matter of public concern. Parents who bred too exuberantly would leave fewer descendants, not more, because they would be unable to care adequately for their children. David Lack and others have found that such a negative feedback demonstrably controls the fecundity of birds.[4] But men are not birds, and have not acted like them for millenniums, at least.

If each human family were dependent only on its own resources; if the children of improvident parents starved to death; if, thus, overbreeding brought its own "punishment" to the germ line—then there would be no public interest in controlling the breeding of families. But our society is deeply committed to the welfare state,[5] and hence is confronted with another aspect of the tragedy of the commons.

In a welfare state, how shall we deal with the family, the religion, the race, or the class (or indeed any distinguishable and cohesive group) that adopts overbreeding as a policy to secure its own aggrandizement?[6] To couple the concept of freedom to breed with the belief that everyone born has an equal right to the commons is to lock the world into a tragic course of action. . . .

Conscience Is Self-Eliminating

It is a mistake to think that we can control the breeding of mankind in the long run by an appeal to conscience. . . .

People vary. Confronted with appeals to limit breeding, some people will undoubtedly respond to the plea more than others. Those who have more children will produce a larger fraction of the next generation than those with more susceptible consciences. The difference will be accentuated, generation by generation. . . . The argument has here been stated in the context of the population problem, but it applies equally well to any instance in which society appeals to an individual exploiting a commons to restrain himself for the general good—by means of his conscience. To make such an appeal is to set up a selective system that works toward the elimination of conscience from the race.

Pathogenic Effects of Conscience

. . . To conjure up a conscience in others is tempting to anyone who wishes to extend his control beyond the legal limits. Leaders at the highest level succumb to this temptation. Has any President during the past generation failed to call on labor unions to moderate voluntarily their demands for higher wages, or to steel companies to honor voluntary guidelines on prices? I can recall none. The rhetoric used on such occasions is designed to produce feelings of guilt in noncooperators.

For centuries it was assumed without proof that guilt was a valuable, perhaps even an indispensable, ingredient of the civilized life. Now, in this post-Freudian world, we doubt it.

Paul Goodman speaks from the modern point of view when he says: "No good has ever come from feeling guilty, neither intelligence, policy, nor compassion. The guilty do not pay attention to the object but only to themselves, and not even to their own interests, which might make sense, but to their anxieties."[7]

One does not have to be a professional psychiatrist to see the consequences of anxiety. We in the Western world are just emerging from a dreadful two-centuries-long Dark Ages of Eros that was sustained partly by prohibition laws, but perhaps more effectively by the anxiety-generating mechanisms of education. . . .

Since proof is difficult, we may even concede that the results of anxiety may sometimes, from certain points of view, be desirable. The larger question we should ask is whether, as a matter of policy, we should ever encourage the use of a technique the tendency (if not the intention) of which is psychologically pathogenic. We hear much talk these days of responsible parenthood; the coupled words are incorporated into the titles of some organizations devoted to birth control. Some people have proposed massive propaganda campaigns to instill responsibility into the nation's (or the world's) breeders. But what is the meaning of the word responsibility in this context? Is it not merely a synonym for the word conscience? When we use the word responsibility in the absence of substantial sanctions are we not trying to browbeat a free man in a commons into acting against his own interest? Responsibility is a verbal counterfeit for a substantial quid pro quo. It is an attempt to get something for nothing.

If the word responsibility is to be used at all, I suggest that it be in the sense Charles Frankel uses it.[8] "Responsibility," says this philosopher, "is the product of definite social arrangements." Notice that Frankel calls for social arrangements—not propaganda.

Mutual Coercion Mutually Agreed Upon

The social arrangements that produce responsibility are arrangements that create coercion, of some sort. Consider bank-robbing. The man who takes money from a bank acts as if the bank were a commons. How do we prevent such action? Certainly not by trying to control his behavior solely by a verbal appeal to his sense of responsibility. Rather than rely on propaganda we follow Frankel's lead and insist that a bank is not a commons; we seek the definite social arrangements that will keep it from becoming a commons. That we thereby infringe on the freedom of would-be robbers we neither deny nor regret.

The morality of bank-robbing is particularly easy to understand because we accept complete prohibition of this activity. We are willing to say "Thou shalt not rob banks," without providing for exceptions. But temperance also can be created by coercion. Taxing is a good coercive device. To keep downtown shoppers temperate in their use of parking space we introduce parking meters for short periods, and traffic fines for longer ones. We need not actually forbid a citizen to park as long as he wants to; we need merely make it increasingly expensive for him to do so. Not prohibition, but carefully biased options are what we offer him. A Madison Avenue man might call this persuasion; I prefer the greater candor of the word coercion.

Coercion is a dirty word to most liberals now, but it need not forever be so. As with the four-letter words, its dirtiness can be cleansed away by exposure to the light, by saying it over and over without apology or embarrassment. To many, the word coercion implies arbitrary decisions of distant and irresponsible bureaucrats; but this is not a necessary part of its meaning. The only kind of coercion I recommend is mutual coercion, mutually agreed upon by the majority of the people affected.

To say that we mutually agree to coercion is not to say that we are required to enjoy it, or even to pretend we enjoy it. Who enjoys taxes? We all grumble about them. But we accept compulsory taxes because we recognize that voluntary taxes would favor the conscienceless. We institute and (grumblingly) support taxes and other coercive devices to escape the horror of the commons.

An alternative to the commons need not be perfectly just to be preferable. . . . The alternative of the commons is too horrifying to contemplate. Injustice is preferable to total ruin.

It is one of the peculiarities of the warfare between reform and the status quo that it is thoughtlessly governed by a double standard. Whenever a reform measure is proposed it is often defeated when its opponents triumphantly discover a flaw in it. As Kingsley Davis has pointed out,[9] worshippers of the status quo sometimes imply that no reform is possible without unanimous agreement, an implication contrary to historical fact. As nearly as I can make out, automatic rejection of proposed reforms is based on one of two unconscious assumptions: (i) that the status quo is perfect; or (ii) that the choice we face is between reform and no action; if the proposed reform is imperfect, we presumably should take no action at all, while we wait for a perfect proposal.

But we can never do nothing. That which we have done for thousands of years is also action. It also produces evils. Once we are aware that the status quo is action, we can then compare its discoverable advantages and disadvantages with the predicted advantages and disadvantages of the proposed reform, discounting as best we can for our lack of experience. On the basis of such a comparison, we can make a rational decision which will not involve the unworkable assumption that only perfect systems are tolerable.

Recognition of Necessity

Perhaps the simplest summary of this analysis of man's population problems is this: the commons, if justifiable at all, is justifiable only under conditions of low-population density. As the human population has increased, the commons has had to be abandoned in one aspect after another.

First we abandoned the commons in food gathering, enclosing farmland and restricting pastures and hunting and fishing areas. These restrictions are still not complete throughout the world.

Somewhat later we saw that the commons as a place for waste disposal would also have to be abandoned. Restrictions on the disposal of domestic sewage are widely accepted in the Western world; we are still struggling to close the commons to pollution by automobiles, factories, insecticide sprayers, fertilizing operations, and atomic energy installations.

In a still more embryonic state is our recognition of the evils of the commons in matters of pleasure. There is almost no restriction on the propagation of sound waves in the public medium. The shopping public is assaulted with mindless music, without its consent. Our government is paying out billions of dollars to create supersonic transport which will disturb 50,000 people for every one person who is whisked from coast to coast 3 hours faster. Advertisers muddy the airwaves of radio and television and pollute the view of travelers. We are a long way from outlawing the commons in matters of pleasure. Is this because our Puritan inheritance makes us view pleasure as something of a sin, and pain (that is, the pollution of advertising) as the sign of virtue?

Every new enclosure of the commons involves the infringement of somebody's personal liberty. Infringements made in the distant past are accepted because no contemporary complains of a loss. It is the newly proposed infringements that we vigorously oppose; cries of "rights" and "freedom" fill the air. But what does "freedom" mean? When men mutually agreed to pass laws against robbing, mankind became more free, not less so. Individuals locked into the logic of the commons are free only to bring on universal ruin; once they see the necessity of mutual coercion, they become free to pursue other goals. I believe it was Hegel who said, "Freedom is the recognition of necessity."

The most important aspect of necessity that we must now recognize is the necessity of abandoning the commons in breeding. No technical solution can rescue us from the misery of overpopulation. Freedom to breed will bring ruin to all. At the moment, to avoid hard decisions many of us are tempted to propagandize for conscience and responsible parenthood. The temptation must be resisted, because an appeal to independently acting consciences selects for life disappearance of all conscience in the long run, and an increase in anxiety in the short.

The only way we can preserve and nurture other and more precious freedoms is by relinquishing the freedom to breed, and that very soon. "Freedom is the recognition of necessity"—and it is the role of education to reveal to all the necessity of abandoning the freedom to breed. Only so, can we put an end to this aspect of the tragedy of the commons.

Notes

1. G. Hardin, ed., *Population, Evolution, and Birth Control* (Freeman, San Francisco, 1964), p. 56.

2. S. McVay, *Scientific America* 216 (No. 8), 13 (1966).

3. J. Fletcher, *Situation Ethics* (Westminster, Philadelphia, 1966).

4. D. Lack, *The Natural Regulation of Animal Numbers* (Clarendon Press, Oxford, 1954).

5. H. Girvetz, *From Wealth to Welfare* (Stanford Univ. Press, Stanford, Calif., 1950).

6. G. Hardin, *Perspec. Biol. Med.* 6, 366 (1963).

7. P. Goodman, *New York Rev. Books* 10(8), 22 (23 May 1968).

8. C. Frankel, *The Case for Modern Man* (Harper, New York, 1955), p. 203.

9. J. D. Rolansky, *Genetics and the Future of Man* (Appleton-Century-Crofts, New York, 1966), p. 177.

4

NO TRAGEDY
ON THE COMMONS

SUSAN J. BUCK*

Introduction

In 1951, Josephine Tey published her classic detective story *Daughter of Time*. In this defense of Richard III, she coined the term *Tonypandy*, which is the regrettable situation which occurs when a historical event is reported and memorialized inaccurately but consistently until the resulting fiction is believed to be the truth.[1] History is not the only field in which Tonypandy occurs. A prime example of Tonypandy in the field of economics is the "tragedy of the commons."

Academics are often too facile in labeling an article as "seminal," but Garrett Hardin's 1968 article, "The Tragedy of the Commons," deserves the accolade.[2] The article has been reprinted over fifty times,[3] and entire books have been devoted to exploring the meaning and implications of Hardin's memorable title.[4] The phrase "tragedy of the commons" has slipped into common parlance at colleges and universities and is rapidly becoming public property.[5] Discussion of the inevitability of such a tragedy is the lawful prey of economists, sociologists, philosophers, and theologians. Certainly we cannot deny that the phenomenon exists: the ruination of a limited resource when confronted with unlimited access by an expanding population. Where, then, lies Tonypandy in the tragedy of the commons?

Although the tragedy of the commons may occur, that it regularly occurred on the common lands of medieval and post-medieval England is not true; the historical antecedents of the tragedy of the commons as developed by Hardin and others following the 1968 article, and as commonly understood by students and profes-

* Originally published in *Environmental Ethics* 7 (Spring 1985): 49-61. Reprinted with permission.

sors, are inaccurate.[6] . . . Decline was not the result of unlimited access, but rather was the result of the historical forces of the industrial revolution, agrarian reform, and improved agricultural practices.

"The Tragedy of the Commons" Defined

. . . [Hardin's original] language is relatively free of cultural phenomena. . . . Later references to Hardin's tragedy of the commons, however, reflect a more explicit historical perspective. In 1977 Hardin used allusions to the Enclosure Acts of the late eighteenth and early nineteenth centuries to explain how the tragedy might be cured.[7] In 1969, Beryl Crowe wrote:

> The commons is a fundamental social institution that has a history going back through our own colonial experience to a body of English common law which antedates the Roman conquest. That law recognized that in societies there are some environmental objects which have never been, and should never be, exclusively appropriated to any individual or group of individuals. In England the classic example of the commons is the pasturage set aside for public use, and the "tragedy of the commons" to which Hardin refers was a tragedy of overgrazing and lack of care and fertilization which resulted in erosion and underproduction so destructive that there developed in the late 19th century an enclosure movement.[8]

. . . Perhaps the most extensive anglicization of the commons is found in *This Endangered Planet* by Richard Falk. He writes that Hardin "has evolved an effective metaphor of [the paradox of aggregation] from a historical experience, the destruction of the common pastures of English country towns in the 1700s and 1800s through overgrazing herds."[9]

Further examples can be found, almost ad infinitum and certainly ad nauseam. Moreover, questioning of graduate students in economics or planning or public administration elicits the same historical background on the tragedy of the commons as described by Falk. Such evidence suggests that there is a general impression among most people today that the tragedy was a regular occurrence on the common lands of the villages in medieval and post-medieval England—a belief which, despite its wide acceptance as fact, is historically false.

The Commons Defined

In order to dispel the myth of the tragedy of the commons, we must first discover the definition of commons as it was understood in medieval England. The legal right of common is "a right which one or more persons have to take or use some portion of that which another's soil produces . . . and is a right to part of the profits of the soil, and to part only, the right of the soil lying with another and not with the person who claims common."[10] This right is an ancient one: "Recent archaeological and historical work indicates that in many places nucleated villages did not come into being until the ninth, tenth, or even the eleventh centuries. . . . But whatever their origins, the classic common field system probably developed with them. . . ."[11] These rights "were not something specifically granted by a generous landlord, but were the residue of rights that were much more extensive, rights that are in all probability older than the modern conception of private property. They probably antedate the idea of private property in land, and are therefore of vast antiquity."[12] The right of common was a right granted to specific persons because these persons had some prior claim to the land or because the actual owner of the land granted them that right in return for their services.

Our modern-day notions of *common* as a public right does not accurately describe the medieval commons. Gonner wrote in 1912:

> [Common] now is taken as denoting the claims, somewhat vague and precarious, of the public as against those holding the land and engaged in its cultivation. But this finds no sanction in a time when over very many, if not most, cultivated districts common was a result of claim to land, and formed a necessary condition of its proper management. . . . The early rights of common were anything but vague, and were invariably vested in those employed in cultivation of their representatives; they were anything rather than a general claim on the part of the public. . . . [Common rights] were a necessary element in the agricultural system, they were involved in the ownership and cultivation of the land, and they were largely the source of the profits obtained from the land and the means of rendering its cultivation effective.[13]

Clearly our use of common to describe public access to national parks or to deep-sea fishing is at variance with the original use of the term. . . .

We thus have a picture of the legal status of a common. Either by common-law right as freehold tenant or through usage and grants, a villager was entitled to pasture limited numbers of specific animals on the lord's waste. It is important to note that even from the beginning, the use of the common was not unrestricted: "Common pasture of stubble and fallow was a feature of open-field husbandry from the start . . . and with it went communal control."[14] The English common was not available to the general public but was only available to certain individuals who owned or were granted the right to use it. Use of the common even by these people was not unregulated. The types and in some cases the numbers of animals each tenant could pasture were limited, based at least partly on a recognition of the limited carrying capacity of the land.

The Management
of the Commons

The earliest records for communal farming regulations are the manor court rolls of the mid-thirteenth century.[15] The earliest record for a village meeting is the fourteenth century. Joan Thirsk writes:

> From these dates the evidence points unequivocally to the autonomy of village communities in determining the form of, and the rules governing their field system. . . . In villages which possessed no more than one manor, matters were agreed in the manorial court, and the decisions sometimes, but not always, recorded on the court roll. Decisions affecting villages which shared the use of commons were taken at the court of the chief lord, at which all the villages were represented. In villages where more than one manor existed, agreement might be reached at a village meeting at which all tenants and lords were present or represented.[16]

. . . Such agreements among the neighbors are recorded in the village bylaws. These bylaws "emphasize the degree to which . . . agricultural practice was directed and controlled by an assembly of cultivators, the manorial court, who coordinated and regulated the season-by-season activities of the whole community. Arable and meadowland were normally thrown open for common pasturing by the stock of all the commoners after harvest and in fallow times, and this necessitated some rules about cropping, fencing, and grazing beasts. Similarly, all the cultivators of the intermixed strips enjoyed common pasturage in the waste, and in addition, the rights to gather timber, peat and other commodities were essential concomitants of the possession of arable and meadow shares."[17] There was, however, an extraordinary diversity of bylaws among the various regions of England. In one Lincolnshire fenland village, for example, "strangers coming into the town but having no land could enjoy free common for their cattle for one year. After that they had to abide by the rules governing all other inhabitants. These were generous provisions that reflected the abundance of grazing."[18] In contrast, in 1440, the village of Launton decreed that "any tenant who has a parcel of meadow in East Brokemede shall not mow there now or ever until his neighbors are agreed under pain of 3s.4d.,"[19] a clear reflection of the need to conserve and to regulate. What is important to note here is the detail with which the open fields were regulated. Ault notes that bylaws covered such points as where fieldworkers were paid (at the granary rather than in the field, where payment in kind might lead to accusations of theft), and at what age boys could begin to pasture sheep on the common (sixteen). The commons were carefully and painstakingly regulated, and those instances in which the common deteriorated were most often due to lawbreaking and to oppression of the poorer tenant rather than to egoistic abuse of a common resource.

Abuses of the Commons

The commons were subject to several forms of abuse. Often the regulations governing the commons were broken, as when greedy farmers took in unauthorized animals, or when wealthy landowners or squatters took grazing to which they were not entitled because of lack of agreement among the tenants. The common thread in these abuses is their illegality.

One of the methods of controlling grazing was "stinting," allocating the number and type of beasts that could be grazed on the waste. Stinting developed more from lack of winter feed when stock was pastured on the arable land than from a desire to protect the summer grazing. This summer grazing "was as carefully controlled as the manorial courts could make it."[20] . . . In Westmorland in 1695, "Occasionally, these stinting rules were broken, resulting in the 'Townfield . . . being sore abused and misorderly eaten.' The remedy was to employ a pounder who had to make sure the stints were carefully maintained."[21] Hence, we have one abuse of the common: simple lawbreaking which was remedied by resort to the law.

A similar problem with a less happy solution occurred when the wealthier landholders took advantage of the poorer tenants. In the early sixteenth century, Fitzherbert noted that the rich man benefitted from overcharging the common.[22] According to Gonner, it was "pointed out alike in the sixteenth, seventeenth and eighteenth centuries that the poor owning rights may be largely kept out of their rights by the action of large farmers who exceed their rights and thus surcharge the common to the detriment of all, or by the lack of winter feed in the absence of which summer grazing could be of little worth. . . . The unfortunate poor tenant was denied his remedy at law for the illegal abuses of the more powerful landowners. The ultimate conclusion was the enclosure of the common land, most effective in the parliamentary enclosure acts from 1720 to 1880."[23] Such change was perhaps inevitable, but it is social change and the perennial exploitation of the poor by the less poor rather than Hardin's tragedy.[24]

A third problem arose on unstinted land. In the sixteenth century the "unstinted common was almost invariably overburdened. . . . This state of things was largely to the advantage of rich commoners or the lord of the manor, who got together large flocks and herds and pastured them in the common lands to the detriment of the poorer commoners, who, unlike them, could do little in the way of providing winter feed, and now found themselves ousted even from their slender privileges in the commons."[25] . . . By 1800 in the East Riding, "there was a good deal of overstocking. Some of the commons were stinted but others were not, and it was here that overstocking occurred. Many of the commons were frequently waterlogged when a small expenditure would have drained them, but what was everyone's business was nobody's business."[26] Of course, by 1800 parliamentary enclosure was well under way and this report from East Riding was made by an employee of the newly formed board of agriculture, established in response to a "widespread campaign for the more effective use of the land-resources of the country, with particular reference to the large areas of remaining open fields and to the vast areas of common lands and wastes."[27] Sponsored by wealthy landowners, the land reform was frequently no more than a sophisticated land-grab, justified in part by the admittedly striking increase in productivity of enclosed common land.

The Inevitable Decline of the Commons

The increased productivity was often touted by land reformers—wealthy or otherwise—as proof of the evils of the commons system. However, the change was the result of many factors, and not just of enclosure. Some of the increase would probably have occurred without enclosure, but enclosure hastened the process. The common land was not the best land. The lord's waste was often reclaimed land, cultivated from forest and marsh. . . . Enclosure took the better land and subjected it to the new and improved methods of agriculture which had been all but impossible under the common system, for the management of the common could not be changed unless all commoners agreed and, just as important, remained agreed.[28] Improved roads and transportation facilities made marketing easier, and of course, the land had fewer people to support. Economies of scale made it profitable to use improved stock. In 1760, Robert Bakewell, the founder of modern methods of livestock improvement, began selective breeding of farm animals.[29] Previously forbidden by ecclesiastical authorities as incest, inbreeding of animals with desirable qualities soon led to dramatic improvements in stock.[30] Planting the enclosure with nitrogen-fixing crops such as clover improved the soil; drainage improved livestock health. Animals were disturbed less by driving to and from land pasture. All of these factors combined to improve the productivity of the formerly common land.

That enclosure improved productivity is neither a surprise nor a shame to the commons. The commons system "was falling into disuse, a new system was taking its place, and with the change the actual use made of the common or common rights declined. It might indeed have been retorted [to advocates of inclosure] that what was wanted was a stricter enforcement of the whole common right system."[31] A related view was expressed in 1974 by Van Rensselaer Potter:

> When I first read Hardin's article [on the tragedy of the commons], I wondered if the users of the early English commons weren't prevented from committing the fatal error of overgrazing by a kind of "bioethics" enforced by the moral pressure of their neighbors. Indeed, the commons system operated successfully in England for several hundred years. Now we read that, before the colonial era in the Sahel, "overpasturage was avoided" by rules worked out by tribal chiefs. When deep wells were drilled to obtain water "the boreholes threw into chaos the traditional system of pasture use based on agreements among tribal chieftains." Thus, we see the tragedy of the commons not as a defect in the concept of a "commons" but as a result of the disastrous transition period between the loss of an effective bioethic and its replacement by a new bioethic that could once again bring biological realities and human values into a viable balance.[32]

Conclusion

Hardin writes that the "view that whatever is owned by many people should be free for the taking by anyone who feels a need for it . . . is precisely the idea of the commons."[33] Why should it matter if this "idea of the commons" is historically inaccurate?

Any academic should feel an aversion to Tonypandy, but the issue is more important than a possible pedantic dislike of inaccuracy. It is beyond dispute that issues such as depletion of limited resources, environmental quality, fisheries economics, and national land management are of great and increasing concern. How those issues are dealt with depends in large part on our perceptions of the disposition of similar issues in the past. If we misunderstand the true nature of the commons, we also misunderstand the implications of the demise of the traditional commons system. Perhaps what existed in fact was not a "tragedy of the commons" but rather a triumph: that for hundreds of years—and perhaps thousands, although written records do not exist to prove the longer era—land was managed successfully by communities. That the system failed to survive the industrial revolution, agrarian reform, and transfigured farming practices is hardly to be wondered at.

Our reexamination of the commons requires a dual focus. The first is to search for the ideas and practices which led to successful commoning for centuries and to try to find lessons and applications for our own times. The second focus is epistemological: are our perceptions of the nature of humankind awry? Since it seems quite likely if "economic man" had been managing the commons that tragedy really would have occurred, perhaps someone else was running the common.

In 1968, Hardin wrote that "'ruin' is the destruction toward which all men rush, each pursuing his own best interest in a society that believes in the freedom of the commons. Freedom in a common brings ruin to all."[34] But the common is not free and never was free. Perhaps in the changed perception of the common lies a remedy for ruin.

Notes

1. Tonypandy was a Welsh mining town where, in 1910, Winston Churchill sent unarmed London policemen to quell rioting strikers. The version popularly believed in Wales is that government troops shot Welsh miners who were striking for their workers' rights. In precise Tey-usage, Tonypandy exists when such a fiction is allowed to persist even by those people who know better. An example of Tonypandy in American history is the Boston Massacre. Josephine Tey, *Daughter of Time* (New York: Macmillan, 1951).

2. Garrett Hardin, "The Tragedy of the Commons," *Science* 162 (1968): 1243–48.

3. Gordon Foxall, "A Note on the Management of 'Commons,'" *Journal of Agricultural Economics* 30 (1979): 55.

4. For example, Garrett Hardin and John Baden, eds., *Managing the Commons* (San Francisco: Freeman, 1977).

5. Who could mistake the content—or inspiration—of articles such as "The Use of the Commons Dilemma in Examining the Allocation of Common Resources" (R. Kenneth Godwin and W. Brace Shepard, Resources for the Future Reprint 179), or "Legislating Commons: The Navajo Tribal Council and the Navajo Range" (Gary D. Libecap and Ronald N. Johnson, *Economic Inquiry* 18 [1980]: 69–86), or Hardin and Baden, *Managing the Commons*. See also basic American government texts such as Robert Lineberry, *Government in America*, 2nd ed. (Boston: Little, Brown, 1983), in which he identifies the tragedy of the commons as "a parable about sheep overgrazing a common meadow" (pp. 579–80).

6. This is not to imply that the tragedy of the commons never occurred in those centuries; records are incomplete and to assert positively that something never occurred is to court contradiction and exposure.

7. Garrett Hardin, "Denial and Disguise," in Hardin and Baden, *Managing the Commons*, pp. 45–52. Hardin acknowledges the injustice of the Enclosure Acts but applauds the increase in agricultural productivity that they entailed.

8. Beryl Crowe, "The Tragedy of the Commons Revisited," in Hardin and Baden, *Managing the Commons*, pp. 54–55.

9. Richard A. Falk, *This Endangered Planet* (New York: Random, 1971), p. 48.

10. E. C. K. Gonner, *Common Land and Inclosure*, 2nd ed. (London: Cass, 1966). The first portion of this quote is quoted by Gonner without attribution. This is not, however, an outmoded or esoteric definition: basic American college dictionaries provide the same definition.

11. C. C. Taylor, "Archaeology and the Origins of Open-Field Agriculture," in Trevor Rowley, ed., *The Origins of Open-Field Agriculture* (London: Groom Helm, 1981), p. 21. See also Della Hooke, "Open-field Agriculture—The Evidence from the Pre-Conquest Charters of the West Midlands," ibid., p. 58: "Land held in common by a community is clearly in evidence by the tenth century."

12. W. G. Hoskins and L. Dudley Stamp, *The Common Lands of England and Wales* (London: Collins, 1965), p. 6.

13. Gonner, *Common Land*, pp. 3–4.

14. W. O. Ault, *Open-Field Farming in Medieval England* (London: Allen and Unwin, 1972), p. 17.

15. Ibid., p. 18. Ault gives 1246 as the earliest manor court rolls; the earliest manorial reeve's accounts are for 1208–9.

16. Joan Thirsk, "Field Systems of the East Midlands," in Alan R. H. Baker and Robin A. Butlin, eds., *Studies of Field Systems in the British Isles* (Cambridge, England: Cambridge University Press, 1973), p. 232.

17. B. K. Roberts, "Field Systems of the West Midlands," in Baker and Butlin, *Studies*, p. 199.

18. Thirsk, "Field Systems," p. 251.

19. Westminster Muniments, 1550; quoted in Ault, *Open-Field Farming*, p. 26.

20. G. Elliot, "Field Systems of Northwest England," in Baker and Butlin, *Studies*, p. 67. As an example, in Denwick in 1567 the stint of "each husbandland was 6 old beasts above two years old, 37 sheep above one year old besides lambs and other young cattle, four pigs above one year old, two geese and one horse or mare" (R. A. Butlin, "Field Systems of Northumberland and Durham," in Baker and Butlin, *Studies*, p. 138).

21. Elliot, "Field Systems," p. 83. The internal quote is from the Westmorland Record office, Musgrave D. P., Court Rolls 1695.

22. Edward Scrutton, *Commons and Common Fields* (1887; reprint ed., New York: Lenox Hill, 1970), p. 122.

23. Roberts, "Field Systems," p. 190.

24. A classic example of exploitation is the Statute of Merton (1236), which allowed "chief tenants to assart land for their own or their villeins' exclusive use, provided that 'sufficient' common land was left for the needs of the village community." June A. Sheppard, "Field Systems of Yorkshire," in Baker and Bullin, *Studies*, pp. 176–77.

25. Gonner, *Common Land*, p. 103.

26. Hoskins and Stamp, *Common Lands*, p. 55.

27. Ibid., p. 54.

28. Scrutton, *Commons*, pp. 120–21. For example, all the farmers might agree to let one field lie fallow against custom for two years. If, in the second year, one tenant decided to return to the customary management and to graze his cattle in the field, the rest were powerless to stop him, and of course, the result would be the use of the field by all the tenants.

29. Victor Rice, Frederick Andrews, Everett Warwick, and James Legates, *Breeding and Improvement of Farm Animals* (New York: McGraw-Hill, 1957), p. 16.

30. For example, between 1710 and 1790, the weight at Smithfield of cattle changed from 370 pounds to 800 pounds, of calves from 50 to 148, of sheep from 28 to 80, and of lambs from 18 to 50. This weight change is of course due to a multitude of causes. Scrutton, *Commons*, p. 121.

31. Gonner, *Common Land*, pp. 306–7.

32. Van Rensselaer Potter, *Science* 185 (1974): 813.

33. Garrett Hardin, "Denial and Disguise," in Hardin and Baden, *Managing the Commons*, p. 47.

34. Hardin, "Tragedy of the Commons," in Hardin and Baden, *Managing the Commons*, p. 20.

PART TWO

ECOLOGY AND THE STRUCTURE OF THE INTERNATIONAL SYSTEM

As discussed in the introductory chapter to this volume, environmental problems are the result of a complex array of social forces, including technology, political and economic institutions, social structures, and people's values. In this part we are particularly interested in the subset of causes that can be attributed to the structure of the international system. Scholars in international relations sometimes use the term "structure" to refer to the international distribution of power among states. Thus, during the Cold War, the structure of the system was often said to be bipolar in that the two superpowers wielded by far the most power in international affairs. Here we use the term more generally to refer to the relatively stable, unchanging characteristics of world politics, such as the political division of the world into sovereign states, or the capitalist global economy, which shapes transactions among societies.[1] These relatively permanent features of the world system give shape and definition to the interactions among governments, international organizations, multinational corporations, nongovernmental organizations, and other agents of world politics.

A few aspects of system structure seem particularly important in shaping the array of global environmental problems we face and the possibilities for responding to those problems. The first is state sovereignty, which many scholars take to be the central feature of world politics. As the World Commission on Environment and Development put it, "The Earth is one, but the world is not."[2] One of the main reasons for this absence of unity is the sovereignty of individual states, which gives them, at least in principle, decisionmaking autonomy over matters falling within their territorial jurisdiction.

The tensions between ecology and sovereignty are due in part to the fact that the boundaries of states and the boundaries of ecosystems do not perfectly coincide, meaning that individual states cannot effectively manage many of their most serious environmental problems. Most large-scale environmental problems cross national borders; many are tied to global systems, such as the atmosphere and oceans, which are beyond the control of individual states.

Yet governments have clung tenaciously to the notion that they retain exclusive authority over the activities within their territory that affect the global environment. The primacy of state sovereignty was one of the few points on which governments could agree during the contentious Stockholm conference:

States have . . . the sovereign right to exploit their own resources pursuant to their own environmental policies, and the responsibility to ensure that activities within their jurisdiction or control do not cause damage to the environment of other states or of areas beyond the limits of their national jurisdiction.[3]

Although this principle refers not only to the sovereign rights of states but also to their responsibilities, it has generally been seen as a reinforcement of state sovereignty. In most instances, states have guarded this right emphatically when pressured by the global community—whether the state in question is a tropical rain-forest country, such as Brazil, or a leading emitter of greenhouse gases, such as the United States.

Some observers see global environmental challenges as eroding sovereignty, as states are forced to accept restrictions on domestic actions. Others argue that international environmental cooperation is boosting the problem-solving abilities of many states, thereby reaffirming their sovereign authority. But as Ken Conca points out, sovereignty is more complex than simply the right of nations to do as they please or the authority of governments to act. Conca argues that sovereignty is indeed being changed by global ecological interdependence, but in many ways at once. Using the example of the Brazilian Amazon, Conca sees Brazilian sovereignty as simultaneously being bounded by new international norms, broadened as the state is made the foundation for forest protection strategies, and rendered more brittle as the enormity of the task and likelihood of failure put state legitimacy at risk. Seen in this light, sovereignty is not an unchanging structural feature of the world system but rather a historical social institution that may or may not successfully adapt to global ecological interdependence.

A second crucial feature of system structure is the existence of an increasingly interconnected capitalist world economy. If nature refuses to sit still for governance within national borders, so too does commerce. It has long been apparent that the world's major centers of industrial production and consumption, including the United States, Europe, and Japan, are not "ecologically self-contained."[4] These regions rely upon imports of a wide range of commodities, both as raw materials for production and as food for consumption. As a result, the core industrial regions of the world economy draw upon the "ecological capital" of the places that supply those inputs. The production that takes place in the industrialized world thus casts an ecological shadow far beyond the borders of individual industrialized countries.

To be sure, we have had a world-scale economic system since at least the colonial era. Nevertheless, economic interconnectedness is being deepened and broadened dramatically by the increasing mobility of goods, services, money, people, technology, ideas, and symbols—

the phenomenon often referred to as globalization. What are the ramifications of globalization for the environment? One is the greater dispersion of both positive and negative repercussions: negative in the sense of invasive species and cross-border pollutant flows; positive in the sense of cross-border environmental cooperation of the sort discussed in later sections.

Also, globalization seems to both lengthen and shorten socio-geographic distances. On the one hand, globalization means the growth of genuinely global-scale production chains that snake in and out of nominally sovereign territories. People at any one node along that chain—be they citizens, consumers, workers, activists, government regulators—are further "distanced" from the other nodes.[5] Most modern consumers, for example, have almost no knowledge of the environmental impact attached to the production of that which they consume, be it an auto or an apple. On the other hand, the communications revolution forges important new linkages that shorten virtual distances, making some forms of knowledge exchange, cooperation, and coalition building possible on a far broader scale.

Rather than attempt to resolve the many controversies about the effects of globalization, Adil Najam and colleagues at the International Institute for Sustainable Development pose a series of propositions about the challenges that globalization poses for sustainability, and the critical entry points for turning its influence in positive directions. For these authors, key effects of globalization include its resource-intensive growth implications and its potential to destabilize livelihoods (particularly for the poor and vulnerable), as well as the world economy's growing vulnerability to disruption via environmental degradation. Foreshadowing a theme we take up in Part Four, they also focus central attention on patterns of consumption as the key to a more sustainable future.

The transnational character of modern capitalism also raises important questions of responsibility. Who is responsible for the destruction of tropical rain forests, when the "causes" of that destruction range from the chain saws in the hands of local timber cutters to the global economic system that creates a demand for tropical timber products? Do we blame local people, the transnational banks and corporations that carry economic practices across borders, distant people who may benefit from these activities, or the structure of the world capitalist economy as a whole?

Just as state sovereignty imposes a pattern of political authority that does not correspond exactly to the underlying ecological reality, so transnational capitalism imposes patterns of economic activity that do not wholly correspond to the prevailing pattern of political authority. Both features of system structure give environmental problems an inherently transnational dimension, and both greatly complicate the prospects for global cooperation. Yet it is important to keep in mind that these "structural" properties of the international system are not natural or automatic features of world politics—they are the results of human choice and behavior. This leads us to the question of how ideas, beliefs, and worldviews give structure to the behavior of various actors in world politics. Obviously, sovereignty and capitalism are two ideas that have had a powerful structuring influence. Some observers have argued that these two ideas are embedded in the more fundamental ethos of "modernity"—a complex set of beliefs that came to dominate European culture in the modern era and subsequently spread to the Americas, Africa, and Asia via colonialism and other manifestations of European power.[6] Some of the principal ideas that make up the modern worldview involve beliefs about the autonomy of the individual, the power of science and technology, the desirability of increased consumption, and the inevitability of progress. Thus, the ideological bedrock of modernity is as important a feature of world politics as the political structure of state sovereignty and the economic structure of global capitalism.[7]

But not all actors embrace the dominant social paradigm. Indeed, many environmentalists argue that environmentalism is a social movement that rejects core features of the dominant paradigm. Is this the case? Does environmentalism transcend the limits of state sovereignty, oppose the unfettered operation of global capitalism, and reject many central tenets of the modern worldview? Is it possible that the idea of environmentalism is itself building a new global structure: a network of individuals and groups with an "antisystemic" orientation in the sense that they reject many values and preferences of the dominant social paradigm?[8] Or is environmentalism better understood as a set of ideas that fits comfortably within the confines of a statist, capitalist, modernist world? These questions are hotly debated by environmentalists and their critics, and there may be no single answer: The environmental movement consists of a patchwork of groups with widely differing goals and views, working at levels ranging from local to global. As Parts Four, Five, and Six make clear, the diversity of ideas driving various forms of environmental advocacy can make collaboration among environmentalists as difficult as collaboration among sovereign states.

Nevertheless, the environmental movement has emerged as a force to be reckoned with in international affairs. We conclude this part with essays that present some important ways in which environmental NGOs and movement groups are changing world politics, including domestic political struggles, transnational networking, and the promotion of large-scale sociocultural change.

The autobiography of Brazilian activist Chico Mendes reminds us that environmentalism around the world has historically drawn most of its energy from the grass roots. Despite the growing international-ization of environmental politics, domestic political struggles remain the most important pathway to change. Mendes was a labor activist and environmentalist working in the western Amazon state of Acre. He led a movement for the preservation of the Amazon forest and the livelihood of its occupants. Mendes advocated a brand of environ-mentalism that struggled as much against the oppression of people as the destruction of nature. Mendes was killed in 1988, assassinated by powerful local landowning interests that were threatened by his ef-forts to organize rural workers in the region. The powerful vision he expressed, which made him an important political leader of the forest peoples' movement in Brazil, also made him in death a martyr and an international symbol. The global outcry following his murder greatly enhanced the pressures on the Brazilian government to reverse poli-cies that promote deforestation in the Amazon region.[9]

We also include a short interview with Kenyan environmental activist Wangari Maathai, another local activist who has become famous around the world for her efforts to protect forests and their people. Kenyan and Brazilian forest politics differ dramatically, and Mendes and Maathai come from very different personal backgrounds. Yet some of the similar themes in their experiences—including the emphasis on peo-ple's livelihoods, the centrality of struggle, and the challenges of orga-nizing and mobilizing a sustained movement—should be apparent. Maathai, who won the Nobel Prize in 2004, also points to the significant role of gender dynamics, a theme taken up in more detail in Part Six.

Tellingly, even as economic globalization has intensified pressures on many local communities and spawned the sort of activism char-acteristic of the movements Mendes and Maathai led, so too has it promoted growing transnational linkages among activists with a common cause. Recognizing that struggles to determine the future of resource use, livelihoods, community, and environmental quality have a transnational dimension, many networks, coalitions, and full-blown social movements have sprung up linking activists across borders.[10] Longtime activist Smitu Kothari describes one such campaign here. Activists in India seeking to block the Sardar Sarovar mega-dam project in the Narmada valley partnered with international environmental and human rights organizations to pressure not only the Indian gov-ernment but also aid donors and the World Bank. Their activities re-verse one of the traditional axioms of environmentalism: These communities are thinking locally but acting globally. To be sure, ques-tions remain about the strength of such efforts. In the Narmada case, activists were able to drive World Bank funding for the project and to pressure the government to compensate victimized communities that were flooded out by the dam—but they did not block the dam from being built or the villages from being inundated. Kothari's essay not only describes the campaign but also reflects on the many challenges facing transnational activist networks and coalitions.

If a sustained global movement of environmentalism is to exert political power, it will be because movement groups as diverse as those seen in these Brazilian, Kenyan, and Indian examples can find ways to establish effective and durable international networks to coordinate efforts, exchange information, and pool resources. The barriers to such cooperation are formidable: a lack of resources compared to the activities they oppose; the frequent opposition of governments, corporations, and other powerful actors; conflicting viewpoints on goals and means; and unequal power between relatively well-heeled and influential groups from the North and some of the less institutionalized, grassroots groups of both the North and the South. Nor can we assume that international environmentalism automatically produces environmental or social benefits; Part Six presents troubling cases in which transnational environmental groups have sometimes sought to preserve Latin American rain forests or African wildlife in ways that fail to involve local communities, perhaps even contributing to their continued oppression.

Despite these obstacles and potential pitfalls, there have been examples of effective international networking among environmentalists, as in the case of the internationally coordinated campaigns to change the environmental practices of the World Bank or confront unfettered trade liberalization (see Part Three). Moreover, the activities of transnational environmental networks need not be limited to lobbying efforts by well-heeled organizations with access to power. As Ronnie Lipschutz suggests,

> The notion of "civil society" is one with a long history, but it generally refers to those forms of association among individuals that are explicitly not part of the public, state apparatus, the private, household realm or the atomistic market. Civil society is important in global politics in that it is a sector of the state-society complex where social change often begins. This does not mean that global civil society is a unity; it is riven by many divisions, more than one finds in even the international state system. Nonetheless, there are segments of this global civil society that are oriented in ways that specifically promote social and political change.[11]

Whether it makes sense to extend to the global realm the idea of "civil society," which originated with the study of domestic politics in industrial democracies, remains the subject of much debate. But even for skeptics, the idea serves as an important reminder that the state is not the sole or even the primary source of political, social, and cultural change.

Thinking Critically

1. Are the problems confronting the Brazilian state in the Amazon generalizable? Is the pattern of transformation of Brazilian sovereignty hypothesized in Conca's essay likely to be found on a broader scale? What makes sovereignty endure in the face of such pressures?

2. Does globalization promote or inhibit international environmental cooperation? Which seems to be growing more quickly—the pressures on countries to solve problems collectively or the loss of control in an increasingly transnationalized world economy?

3. Are Mendes and Maathai describing similar struggles? What are the constants and what are the variables? In other words, what aspects of these movements, their obstacles, and the context in which they operate are likely to be inherent to such struggles? What aspects are likely to be place-specific?

4. Contrast the activities of the environmental organizations and movement groups discussed by activists Mendes, Maathai, and Kothari. Are the forces that push people to mobilize politically the same in each case? Are the political resources available to these groups the same in each case? What gives these groups power? What limits their power?

5. Do the cases from India, Kenya, and Brazil provide evidence for the idea that we are seeing the emergence of a global civil society? Or do they describe locally grounded political struggles that have little in common beyond occasional, expedient cooperation?

Notes

1. The term "structure" is used in this sense in Ken Conca, "Environmental Change and the Deep Structure of World Politics," in Ronnie D. Lipschutz and Ken Conca, eds., *The State and Social Power in Global Environmental Politics* (New York: Columbia University Press, 1993).

2. World Commission on Environment and Development, *Our Common Future* (New York: Oxford University Press, 1987).

3. Mostafa K. Tolba, Osama A. El-Kholy, E. El-Hinnawi, M. W. Holdgate, D. F. McMichael, and R. E. Munn, *The World Environment, 1972–1992: Two Decades of Challenge* (London: Chapman & Hall, 1992), p. 808. This principle was reiterated twenty years later at the Earth Summit; see "Rio Declaration on Environment and Development," United Nations Conference on Environment and Development, UN Doc. A/CONF.151/5/Rev. 1(1992).

4. Jim MacNeill, Pieter Winsemius, and Taizo Yakushiji, *Beyond Interdependence* (New York: Oxford University Press, 1991).

5. See Ken Conca, "Consumption and Environment in a Global Economy," *Global Environmental Politics* 1, no. 3 (Summer 2001): 53–71.

6. On the role of colonialism in promoting the spread of European values, see Edward Said, *Culture and Imperialism* (New York: Random House, 1993).

7. This theme is developed in Conca, "Environmental Change and the Deep Structure of World Politics."

8. The term "antisystemic movement" is taken from G. Arrighi, T. K. Hopkins, and I. Wallerstein, *Antisystemic Movements* (London: Verso, 1989).

9. On the international pressures surrounding deforestation in the Amazon, see Susanna Hecht and Alexander Cockburn, *The Fate of the Forest: Developers, Destroyers, and Defenders of the Amazon* (New York: HarperCollins, 1990).

10. See Margaret Keck and Kathryn Sikkink, *Activist Beyond Borders: Advocacy Networks in International Politics* (Ithaca, NY: Cornell University Press, 1998); Sanjeev Khagram, James V. Riker, and Kathryn Sikkink, eds., *Restructuring World Politics: Transnational Social Movements, Networks, and Norms* (Minneapolis: University of Minnesota Press, 2002).

11. Ronnie D. Lipschutz with Judith Mayer, *Global Civil Society and Global Environmental Governance: The Politics of Nature from Place to Planet* (Albany: SUNY Press, 1996), p. 2.

5

RETHINKING THE ECOLOGY-SOVEREIGNTY DEBATE

KEN CONCA*

How do mounting international pressures for environmental protection affect state sovereignty? Does it even make sense to speak of sovereignty in a world marked by tight ecological interdependence, massive transboundary pollutant flows, and severe threats to key global environmental services? How will the evolving roles, rules, and understandings that have institutionalized sovereignty adapt to these new ecological realities?

These questions are of particular concern in the South, where the full range of rights and opportunities promised by sovereignty have rarely been realized to the extent enjoyed in the industrialized world. When Third World governments have voiced resistance to the institutionalization of new standards of environmental behavior, they have often done so on the grounds that such rules violate their sovereignty.[1]

In this paper I present a critique of prevailing perspectives on the sovereignty-ecology link. Though the focus is not exclusively on the Third World, the critique illustrates the limited utility of prevailing formulations in a Third World context. I also point the way toward some elements of an alternative conceptualization, and illustrate these propositions with a brief discussion of the case of the Brazilian Amazon.

*   Originally published as Ken Conca, "Rethinking the Ecology-Sovereignty Debate," *Millennium* 23, no. 3. Copyright © 1994 by SAGE. Reprinted by permission of SAGE.

Two Perspectives on Ecology and Sovereignty

My reading of the ecology-sovereignty literature is that two perspectives dominate the debate. The first argues that we are in fact seeing an erosion or weakening of sovereignty. Environmental concerns are said to be erecting new and effectively global standards for state behavior. These new global standards are said to manifest themselves in several ways: in formal dealings among states (such as the creation of international environmental regimes); in rules of environmental conditionality, attached to the actions of international organizations such as the World Bank;[2] in the evolving norms of a growing body of international environmental law;[3] and in the political pressures brought to bear on governments by increasingly transnational environmental movements, citizens' networks, and non-governmental organizations.[4] Such pressures and constraints are unevenly applied and imperfectly enforced, to be sure; but they are beginning, it is claimed, to constrain the autonomy of state action by imposing limits on the menu of policy choices available to states.

This perspective is sometimes, though not inevitably, tied to the view that sovereignty and ecology are inherently at odds. Because ecosystems and environmental processes do not respect state borders, sovereignty itself becomes a key institution of global-scale environmental destruction. It creates a scale for decision-making, adjudication, and authority that does not coincide with fundamental ecological realities, and thus frustrates ecologically responsible management.[5]

These claims about eroding sovereignty can be contrasted with a second identifiable point of view in the literature. Here the claim is that international processes and, in particular, the emergence of multilateral institutions for environmental protection do not inevitably erode state sovereignty and may even strengthen it. By placing states at the center of institutional responses and strengthening their capacity to act collectively, it is argued, the menu of choices available to states is being expanded, not restricted.

For example, Levy, Keohane, and Haas have argued that although environmental regimes may limit the scope of governments to act unilaterally, they also facilitate collective state-based problem solving.[6] The authors draw a distinction between "operational" sovereignty, defined as the legal freedom of the state to act under international law, and "formal" sovereignty, defined in terms of the state's legal supremacy and independence.[7] International environmental institutions constrain operational sovereignty, but formal sovereignty remains largely intact. Implicit in this reasoning is the argument that enhanced problem-solving capabilities more than offset the external limitations on the scope of state authority.

A Critique

These two perspectives inevitably embody normative stances toward the state. In one view, the state is a large part of the problem, whereas in the other it is the foundation for solutions—or, at the very least, a central feature of the terrain on which solutions will have to be built. We can also examine them, however, as claims of what is happening to sovereignty, for better or for worse. Here, although they do make different sets of claims, the two are not necessarily irreconcilable. It is perfectly plausible, for example, that the scope of state autonomy is being narrowed (as the first claim would suggest) at the same time that the problem-solving capacity of states is increasing (as the second claim would argue).

However, before concluding that this represents the full range of consequences for sovereignty in an ecologically interdependent world, several observations are in order. The picture sketched above is in fact seriously incomplete, particularly when applied to contemporary international politics in the Third World. I hypothesize that for many Third World states, sovereignty is in fact being transformed as a result of global ecological interdependence, but not in the manner sketched by either of the above claims, or even by the net effect of the two taken together.

I base this hypothesis on two sets of observations. First, both arguments fail to disaggregate what is in fact a complex and highly unevenly distributed set of international pressures on states to solve environmental problems. Second, both are based on an incomplete characterization of sovereignty itself. They only partially capture what has made sovereignty endure over time, and therefore misrepresent what sovereignty has actually meant for most states.

Let me stress here that the point is not to set up two straw arguments for easy dismissal. There are important insights in both of these perspectives. But they also appear to miss some potentially important effects on sovereignty, in part because their conceptual approaches to sovereignty limit the range of hypotheses they entertain.

Characterization of Environmental Pressures on the State

One problem is an overly general representation of the types of environmental pressure states feel. Clearly, governments do feel mounting pressure to respond to international environmental problems. Cross-national comparisons of public opinion data show consistently high levels of public awareness and concern.[8] While not all peoples, classes, regions, and cultures define the problem in exactly the same terms, widespread concerns about environmental quality cut across simplistic distinctions between rich and poor, North and South, overdeveloped and underdeveloped.[9] The growth of pressures on states can also be seen in the contrast between the 1992 UNCED Conference in Rio de Janeiro and the UN Conference on the Human Environment, held two decades earlier in Stockholm. Stockholm was a gathering of 114 nations but was attended by only 2 heads of state; Rio represented an assemblage of more than 150 nations, including over 100 heads of state. The 134 non-governmental organizations at Stockholm were dwarfed by the 1400 non-governmental organizations and more than 8000 journalists from 111 countries who attended the Rio Conference.[10]

If it is clear that pressures are mounting, it is also clear that there have been consequences for the range of choices available to states. It has become much more difficult (though by no means impossible) to construct large dams, indiscriminately export toxic wastes, clear-cut forests, traffic in endangered species, or emit unlimited quantities of chemicals that destroy the ozone layer. That governments of both the North and the South so often see these limits (at least when applied to them) as interference in their sovereign right to use natural resources as they see fit indicates a strong perception that the consequences are real.

However, while we may very well be seeing the birth of a generalizable, universal norm of environmental responsibility, the specific pressures on states have thus far followed a much more selective pattern. First, to the extent that a new norm is emerging, it is manifest in a highly segmented set of activities, including the lobbying of scientists, the pressure of public opinion, the calculations of governments, and the targeted political pressures of eco-activists. There is no reason to suppose that these all carry the same implications for sovereignty, or even push in the same general direction.

Second, regardless of their origin, the pressures states are feeling typically flow through multiple channels, including intergovernmental relations, dealings with international organizations, transnational linkages among environmental groups, and the workings of the media. Can pressures to join state-based international regimes be assumed to affect sovereignty in the same manner as pressures to accept the World Bank's environmental conditions on lending?

Third, current pressures clearly do not touch all states equally. Instead, what we have seen is something akin to assigning ecological pariah status to specific states on specific issues, whether it be Brazil and Indonesia in the case of tropical deforestation, China and India on dam construction, Japan on the trade in endangered species, or the former Soviet Union on reactor safety. Whatever the implications for sovereignty, they are unevenly distributed.

Fourth, and perhaps most important, responding to international environmental pressures can create resources and purchase legitimacy at the same time that it may constrain the menu of policy choices. This is in fact generally acknowledged when the gains for states are directly linked to efforts at environmental management. But these are not the only plausible effects; some of the resources gained or legitimacy purchased may speak to more general questions of the state's legitimacy and capacity to govern.[11]

Conceptions of Sovereignty

A second set of problems involves the specific conceptualization of sovereignty itself that underlies these perspectives. One problem is that both sovereignty and the challenge to it are viewed in essentially functionalist terms. By this reasoning, states exist because they perform key functions better than alternative forms of social organization, and pressures on the state exist because one increasingly important function—environmental protection—is being performed inadequately. The problems with functionalist arguments are well known, and stem from their post hoc character: causes are imputed from observed effects.[12] Problems emerge when the function is incorrectly specified—that is, when causal significance is given to an observed effect that is in reality an unintended consequence or less-than-central function. A straightforward example: the notion that international environmental regimes exist because states want to solve environmental problems may in fact be wrong. Regimes may be thrust on states by increasingly powerful non-state actors, or they may serve other fundamental purposes of state, e.g., those having to do with state legitimacy and perceptions of effectiveness. Functionalist interpretations based on each of these widely differing "functions" would lead us to dramatically different conclusions about the implications for sovereignty.

The conceptualization of sovereignty is also excessively general. Sovereignty in historical practice has carried with it the presumption of a complex bundle of rights: equality among states, non-intervention, exclusive territorial jurisdiction, the presumption of state competence, restrictions on binding adjudication without consent, exclusive rights to wield violence, and the embeddedness of international law in the free will of states.[13]

There is no reason to expect that a particular set of international pressures affects these various component norms of sovereignty equally or in parallel fashion. Indeed, to the extent that ecological interdependence highlights tensions among such norms, one would expect just the opposite—that some normative pillars of sovereignty can be strengthened as others are undermined or eroded. Consider transboundary pollutant flows: institutional mechanisms to control them could erode the sovereign right to exclusive territorial jurisdiction, but at the same time strengthen aspects of the principle of non-intervention, if the flows themselves are viewed as unjustified interventions.

Third, the view of sovereignty is largely ahistorical. What rules, practices, or beliefs reproduce sovereignty as an institution? Has this process of reproduction been broadly similar in all entities we regard as states, or is there more than one way to reproduce oneself as a sovereign entity? Are there differences in what sovereignty has meant for states whose organized existence is largely a product of colonialism? Does the territorial basis of the state differ fundamentally in frontier societies or in multiethnic ones? Clearly, the answers are unlikely to be uniform across time and for all states. This suggests that we cannot describe in universal terms either the processes rendering states sovereign or the way in which they may be changing as a result of ecological interdependence. Sovereignty as a global institution changes because of what happens to different states over time, at different rates and in different ways.

These weaknesses—functionalist logic, excessive generality, and ahistorical character—are symptoms of more fundamental conceptual problems. One of these is the unresolved tension over whether sovereignty represents, as Robert Jackson has put it, "a norm or a fact." In other words, is sovereignty based on the "fact" of material capabilities that enable organized entities to claim standing as states? Or is it based on the selective extension of recognition as a legitimate state? As Jackson and others have argued, we need to understand sovereignty as at once *both* "fact" *and* "norm."[14]

The perspectives examined here tend instead to fall on one or the other side of this divide. The ecology-erodes-sovereignty view typically frames sovereignty as a formal legal right, de-emphasizing the foundations of the state that make it able to claim domestic authority and international standing. Alternately, the claim of enduring sovereignty in the face of environmental pressures stresses states as problem-solvers (albeit with varying degrees of capability). It thus emphasizes sovereignty as the maintenance of a certain set of capabilities with which to act.

Finally, and perhaps most importantly, sovereignty in both perspectives is essentially conceived as freedom from external constraints on state action and choice. This one-dimensional view overlooks the fact that sovereignty looks inward as well as outward. It finds its basis not only in autonomy relative to external actors, but also in the state's jurisdictional power over civil society. According to Ruth Lapidoth:

> Usually, a distinction is made between the internal and external aspect of sovereignty. The former [internal] means the highest, original—as opposed to derivative—power within a territorial jurisdiction; this power is not subject to the executive, legislative, or judicial jurisdiction of a foreign state or any foreign law other than public international law. The external aspect of sovereignty underlines the independence and equality of states and the fact that they are direct and immediate subjects of international law.[15]

John Ruggie's definition of sovereignty as "the institutionalization of public authority within mutually exclusive jurisdictional domains" also captures this internal dimension.[16]

Historically, the ability to control rules of access to the environment and natural resources—to define who may alter, and to what extent, which specific natural materials, systems, and processes—has been a central component of state authority and legitimacy.[17] Thus the full effects of international environmental pressures on state sovereignty as a collective institution cannot be understood without examining this inward-looking dimension. This is particularly so for much of the South, given the legacy of colonialism and the orientation of so many Third World political economies toward commodity exports.

Like the outward-looking dimension, the state-society dimension of sovereignty represents both fact and norm. It demands not only some minimal level of social recognition of the state's legitimacy, but also a complex bundle of state capabilities. Joel Migdal, for example, disaggregates the notion of state capacity into such varied components as the penetration of civil society, the regulation of social relations, the extraction of resources from civil society, and the use of those resources for defined state purposes.[18] International pressures, whether manifest in state-state, state-IO, or state-NGO interactions, are unlikely to affect these varied capabilities equally. Moreover, state capacity and social legitimacy may be at odds, as appears to be the case when coercive means are used to "protect" ecosystems from local use and encroachment.[19]

Toward an Alternative View of the Sovereignty-Ecology Link

What would an alternative conceptualization look like? Clearly, it will require a multidimensional, less readily operational definition of sovereignty. Sovereignty must be conceived as having both external and internal dimensions; it must be seen as having a basis in both norms of recognition and material capabilities; and both its normative and material bases must be seen as consisting of multifaceted bundles of norms and capabilities, respectively. These complexities should make us humble about drawing general conclusions outside the context of specific cases. A corollary is that there is little to be gained in speaking in general unified terms about sovereignty being "strengthened," "eroded," or "maintained," either with regard to specific states or the institution of state sovereignty as a whole.

The multiple dimensions of sovereignty should not, however, automatically lead us down the path of static 2×3 matrices and reductionist thinking. The focus should be on whether and how *specific* state actions and *specific* aspects of state-society relations create the conditions of authority, legitimacy, and capability necessary for states to make effectively sovereign claims. When the Brazilian government builds a road through the jungle, this must be seen as an act that speaks to each of the dimensions of sovereignty alluded to above: legitimacy as well as capability, international as well as domestic. If the idea of a two-level game is an apt metaphor (and it may not be, for this reason), it is a game in which most of the moves resonate on both boards at once.

An Example: The Brazilian Amazon

Consider the example of the Brazilian Amazon, perhaps the single most widely noted and contentious case to date in the ecology-sovereignty debate.[20] Before the ink had dried on the major agreements signed at the 1992 UNCED Conference in Rio de Janeiro, Brazilian diplomat Marcos Azambuja offered the following analysis:

> Brazilian interests are reinforced in the majority of the documents. At no time did we face opposition to our basic interests. . . . (W)e came out of the negotiations without the slightest scratch to our sovereignty.[21]

As evidence, the ambassador could have pointed to the conference declaration of principles on environment and development. Here the sovereign right of states to "exploit their own resources" is reaffirmed using exactly the same language enshrined in the well-known Principle 21 of the Stockholm Conference 20 years earlier.[22] Or, the ambassador could turn to the specific agreements on climate and biodiversity, which did little to contradict this principle.

The absence of "scratches" on the wall of Brazilian sovereignty was particularly noteworthy with respect to the issue of predominant concern to the Brazilians at the conference: the fate of tropical rain forests, and of the Amazon in particular. Efforts to scratch that wall, by constructing a regime for the preservation (or at least controlled depletion) of the world's remaining rain forests, were soundly defeated. Key points of disagreement included whether to link the regime specifically to an agreement on climate change and whether to cover temperate as well as tropical forests.

But walls have two surfaces, and in the Brazilian case the inside surface has suffered more than a slight scratch. Consider the following testimony of one veteran field researcher in the Amazon:

> Wherever one looks in the Amazonian economy, the state is in retreat: unable to finance tax breaks or build highways without the aid of multilateral banks, unable to include more than one per cent of the rural population in official colonisation schemes, unable to control land titling or land conflicts, unable to register or tax the greater part of the Amazonian economy, unable to enforce federal law on more than a sporadic basis.[23]

The irony is that this assessment of the limits of state capabilities comes at a time when the Brazilian state has been placed squarely at the center of most schemes for sustainable development in the region. Clearly, some state actions have been proscribed by international pressures. But, far from prohibiting state action, the net effect of international pressures has been to stimulate a more active, interventionist state role in the region, under the rubric of supporting sustainable development. Far from simply "eroding" sovereignty, these pressures strengthen the presence of the state in the region and in Brazilian society as a whole. They also create opportunities for state actors to pursue long-standing goals having little to do with ecology. In the specifically Brazilian case such goals include the control of remote territories or indigenous peoples, the demarcation and fortification of Brazil's borders, and the reorganization of existing patterns of land tenure.[24]

These extensions of the state are not without cost, however; they can only be realized at substantial risk to state legitimacy, given the enormous complexity of the task of sustainable development and the limited effectiveness of many state actions as sketched in the above quote. Moreover, the risk to state legitimacy may extend beyond the relatively narrow realm of environmental management. Consider the following commentary in the leading Brazilian newsweekly, *Veja*, discussing the highly publicized murder of a group of indigenous people at the Haximu settlement. "The Haximu massacre shows that, in reality, these minorities [indigenous peoples] are protected with the same courage and efficiency that guard the public hospital network and the pensions of the retired."[25] The state's inability to protect the lives and land of indigenous peoples is being linked directly to its other widely perceived inadequacies.

Under such circumstances, it means little to say that Brazilian sovereignty over the Amazon is eroding, strengthening, or maintaining the status quo. Rather, it seems that we are seeing a more complex, dynamic process in which sovereignty is simultaneously being narrowed in scope (by international prohibitions), deepened (by strengthening state capacities and state penetration of civil society), and rendered more brittle (by eroding state legitimacy).

Conclusion

. . . A strong case can be made for both of the perspectives sketched at the outset of this paper. Clearly, the freedom of states to undertake, promote, or tolerate processes of environmental degradation is being limited, and many of the limits emanate from sources external to the state itself. At the same time, there is little doubt that new international institutions have made some governments more effective problem solvers (although we should always be careful about assumptions that the problem to be solved is, from the point of view of state actors, environmental and not political). That both effects could be happening at once is testimony to the multifaceted character of sovereignty.

Whether these represent the full set of effects is another matter. Consider an analogy to the origins of the modern welfare state. States were faced with a new set of challenges (macroeconomic stabilization, creating a social safety net, and so on). In response, states evolved new institutions, some national and some international, and in the process thrust themselves into a whole new set of state-society relationships. The consequences were hardly a lessening of the state's penetration of civil society or a decline in the size and reach of state institutions. At the same time, however, by assuming these new tasks, state legitimacy (both domestic and international) was put substantially at risk. The entire process was of course intensely politicized and political, with both state and non-state actors seeking to turn the new agenda to maximum advantage.

Much the same process may be at work with the challenge of environmental protection. New tasks, for which states are poorly suited and to which they are often opposed, have been thrust upon them by rising social demands. This challenge renders some choices more remote, but it also creates new opportunities, in the form of international resources for state responses and new mandates for state management and regulation. However, because most of the solutions being promulgated have a strongly statist cast, state legitimacy is put at substantial risk. A growing body of evidence suggests that participation, democracy, and legitimate authority are the keys to solving environmental problems. If so, the implications for state legitimacy may ultimately be the greatest consequence, both for sovereignty and for ecology.

Notes

1. See, for example, the comments of the Malaysian Prime Minister, Mahathir Mohamad, at the 1992 U.N. Conference on Environment and Development (UNCED), in *Environmental Policy and Law* 22, no. 4 (1992), p. 232, and Somaya Saad, "For Whose Benefit? Redefining Security," *Ecodecisions* (September 1991), pp. 59–60. See also the "Beijing Declaration of 41 Developing Countries," 18–19 June 1991, reprinted in *China Daily* (20 June 1991), p. 4, cited in the introduction to Andrew Hurrell and Benedict Kingsbury, eds., *The International Politics of the Environment* (Oxford, UK: Clarendon Press, 1992), p. 39, note 60.

2. On environmental conditionality, see Andrew Hurrell, "Green Conditionality," Overseas Development Council Policy Paper, March 1993 (Washington, DC: Overseas Development Council, 1993).

3. See Patricia Birnie, "International Environmental Law: Its Adequacy for Present and Future Needs," in Hurrell and Kingsbury, eds., *The International Politics of the Environment*, p. 84, note 1. Birnie refers to what has been described as an emerging, bounded concept of "reasonable sovereignty."

4. On emergent global environmental values carried by transnational networks of activists and advocates see Margaret Keck and Kathryn Sikkink, "International Issue Networks in the Environment and Human Rights," a paper presented at the 17th Congress of the Latin American Studies Association, Los Angeles, California, 24–27 September 1992. See also Kathryn Sikkink, "Human Rights, Principled Issue-networks, and Sovereignty in Latin America," *International Organization* 47, no. 3 (Summer 1993), pp. 411–441, and Ronnie D. Lipschutz, "Reconstructing World Politics: The Emergence of Global Civil Society," *Millennium: Journal of International Studies* 21, no. 3 (Winter 1992), pp. 389–420.

5. For a discussion of this view, see Hurrell and Kingsbury, "Introduction," in Hurrell and Kingsbury, eds., *International Politics of the Environment*, pp. 6–8. The authors cite the work of Richard Falk and John Dryzek as representative examples.

6. Mark A. Levy, Robert O. Keohane, and Peter M. Haas, "Improving the Effectiveness of International Environmental Institutions," in Haas, Keohane, and Levy, eds., *Institutions for the Earth: Sources of Effective International Environmental Protection* (Cambridge, MA: MIT Press, 1993), especially pp. 415–417.

7. Ibid., p. 416.

8. See Riley E. Dunlap et al., "Of Global Concern: Results of the Health of the Planet Survey," *Environment* 35, no. 9 (November 1993), pp. 6–15 and 33–39.

9. One interesting result of the study by Dunlap and colleagues was the strikingly similar pattern of environmental concerns found in polling data across twenty-four countries of widely differing income levels (see Dunlap et al., "Of Global Concern").

10. These figures are from Peter M. Haas, Marc A. Levy, and Edward A. Parson, "Appraising the Earth Summit: How Should We Judge UNCED's Success?" *Environment* 34, no. 6 (October 1992), pp. 7–11 and 26–33.

11. This observation points to the basically functionalist logic of much of the ecology-sovereignty debate, a theme to which I return below.

12. For a discussion of the limits of functionalist theories, see Robert O. Keohane, *After Hegemony: Cooperation and Discord in the World Political Economy* (Princeton, NJ: Princeton University Press, 1984), pp. 80–83.

13. This list is from Ruth Lapidoth, "Sovereignty in Transition," *Journal of International Affairs* 45, no. 2 (Winter 1992), pp. 325–346.

14. Robert Jackson, *Quasi-States: Sovereignty, International Relations, and the Third World* (Cambridge, UK: Cambridge University Press, 1990), chapter 3.

15. Ibid., p. 327.

16. John G. Ruggie, "Continuity and Transformation in the World Polity: Toward a Neorealist Synthesis," in Robert O. Keohane, ed., *Neorealism and Its Critics* (New York: Columbia University Press, 1986), p. 143, as cited in J. Samuel Barkin and Bruce Cronin, "The State and the Nation: Changing Norms and the Rules of Sovereignty in International Relations," *International Organization* 48, no. 1 (Winter 1994), pp. 107–130.

17. See Ronnie D. Lipschutz and Judith Mayer, "Not Seeing the Forest for the Trees: Rights, Rules, and the Renegotiation of Resource Management Regimes," in Ronnie D. Lipschutz and Ken Conca, eds., *The State and Social Power in Global Environmental Politics* (New York: Columbia University Press, 1993), pp. 246–273.

18. Joel Migdal, *Strong Societies and Weak States* (Princeton, NJ: Princeton University Press, 1988).

19. For a discussion of this effect in the specific context of wildlife in Kenya and forests in Indonesia, see Nancy Peluso, "Coercing Conservation," in Lipschutz and Conca, eds., *The State and Social Power*, pp. 46–70.

20. I discuss this case in greater detail in Ken Conca, "Environmental Protection, International Norms, and National Sovereignty: The Case of the Brazilian Amazon," in Gene Lyons and Michael Mastanduno, eds., *Beyond Westphalia? National Sovereignty and International Intervention* (Baltimore, MD: Johns Hopkins University Press, 1995).

21. "Summit Documents Safeguard Brazilian Interests," *Daily Report: Latin America*, FBIS-LAT–92–114-S, 12 June 1992, p. 27 (supplement); original source *O Globo*, 11 June 1992, Rio '92 section, p. 1.

22. Principle 2: "States have, in accordance with the Charter of the United Nations and the principles of international law, the sovereign right to exploit their own resources, pursuant to their own environmental and developmental policies, and the responsibility to ensure that activities within their jurisdiction or control do not cause damage to the environment of other States or of areas beyond the limits of national jurisdiction." See "Rio Declaration on Environment and Development," United Nations Conference on Environment and Development, U.N. Document A/CONF.151/5/Rev.1 (1992).

23. David Cleary, "After the Frontier: Problems with Political Economy in the Modern Brazilian Amazon," *Journal of Latin American Studies* 25, part 2 (May 1993), pp. 331–349.

24. These themes are discussed in detail in Conca, "Environmental Protection, International Norms, and National Sovereignty."

25. "Um Grito do Fundo da Selva," *Veja* (August 25, 1993), p. 27. The translation is mine.

6

ENVIRONMENT AND GLOBALIZATION: FIVE PROPOSITIONS

ADIL NAJAM, DAVID RUNNALS,
AND MARK HALLE*

The Five Propositions

By way of exploring the linkages between environment and globalization, let us posit five key propositions on how these two areas are linked, with a special focus on those linkages that are particularly pertinent for policy-making and policy-makers. The purpose of these propositions is to highlight the possible implications of the dominant trends. This is neither an exhaustive list nor a set of predictions. It is, rather, an identification of the five important trajectories which are of particular importance to policy-makers because (a) these are areas that have a direct bearing on national and international policy and, (b) importantly, they *can* be influenced by national and international policy.

PROPOSITION 1: The rapid acceleration in global economic activity and our dramatically increased demands for critical, finite natural resources undermine our pursuit of continued economic prosperity.

---

* Excerpted from Adil Najam, David Runnals, and Mark Halle, *Environment and Globalization: Five Propositions*. © 2007 International Institute for Sustainable Development. www.iisd.org. Reprinted with permission.

The premise of this proposition is that a sound environment is essential to realizing the full potential of globalization. Conversely, the absence of a sound environment can significantly undermine the promise of economic prosperity through globalization.

The notion that rising pressures on, and dwindling stocks of, critical natural resources can dramatically restrain the motors of economic growth is not new.[14] What *is* new, however, is the realization that the spectacular economic expansion we have been seeing has made the resource crunch a pressing reality that could easily become the single biggest challenge to continued economic prosperity.

The premise of the proposition is fairly simple. First, natural resources—oil, timber, metals, etc.—are the raw materials behind much of global economic growth. Second, there is ultimately a finite amount of these resources available for human use. Third, and importantly, the quantum of resources being used has grown exponentially in recent years, especially with the spectacular economic expansion of large developing economies—such as India and China—and increasing global prosperity. Fourth, we are already witnessing increasing global competition for such resources; and not just market but geopolitical forces are being mobilized to ensure continued supplies and controls over critical resources.[15]

Add these facts together and you arrive at a realization that sooner rather than later the degradation of ecological processes—especially fragile ecological systems that are central to the preservation of our essential life systems—could cause a major hiccup in continued global economic growth, and possibly become the single most important threat to the continuation of current globalization trajectories.[16] The dynamic is not new, but it has suddenly become more real and more immediate. Growth, of course, is a paradox in the context of sustainable development.[17] We need growth in order to meet the needs of people, especially the poorest among us; but permanent global growth is impossible in a finite system. Studies demonstrate that we already exceed the productive capacity of nature by 25[18] to 30 percent,[19] and that 60 percent[20] of the ecosystems are currently overused.

Although scares about "limits to growth"[21] have proved less than credible in the past, simple economic logic (and available trends) argues that as competition for scarce natural resources increases, prices will be driven up—and sooner than we might have assumed. In the past, technology has helped—and in the future, it certainly could help—to alleviate some of these pressures by developing new solutions and by more widely deploying existing technological solutions. However, the prospects of higher demand, growing prices and dwindling stocks are already propelling new races for control over key resources. The race is now on not just for oil, but for metals, minerals, timber and even for recyclable waste.[22] For many developing countries endowed with critical resources in high demand, this provides an opportunity to harness the power of globalization and pull themselves out of poverty. Past experience suggests that national and global economies have not been particularly good at allowing for the benefits of resources to flow down to the poor;[23] the challenge today is to find the ways and means to do exactly that.

A parallel challenge is to decrease the adverse effects of resource competition on the poor.[24] For example, "fish prices are expected to rise, reducing the availability and affordability of fish for low income families in developing countries."[25] In areas like the Mekong River basin in Southeast Asia, where 50 million people depend on fish for their food and their livelihoods,[26] poor families will lose food security while the wealthy, both domestically and globally, bid up the price of food the poor cannot afford. Populations dependent on the extraction or exploitation of natural resources, or on natural systems and ecosystem services, could lose their livelihoods as local sources are depleted (fisheries, forests, etc.) or degraded (soil fertility for agriculture) and will need assistance to make the transition to alternative employment.

While market mechanisms and technology could possibly assist in handling increasing resource competition, they offer no solutions for running out of ecosystem services.[27] This is a critical threat to the continuation of current globalization trajectories and the preservation of our lives on the planet. Many critical ecosystem services—including watershed filtration, soil fertility and climate stability—are unvalued (or *under*valued) and, therefore, as these ecological services are threatened, there are no market signals that would spur technological development of alternative supplies. More importantly, we do not have the technological ability to create substitutes for ecological services at the volume or at the costs that would be needed.

Environmental degradation could also impact productivity through damages to health. For example, international agencies found that 2.5 million people in the Asia-Pacific region die every year due to environmental problems including air pollution, unsafe water and poor sanitation.[28] Ignoring environmental costs destroys value. The "natural capital" of ecosystem services (such as watersheds, which provide clean water) is drawn down, creating a need to pay for services (like water filtration plants) that could have been provided for free, in perpetuity, if sustainably managed.[29] Similarly, environmental degradation, global and local, will affect the agricultural sector, on which the majority of the world's poor depend directly for their survival. For example, recent data suggest that global climate change could reduce South Asia's wheat area by half.[30] While gains in productivity in temperate areas could partially offset the difference, whether poorer tropical countries could afford to buy food from richer regions of the world is uncertain. To avoid famine, the Consultative Group on International Agricultural Research has already called for accelerated efforts to develop drought-, heat- and flood-resistant strains of staple crops.[31] The Worldwatch Institute estimates that 17 percent of cropland in China, and a staggering 28 percent in India, is seriously degraded by erosion, water-logging, desertification and other forms of degradation.[32]

It is most likely, therefore, that decreased environmental stability will create more hostile conditions for economic growth and also place new pressures on international cooperation. Two recent reports have documented and drawn global attention to this discussed "possibility," which has started to become a reality. On one hand, the *Millennium Ecosystem Assessment*[33] has meticulously documented the slide in the environmental health of the planet and how we are pushing the limits of many critical resources. The recent rise in oil prices has had the effect of making this connection tangible and recognizable even to ordinary citizens. On the other hand, the recently released *Stern Review*[34] has bluntly suggested that these environmental pressures have now begun impacting global economic processes and that impacts of climate change could create losses of 5–10 percent of global GDP, and decrease welfare by up to 20 percent if damages include non-market impacts and are weighted for ethical/distribution effects. This calculation includes estimations of damages caused by flooding, lower crop yields, extreme weather-related damages and other direct impacts on the environment and human health.

Together, and in the context of galloping economic growth in Asia and elsewhere, these and other such findings suggest that mounting environmental degradation could impose very significant costs on globalization and economic growth. But they also hold the promise that an improved environment is central to human well-being in ecological as well as in economic terms.

PROPOSITION 2: The linked processes of globalization and environmental degradation pose new security threats to an already insecure world. They impact the vulnerability of ecosystems and societies, and the least resilient ecosystems. The livelihoods of the poorest communities are most at risk.

With globalization, when insecurity increases and violence erupts, the ramifications become global in reach. The forces of globalization, when coupled with those of environmental degradation, expand concepts of threat and security, both individually and through their connections. We have already begun recognizing new global threats from non-state groups and individuals, and security is now being defined more broadly to include, among others, wars between and within states, transnational organized crime, internal displacements and migration, nuclear and other weapons, poverty, infectious disease, and environmental degradation.[35]

To take one pressing example, the World Resources Institute (WRI)[36] reports that:

> Water scarcity is already a major problem for the world's poor, and changes in rainfall and temperature associated with climate change will likely make this worse. Even without climate change, the number of people affected by water scarcity is projected to increase from 1.7 billion today to 5 billion by 2025.[37] In addition, crop yields are expected to decline in most tropical and sub-tropical regions as rainfall and temperature patterns change with a changing climate.[38] A recent report by the Food and Agriculture Organization estimates that developing nations may experience an 11 percent decrease in lands suitable for rain-fed agriculture by 2080 due to climate change.[39] There is also some evidence that disease vectors such as malaria-bearing mosquitoes will spread more widely.[40] At the same time, global warming may bring an increase in severe weather events like cyclones and torrential rains.

All of this imperils human security, which in turn drives societal insecurity and, in many cases, violence. Placed in the context of globalization, violence and insecurity can spill out since now they can travel further, just as people, goods and services can.

Security is about protecting people from critical and pervasive threats.[41] This ranges from the security of nations to that of individuals and of societies. Human security is about creating systems that give individuals and communities the building blocks to live with dignity. Livelihoods are, therefore, an essential element of human security. Acting together, globalization and environmental stress may directly threaten the livelihoods of the poor, i.e., the capabilities, material and social assets and activities required for a means of living, and decrease their ability to cope with, and recover from, environmental stresses and shocks.

For "winners" of the process, globalization becomes an integrating phenomenon— one that brings together markets, ideas, individuals, goods, services and communications. For the "losers" in the process, however, it can be a marginalizing phenomenon.[42] Just as the winners come closer to each other they become more "distant" from the losers. The dependence within society on each other becomes diminished as transboundary dependence increases. To use a basic example, as West African consumers develop a liking for imported rice, their "links" to farmers on other continents who export rice to them increase even as their "links" to farmers in their own country growing cassava decrease. Environmental stress can have a similarly marginalizing impact on the vulnerable and the weak. It is quite clear from the evidence now that even though climate change will eventually impact everyone, it will impact the poorest communities first and hardest. In the case of desertification, we already see the poorest and most vulnerable communities being displaced the most.[43] In essence, the already insecure and vulnerable are pushed to greater depths of insecurity and vulnerability.

The combined effects of globalization-related marginalization and environment-related marginalization can wreak havoc on whatever resilience poor communities might otherwise have possessed. An illustrative example is the case of small fishers in the Caribbean.[44] On one hand, globalization forces of advanced extraction technologies, reduced transportation costs, increased ability to keep fishstock fresh over long distances and increasing global demands from faraway markets combine to drive the small fisher out of the market. On the other, the very same forces dramatically decrease the amount of fish in the ocean, thereby further reducing the resilience of the small fisher. As globalization changes the patterns of environmental dependence, it may marginalize parts of Caribbean society and disintegrate local security networks.

In many ways, climate change is the ultimate threat to global security because it can existentially threaten security at every level from the individual to the planetary.[45] In a world where one-quarter of the people in developing countries (1.3 billion) already survive on fragile lands,[46] and where approximately 60 percent of ecosystem services examined are being degraded or used unsustainably, including freshwater; capture fisheries; air and water purification; and climate regulation,[47] the implications of global climate change are becoming evident among the already vulnerable. For example, impacts of climate change on Inuit livelihoods have been recorded; evacuations of low-lying coastal populations, such as Vanuatu's, have begun; and more dramatic adaptation and survival challenges in vulnerable states such as Bangladesh are expected. Climate change–related sea level rise and agricultural disruption could cause 150 million environmental refugees in the year 2050, which could exacerbate insecurity in host countries and regionally.[48] The death of low-lying coastal states and changes in their economic zones and maritime boundaries may cause further instability.

Three key security challenges in the context of climate change are water scarcity, food shortages and disrupted access to strategic minerals such as oil. Historically, these have been the cause of violence and war. International experience with the linkage between natural resources and conflict calls for resolute action as natural resources can fuel and motivate violent conflict (e.g., conflict diamonds funding rebel groups in Angola and Sierra Leone; conflicts over distribution of resource profits from timber and natural gas in Indonesia; oil as key factor in Iraqi invasion of Kuwait).[49] Environmental stress unleashed by potential climate change could trigger international migration and, possibly, civil wars. In fragile circumstances, environmental stress could act as an additional destabilizing factor exacerbating conflict as it combines with other political and social factors.

Conditions of insecurity and conflict impose high costs on the pursuit of sustainable development just as they impose hurdles in the way of globalization.[50] Both processes require a measure of stability without which only survival considerations will be pursued. Conflict sets back the prospects for sustainable development, often by decades, by setting in motion a negative spiral—environmental degradation leads to more competition for scarce resources, leading the powerful to secure the resources for their use, leading to conflict, which leads to worsened social relations, smash-and-grab resource use, greater resentment, etc. Security—from national to human—is, therefore, a prerequisite for realizing the benefits of sustainable development as well as those of globalization.

PROPOSITION 3: The newly prosperous and the established wealthy will have to come to terms with the limitations of the ecological space in which both must operate, and also with the needs and rights of those who have not been as lucky.

Consider the following:

- Emerging economies now dominate and drive global growth.[51] Last year [2006] their combined output accounted for more than half of total world GDP.
- China has become a major importer of just about all natural resources. It is now also the world's largest importer of recyclable waste material.[52]
- "About 700,000 Chinese tourists visited France last year and the number is climbing annually. By 2020, the World Tourism Organization estimates, 100 million Chinese will make foreign trips each year."[53]

- Mittal Steel, a company born in India, with its recent hostile takeover of Arcelor, is now the world's largest and most global steel company.[54] While the company's financial headquarters is in Europe, much of the company's growth has been in emerging markets—India and China, but also Latin America and elsewhere in Asia.
- "By one calculation, there are now more than 1.7 billion members of 'the consumer class'—nearly half of them in the developing world. A lifestyle and culture that became common in Europe, North America, Japan and a few other pockets of the world in the twentieth century is going global in the twenty-first."[55] "China and India alone claim more than 20 per cent of the global [consumer class] total—with a combined consumer class of 362 million, more than in all of Western Europe."[56]

The point of the above is that the key decisions that will affect—and are already affecting—the trajectories of globalization as well as environmental processes are no longer solely Northern. They are increasingly coming from a few large developing countries, especially China and India, but also a handful of other large developing countries. A palpable excitement accompanies this dramatic rise, but there are challenges as well as opportunities.

The dramatic growth in these new economies has forced them to think about the management of that growth, including its environmental dimensions. In many cases, they are doing so on their own terms and in the context of their own specific realities. China, for example, has embarked on substantial environmental programs. Some immediate programs are fueled by the upcoming Olympic Games to be held in China,[57] but many are much longer-term initiatives that emerge from an explicit realization by China that the costs of environmental degradation are a major strain on the country's prospects for continued prosperity, and threaten to affect its standing in the world.

The rapid rise of this set of erstwhile developing countries should also trigger reflection within established industrialized economies on the questions of growth and consumption. It is not viable—nor was it ever—to urge consumption restraint on the newly prosperous while continuing on paths of high consumption oneself. While the question of consumption will be discussed more specifically later, the point to be made here is that the newly prosperous as well as those who have been affluent for much longer will now have to come to terms with the limitations of the ecological space in which both must operate and also with the needs and rights of those who have not been as lucky.

The interaction of globalization and environment are writ large in the new realities unleashed by the focus of global possibilities in terms of both processes moving southwards. For example, it is popular to say that "China is the workshop to the world";[58] but it is also worth asking "who is the customer of this workshop's products?" and "who are the suppliers to the workshop?" Of course, China is used here as a metaphor because it is the most dominant example of a host of rapidly developing countries providing manufacturing to the whole world, industrialized as well as developing. But to the extent that China (and some other countries) have emerged as the new "workshop" of the world, the suppliers to this workshop are the still poor raw material–based economies in Asia, Africa and Latin America; and the customers of the products from this workshop are the populations in the North and within the affluent pockets in the South. To consider the "workshop" metaphor seriously requires placing the "workshop" within a supply chain that is (a) truly global in nature, and (b) not just an economic supply chain, but an environmental one.

None of the above, however, must distract our attention from the fact that countries that industrialized earlier—in North America, Europe and East Asia/Oceania—are still major movers of globalization and environmental processes[59] and have long-standing and continuing responsibilities in this regard. Many of the most pressing environmental problems that the world faces today are not caused by developing countries and, in fact, belong to a different industrialization era. The rise, and the scale of the rise, of new emerging economies in Asia should be a moment of reflection for the "old" rich countries about their own consumption and resource-use patterns. The ecological space for the North is constricting and societies that continue on the path of highly consumptive growth themselves have no right or standing to ask the "new" rich to restrain their appetites. Certainly not until they themselves have done so.

At the same time, today it does mean that emerging economies at least have the opportunity to shape the future in ways that they did not have before. They could choose to follow distinct and different paths of their own that stem from their own particular developmental conditions as well as an understanding of today's world. In essence, they have an opportunity—and hopefully the motivation—to bend the curve[60] in ways that "old" industrialization did not or could not.

China, for example, is a particularly interesting and important example of the opportunities for paradigm shifts that might emerge from this shift in the global center of gravity. Not only is China a major importer of just about all natural resources (and so it will remain), it is emerging as a new hub of recycling.[61] China—and, increasingly, India—lie at the cusp of a new set of challenges and opportunities. They seem aware of the opportunity they have to do things differently from countries that industrialized earlier and under different circumstances. The most pressing global environmental problems that the world faces today are not of their making; but they have a real opportunity to undo these problems by "bending" the proverbial curve that expresses the relationship between growth and environmental degradation. The question is whether these emerging economies of the South will have the foresight to embrace the opportunity and to chart a development path that is different from that which had been followed by those who came before them, and whether the "old" affluent economies of the North will demonstrate a shared commitment to assist the developing world in charting such a path and by demonstrably taking the lead in curtailing their own unsustainable patterns.[62]

PROPOSITION 4: Consumption—in both the North and the South—will define the future of globalization as well as the global environment.

To put this proposition most bluntly, the central challenge to the future of environment and globalization is consumption, not growth. Fueled by the aspirational "norms" of consumption[63] that also become globalized through, in part, the global media and advertising, consumption changes magnify the footprints of growth. For example, while global population doubled between 1950 and 2004, global wood use more than doubled, global water use roughly tripled, and consumption of coal, oil and natural gas increased nearly five times.[64]

A focus on consumption immediately draws our attention to the challenge of inequity. That challenge cannot be brushed aside. A simple but powerful illustration suggests that on average, in 2000, one American consumed as much energy as 2.1 Germans, 12.1 Colombians, 28.9 Indians, 127 Haitians or 395 Ethiopians.[65] These numbers are, of course, stylized but they do help make the point that we live in a massively unequal world and that these inequities are central to the future of globalization as well as the environment. Also, one should note that national averages hide massive consumption inequity within nearly all societies. The very affluent within developing countries overconsume just as the poor within affluent countries underconsume.

The scope of the challenge is highlighted by the *2006 Living Planet Report*,[66] which points out that, based on current projections, humanity will be using two planets' worth of natural resources by 2050—if those resources have not run out by then. Humanity's ecological footprint—the demand people place upon the natural world—has increased to the point where the Earth is unable to keep up in the struggle to regenerate. The key to resolving this challenge is to de-link consumption from growth, and growth from development:[67] to provide the poor with the opportunity to increase their use of resources even as the affluent reduce their share so that a sustainable level and global equity can be achieved.[68]

Technology is one key element in meeting this challenge. The policy decisions we now take that will influence future trajectories of technology development and deployment—and of consumption choices—will shape the interaction between globalization and the global environment. The good news is that these trajectories *can* be shaped by policy. Technology has been one of the great drivers of modern globalization.[69] It has also become one of the principal drivers of environmental processes. Transport technologies, for example, have not only made the world a smaller and more "global" planet, they have also resulted in new environmental stress, especially through increased atmospheric carbon concentrations. Technology has sped up prosperity for many, but it has also allowed extraction of resources—fish, timber, metals, minerals, etc.—at unprecedented rates, thereby placing new and massive pressures on stocks.

At the same time, technological advances have allowed, in some areas, reduced environmental stress. Evidence suggests, for example, that China's economic growth has come with a relatively lesser increase in emissions than what had happened earlier in Europe and North America because China has been able to "leapfrog" to technologies that are much cleaner than Europe and North America were using at similar stages in their development. Although its emission rates per GDP are still high, they are decreasing and have been halved in the last decade.[70] For example, their fuel economy standards are higher than those of the United States.[71]

Technological solutions will inevitably determine the future of globalization as well as the global environment. But they will do so within the context of global consumption demands. Technology cannot change the demands or help us satisfy all of them but it can, through globalization, help meet these demands in a more planet-friendly way.

Automobiles, in fact, are an interesting area of interplay between technological advances and consumption growth. Although the far greater number of automobiles more than makes up for these advances, the fact is that the automobile today is many orders of magnitude cleaner in environmental terms than automobiles were 30 or 40 years ago. The promise of technology also lies in the fact that, even with existing knowledge, we have the ability to make automobiles an order of magnitude cleaner than they are today. The point, of course, is that technology does not operate in a vacuum. In particular, it cannot be understood outside of the context of consumption.[72]

Ultimately, the trajectories of the future—as well as the technologies available— will be shaped by our aspirations of what a "good life" really is.[73] The moral and spiritual dimension of planetary aspirations may not seem like an appropriate subject for policy discussions, but it lies at the very heart of the type of global society that we want to live in and the type of global society that we are constructing. Not only are policy discussions impacted by aspirational decisions of society, they can in fact shape these aspirations. The Brundtland Report[74] released 20 years ago was very much an attempt to shape global aspirations on environment as well as what we now call globalization. Agenda 21, which emerged from the Rio Earth Summit 15 years ago, was another such attempt.[75] Since then, an array of other influential ideas have come from governments, civil society and business. For example, concepts of "natural capitalism," industrial ecology, ecoefficiency, "Factor Ten" efficiency improvements, and "Global Transitions" have been proposed and some have gained currency in civic discourse, business strategy and government policy.[76]

The European Union has launched an initiative that aims to "reduce the negative environmental impacts generated by the use of natural resources in a growing economy," decoupling growth and environmental impact.[77] Similarly, the U.K. has signaled a shift towards a "One Planet Economy," with the launch of the government's new U.K. Sustainable Development Framework.[78] Sweden has pledged to become the first "oil-free nation" by 2020 by switching to alternative fuels.[79] In short, key actors have begun to recognize—and some to implement—the notion that ultimately consumption will have to be constrained.

The purpose of this proposition, therefore, is not simply to say that consumption is the key to understanding globalization and the environment. It is to propose that de-linking consumption from growth, and growth from development is possible. That the promise of sustainable development is—or can be—an honest promise; honestly kept. It is also to suggest that policy interventions are necessary to make this transition and to offer the hope that slowly—albeit too slowly—this realization is coming to be accepted by decision-makers. The challenge, of course, is whether this slow realization will be able to trigger the much larger change in global consumption trajectories before it is too late.

PROPOSITION 5: Concerns about the global market and global environment will become even more intertwined and each will become increasingly dependent on the other.

Although still unrecognized by many, it is nonetheless a fact that a large proportion of existing global environmental policy is, in fact, based on creating, regulating and managing markets. The most obvious examples are direct trade-related instruments like the Convention on International Trade in Endangered Species of Wild Fauna and Flora (CITES) or the Basel Convention on Trade in Hazardous Waste. But even less obvious instruments such as the Climate Convention (especially through its emission trading provisions) or the Biodiversity Convention (through, for example, the Cartagena Protocol on living modified organisms) operate within created or existing marketplaces and markets are a central element of their design and implementation.

For their part, the managers of market interactions—most prominently in the area of international trade, but also in investment, subsidies, etc.—have also belatedly come to the conclusion that they cannot divorce market policies from environmental policy for long. To take international trade as an example, we see that a significant part of international trade is in environment-related goods—ranging from trade in resources such as timber or fish to flowers and species, and much more. Moreover, trade in just about all goods has environmental relevance in the manufacture, transport, disposal and use of those goods. The Preamble to the Marrakech Agreements establishing the World Trade Organization (WTO) recognizes this clearly. And following its lead, the Doha Round of WTO negotiations has also acknowledged this intrinsic connection by placing environment squarely on the trade negotiation agenda.[80] Although those negotiations are currently stalled, the principle of the inclusion of environmental concerns on the trade agenda is no longer in question and is not in doubt.

Importantly, there is a synergy in the stated goals of the trade and the environment system. Both claim to work in the context of, and for the attainment of, sustainable development.[81] Given that international trade is a principal motor of globalization, one can argue that sustainable development should be considered an ultimate goal of globalization, just as it is the stated end-goal of the international trading system.

This integration of environment into trade policy and trade into environmental policy will only intensify. The hope, of course, is that not only the two policy issues, but also the two policy arenas, will interact more than they have to date; that each will recognize that they share the meta-goal of sustainable development; and that both will seek to reach that goal through collaboration. One must start, therefore, with the acceptance that policies that impact markets go beyond the

WTO (e.g., supply chains, regional and bilateral arrangements, etc.) just as policies that impact the environment go beyond UNEP (e.g., national and local initiatives, private sector and civil society initiatives, etc.). Our concern here, therefore, is larger than the future of WTO and UNEP; it is how environmental and market dynamics interact to reap the potential of globalization and environmental improvement.

One interesting example of how the interactions between markets and environment may play out beyond international trade is in the area of electronic waste.[82] The manufacture of electronic equipment is one of the world's fastest-growing industries. Yet, with the proliferation of such equipment also comes the growing environmental challenge of proper management of the equipment at the end of its useful life. As technology advances and the demands by consumers for new and advanced equipment soar, proper management of the waste will be of paramount importance. In 2004 alone, about 315 million personal computers became obsolete.[83] Despite efforts by many countries to tighten control over acceptable disposal methods, adopt processes to recover valuable constituents and use safe practices to deal with the hazardous constituents in e-wastes (e.g., cadmium, lead, beryllium, CFCs, brominated flame retardants, mercury, nickel and certain organic compounds), many difficulties lie ahead.

One interesting subcomponent of this is the trade in refurbished mobile phones. Phones that are used and discarded in advanced industrialized countries (and some fast-industrializing developing countries) end up in poorer countries where they are refurbished and resold, soon to become useless and electronic-waste. By this time, however, there are few options for proper disposal and few affordable opportunities to return items to the original producer. Resolving this growing problem will require us to think outside of the confined boxes of "markets" and "environment." For example, a mechanism could be established to fund the buy-back of mobile phone waste in developing countries wherein the funds are collected from producing companies (based on their average cost of buyback) and donors. The collection itself could be done by the same small entrepreneur who sells used phones, thereby contributing to livelihood, with the network of collection and compensation managed with civil society assistance, since they have far better access to local markets and entrepreneurs than large multinationals. Such a mechanism illustrates how a creative and integrated approach and the inclusion of relevant market actors can bring the benefits of global markets to the poorest communities in ways that are beneficial to the environment and lead to the shared goal of sustainable development.

Looking at the larger picture, one does begin to see the emerging recognition of the need for better integration among the key players. On the trade side, for example, the Doha Declaration and its reaffirmation of sustainable development as the meta-goal of global trade policy was a manifestation of this recognition. Soon afterwards, the World Summit on Sustainable Development (WSSD) of 2002 also reaffirmed the centrality of the trade and environment connections in its Declaration and all its deliberations. However, the move from the declaratory to the regulatory remains mired in institutional challenges since our systems of global governance have been designed to keep the two issues apart rather than to inspire collaboration for the achievement of common goals.[84]

The central point of this proposition, then, is that even though the reality of the global marketplace and the global environment are intrinsically intertwined and becoming ever more so—through the mechanisms of international trade; manifestations of environmental stress; the changes in peoples' livelihoods; and the actions of business and civil society—the processes of decision-making in these two areas are still far apart and only occasionally interact. The good news is that recent developments have nudged policy-makers in the two areas to talk to each other just a little bit more. To be meaningful, however, this nudge must soon convert into a real push and the stated common goal of sustainable development should become a central driver of coordinated policies.

References

Abbott, C., P. Rogers and J. Sloboda, 2006. *Global Responses to Global Threats: Sustainable Security for the 21st Century*. Oxford, U.K.: Oxford Research Group.

Allen, J. and M. Nelson, 1999. "Biospherics and Biosphere 2, Mission One (1991–1993)." *Ecological Engineering* 13, 15–29.

Auty, R. M., 1993. *Sustaining Development in Mineral Economies: The Resource Curse Thesis*. London, U.K.: Routledge.

Basu, K., 2005. *Globalization, Poverty and Inequality: What is the Relationship? What Can be Done?* Research Paper No. 2005/32. Helsinki, Finland: UNU-WIDER.

Black, R., 2006. "New crops needed to avoid famines." On BBC News Web site, December 3, 2006. Available at http://news.bbc.co.uk/2/hi/science/nature/6200114.stm.

Bleischwitz, R., and P. Hennicke (eds.), 2004. *Eco-efficiency, Regulation and Sustainable Business: Towards a Governance Structure for Sustainable Development*. Cheltenham, U.K., and Northampton, MA: Edward Elgar.

Breton, Y., *et al.*, 2006. *Coastal Resource Management in the Wider Caribbean: Resilience, Adaptation, and Community Diversity*. Kingston, Miami: Ian Randle Publishers, and Ottawa, Canada: IDRC.

Bromley, D., 2006. "Toward Understanding Global Tension: Natural Resources and Competing Economic Histories." *Resource Policies: Effectiveness, Efficiency, and Equity*. 2006 Berlin Conference on the Human Dimensions of Global Environmental Change 17–18 November.

Brown, L., 2006. *Plan B 2.0: Rescuing a Planet under Stress and a Civilization in Trouble*. New York: W. W. Norton and Company.

Brundtland, G. H. (ed.), 1987. *Our Common Future: Report of the World Commission on Environment and Development*. Oxford, U.K.: Oxford University Press.

Castells, M., 1999. *Information Technology, Globalization and Social Development. United Nations Research Institute for Social Development* (UNRISD). Geneva, Switzerland: UNRISD Publications.

Costanza, R., *et al.*, 1997. "The Value of the World's Ecosystem Services and Natural Capital." *Nature* 387.

Daily, G. C., 1997. *Nature's Services: Societal Dependence on Natural Ecosystems*. Washington, DC: Island Press.

Daly, H. E., 1996. *Beyond Growth*. Boston: Beacon Press.

Durning, A., 1992. *How Much is Enough? The Consumer Society and the Future of the Earth*. New York: W. W. Norton and Company.

Economist, The, 2006. "*Economist* Survey: World Economy." September 14.

European Commission, 2005. *Thematic Strategy on the Sustainable Use of Natural Resources*. Brussels, Belgium: European Commission. December 21.

Fisher-Vanden, K., *et al.*, 2004. "What is Driving China's Decline in Energy Intensity?" *Resource and Energy Economics* 26: 77–97.

Georgiescu-Roegen, N., 1971. *The Entropy Law and the Economic Process*. Cambridge, MA: Harvard University Press.

Gleditsch, N. P., 2001. "Environmental Change, Security, and Conflict." In Crocker, C. A., F. O. Hampson and P. Aall (eds.), *Turbulent Peace: the Challenges of Managing International Conflict*. Washington, DC: USIP, 55–69.

Godoy, J., 2006. "China Reaches into Europe's Resource-Rich 'Backyard.'" Inter Press Service News Agency, November 15.

Halle, M., 2005. *Where Are We in the Doha Round?* Winnipeg, Canada: International Institute for Sustainable Development. Available at http://www.iisd.org.

Hawken, P., 1994. *The Ecology of Commerce: A Declaration of Sustainability*. New York: HarperCollins Publishers.

Hawken, P., A. Lovins and L. H. Lovins, 2000. *Natural Capitalism*. Boston: Back Bay Books.

Homer-Dixon, T., 1995. "The Ingenuity Gap: Can Poor Countries Adapt to Resource Scarcity?" *Population and Development Review* 21(3).

Human Security Centre, 2006. *Human Security Report 2005: War and Peace in the 21st Century*. New York: Oxford University Press.

Intergovernmental Panel on Climate Change (IPCC), 2001. *Third Assessment Report: Working Group II: Impacts, Adaptation and Vulnerability*. Oxford, UK: Oxford University Press.

James, J., 2002. *Technology, Globalization and Poverty*. Cheltenham, U.K., and Northampton, MA: Edward Elgar.

Johnson, M., K. Mayrand and M. Paquin, 2006. *Governing Global Desertification: Linking Environmental Degradation, Poverty and Participation*. Hampshire, U.K.: Ashgate Publishing, Ltd.

Lay, J., R. Thiele and M. Wiebelt, 2006. *Resource Booms, Inequality and Poverty: The Case of Gas in Bolivia*. Kiel Working Paper No. 1287. Kiel, Germany: The Kiel Institute for the World Economy.

Lees, G., 2006. "India and China Compete for Burma's Resources." *World Politics Watch Exclusive*, August 21.

Macfadyen, G. and E. Corcoran, 2002. *Literature Review of Studies on Poverty in Fishing Communities and of Lessons Learned in Using the Sustainable Livelihoods Approach in Poverty Alleviation Strategies and Projects*. FAO Fisheries Circular No. 979 FIPP/C979. Rome, Italy: FAO.

Malthus, T., 1798. *An Essay on the Principle of Population, as it Affects the Future Improvement of Society*. With Remarks on the Speculations of Mr. Godwin, M. Condorcet and Other Writers. London, U.K.: Printed for J. Johnson, in St. Paul's Church Yard.

Matthew, R. A., M. Halle and J. Switzer, 2002. *Conserving the Peace: Resources, Livelihoods and Security*. Winnipeg, Canada: IISD.

McDonough, W., and M. Braungart, 2002. *Cradle to Cradle: Remaking the Way We Make Things*. New York: North Point Press.

Meadows, D. H., *et al.*, 1972. *The Limits to Growth*. New York: Universe Books.

Meadows, D. H., J. Randers and D. L. Meadows, 2004. *Limits to Growth: The Thirty-Year Update*. White River Jct., VT: Chelsea Green Publishing Company.

Millennium Ecosystem Assessment, 2005. *Ecosystems and Human Well-Being: Synthesis Reports*. Washington, DC: MA, WRI and Island Press.

Myers, N., 1993. *Ultimate Security: The Environmental Basis of Political Stability*. New York and London: W. W. Norton.

Najam, A. (ed.), 2003. *Environment, Development and Human Security: Perspectives from South Asia*. Lanham, MD: University Press of America.

Najam, A., 2004. "Trade and Environment Negotiations after Doha: Southern Priorities and Options." In *Sustainable Development: Bridging the Research/Policy Gaps in Southern Contexts* edited by Sustainable Development Policy Institute, Pakistan. Pp. 183–195. Karachi, Pakistan: Oxford University Press.

Najam, A., M. Papa and N. Taiyab, 2006. *Global Environmental Governance: A Reform Agenda*. Winnipeg, Canada: IISD.

Organisation for Economic Co-operation and Development (OECD), 1998. *Eco-Efficiency*. Paris, France: OECD Publications.

Pirages, D., and K. Cousins, 2005. *From Resource Scarcity to Ecological Security: Exploring New Limits to Growth*. Cambridge, MA: MIT Press.

Polaski, S., 2006. *Winners and Losers: Impact of the Doha Round on Developing Countries*. Carnegie Endowment Report, March. Washington, DC: Carnegie Endowment.

Prescott-Allen, R., 2001. *The Well-Being of Nations*. San Francisco: Island Press.

Raskin, P., T. Banuri, G. Gallopin and P. Gutman, 2002. *Great Transitions: The Promise and Lure of the Times Ahead (a report of the Global Scenario Group)*. Boston: Stockholm Environment Institute.

Ross, M., 2004. "How Do Natural Resources Influence Civil War? Evidence from Thirteen Cases," *International Organization* 58 (Winter): 35–67.

Roughneen, S., 2006. "Influence Anxiety: China's Role in Africa." *ISN Security Watch*. May 15.

Saltmarsh, M., 2006. "Getting in early as China cleans up." *International Herald Tribune*, January 8.

Schor, J., 1991. "Global Equity and Environmental Crisis: An Argument for Reducing Working Hours in the North." *World Development* 19(1).

Schor, J. B., and D. B. Holt (eds.), 2000. *The Consumer Society Reader*. New York: W. W. Norton and Company.

Selin, H., and S. VanDeveer, 2006. "Raising Global Standards: Hazardous Substances and E-waste Management in the European Union," in *Environment* 48(10): 6–18.

Simon, J. L., 1981. *The Ultimate Resource*. Princeton, NJ: Princeton University Press.

Sindico, F., 2005. "Ex-Post and Ex-Ante [Legal] Approaches to Climate Change Threats to the International Community." *New Zealand Journal for Environmental Law* 9: 209–238.

Smith, C., 2006. "Chinese Speak the International Language of Shopping." *New York Times*, November 7.

Stedman, S. J., 1997. "Spoiler Problems in Peace Processes," *International Security* 22 (Fall): 5–53.

Stern, N., 2006. *Stern Review on the Economics of Climate Change*. Report to Her Majesty's Treasury. 30 October. Cambridge, U.K.: Cambridge University Press.

Story, J., 2005. "China—Workshop of the World?" *Journal of Chinese Business and Economic Studies* 3(2): 95–109.

Sturm, A., and M. Wackernagel, 2003. *The Winners and Losers in Global Competition: Why Eco-Efficiency Reinforces Competitiveness: A Study of 44 Nations*. Ashland, OH: Purdue University Press.

Sun, X., E. Katsigris and A. White, 2004. "Meeting China's Demand for Forest Products: An Overview," in *International Forestry Review* 6(3–4): 227–236.

Terazono, A., A. Yoshida, J. Yang, Y. Moriguchi and S. Sakai, 2004. "Material Cycles in Asia: Especially the Recycling Loop between Japan and China," in *Material Cycles and Waste Management* 6(2): 82–96.

Tussie, D. (ed.), 1999. *The Environment and International Trade Negotiations: Developing Country Stakes*. Basingstroke, U.K.: Macmillan.

United Nations Secretary General (UNSG), 1999. *Comprehensive Review of Changing Consumption and Production Patterns*. E/CN.17/1999/2, January 13.

UNSG, 2004. *A More Secure World: Our Shared Responsibility*. Report of the U.N. Secretary-General's High Level Panel on Threats, Challenges and Change. New York: United Nations A/59/565.

Weizsäcker, E. U., A. B. Lovins and L. H. Lovins, 1997. *Factor Four. Doubling Wealth—Halving Resource Use*. London, U.K.: Earthscan.

Williams, M., 2005. "The Third World and Global Environmental Negotiations: Interests, Institutions and Ideas." *Global Environmental Politics* 5(3): 48–69.

World Bank, 2003. *World Development Report 2003: Sustainable Development in a Dynamic World: Transforming Institutions, Growth, and Quality of Life*. Washington, DC: World Bank Publications.

World Conservation Union, 2002. *State of the Art Review on Environment, Security and Development Cooperation*. Prepared for the OECD Development Assistance Committee. Gland, Switzerland: IUCN.

World Resources Institute (WRI), 2004. "WRI Report Outlines Impacts of New Chinese Fuel Economy Standards on Automakers." News Release November 9. Washington, DC: WRI.

WRI, UNDP, UNEP and the World Bank, 2005. *World Resources 2005: The Wealth of the Poor: Managing Ecosystems to Fight Poverty*. Washington, DC: WRI.

Worldwatch Institute, 2006. *State of the World 2006, Special Focus: China and India*. New York: W. W. Norton and Company.

WWF and Ecofys, 2005. *WWF Climate Scorecards: Comparison of the Climate Performance of the G8 Countries*. July. Gland, Switzerland: WWF.

WWF, 2006. *Living Planet Report 2006*. Gland, Switzerland: WWF.

WWF-UK, 2005. "Tony Blair signals radical move towards 'One Planet Economy.'" Press Briefing, March 7. Godalming, Surrey, U.K.: WWF-UK.

Young, O., *et al.*, 2006. "The Globalization of Socio-Ecological Systems: An Agenda for Scientific Research." *Global Environmental Change* 16(3).

Notes

14. Even 18th century scientists were preoccupied with the effects of resource scarcity on the future improvement of society, e.g., see Malthus, 1798.

15. Bromley, 2006; Sturm and Wackernagel, 2003; Roughneen, 2006; Godoy, 2006.

16. See Young *et al.*, 2006, for the effects of globalization on the resilience, vulnerability and adaptability of socio-ecological systems. See Pirages and Cousins, 2005, for the evolution of the "new limits to growth."

17. The authors are thankful to Phillipe Roch for this insight and some of the text on growth in this and other sections.

18. See http://www.footprintnetwork.org.

19. WWF, 2006.

20. Millennium Ecosystem Assessment, 2005.

21. See Meadows, 1972; Meadows *et al.*, 2004, for the concept of "limits." The concept as originally presented was widely challenged (see Simon, 1981), but as a general concept it is widely accepted that there are ultimate limits to all finite resources. Also see Georgiescu-Roegen, 1971.

22. See, for example, Lees, 2006. The race also increases our interest in mining the oceans and the skies.

23. On "resource curse" thesis and implications see Auty, 1993; Lay *et al.*, 2006; for policy solutions see WRI, 2005.

24. Homer-Dixon, 1995.

25. 21 UNSG, 1999.

26. Worldwatch Institute, 2006: 41.

27. Constanza *et al.*, 1997; Allen and Nelson, 1999.

28. Worldwatch Institute, 2006, xxiv.

29. See Daily, 1997; Hawken *et al.*, 2000. For estimated saving of watershed management as an alternative to filtration plants see Worldwatch Institute, 2006: 49.

30. Black, 2006.

31. Black, 2006.

32. Worldwatch Institute, 2006: 15.

33. Millennium Ecosystem Assessment, 2005.

34. Stern, 2006.

35. UNSG, 2004.

36. See discussion in WRI *et al.*, 2005: Chapter 1, "Nature, Power and Poverty," 17.

37. IPCC, 2001: 9 in WRI, 2005.

38. IPCC, 2001: 84 in WRI, 2005.

39. FAO, 2005: 2 in WRI, 2005.

40. IPCC, 2001: 455 in WRI, 2005.

41. More on the concept of "human security" in Human Security Centre, 2006 report. Also see Najam, 2003.

42. On the relationship between globalization, inequality and marginalization within and across nations, see e.g., Basu, 2005.

43. Johnson *et al.*, 2006; Najam, 2004a.

44. See also e.g., Breton *et al.*, 2006; Macfadyen and Corcoran, 2002.

45. Sindico, 2005; Abbott *et al.*, 2006.

46. World Bank, 2003.

47. Millennium Ecosystem Assessment, 2005.

48. Myers, 1993; IPCC, 2001.

49. For an overview of the environment-security nexus see Gleditsch, 2001; Stedman, 1997; Najam, 2003; Ross, 2004.

50. World Conservation Union, 2002; Matthew, Halle and Switzer, 2002; Najam, 2003.

51. Measured at PPP, *The Economist*, 2006.

52. Sun *et al.*, 2004; Terazono *et al.*, 2004.

53. Smith, 2006.

54. BBC, 2006.

55. See "The Rise and Spread of the Consumer Class" at http://www.worldwatch.org/node/810-.

56. See Chapter 1, "The State of Consumption Today," Worldwatch State of the World 2004.

57. Saltmarsh, 2006.

58. Story, 2005.

59. Polaski, 2006; Williams, 2005; Tussie, 1999.

60. This refers to the linkage between economic growth and growth in emissions.

61. Sun *et al.*, 2004; Terazono *et al.*, 2004.

62. Fisher-Vanden *et al.*, 2004.

63. See e.g., Durning, 1992.

64. State of the World 2006: 44.

65. See Sierra Club Web site; http://www.sierraclub.org/population/consumption/.

66. WWF, 2006.

67. See e.g., Daly, 1996.

68. Schor, 1991.

69. James, 2002; Castells, 1999.

70. WWF and Ecofys, 2005.

71. Bradsher, 2003. Also see WRI, 2004.

72. Brown, 2006.

73. *The Economist*, 2006; Schor, 2000; Gasper, 2005; Binswanger, 2006; Galati *et al.*, 2006; Grahm and Pettiano, 2006; Prescott-Allen, 2001.

74. Brundtland, 1987.

75. Agenda 21, 1992.

76. On factor four: Weizsäcker, Lovins and Lovins, 1997; on natural capitalism: Hawken, Lovins and Lovins 2000; on eco-efficiency/industrial ecology: McDonough and Braungart, 2002, Bleischwitz and Hennicke, 2004, OECD, 1998; on the ecology of commerce: Hawken, 1994; on Great Transition: Raskin *et al.*, 2002.

77. European Commission, 2005.

78. WWF-UK, 2005.

79. Making Sweden an Oil-free Society. Report of the Swedish Government Commission on Oil Independence. 21 June 2006. http://www.sweden.gov.se/content/1/c6/06/70/96/7f04f437.pdf.

80. For full text of these documents see http://www.wto.org. See preamble in Marrakech Agreement Establishing the World Trade Organization, as well as Article XX chapeau and sub-points for environmental exceptions in the General Agreement on Tariffs and Trade.

81. Najam, 2004; Halle, 2005.

82. Selin and VanDeveer, 2006.

83. See http://www.ban.org/ban_news/2006/060921_toxic_shock.html. Also see, for related figures, Selin and VanDeveer, 2006.

84. Najam, Papa and Taiyab, 2006; Najam, 2004.

7

FIGHT FOR
THE FOREST

CHICO MENDES
(WITH TONY GROSS)*

Building Bridges

We realized that in order to guarantee the future of the Amazon we had to find a way to preserve the forest while at the same time developing the region's economy.

So what were our thoughts originally? We accepted that the Amazon could not be turned into some kind of sanctuary that nobody could touch. On the other hand, we knew it was important to stop the deforestation that is threatening the Amazon and all human life on the planet. We felt our alternative should involve preserving the forest, but it should also include a plan to develop the economy. So we came up with the idea of extractive reserves.

What do we mean by an extractive reserve? We mean the land is under public ownership but the rubber tappers and other workers that live on that land should have the right to live and work there. I say "other workers" because there are not only rubber tappers in the forest. In our area, rubber tappers also harvest Brazil nuts, but in other parts of the Amazon there are people who earn a living solely from harvesting nuts, while there are others who harvest babaçu and jute. . . .

Where did we get the idea of setting up the CNS [National Council of Rubber Tappers]? We discovered there is something called the National Rubber Council which represents the interests of landowners and businessmen but not the interests of the rubber tappers, so we thought, why not create an organization as a

* Originally published in Chico Mendes with Tony Gross, *Fight for the Forest: Chico Mendes in His Own Words* (London: Latin America Bureau, 1989). Reprinted with permission.

counterweight to all that bureaucracy and try to stop the government messing the rubber tappers about? The First National Congress set up the CNS and elected a provisional executive committee.

The CNS is not meant to be a kind of parallel trade union, replacing the Xapuri Rural Workers' Union, for example. [Editors' note: Xapuri is the town where Mendes lived and worked until his assassination in December 1988. It is located in the western Amazonian state of Acre, near the Brazilian border with Bolivia.] It is just an organization for rubber tappers. The growth of the trade unions was very important for us, but other agricultural workers including day laborers and so on are also members of the same union. Other kinds of agricultural workers have been seen as having particular needs and interests, but not rubber tappers; it's as though we were something that existed only in the past. So one of the reasons for creating the CNS was to recognize the rubber tappers as a particular group of workers fighting for a very important objective—the defense of the Amazon forest. The idea went down very well.

The Indians

We also wanted to seek out the leaders of the Indian peoples in Acre and discuss how to unite our resistance movements, especially since Indians and rubber tappers have been at odds with each other for centuries. In Acre the leaders of the rubber tappers and Indian peoples met and concluded that neither of us was to blame for this. The real culprits were the rubber estate owners, the bankers and all the other powerful interest groups that had exploited us both.

People understood this very quickly, and from the beginning of 1986 the alliance of the peoples of the forest got stronger and stronger. Our links with the Indians have grown even further this year. For example, a meeting of the Tarauacá rubber tappers was attended by 200 Indians and six of them were elected to the Tarauacá Rubber Tappers' Commission. Indians are now beginning to participate in the CNS organizing commissions. In Cruzeiro do Sul about 200 Indians are active in the movement and this year they have even joined in our *empates*. [Editors' note: The term *empate* means "tie" or "standoff" in Portuguese. It refers here to a common tactic of the movement in which local people physically occupy the area threatened by deforesters. The goals are to inhibit the destruction of the forest and to convince the workers involved in deforestation that their interests lie in forest preservation.]

Our proposals are now not just ours alone, they are put forward together by Indians and rubber tappers. Our fight is the fight of all the peoples of the forest.

When the Minister of Agriculture met a joint commission of Indians and rubber tappers in his office, he was really taken aback. "What's going on?" he said. "Indians and rubber tappers have been fighting each other since the last century! Why is it that today you come here together?"

We told him things had changed and this meant the fight to defend the Amazon was stronger. People really took notice of that. . . .

The Landowners Strike Back

We know we face powerful opposition. As well as the landowners and businessmen who dominate the Amazon region, we are up against the power of those who voted against land reform in the Constituent Assembly. The voting power of these people in Congress has been a problem for us and has encouraged the growth of the right-wing landowners' movement, the Rural Democratic Union (UDR). The defeat of the land reform proposal was a big victory for the landowners and land speculators. Now, since the establishment of the UDR in Acre, we've got a real fight on our hands. However, we also believe our movement has never been stronger.

You can already see how strong the UDR is in Acre—it's just organized its first cattle auction to raise funds. We know, through people who have been to UDR meetings here, that their aim is to destroy the Xapuri union by striking at the grassroots organizations of the Xapuri rubber tappers. They think if they can defeat Xapuri they can impose their terms on the whole state and further afield in the Amazon region as well. The Governor of Acre himself told me this. Just to give you an idea, it was after the UDR's official launch here in Acre that the first drops of blood were spilt in Xapuri. . . .

The Government Takes Sides

There was a time when the state government seemed to be paying a lot of attention to environmental problems and to the rubber tappers. But we soon realized it was just putting on a show of defending the environment so the international banks and other international organizations would approve its development projects.

We can't see how the authorities can say they defend the ecological system while at the same time deploying police to protect those who are destroying the forest. That happened, for example, in the case of the Ecuador rubber estate where there were many nut and rubber trees. The Governor was warned several times about what was going on there. In fact, I personally warned him and suggested he go and look at what was happening for himself. I told him he was being very hasty in sending police there. Fifty acres of virgin forest were cut down, but thanks to the pressure, thanks to the hundreds of telegrams sent to the Governor by national and international organizations, we managed to get him to withdraw the police from the area and so saved about 300 hectares of forest.

In the area they destroyed there, the last harvest produced 1,400 cans of Brazil nuts, a good crop. We challenged the owner of the land and the Governor himself to work out the annual income per hectare produced by forest products such as Brazil nuts and rubber and then compare it with that produced by grazing cattle there. They refused because they knew we could prove the income from one hectare of forest is 20 times greater than when the forest is cleared and given over to cattle.

We quoted decree law 7.511 of 30 July 1986 and regulation 486 of 28 October 1986 which prohibit the cutting down and sale of Brazil nut and rubber trees and the deforestation of hillsides. There were two hillsides in the area being cut down on the Ecuador rubber estate and the law was completely flouted. After the second *empate*, when the rubber tappers managed to stop work going ahead, the local IBDF [Brazilian Forestry Development Institute] representative appeared and without even inspecting what was going on, told the landowner he could go ahead and clear the forest. He gave the landowner a license even though the landowner did not present, as he should have done, a written plan for managing the area.

Another law—I can't remember its number—says you can only clear up to 50 hectares of forest without presenting a forestry management plan. Further on it adds that it's forbidden to cut down any area of forest on hillsides or where there is a concentration of Brazil nut and rubber trees. None of these laws were respected. The Governor himself didn't even consider them and the IBDF certainly didn't.

We do have a good relationship with the Acre Technology Foundation (FUNTAC) which is a state government agency. They really understand how difficult the lives of rubber tappers are and recognize that deforestation is a problem. But despite the good relationship we've got with FUNTAC, we have no confidence left in the state government. How can we believe a Governor who says he defends the forest, and visits Rio and Japan to talk about defending the forest, but who then orders the police to go and protect the people who are destroying it? He ought to be using the political power that his office gives him. If he used his power in favor of the workers he'd certainly get their support. . . .

The rubber tappers aren't saying that nobody should lay a finger on the Amazon. No. We've got our own proposals for organizing production. The rubber tappers and the Indians have always grown their subsistence crops but they've never threatened the existence of the forest. It's the deforestation carried out by the big landowners to open up pasture for their cattle that is threatening the forest. Often, these people are just speculating with the land. What happens in Xapuri and other parts of the Amazon is that these people cut down 10,000 hectares, turn half of it into pasture for their cattle and let the other half grow wild. They are really just involved in land speculation.

The landowners use all the economic power at their disposal. They bribe the authorities; it's common knowledge that they've bought off the IBDF staff in the Amazon region. They also use the law. They request police protection for the workers hired to cut down the trees, saying it is their land so they can do whatever they like with it. They accuse the rubber tappers of trespassing when we try and stop the deforestation. They turn to the courts for support and protection, claiming the land is private property. But the rubber tappers have been here for centuries!

There has been less pressure from the police in the last two years because we are able to present reasoned arguments to them. When we organize an *empate*, the main argument we use is that the law is being flouted by the landowners and our *empate* is only trying to make sure the law is respected.

The other tactic the landowners use, and it's a very effective one, is to use hired guns to intimidate us. Our movement's leaders, not just myself but quite a few others as well, have been threatened a lot this year. We are all on the death list of the UDR's assassination squads. Here in Xapuri, these squads are led by Darlí and Alvarino Alves da Silva, owners of the Paraná and other ranches round here. They lead a gang of about 30 gunmen—I say 30 because we've counted them as they patrol the town. Things have changed recently because we managed to get an arrest warrant issued in Umuarama, in the state of Paraná, for the two of them. I don't know whether it was the federal police, but somebody tipped them off. Now they're both in hiding and have said they'll only give themselves up when I'm dead.

We are sure this will be the landowners' main tactic from now on. They are going to fight our movement with violence and intimidation. There's no doubt in our minds about that. The level of violence that has been common in the south of the state of Pará is already spreading to Xapuri, to Acre.

8

KENYA'S GREEN MILITANT: AN INTERVIEW WITH WANGARI MUTA MAATHAI

INTERVIEW BY ETHIRAJAN ANBARASAN
OF THE *UNESCO COURIER**

In a country where women play a marginal role in political and social affairs, fifty-nine-year-old Wangari Muta Maathai's achievements stand out as an exception. A biologist, she was the first woman from East Africa to receive a doctorate, to become a professor and chair a department—all at the University of Nairobi.

Maathai began to be active in the National Council of Women of Kenya in 1976 and it was through the council that she launched a tree-planting project called "Save the Land Harambee" (a Swahili word meaning let's all pull together). The project was renamed the Green Belt Movement (GBM) in 1977.

The GBM initiated programs to promote and protect biodiversity, to protect the soil, to create jobs especially in rural areas, to give women a positive image in the community and to assert their leadership qualities.

The overall aim of the GBM has been to create public awareness of the need to protect the environment through tree planting and sustainable management. Nearly 80 percent of the 20 million trees planted by the GBM have survived. At present the GBM has over 3,000 nurseries, giving job opportunities to about 80,000 people, most of them rural women.

In 1986 the GBM established a Pan-African Green Belt Network and has organized workshops and training programs on environmental awareness for scores of individuals from other African countries. This has led to the adoption of Green Belt methods in Tanzania, Uganda, Malawi, Lesotho, Ethiopia, and Zimbabwe. Maathai, who is a member of the UN Secretary-General's Advisory Board

---

* Originally published in *UNESCO Courier,* December 1999. Reprinted with permission.

on Disarmament, has won fourteen international awards, including the prestigious Right Livelihood Award. She won the award, presented by a Swedish foundation and often referred to as an Alternative Nobel Prize, in recognition of her "contributions to the well-being of humankind."

In a country where single-party rule prevailed for decades, Maathai has been teargassed and severely beaten by police during demonstrations to protect Kenya's forests. "The government thinks that by threatening me and bashing me they can silence me," says Maathai. "But I have an elephant's skin. And somebody must raise their voice."

Maathai, a mother of three children, is currently involved in a struggle to save the 2,500-acre Karura forests, northwest of Nairobi, where the government wants to build housing complexes.

You once said that the quality of the environment cannot be improved unless and until the living conditions of ordinary people are improved. Could you enlarge on this?
If you want to save the environment you should protect the people first, because human beings are part of biological diversity. And if we can't protect our own species, what's the point of protecting tree species?

It sometimes looks as if poor people are destroying the environment. But they are so preoccupied with their survival that they are not concerned about the long-term damage they are doing to the environment simply to meet their most basic needs.

So it is ironic that the poor people who depend on the environment are also partly responsible for its destruction. That's why I insist that the living conditions of the poor must be improved if we really want to save our environment. For example, in certain regions of Kenya, women walk for miles to get firewood from the forests, as there are no trees left nearby. When fuel is in short supply, women have to walk further and further to find it. Hot meals are served less frequently, nutrition suffers, and hunger increases. If these women had enough resources they would not be depleting valuable forest.

What is at stake in the forests of Kenya and East Africa today?
Since the beginning of this century, there has been a clear tendency to cut down indigenous forests and to replace them with exotic species for commercial exploitation. We've now become more aware of what this involves and have realized that it was wrong to cut down indigenous forests, thereby destroying our rich biological diversity. But much damage has already been done.

When the Green Belt Movement started its campaign in 1977 to plant trees, Kenya had about 2.9 percent of forest cover. Today the forested area has further dwindled to around 2 percent. We are losing more trees than we are planting.

The other important issue is that the East African environment is very vulnerable. We are very close to the Sahara Desert, and experts have been warning that the desert could expand southward like a flood if we keep on felling trees indiscriminately, since trees prevent soil erosion caused by rain and wind. By clearing remaining patches of forests we are in essence creating many micro–Sahara Deserts. We can already see evidence of this phenomenon.

We hold civic education seminars for rural people, especially farmers, as part of campaigns to raise public awareness about environmental issues. If you were to ask a hundred farmers how many of them remember a spring or a stream that has dried up in their lifetime, almost thirty of them would raise their hands.

What has your Green Belt Movement (GBM) achieved and in particular to what extent has it prevented environmental degradation in Kenya?

The most notable achievement of the GBM in my view has been in raising environmental awareness among ordinary citizens, especially rural people. Different groups of people now realize that the environment is a concern for everybody and not simply a concern for the government. It is partly because of this awareness that we are now able to reach out to decisionmakers in the government. Ordinary citizens are challenging them to protect the environment.

Secondly, the GBM introduced the idea of environmental conservation through trees because trees meet many basic needs of rural communities. We started out by planting seven trees in a small park in Nairobi in 1977. At that time we had no tree nursery, no staff and no funds, only a conviction that ordinary country people had a role to play in solving environmental problems. We went on from there and now we have planted over 20 million trees all over Kenya.

The act of planting trees conveys a simple message. It suggests that at the very least you can plant a tree and improve your habitat. It increases people's awareness that they can take control of their environment, which is the first step toward greater participation in society. Since the trees we have planted are visible, they are the greatest ambassadors for our movement.

Despite the Rio earth summit of 1992 and the Kyoto climate summit in 1997, there has been no significant progress in environmental protection programs and campaigns at a global level. Why?

Unfortunately, for many world leaders development still means extensive farming of cash crops, expensive hydroelectric dams, hotels, supermarkets and luxury items, which plunder human and natural resources. This is shortsighted and does not meet people's basic needs—for adequate food, clean water, shelter, local clinics, information and freedom.

As a result of this craze for so-called development, environmental protection has taken a backseat. The problem is that the people who are responsible for much of the destruction of the environment are precisely those who should be providing leadership in environmental protection campaigns. But they are not doing so.

Also, political power now is wielded by those who have business interests and close links with multinational corporations (MNCs). The only aim of these

MNCs is to make profit at the expense of the environment and people. We also know that many world political leaders are persuaded by MNCs not to pay attention to declarations made in international environmental conferences. I strongly believe that as citizens we should refuse to be at the mercy of these corporations. Corporations can be extremely merciless, as they have no human face.

You started your career as an academic. Later you became an environmentalist, and now you are called a pro-democracy activist. How would you describe your evolution in the last twenty-five years?
Few environmentalists today are worried about the welfare of bees, butterflies and trees alone. They know that it is not possible to keep the environment pure if you have a government that does not control polluting industries and deforestation.

In Kenya, for example, real estate developers have been allowed to go into the middle of indigenous forests and build expensive houses. As concerned individuals we should oppose that. When you start intervening at that level, you find yourself in direct confrontation with policymakers and you start to be called an activist.

I was teaching at the University of Nairobi in the 1970s, when I felt that the academic rights of women professors were not being respected because they were women. I became an activist at the university, insisting that I wanted my rights as an academic.

Meanwhile, I found myself confronted by other issues that were directly related to my work but were not clear to me at the outset, like human rights. This directly led me to another area, governance. As a result I was drafted into the pro-democracy campaign.

I realized in the 1970s that in a young democracy like ours it was very easy for leaders to become dictators. As this happened they started using national resources as though they were their personal property. I realized that the constitution had given them powers to misuse official machinery.

So I became involved in the pro-democracy movement and pressed for constitutional reforms and political space to ensure freedom of thought and expression. We cannot live with a political system that kills creativity and produces cowardly people.

With your academic qualifications you could have lived a comfortable life in the United States or elsewhere in the West. But you decided to come back and settle down in Kenya. In the last twenty-five years, you have been verbally abused, threatened, beaten, put behind bars and on many occasions forbidden to leave the country. Have you ever regretted returning to Kenya and becoming an activist?
I did not deliberately decide to become an activist, but I have never regretted the fact that I decided to stay here and to contribute to the development of this country and my region. I know that I have made a little difference. Many people come up to me and tell me that my work has inspired them. This gives me great satisfaction because in the earlier days, especially during the dictatorship, it was difficult to speak.

Until a few years ago, people used to come up to me in the street and whisper "I am with you and I am praying for you." They were so scared of being identified with me that they did not want to be heard. I know a lot of people were afraid of talking to me and being seen with me because they might be punished.

I have been a greater positive force by staying here and going through trials and tribulations than if I had gone to other countries. It would have been very different to live in the West and say my country should do this and that. By being here I encourage many more people.

Do you think you were subjected to virulent attacks and abuses because you questioned men's decisions?

Our men think African women should be dependent and submissive, definitely not better than their husbands. There is no doubt that at first many people opposed me because I am a woman and resented the idea that I had strong opinions.

I know that at times men in positions of influence, including President Daniel Arap Moi, ridiculed me. At one time Members of Parliament accused me and ridiculed me for being a divorced woman. I have felt that deep inside they were hoping that by calling into question my womanhood I would be subdued. Later they realized they were wrong. In 1989, for example, we had a big confrontation with the authorities when we were fighting to save Uhuru Park in Nairobi. I argued that it would be ridiculous to destroy this beautiful park in the center of the city and replace it with a multistoried complex.

Uhuru Park was the only place in Nairobi where people could spend time with their families outdoors. The park was a wonderful place for people to go because it was a place where no one bothered them.

When I launched the campaign opposing the construction of the "Park-monster," as the project later came to be known, I was ridiculed and accused of not understanding development. I didn't study development but I do know that you need space in a city. Fortunately other nongovernmental organizations and thousands of ordinary people joined our protests and finally the park was saved. The government, which wanted to destroy that park, has since declared it a national heritage. That's wonderful. They could have done that without fighting and without ridiculing me.

What made you stand in the presidential elections in 1997? Despite your popularity, why didn't you win a sizeable number of votes?

I decided to stand for election for several reasons. In 1992, when a multiparty system was legalized in Kenya for the first time, I tried very hard with other political groups to unite the opposition, but in vain. When there were many opposition candidates running for the presidency, I withdrew from the campaign.

As expected, the opposition lost those elections and everybody now accepts that the campaign we launched for them to unite was right. We wanted to form a government of national unity within the opposition in 1992. This is exactly what they are now clamoring for.

In the 1997 general elections, my idea was to persuade the opposition to unite and field a strong candidate from one ethnic community against the ruling Kenya African National Union (KANU). But I was called a tribalist by some opposition groups for proposing that idea. When all my efforts to unite the opposition failed, I decided to run for president.

But during the campaign I also came to realize that in this country it is very difficult to get elected without money. I didn't have money. I realized that it doesn't matter how good you are, how honest you are and how pro-democratic you are, if you don't have money to give to the voter you won't get elected. So I lost.

All this gave me a new experience. Now I can speak as an insider. I also realized that people here are not yet ready for democracy and we need a lot of civic education and political consciousness. People here are still controlled by ethnicity and vote along ethnic lines. The ethnic question became a very important issue during the last elections.

Despite having enormous natural resources Africa still lags behind other continents in terms of development and growth. Why is this?

Poor leadership, without any doubt. This generation of African leaders will go down in history as a very irresponsible one that has brought Africa to its knees. During the past three decades, Africa has suffered from a lack of visionary and altruistic leaders committed to the welfare of their people.

There are historical reasons for this. Just before independence was granted to many African countries, young Africans were promoted by colonial rulers to positions until then unoccupied by the local people and were trained to take over power from the colonial administration. The new black administrators and burgeoning elites enjoyed the same economic and social lifestyles and privileges that the imperial administrators enjoyed. The only difference between the two in terms of the objectives for the country was the color of their skin.

In the process, the African leaders abandoned their people, and in order to maintain their hold on power they did exactly what the colonial system was doing, namely, to pit one community against another. This internal conflict continued for decades in many African countries, draining their scarce resources.

So what we need is to improve our leadership. If we don't there is no hope, because history teaches us that if you cannot protect what is your own, somebody will come and take it. If our people cannot protect themselves they will continue to be exploited. Their resources will continue to be exploited.

It is also true that Western powers, especially the former colonial masters of this region, have continued to exploit Africa and have continued to work very closely with these dictators and irresponsible leaders. That is why we are now deep in debt, which we cannot repay.

Africa also needs assistance from international governments to improve its economic standing. For example, most foreign aid to Africa comes in the form of curative social welfare programs such as famine relief, food aid, population control programs, refugee camps, peacekeeping forces and humanitarian missions.

At the same time, hardly any resources are available for sustainable human development programs such as functional education and training, development of infrastructure, food production and promotion of entrepreneurship. There are no funds for the development of cultural and social programs which would empower people and release their creative energy.

I am hoping that in the new millennium a new leadership will emerge in Africa, and I hope this new leadership will show more concern for the people and utilize the continent's resources to help Africans get out of poverty.

9

GLOBALIZATION, GLOBAL ALLIANCES, AND THE NARMADA MOVEMENT

SMITU KOTHARI*

The past decade has witnessed several significant regional and global efforts to build horizontal linkages that transcend national boundaries. Prior to this, most earlier nongovernmental efforts were focused on building international solidarity (e.g., the Socialist International, the various Communist Internationals, or the forums of the working class), were based on single issues (e.g., the women's movement), or were regional (e.g., the solidarity efforts against imperialist intervention at home in many of the countries of Central and South America).

This recent past has seen the evolution of very different transborder alliances—from hesitant efforts seeking small concessions from dominant and dominating institutions, to initiatives that challenge global power interests, current patterns of economic development, and cultural control. This brief note will concern itself primarily with the latter two since that is the evolving thinking with the Narmada Bachao Andolan (NBA, the Movement to Save the Narmada).[1] Of course, global alliances like the ones that have been built around the struggles for justice in the Narmada Valley are still at a nascent stage since any significant challenge to dominant structures and the building of *countervailing* power requires a political coherence that movements, groups, and party activists (the world over) still lack. But, it is clear from recent analysis and action in and around the Narmada movements ... that the challenge is being increasingly recognized and the strategies of resistance and of articulating and building alternatives are actively on (Kothari 1995;

* Originally published in Sanjeev Khagram, James V. Riker, and Kathryn Sikkink, eds., *Restructuring World Politics: Transnational Social Movements, Networks, and Norms*, pp. 231–244. © 2002 University of Minnesota Press. Reprinted with permission.

Patkar and Kothari 1995; "Fifty Years of Bretton Woods Institutions: Enough" 1994; Kothari 2000; Alvarez, Escobar, and Escobar 1998).

Before specifically discussing the Narmada experience, it is critical to situate it in the larger context of globalization. It is also important to outline some issues that still seem to be neglected in the process of creating better coordination among and between emerging global alliances seeking to transform the dominant economic and political systems.

The Wider Context

Much of the alliance building around the Narmada issue has attempted to make the donor governments, transnational corporations seeking to invest in projects on the Narmada River, and the World Bank accountable to international norms and to the international human rights regime. In the case of the World Bank, it is also to its own policies, which on paper have evolved in directions that are much closer to social movement concerns than before. However, recent thinking in the movement—which is not equally shared by all constituents of the alliance and thus, consequently, raises several crucial issues—recognizes that the World Bank and other Bretton Woods institutions, as powerful as they are, are still only the more visible symbols of a power configuration that is firmly embedded in the contemporary structures of corporate capitalism. The gulf between the extent of morality and responsibility that these institutions overtly display and what is actually internalized is therefore a function of this basic structural reality. There is, therefore, a growing belief that critiques and campaigns must evolve and strengthen strategies that challenge the structures themselves. In fact, at the moment, even if the World Bank were forced to shut down, in the absence of other structural changes in the global economic order, another similar institution (or institutions) would take its place.

These institutions are aligned in more or less the same way as the current configuration of economic (and military) power, with the G-7 nations (*and* the interests that they represent) dominating the hierarchy. Very few individuals involved in building horizontal linkages of citizens' initiatives and people's movements address the deeper systemic and structural issues. This is partly because so much energy is expended in the local space, in "fire fighting," and in ensuring that some of the changes accepted by dominant institutions after an intense period of campaigning and advocacy actually get implemented. But partly it is also because the deeper questions are harder to deal with; they confront very fundamental aspects of our own lives and challenge us in turn by exposing our institutional and personal weaknesses. This is not to minimize the significance of efforts to hold those in power accountable. Each effort and each step forward helps create democratic space where the potential to nurture political struggle is strengthened (Kothari 2002).

The other challenge that those in the process of building these alliances must face is that while there is a committed base and ample idealism within each participating movement or group, most efforts are still dispersed, fragmented, and scattered. Take, for example, the resistance in India against Cargill or Monsanto (hybrid and transgenic seeds), Union Carbide (the Bhopal tragedy), and the Sardar Sarovar project (SSP). Not only is there very little coordination between groups and movements involved in the opposition to the specific corporations and the dam project, there is little sustained work in responding to the larger political threat that the current patterns of globalization are posing. (And most groups now realize that strengthening the local alone is a necessary but insufficient condition for resisting the global.) This lack of political consolidation presents a major challenge to domestic and transnational networks since the forces of national and transnational capital are increasingly demonstrating significant coherence and consistency in their policies and practice.

Many efforts to challenge the forces of transnational capital have met with criticism from within India. It is argued that focusing on global institutions that have an adverse impact on India detracts from the more basic task of mobilizing within the country and of holding the Indian state accountable to its social and constitutional obligations as well as its obligations to the United Nations charter and instruments to which it is a signatory. Additionally, the argument states that these critiques detract us from the task of compelling the state to become an agency of controlling (or regulating) both global capital and other destabilizing or disrupting political interests. While much of this analysis is true, it can be argued that the time has come to pursue both strategies—the national and the global—with better coordination and transparency.

Can this coordinated action across movements and concerned groups take place without radicalizing political parties or participating in electoral politics? In most countries, both in the Third World and the First World, groups have found the process of sensitizing political parties an enormously difficult one. In countries that have a functioning electoral system, this limitation inevitably inhibits the creation of public debate. The lack of response from parties is not just because their caste-class affiliations obstruct or constrain a focused response to the threats— after all, many Third World societies still have active socialist and Marxist parties. Granted, however, that with the end of the Cold War, any political strategy adopted by a political party has to contend with an even more aggressive capitalist enterprise and consequently, the task of convincing constituencies of the importance of an alternative vision is all the more difficult. Precisely because of this political dynamic, the need for a deeper debate within parties regarding the dangers of predatory capital (both global and national and the tactical and strategic alliances between the two) and the adverse implications of greater dependency on undemocratic, secretive, and unjust global institutions like the World Bank and the IMF continue to be urgent.

Equally, an overwhelming proportion of the poor and the oppressed as well as the victims of the development process are not organized and, in many ways, continue to depend on a patronizing political and economic establishment that can no longer deliver even the crumbs of the past. Similarly, the middle classes, both in the Third World and the First World, are still largely oblivious not just to the role of the World Bank and the IMF in imposing a new hegemonic order, but to the real conditions, contexts, and roots of poverty, ecological degradation, and social injustice found within and across states.

Unfortunately, most Third World nation-states have been usurped by their ruling elites. A significant proportion of their bureaucratic, political, and military elites are almost no better than agents and carriers of elites in the First World. This criticism might seem too strong, but if we look at the evidence (despite occasional "hard lines" that are taken by Third World leaders), we can witness a growing affinity between elites across the world and a consequent distancing from the base of their own societies, as well as from the struggles for social justice. This process clearly reflects a decline in nationalistic idealism, which continues to survive in a few scattered groups and continues to have a persistent appeal for a significant proportion of the masses in the country who have, however, been confused and oppressed by obscure economic discourses and the rhetoric of progress and prosperity.

This task acquires more seriousness particularly since international economic institutions and national governments are becoming far more sophisticated in "dealing" with criticism and dissent. The large sums of donor money available for NGOs, the cooptation and "management" of dissenting or alternative language (one of the best examples is the concept of "sustainable development," for within the present patterns of economic growth, sustainable development will remain an oxymoron, a contradiction in terms), as well as the possibilities for lucrative contracts and consultancies have effectively muffled and divided dissenting voices. Too much of active dissent is co-opted, contained, or derailed; as a result, the roots of present political and economic control remain largely unaddressed. It is only recently that a renewed mobilization within and across borders is becoming evident, and looking at its growth and the resulting nervousness among ruling elites and the dominant structures of governance, it is obvious that this countervailing process is clearly beginning to take root. As it does, it will have to draw on the learning of the past and innovate new strategies and tactics of transnational engagement. This interplay and contestation will be one of the many crucial developments in the political and cultural landscape of the globe.[2]

This landscape will also witness significant changes in political theory and action as global production, the mobility of global capital and finance, and the creation of megacorporations contest and even attempt to smother nationally bound labor-capital relations. The role of the state in transforming relations, as well as its reconceptualization as capital seeks to use it for its ends and international and transnational democratic forces pressure the state to democratize itself, will also increasingly occupy political and social consciousness and action. At the moment, however, in the name of good governance,[3] the dominant logic is that the state must embrace market-friendly policies, ensure a stable climate for global investment, and implement massive programs of infrastructure development that facilitate free play to the neoliberal agenda.

All this—the changing face of dominant processes of globalization; the unity of ruling elites; the fragmentation and dispersal of popular movements; the lack of strategies to sensitize the political parties, the poor, and the middle classes; the consequent decline of radical politics; the emerging mobilization and transnational alliances; and the innovation and creativity that is emerging in the debates and actions of those involved in building and strengthening transnational linkages—all these form the backdrop to understanding the building of the global alliance for justice and human rights in the Narmada Valley.

A Brief History of the Alliance

During the mid-1990s, when the Narmada movement was gradually expanding its mass base and picking up momentum, the predominant strategy was to seek reforms from the state and central governments. It was believed that most issues could be resolved through a process of dialogue. Every avenue of pursuing this was explored and it gradually became evident that as far as the governments were concerned, the gap between rhetoric and practice was continuing to grow. A wide range of nonviolent strategies were adopted and the country's intelligentsia and political opinion makers, as well as other democratic movements in the country, were mobilized. This resulted in generating significant countervailing pressure that compelled successive chief ministers and prime ministers to meet with movement leaders. Assurances to resolve outstanding problems were secured from these political leaders. These meetings, however, resulted only in unfulfilled expectations.

It was during this time that several World Bank missions visited the valley. The mobilization of those who were to be displaced by the dam had created enough public awareness that the World Bank could not easily disregard the organized voices of those who faced displacement and other issues of social and environmental impacts. Nevertheless, even the World Bank was unsuccessful *and* unwilling to make its disbursements conditional on a demonstrated commitment by the various governments to implement policies that had evolved over the past two decades.

Additionally, the Japanese government was evaluating its involvement in the project. The realization among Narmada Bachao Andolan (NBA) activists that the local and national campaign would have to extend itself beyond the national boundaries created intense debate within the movement. Should movement representatives go abroad to pressure the World Bank or could this be done from within? Since there was no discussion of an alliance then, should a relationship be forged with organizations based in the United States, Europe, and Japan?[4] What should the basis of such a relationship be, particularly since there were significant economic, cultural, and social differences? Who should represent the movement? How should that representation be defined?

The first testimonies before subcommittees of the U.S. Congress were organized by the Washington-based Environmental Defense Fund (EDF). One of the main leaders of the movement, Medha Patkar, and myself were among the first to make presentations on the adverse social and environmental implications of World Bank funding and the need for the U.S. government to exercise its influence within the World Bank to make it more socially and environmentally responsible in the context of the Sardar Sarovar project.

Gradually, EDF, as well as a wide range of U.S.-based organizations, testified before Congress and used a complex set of advocacy strategies to pressure the World Bank. In Japan, Friends of the Earth (Japan) launched a major campaign, initially organizing two public hearings. Japanese academics, activists, and press correspondents made site visits in India. Most of them reported on the grave consequences of the project and on the vast gaps between promise and performance on the part of the governments and dam-building authorities. A media campaign, coupled with pressures on key members of the Japanese Diet (parliament) and relevant central ministries, created a public embarrassment for the government. In Europe, activist groups were meeting their parliamentarians and pressuring their respective executive directors in the World Bank. By 1991, 60 percent of Swedish and 80 percent of Finnish parliamentarians had signed a memorandum to the president of the World Bank seeking a review of the SSP.

A series of unprecedented responses ensued. The Japanese government announced that it was withdrawing its commitment to provide loans to the SSP. The World Bank reluctantly announced that it was setting up, for the first time in its history, an independent review committee under the chairpersonship of Bradford Morse, who had recently stepped down as an administrator of UNDP. Their report, *Sardar Sarovar: Report of the Independent Review,* was a path-breaking document that called on the World Bank "to step back" (Morse and Berger 1992). However, the World Bank did not heed this recommendation and issued a note called "The Next Steps." The collective pressure from the alliance was stepped up, including full-page advertisements in major newspapers signed by over eight hundred organizations from all over the world calling on the president of the World Bank to withdraw funding. In less than six months, the Indian government and the World Bank, recognizing that the Next Steps could not be satisfactorily implemented, decided on a face-saving decision—that the World Bank should be asked to withdraw from the project. It was one of the first times that the World Bank was compelled to withdraw from such a prestigious project that it had defended so vociferously and for so long.

It needs to be stressed here that much of this would not have been possible without the successful mass mobilization in the Narmada Valley. Estimates of the number of people in the movement range from 70 to 80 percent of those to be affected by the project (approximately 150,000 people in over two hundred villages in the three states of Madhya Pradesh, Maharashtra, and Gujarat).

By this time the global alliance had extended itself to other parts of Europe and the rest of the world. Newer strategies had to be planned to respond more rapidly to the growing human rights violations in the valley. One initiative that took shape in 1993 was the formation of an International Panel on Human Rights, which has regularly sent a representative from the human rights community to spend between a week and a fortnight to report, from the point of view of established human rights conventions and covenants, the violations taking place. One of the most difficult tasks for communities affected by the processes of globalization has been to make the representative institutions accountable to the international human rights regime. The World Bank and the IMF, even though they were formed under the UN, continue to be diffident in respecting established standards. In fact, many within these institutions see the norms as a hindrance to the successful implementation of their structural adjustment programs and other institutional changes that seek to create a viable global marketplace.

The alliance has gone on to challenge the involvement of corporations and financiers in other projects in the Narmada Valley.[5] Many of the partnerships that have been forged in the process of the alliance building have led to solidarities on issues beyond the struggle against a cluster of dams.

One of the most dramatic achievements of the movement in the Narmada Valley has been its central influence in the formation and direction of the World Commission on Dams (WCD). An innovative institutional innovation on a contemporary controversy, the WCD is a pioneering step in defining the structure of institutions of global governance that would mediate contentious global or regional issues in the future. The years since it was formed in 1998 have witnessed some of the best coordinated global efforts by social movements and people's organizations to make inputs before a group of commissioners who represent the entire spectrum of "stakeholders"—from leaders of anti-dam movements and indigenous peoples to senior representatives of financial institutions and corporations. Other stakeholders have also made crucial submissions, but the sustained and coordinated efforts by transboundary networks of dam-affected communities, support groups, and the extended global alliances have had a dramatic influence in highlighting the comprehensive adverse impacts of large dams, as well as in democratizing the work of the commission itself. A comprehensive independent assessment of the WCD locates the commission historically, critically maps the process, and looks at the lessons this process has for future commissions, multistakeholder processes, and transnational alliances.[6]

Numerous questions have been raised in this process of building the alliance. Debates on governance and development policy within India have increasingly focused on the need to transform the very structures of power. In a class- and caste-based society, processes of economic globalization inevitably compound the loss of control of local communities over their resources and their lives, which may exacerbate conditions of social unrest and conflict or lead to the growth of insecurity among cultural and political identities. Without this control, transforming the dominant processes of policymaking—nationally and globally—is an almost impossible task. (This underscores . . . the need to attend simultane-

ously to both domestic and international processes when evaluating or responding to transnational networks.) Additionally, to what extent can global alliances
transit from seeking concessions from international institutions and national
governments to concentrating on issues of social and ecological justice in both
the First and Third Worlds?

Global Alliances:
Some Challenges

Like the NBA, more and more groups and movements from the Third World now
feel that solidarities need to be created not just by expressions of compassion, but
in a climate of collective and individual self-introspection and change. Relationships should be marked not by a patronizing attitude, but by a spirit of fellowship.
This is more difficult than it sounds because even among alliance members there
are significant class and privilege differences. Collectively molding an authentic
alternative vision is an enormously arduous task. In fact, it is a much greater challenge for those in the First World, who will have to fight greater personal battles,
than for elites in our milieu. Additionally, for them there is a further need to be
rooted authentically within their own societies, as indeed we need to root ourselves in ours. In fact, participation in global initiatives needs to move beyond the
better-known, more visible, primarily elite activists.

All this calls for urgent political consolidation. Given the growing stirring for
justice and democracy all over the world, one of the biggest challenges for individual struggles and for nascent global alliances is to convert sentiment, anger, and assertion against dominant institutions into effective and sustained political
strategies. It also calls for a rethinking of rigid ideological orientations and greater
humility in the task of building a broad democratic front that does not imply the
submergence of plural institutional identities. The collective task of politicizing diverse constituencies—in both the North and the South—is now as urgent as ever.

It also presents challenges for a new vision of universalism—a universalism
that does not impinge on smaller identities and pluralistic structures and which,
in turn, is not impeded by the struggles of the same. Stated differently, the challenge is how to build international solidarities and links toward a holistic, univer-
salistic worldview that does not impede the cultural flowering of diverse
identities—a process that not only reverses the cultural aggression and hegemonic thrust of dominant institutions, but strengthens the fabric of pluralism,
diversity, and justice.

References

Alvarez, Sonia, Evelina Escobar, and Arturo Escobar. 1998. *Cultures of Politics. Politics of Cultures.* Boulder, CO: Westview Press.
Dubash, Navroz, Mairi Dupar, Smitu Kothari, and Tundu Lissu. 2001. *A Watershed in Global Governance? An Independent Assessment of the World Commission on Dams.*

Delhi: Lokayan; Dar es Salaam: Lawyers Environmental Action Team; and Washington, DC: World Resources Institute.

"Fifty Years of Bretton Woods Institutions: Enough." 1994. *Lokayan Bulletin*, December.

Kothari, Smitu. 1995. "The Damming of the Narmada and the Politics of Development." In *Toward Sustainable Development? Struggling over India's Narmada River*, edited by William F. Fisher. Armonk, NY: M. E. Sharpe.

Kothari, Smitu. 2000. "A Million Mutinies Now: Lesser Known Environmental Movements." *Humanscape*, October.

Kothari, Smitu. 2002. *In Search of Democratic Space*. Delhi: Rainbow Publishers.

Morse, Bradford, and Thomas Berger. 1992. *Sardar Sarovar: Report of the Independent Review*. Ottawa: Resources Futures International.

Patkar, Medha, and Smitu Kothari. 1995. "The Struggle for Participation and Justice: A Historical Narrative." In *Toward Sustainable Development? Struggling over India's Narmada River*, edited by William F. Fisher. Armonk, NY: M. E. Sharpe.

World Commission on Dams. 2000. *Dams and Development: A New Framework for Decision-Making*. London and Sterling, VA: Earthscan Publications.

Notes

This essay presents some brief reflections based on a long-term involvement in the Movement to Save the Narmada (Narmada Bachao Andolan—NBA). Since complete objectivity is in any case a contradiction in terms, I will only say that while the task of writing about a popular struggle that I am involved in requires some distancing from the "subject," I cannot avoid the deeper levels of "subjectivity" that run through the paper. There will also, obviously, be differences between how I "read" the Andolan's history, how it would like the history to be presented, and how different participants in the Andolan understand it.

1. The NBA, while rooted in the Narmada Valley, is a national alliance of organizations jointly campaigning for justice in the valley. It was set up in 1988 to initially seek comprehensive rehabilitation for those displaced by the Sardar Sarovar Project (SSP) in west-central India. By August 1990, the NBA, recognizing the inability of the state and central governments to provide rehabilitation, decided to oppose the building of the project.

2. This is not to say that the defense of economic and cultural globalization is universal among global elites. There are powerful currents in almost all Third World societies and several First World ones that resist the logic and hegemony of globalization and seek to protect both fundamentalist and progressive traditions. What is important, however, is that the potential and role of domestic social and political forces (as they challenge the forces of capital) and the influence of these nationally bound struggles on the nature of transnational alliances and linkages should not be underestimated. Conversely also, transnational alliances often strengthen local social movements by providing a wider arena to pursue advocacy and political strategies that contribute to the democratization of society. There are two crucial lessons: one, the central need for transnational alliances to be rooted in local movements with the active participation of local communities; and two, the profound demand for a major restructuring of contemporary democratic institutions, from the local to the global.

3. One of the more eloquent prescriptive documents that propagates this worldview is the World Bank's World Development Report of 1997, which centers on the role of the state in an era of economic globalization.

4. Movement activists supporting the need to go beyond national boundaries believed that alliances with European and Japanese groups were crucial since the governments of these countries were members of the World Bank and sent influential citizens as their executive directors to the World Bank headquarters in Washington, D.C.

5. In late 1999 and 2000, the existing alliance was reactivated and new actors were brought in as the state of Madhya Pradesh went ahead with its decision to build another dam in the Narmada Valley at Maheshwar. A U.S.-based corporation, Ogden, and German state guarantees to German corporate investments in the project were challenged. The German government was also compelled by an alliance of local and German NGOs to constitute an independent commission. The commission's report left little doubt about the apathy of local corporate partners and government officials to the plight of those to be displaced. It also documented the almost total opposition by local communities to the project. After some delays, the German government decided to withdraw its promised guarantees. Similarly, in the United States, a comprehensive campaign against Ogden has forced another independent investigation, eventually compelling even Ogden to withdraw from the project. See www.narmada.org for details of this process.

6. For details of the commission's work, see World Commission on Dams 2000. Also see their web site, www.dams.org. For a comprehensive report of the process, the lessons, and the limitations of the commission's works, see Dubash et al., 2001. This report and related material are also available at www.wcdassessment.org.

PART THREE

INSTITUTIONS OF GLOBAL ENVIRONMENTAL GOVERNANCE

Effective responses to global environmental problems clearly require international cooperation. Many environmental problems flow across borders; others, such as climate change, deep-ocean pollution, and destruction of the Earth's stratospheric ozone layer, negate the concept of borders entirely; and still others, such as soil erosion, land degradation, and the depletion of fisheries, may add up to yield global-scale socioeconomic effects despite their physically localized character. To respond effectively to these problems, governments and other actors in international society must cooperate.

But the barriers to such cooperation are substantial and include uncertainty, mistrust, conflicting interests, different views of causality, complex linkages to other issues, and the myriad problems of coordinating the behavior of large numbers of actors.[1] For some, the challenge of global environmental governance is to fill the "anarchic" space of an ungoverned world system with laws and rules that can change actors' environmentally destructive behavior; for others, it is to reform or transform deeply embedded political-economic practices that already "govern" the world system: trade, foreign investment, development assistance, multinational corporate activity. With four decades of experience since the Stockholm conference to look back upon, how successful has the international community been in creating new governance mechanisms that promote sustainability and in reforming existing ones that may undermine it?

Answering this question requires an understanding of the concept of institutions. Oran Young has defined institutions as "social practices consisting of easily recognized roles coupled with clusters of rules or conventions governing relations among the occupants of these roles."[2] By this definition, stressing roles and rules, institutions are not synonymous with organizations, which are "material entities possessing physical locations (or seats), offices, personnel, equipment, and budgets."[3] Many institutions have a formal organizational base; others, such as language systems or the family, endure informally, being reproduced over time by the beliefs and practices of individuals and groups.

In this section, we examine a wide range of institutionalized approaches to global environmental governance. We start with what has arguably been the centerpiece of efforts to promote global environmental protection since the Stockholm conference: multilateral environmental treaties. Despite the sometimes formidable barriers to cooperation, international agreements of varying scope and effectiveness now exist on a number of important issues, including the international trade in endangered species, international shipments of toxic waste, ocean dumping, the Antarctic environment, whaling, nuclear safety, and the protection of regional seas. Perhaps the most powerful example of international cooperation is provided by the international agreement on protecting the planet's ozone layer. The successful negotiation of the Montreal Protocol on Substances that Deplete the Ozone Layer in 1987, and its further strengthening in subsequent agreements, signaled what many hoped would be a new era of increased global environmental cooperation.

Certainly that enthusiasm carried over into the 1992 Earth Summit, where governments attempted to hammer out agreements that would slow global climate change, protect biological diversity, and reduce rates of deforestation. But as the international community grappled with these more complex and contentious problems—involving more actors, greater scientific uncertainty, higher stakes, more deeply entrenched interests, and higher costs of adjustment—the momentum for forming ambitious new international environmental regimes stalled in the post-UNCED 1990s. Norichika Kanie provides an overview of the pattern of agreement formation in recent decades. Given the tendency of most accords to tackle narrow, issue-specific problems, she characterizes the resulting "multilateral environmental agreement (MEA) system" as fragmented and decentralized. While there may be advantages of flexibility and pragmatism in such a system, most observers would also agree that it brings problems of overlap, redundancy, and poor coordination. Thus, one of the current debates prompted by this state of affairs is how to promote better integration and coordination among existing agreements.[4]

One obvious instrument for providing such coordination, the UN Environment Programme (UNEP), also faces substantial challenges. As Maria Ivanova explains, UNEP emerged from the 1972 Stockholm conference with a broad mandate to catalyze and coordinate environmental activities within the UN—but without the powers, funding mechanisms, or governance structure to do so effectively. This mandate without means has led some to call for scrapping UNEP in favor of a "World Environment Organization" that would have the authority, monitoring capability, and enforcement muscle lacking in softer institutional arrangements.[5] To date, the idea has gained little traction, with opponents arguing that it would merely generate a layer of global bureaucracy with an unclear mission and dubious prospects for effectiveness.

Richard Bissell summarizes a very different approach to organizing global governance, exemplified by the World Commission on Dams

(WCD). Rather than situate the question at hand in a sovereign inter-state forum such as an international treaty or a UN body, the WCD brought together a group of representative "stakeholders," ranging from environmental and human rights activists to dam-building in-dustrialists and professionals. And rather than beginning with a least-common-denominator foundation of agreement, the WCD placed the core economic, social, and environmental controversies surround-ing large dams at the heart of its work. Its relative success in hammer-ing out a consensus statement on dams and development has led some to see the WCD as a potentially fruitful model for other thorny international controversies.[6] Questions remain, however: Who exactly is a stakeholder? How broadly participatory can and should such processes be? What constitutes legitimate knowledge? At the end of the day, doesn't the fate of the enterprise rest on the willingness of governments and other powerful actors to embrace the findings?

Analysis of the institutionalization of global environmental gover-nance must go beyond environmental treaties and explicitly environ-mental organizations such as UNEP to examine broader patterns of activity in the world system. As international agreements have come into force, it has become clear that their effectiveness can be limited by the environmentally destructive effects of more fundamental eco-nomic and political processes. Practices such as international trade, foreign investment, technology transfer, and development assistance can have effects that cut across issue-specific environmental concerns such as soils, forests, or water quality. The international trade regime—as codified in the General Agreement on Tariffs and Trade (GATT), the World Trade Organization (WTO), and regional arrange-ments such as the European Union and the North American Free Trade Agreement (NAFTA)—is an example of an institution, in Young's sense of roles and rules, with important consequences for the global environment. So too is the so-called development regime, embedded in practices of bilateral foreign aid and the lending activities of mul-tilateral organizations such as the World Bank and the regional de-velopment banks.

Environmentalists began to focus serious attention on links be-tween trade and the environment in the 1990s. They did so for sev-eral reasons, including the increasingly apparent environmental consequences of trade, the growing importance of trade in the world economy, and an emerging flurry of efforts to rewrite the rules of the international trading game through agreements such as NAFTA and GATT. The ensuing trade-environment debate has reflected funda-mentally different perspectives about environmental externalities, about fairness in international trade competition, and about the ap-propriate way to view economic growth.[7]

Some environmentalists take a strongly critical view of the current trade regime. They argue that trade should be understood and judged not as an end in itself but as a means to the larger aim of sustainability; that aggressive trade liberalization promotes materials-intensive, unsustainable economic growth, destabilizes local communities, and worsens the income gap between rich and poor that lies at the heart of many environmental ills; and that current trade rules undermine multilateral environmental agreements (MEAs) that often seek to employ trade restrictions as compliance incentives. Others offer a more reform-minded perspective on the trade-environment linkage. In this view, much of the problem lies not with trade itself, but rather with specific practices embraced by the WTO, which focus inadequate attention on legitimate environmental concerns and operate in a context of excessive exclusion and secrecy.

A reformist agenda centers primarily on procedural changes to facilitate openness and dialogue between trade and environmental advocates, as well as identifying common ground between environmental advocates and trade proponents, such as the elimination of subsidies that are both environmentally harmful as well as trade distorting. In response, advocates of trade liberalization often warn that we must pay careful attention to the stability of the international trading system.[8] In this view, we should not risk trade wars by implementing protectionist measures to promote what are often subjective, culturally specific environmental goals. Instead, environmental goals should be accomplished with diplomacy and domestic legislation that minimize the impact on the trading system. Hugo Cameron of the International Institute for Sustainable Development (IISD) sketches the history of these debates. Cameron stresses the positions of different actors that create "fault lines" in the trade-environment debate, as well as the evolution and growing institutionalization of the debate over time.

The case of development assistance provides an interesting contrast to international trade in that processes of attempted institutional reform for the purposes of environmental protection are already well under way. Both bilateral aid donor governments and multilateral development banks have come under intense pressures to "green" their aid and lending practices. Most have responded by adopting new rules that seek to screen out particularly harmful projects and to increase commitments to positive projects that invest in sustainable development. The chapter by J. Timmons Roberts and colleagues summarizes the results of an unprecedented effort to evaluate the extent of change in foreign aid practices. They evaluated thousands of projects funded by development-assistance grants and loans to assess the extent to which donor governments had lived up to their environmental commitments. Their findings draw a mixed picture: aid has to some extent shifted toward less environmentally impactful projects but has not lived up to the commitments donor governments have made at global summits.

The World Bank, in particular, as the financially and intellectually dominant international organization on the development scene, has felt substantial pressure to change its lending practices. Beginning in the mid-1980s, the World Bank's role in distributing tens of billions of dollars annually for development projects, including many with devastating environmental impacts, made it a target of criticism from nongovernmental organizations in both the North and the South.[9] As a result, the Bank began to institute a series of internal reforms aimed at improving its environmental performance. Despite organizational and procedural changes within the World Bank, even the optimists acknowledge that change in practice has been uneven. As with any large organization, reform in the Bank has collided with bureaucratic inertia and resistance. To underscore both the possibilities of and barriers to change, we include an extended excerpt from a report by the World Bank Inspection Panel, a body that itself was created as a result of criticism directed at the Bank. The Inspection Panel decides whether to investigate grievances brought by citizens in countries with Bank-funded projects; it can issue independent reports on whether the Bank has complied with its own rules and standards on issues such as environmental assessment, forced resettlement of local communities, and the treatment of indigenous people. Bank observers have had differing opinions on whether the panel constitutes evidence of a changing organizational culture.[10] The report excerpted here, on an agricultural colonization project in western China, is one of the panel's strongest criticisms to date of Bank practices. It documents numerous instances in which changed thinking and operational guidelines have not translated fully into good practices on the ground.

Thinking Critically

1. When it comes to international environmental cooperation, do you think the glass is half empty or half full? Given Kanie's description of the pros and cons of the decentralized approach to international environmental treaty formation, would it make sense to attempt to deepen and strengthen this approach, or try something new?

2. Would it make more sense to attempt to reform and strengthen the existing UN Environment Programme or build a new organization

from scratch? In either case, what would the powers, mandate, responsibilities, and design of that organization look like? How would you organize a political constituency for such change?

3. Given the current state of environmental debates on trade, development assistance, the UN Environment Programme, and international environmental treaties, is it worth trying to revive broadly multilateral North-South bargaining on environment and development? Or did the 2002 World Summit on Sustainable Development mark the death of the "global summit" approach to global environmental governance and herald the need for a new approach?

4. In your opinion, how will history judge the world's progress in institutionalizing international environmental cooperation and governance in the period from the Stockholm conference (1972) to the Johannesburg summit (2002)? Imagine that you are a journalist writing about the legacy of this period from the vantage point of someone living in the year 2032. What do you imagine the first paragraph of your story would say?

5. Who is a "stakeholder" in global environmental controversies? If you were constituting, say, a World Commission on Climate along the lines of the World Commission on Dams, how would you decide who should have a voice?

Notes

1. A classic work on barriers to cooperation is Mancur Olson, *The Logic of Collective Action: Public Goods and the Theory of Groups* (Cambridge, MA: Harvard University Press, 1965). For a more optimistic perspective on similar questions, see Elinor Ostrom, *Governing the Commons: The Evolution of Institutions for Collective Action* (London: Cambridge University Press, 1990).

2. See Oran Young, *International Cooperation: Building Regimes for Natural Resources and the Environment* (Ithaca, NY: Cornell University Press, 1989), p. 32.

3. Ibid.

4. See United Nations, *Delivering as One: Report of the High-level Panel on United Nations System-wide Coherence in the Areas of Development, Humanitarian Assistance and the Environment*. UN doc A/61/583, November 2006.

5. On the pros and cons of a WEO, see the debate in *Global Environmental Politics* 1, no. 1 (February 2001).

6. See the symposium "The World Commission on Dams: A Model for Global Environmental Governance?" *Politics and the Life Sciences* 21, no. 1 (March 2002): 37–71; Navroz K. Dubash, Mairi Dupar, Smitu Kothari, and Tundu Lissu, *A Watershed in Global Governance? An Independent Assessment of the World Commission on Dams* (Washington, DC: World Resources Institute, 2001).

7. See, for example, the exchange between Herman Daly and Jagdish Bhagwati in the November 1993 issue of *Scientific American*. See also Ken Conca, "The WTO and the Undermining of Global Environmental Governance," *Review of International Political Economy* 7, no. 3 (Autumn 2000): 484–494.

8. On protectionism and the stability of the international trading system, see Jagdish Bhagwati, *Protectionism* (Cambridge, MA: MIT Press, 1989).

9. The origins of the campaign to change the World Bank are described in Pat Aufderheide and Bruce Rich, "Environmental Reform and the Multilateral Banks," *World Policy Journal* 5, no. 2 (Spring 1988): 301–321.

10. See, for example, Mohamed T. El-Ashry, "The Road from Rio: Implications of the UN Conference on Environment and Development for the World Bank," *Journal of Environment and Development* 2, no. 2 (Summer 1993): 69; the exchange between Paul Nelson and Rodger Payne in *Journal of Peace Research* 34, no. 4 (1997); and Bruce Rich, *Mortgaging the Earth: The World Bank, Environmental Impoverishment, and the Crisis of Development* (Boston: Beacon Press, 1994).

10

GOVERNANCE
WITH MULTILATERAL
ENVIRONMENTAL AGREEMENTS:
A HEALTHY
OR ILL-EQUIPPED
FRAGMENTATION?

NORICHIKA KANIE[*]

Introduction

This chapter focuses on multilateral environmental agreements (MEAs). Unlike other international policy fields such as trade, labor, or health, where international institutions are streamlined, environmental problem solving is centered around a multiple number of multilateral environmental agreements and their institutions (secretariat and conference of the parties). Although existing environmental institutions such as MEAs and UNEP [the United Nations Environment Programme] have achieved a great deal and reduced the speed with which environmental degradation is proceeding, there still are a number of pressing environmental problems prevailing throughout the world, including air and water pollution, the loss of biological diversity, desertification, and climate change. Furthermore, accelerated globalization has caused cross-border environmental problems to increase. Chal-

[*]   Originally published in Lydia Swart and Estelle Siegal Perry, *Global Environmental Governance: Perspectives on the Current Debate.* © 2007 Center for UN Reform Education. Reprinted with permission.

lenges of environmental governance are huge and still growing. What is necessary to improve the system and make it more effective? Could we head for a more effective environmental governance system based on MEAs on the road ahead, or do we need to change direction towards a more streamlined problem-solving system?

Questions in the following three areas are considered below:

1. The first set of questions is about the MEA system itself. What is the MEA system? How and why did it come about? Why are there so many independent multilateral agreements in the field of environment and what are the related problems?
2. The second deals with the performance of the MEA system. What are its strengths and weaknesses? Although evaluating the performance of institutions involves many methodological issues which could lead to an interesting academic debate, this chapter will not delve into this.
3. What reforms are required, what are the options? How large is the gap between needed reform and the current political will? What could narrow this gap?

The MEA System: Why are there so many agreements and what are the related problems?

In this chapter, the definition used for a multilateral environmental agreement is "an intergovernmental document intended as legally binding with a primary stated purpose of preventing or managing human impacts on natural resources."[1] Varying methodologies used for counting MEAs have resulted in different numbers, but many researchers and analysts agree that there is a proliferation of MEAs, constituting a key characteristic of the existing environmental governance system. In the International Environmental Agreements (IEA) database, 405 agreements and 152 protocols have been identified, modified by 236 amendments bringing the total to 794 MEAs that came into existence between 1875 and 2005, although many of these are now defunct.[2] The Ecolex project sponsored by UNEP, FAO [the Food and Agriculture Organization], and IUCN [the World Conservation Union] recognizes in total 519 environmental treaties.[3] Other research identifies more than 500 MEAs registered with the UN, including 61 on atmosphere; 155 on biodiversity; 179 on chemicals, hazardous substances, and waste; 46 land conventions; and 197 on water issues.[4]

This apparent disjointed approach to the current form of environmental governance can largely be attributed to two factors. One is the historical development of environmental institutions, and the second is the very nature and complexity of environmental problems.

Historical Development

When the institutionalization of international environmental policymaking really began in 1972, the issues focused mainly on the conservation and management of natural resources, both living and nonliving. No one could have predicted, or even imagined at that time, the severity or variety of problems that would arise by the twenty-first century, including such previously unrecognized threats as stratospheric ozone depletion and the trade in hazardous wastes. The manner in which environmental institutions have developed in response to these problems has largely been ad hoc and fragmented. Unlike the postwar financial and commercial regimes, which have been organized around a small number of formal institutions with fairly clearly demarcated norms and rules, environmental governance has evolved incrementally over the last 35 years, and now encompasses a wide array of international institutions, laws, and regimes. Collectively, these institutions serve as a reflection of the muddled hierarchy of real-world issues that compete for global attention. Apart from the multitude of MEAs and a plethora of international organizations, doing the best they can to respond to environmental challenges that range from climate change to persistent organic pollutants, new planning doctrines have emerged concerning critical loads, integrated assessment, and public participation and are being applied to multilateral management efforts. More importantly, environmental issues are now viewed within the framework of sustainable development.

The concept of sustainable development calls for simultaneous and concerted efforts to deal with pollution, economic development, unequal distribution of economic resources, and poverty reduction. It contends that most social ills are nondecomposable, and that environmental degradation cannot be addressed without confronting those human activities that give rise to it. Sustainable development dramatically expanded the international agenda by stressing that these issues need to be simultaneously addressed and that policies should seek to focus on the interactive effects between them. One of the sources of the current debate on environmental governance reform stems from the gap between the historical development of environmental institutions and the new institutional requirements posed by the transition from mere environmental protection to sustainable development. MEAs are, of course, no exception in facing these challenges.

The core of the new sustainable development agenda reflects new thinking among the environmental and the developmental communities about the linkages between key issues on the international agenda.[5] Some critics contend that this new agenda threatens to divert attention from the fundamental goals of fighting poverty, reducing military expenditure, increasing respect for human rights, and promoting democracy. Conversely, though, the broad agenda offers the prospect of strategic linkages between small policy networks in the international environmental and developmental communities which previously lacked sufficient autonomous influence to be able to shape agendas or policies. In this sense, the new agenda of sustainable development provides opportunities as well.

Sustainable development has two core components. The first is *substantive*, as discussed above, stressing the need for an integrative approach to economic development that includes environmental protection along with other goals of growth, social equity, and, according to some advocates, democratization. Accordingly, the MEA system, which has evolved incrementally on a somewhat ad-hoc basis over the last 35 years in a rather narrow-scoped issue-specific manner, is now facing a new challenge that requires adjustments. The second is *procedural*. Sustainable development and Agenda 21 call for a radically broader participation in decision making. [Editors' note: Agenda 21 is the extensive blueprint for implementing sustainable development agreed to by nations at the 1992 Earth Summit.] Sustainable development is no longer the pure domain of national sovereignty. Agenda 21 calls for multiple stakeholder participation, or "major groups," at multiple levels of international discussions, including NGOs, scientists, business/industry, farmers, workers/trade unions, local authorities, as well as indigenous people, women, and youth and children. The MEA system is also facing these substantive and procedural challenges.

Issue Complexity

One of the major reasons for utilizing the MEA approach to environmental problems arises from the very nature and complexity of the problems. Environmental processes are governed by laws of nature that are not susceptible to conventional bargaining within the domestic or international policy-making processes. Environmental policy makers have to struggle, from the outset, with the issue of "scientific uncertainty" as well as the incompatibilities between the ethical and political ramifications of the precautionary principle. In many ways, the current international legislative environment is not conducive to the development of coordinated, or synergistic, approaches to collective environmental—and sustainable development—problem solving. Particular international agreements are often negotiated by way of "specific" regimes that are considered in relative isolation. Each agreement is tackled, more or less, by artificially decomposing the causative complexities involved for the sake of practical "manageability." Agreements are negotiated by specialized ministries, or functional organizations, within forums that are detached from the negotiating arenas of other international agreements. Furthermore, the process of consensus building within the context of noncooperative attitudes, which are characteristic of global multilateral treaty-making, involves a great deal of ad-hoc log rolling. This, all too often, obscures the interconnectedness of the goals to be shared among different issue-specific regimes. The treaty-making process is also extremely time-consuming. It typically takes over a decade to advance from the agenda-setting stage, via a framework agreement, to the negotiation of the first operational protocol for collective action. Even after reaching agreement, ratification of the protocol requires governments to create consensus at the domestic level. In case a government turns out to be unwilling to ratify the protocol—thus politically increasing scientific uncertainty again—there always remains the possibility that the whole negotiation process can unexpectedly be brought back to an earlier stage, causing considerable time delays.

To date, international environmental policy making has generally been segregated on the basis of topic, sector, or territory. The result is the negotiation of treaties that often overlap and conflict with one another. This engenders unnecessary complications at the national level as signatories struggle to meet their reporting obligations under multiple agreements. At the international level, some coordination exists between environmental institutions through mechanisms such as the Interagency Coordination Committee and the Commission for Sustainable Development [UNCSD], but these institutions are far too weak to effectively coordinate MEAs, and to integrate the various dimensions of sustainable development. These mechanisms seem to function more as a *pooling regime* than as an effective *coordination regime*.

And yet there is progress. Describing the difficulty of the endeavor should still not blind us, as analysts, to the fact that amazing accomplishments have been achieved multilaterally over the last 30 years. Most governments created environmental agencies and, since 1992, units responsible for sustainable development. Public expenditures on environmental protection and sustainable development in the advanced industrialized countries now routinely run between 2–3 percent of their GNP. The market for pollution control technology is conservatively estimated at 600 billion dollars per year, and this market did not even exist in 1972. It was created as a result of governments adopting policies in order to achieve environmental protection and sustainable development. As mentioned above, hundreds of MEAs have been adopted. Many of these MEAs have actually been effective at improving the environment by inducing states to change policies in a manner conducive to a cleaner environment. Stratospheric ozone pollution has been reduced. European acid rain is greatly reduced. Oil spills in the oceans are down in number and volume. Considering the pace with which economies have grown in the last 30 years, these should be recognized as considerable accomplishments. But the challenge still remains to do better, and to progress from environmental protection to sustainable development.

It is generally recognized that certain inherent links exist between human activities and the natural environment on which they depend. We know, for example, that there are a number of different gases that all lead to climate change, acid rain, and ozone loss. Similarly, we recognize that the climate, forests, oceans, wetlands, and diverse biosystems are naturally codependent within the global ecosystem. The multilateral approach to these issues still remains fragmented, however, in terms of methods and mechanisms of scientific assessment and the development of consensual knowledge. This is also the case in regard to human capacity building and the art of interfacing domestic, regional, and international policy. At present, it is unlikely that the tendency to simply piggyback new institutions on existing ones will provide a coherent holistic approach to the governance of global sustainable development. The debates on sustainable development and institutional reforms to improve its prospects will surely continue for the foreseeable future. It is now widely recognized and appreciated that the principal characteristic of international issues is their complexity. Yet, traditionally international institutions have been designed according to an organizational logic that addresses problems individually. Sustainable development requires a reorientation of collective understanding and of formal institutions to focus on the key intersecting and interacting elements of complex problems.

How well does the MEA system perform?
What are the strengths and weaknesses of the MEA system?

The present international environmental governance system is organized around UNEP, which was established in 1973. But, over the years, many other organizations have acquired environmental responsibilities, including the World Bank, the IPCC [Intergovernmental Panel on Climate Change], the UNCSD, the GEF [Global Environment Facility] and MEA secretariats, as well as numerous non-state actors. Widespread frustration is often expressed about the inflexible and inelastic operation of the current environmental governance system. Those with insufficient information tend to dismiss the ability of this patchwork quilt of governance arrangements to effectively govern, because of the failings of some of its more visible elements. However, to best understand and evaluate the existing system, one must recognize that it consists of a governance system of many interconnected and interactive elements. Nonetheless, one still must acknowledge that environmental treaty-making has often been segregated on the basis of topic, sector, or territory, and the result has sometimes been overlapping and conflicting negotiation processes. It is also the case that the implementation of one treaty can impede on the principle of another. In such cases, conflicting principles should be investigated, analyzed, and revised to achieve a more effective system of environmental governance.

Still, the current environmental governance system also has advantages. Issue-specific regimes have achieved a relatively high level of performance in a wide range of dimensions. As pointed out earlier, the environmental quality of many regional seas has been stabilized, if not improved. We know that depletion of the ozone layer and acid rain in Europe have been reduced. The Convention on International Trade in Endangered Species (CITES) has induced behavioral change by focusing on trade. Scientific understandings of climate change and its solutions have also improved dramatically as a consequence of the performance of UNFCCC [UN Framework Convention on Climate Change] and IPCC. Norms have changed to take into account environmental consideration, as we can tell from the frequent use of the term "sustainable development" in speeches and news articles. Studies on the effectiveness of environmental institutions suggest that these institutions do matter in improving the human environment. In the face of sustained economic growth, these achievements in the last three to four decades are considerable. In addition, research and analysis have shown that the current diffused MEA system has provided at least the following strengths or advantages:

- Current research on institutions has shown that the best institutional design for managing complex problems such as the global environment is a loose, decentralized, and dense network of institutions and actors that are able to relay information and provide *sufficient redundancies* in the performance of functions so that *inactivity of one institution does not jeopardize the entire system.*[6]
- *Multiple forums allow multiple opportunities for multiple actors to hold discussions and to take action.* This increases the visibility of environmental governance and results in norm diffusion.
- A basic principle of the MEA system is to establish one problem-solving rule centered around one MEA. *Specialization* makes it possible to create a tailor-made solution. It is also easier for the public to understand.
- Multiple MEAs and their specific rules of governance *provide civil society with more windows of opportunity for participation in the global debate.*[7] This is actually a very important point in realizing sustainable development in procedural terms.
- A diffused MEA system provides secretariats with *opportunities and flexibility for self-innovation.* It also allows a certain degree of freedom for secretariats to cooperate with agencies dealing with issues other than the environment, where such opportunities exist. Even competition over limited resources often creates positive effects as it encourages the secretariats and other agents to continuously assess their mandates and improve their performances and competencies. Some analysts also see positive effects when host countries of MEA secretariats inject stronger political will in a particular issue (*ownership*).

There are, however, also weaknesses in the current MEA system. In fact, many proponents of environmental governance reform emphasize the shortcomings of the current system, as a coordinated and synergistic approach to solving common problems is lacking. They further argue that inconsistencies in rules and objectives among a large number of MEAs lead to unnecessary duplication. Many analysts have identified the following, greatly interconnected, problems of MEAs.[8]

- As pointed out earlier, it is reported that there are more than 500 MEAs registered with the UN.[9] Many of these are regional in scope or nested within a hierarchical structure of agreements, and a large number are actually defunct, but nonetheless the majority of these operate at the global level. The proliferation of MEAs, with little authority to coordinate activities, leads to *treaty congestion* as well as institutional and policy *incoherence, confusion, and duplication of work. Redundancy leads to inefficiency.* However, the rate with which new conventions have emerged has been decreasing since the late 1990s, which is sometimes described as a result of "negotiation fatigue."[10]

- MEA secretariats tend to develop an institutional interest in expanding their work, which may result in *man-made institutional barriers and may enhance vested interests* over time. In its report entitled "Delivering as One," the Secretary General's High-level Panel on UN System-wide Coherence in the Areas of Development, Humanitarian Assistance, and the Environment also cautioned that fragmentation in environmental governance does not offer an operational framework to address global issues. Illustrating this point, the panel refers to the slight impact more than 20 UN organizations engaged in water and energy issues have been able to make.

- In some cases, MEAs have *conflicting or duplicating agendas*. An often-cited example are the conflicting signals sent by the Montreal Protocol for ozone layer protection and the Kyoto Protocol for climate change: although the former proposes HFCs [hydrofluorocarbons] as an alternative to CFCs [chlorofluorocarbons], the latter considers both gases as greenhouse gases that need to be reduced. Such a conflicting/duplicating agenda is partially due to the nature of multilateral rule-making. Each new negotiation process typically starts with different policy makers and stakeholders who do not have the same institutional and policy-oriented concerns that were present in earlier negotiations on related issues. They often start from scratch and are influenced by their own particular political dynamics. In addition, they tend to end up with ambiguous wording as a result of concessions made in the process of reaching consensus.

- *The proliferation of MEAs increases administrative and institutional costs for member states*, because it leads to an *increased number of meetings, international negotiations, and reporting.* A survey conducted for the aforementioned report "Delivering as One" revealed that the three Rio conventions (climate change, biodiversity, and desertification) have up to 230 meeting days annually. It also points out that adding the figures for seven other major global environmental agreements raises the number to almost 400 days. The increasing administrative and travel *costs are especially burdensome for developing countries, reducing their participation.*

- *The geographically dispersed locations of MEA secretariats may cause MEAs to be reluctant to hold more substantive and frequent coordinating meetings because of travel costs.* To overcome this problem, clustering of MEA secretariats based on issues, themes, functions, or geographical focus have been repeatedly discussed.

- Due to the costs related to attending meetings worldwide, *developing countries tend to be less willing to engage in additional agreements.*

Coordination problems also are apparent in the interaction between science and policy. As environmental policy relies deeply on scientific knowledge, the science-policy interface is key to solving environmental problems. A lot of good scientific information from sources such as the IPCC, the Millennium Ecosystem Assessment, and UNEP's Global Environmental Outlook is available to us. What is lacking is not good information, but a synthesis of the information. In the current situation, multiple sources of information are gathered in multiple ways and relayed to the stakeholders by multiple paths. Such disparate information does not allow for easy integration into the decision-making processes for sustainable development.

Generally speaking, the larger the number of MEAs, the more frequently they need to interact with each other. An MEA frequently influences the development and effectiveness of other MEAs, and in return, it is also influenced by other policy instruments. While the effects of such interlinkages could either be positive (synergistic) or negative (disruptive), recent study has shown that the MEA system creates more synergistic effects of interlinkages than disruptive effects and that "institutional interaction may not primarily be a bad thing that ought to be diminished as much as possible."[11] According to Oberthur and Gehring, institutional interaction led to synergy and improved the institutional effectiveness in more than 60 percent of their sample of 163 cases of institutional interaction in international and European environmental policy.[12] Of course, this does not mean that one can dismiss the 25 percent of cases where disruption does take place. The accumulative impact of disruption is also not clear. Reducing disruptive interlinkages and weaknesses, while enhancing synergistic interlinkages and strengths within the current MEA system, is the way forward towards reform of environmental governance, as discussed in the next section.

What are the reform options?

Over the years, many reform proposals have been circulated.[13] UNEP pursued internal efforts at streamlining its activities and achieving synergies amongst its various projects in its 1990 System Wide Medium Term Environmental Program (SWMTEP). The 1997 Task Force on Environment and Human Settlements, established by UN Secretary-General Kofi Annan, suggested strengthening UNEP by elevating it to a Specialized Agency (and thus entitling it to a fixed and regular budget) and improving its ability to coordinate activities with other specialized agencies, although no clear guidelines were given on how such coordination was to be achieved in the absence of strong political will by member states or the heads of the agencies. This prompted the Task Force to make the recommendation that an "issue management" approach be set up within the UN to address issues that cut across the mandates of specific institutions concerned with environment and sustainable development, such as UNEP and UNDP, and to some extent MEAs. Subsequently, the High-level Advisory Board on Sustainable Development was discontinued and supplemented by the establishment of the Environment Management Group (EMG), chaired by the Executive Director of UNEP.[14] The EMG was formed to assist in the coordination of activities between UNEP, UNDP, and other UN agencies, funds, and programs and MEA secretariats, and "adopt a problem-solving, results-oriented approach that would enable United Nations bodies and their partners to share information, consult on proposed new initiatives and contribute to a planning framework and develop agreed priorities and their respective roles in the implementation of those priorities in order to achieve a more rational and cost-effective use of their resources."[15] However, to date, its coordination functions are not very effective because: (1) there has been little high-level engagement in its work, (2) the negative perception of EMG as UNEP's tool to assert control over the work of other agencies, and (3) lack of a clear sense of outcomes.[16] A revitalized UNEP has also been supported by UNEP's 1997 Nairobi Declaration on the Role and Mandate of the United Nations Environment Programme.[17]

More far-reaching proposals have called for the creation of a new World Environmental Organization (WEO) or Global Environmental Organization (GEO) which would possibly replace UNEP, and be endowed with stronger and more centralized resources and influence. The proponents calling for the creation of a centralized WEO/GEO assign it many of the responsibilities currently distributed throughout the UN system.[18] It would be responsible for articulating environmental and sustainable development policies for the international community, and have resources to verify compliance and enforce sanctions on those in noncompliance. Such a WEO/GEO might even have the legal authority and staff to advocate for the environment in WTO [World Trade Organization] trade and arbitration panels, or claim authority to adjudicate such disputes on its own. In addition, it would consolidate the vast array of MEAs (or environmental regimes) in one place, supplementing weaknesses of the current system by easing the administrative burden on governments trying to keep up with the vast array of international environmental obligations, as well as bolstering the political influence of environmental officials within their own governments because they would be collectively housed in a centralized environmental embassy. Such a WEO/GEO initially received a favorable reception from Brazil, Germany, Singapore, and South Africa. However, the proposal has met with institutional resistance from institutions that would lose responsibilities, and with disinterest by much of the UN community.

A hybrid version of a WEO/GEO combined with a more streamlined UNEP has also received recent attention to encourage "a new governance approach" based on partially decoupled links amongst formal institutional bodies.[19] Some redistribution of authority would occur, as a WEO/GEO would be established to develop policy, to coordinate the MEAs, and to counterbalance the WTO. The WEO/GEO would work loosely with other international institutions and promote non-state participation, while pursuing possible synergies between MEAs and their institutions. UNEP would continue to coordinate international environmental science management.

Various visionary schemes have also been proposed. The Club of Rome and others have suggested transforming the Trusteeship Council into an Environmental or Sustainable Development body. In 1992, Gus Speth raised the prospect of a massive North-South bargain for sustainable development.[20] Mahbub Ul Haq's proposed focus on human security offers a similar grand systemic focus that would reorganize all institutional efforts.[21]

The preparatory process for the 2002 WSSD [World Summit on Sustainable Development] clearly demonstrated the extent to which many governments were willing to undertake extensive institutional reforms. The WSSD process also reaffirmed the importance of MEAs, and the need to keep them intact from WTO challenges. The February 2002 Cartagena meeting resulted in a decision on International Environmental Governance that made it clear that governments wished to retain UNEP as the center of the governance system, around which other efforts would revolve.[22] This meeting concluded a series of six often wishy-washy preparatory meetings held at the Ministerial Level by the Intergovernmental Group of Ministers.[23] The Cartagena decision suggested that "the process (of institutional reform) should be evolutionary in nature. . . . A prudent approach to institutional change is required, with preference given to making better use of existing structures." Moreover, the Ministers proposed:

- Sustainable development requires better coordination between ministries at the national level.
- The increasing complexity and impact of trends in environmental degradation require an enhanced capacity for scientific assessment and monitoring and for provision of early warnings to governments.
- Environmental policy at all levels should be tied to sustainable development policies.
- NGOs, civil society, and the private sector should be involved more extensively with all areas of decision making within and between governments.
- LDCs should be treated "on the basis of common but differentiated responsibility."[24]
- Capacity building and technology transfer are vital elements of governance.
- Retain UNEP/Nairobi as a meeting center.
- Strengthen UNEP with regular financing—elevate to UN specialized agency with "predictable" funding.
- The clustering approach of MEAs should be considered.

The Global Ministerial Environment Forum (GMEF) was established to be the cornerstone of the international institutional structure of international governance of the environment and sustainable development. Since its first meeting in 2000, national environmental ministers have met to discuss high-level policy issues, coinciding with UNEP's Governing Council meetings. Although the GMEF premise remains vague, and its specific architecture remains to be seen, many consider the GMEF to have the potential to become a more effective forum for high-level policy interaction amongst environmental ministers, non-state actors, and between environmental ministers and ministers from non-environmental sectors.[25] At the very least, the GMEF needs to clarify its primary mission, its relationships with the Conference of State Parties of the MEAs, and whether it should have its own permanent secretariat and where it should meet.

Political analysis of the five years since the Johannesburg Summit and the potential for reform

While ongoing pressures for institutional reform are likely to come from NGOs and an internationally organized academic network,[26] the political momentum for multilateral institutional reform for sustainable development is obviously less evident in the post-Johannesburg period when compared to the early 1990s. The negotiation on Chapter Ten of the Johannesburg Summit Plan of Implementation on institutions for sustainable development showed that there exists a will in the international community to discuss sustainable development institutions, but little political will to actually move forward. In fact, around ten paragraphs in Chapter Ten had to be deleted at the end of the negotiation in Johannesburg for lack of agreement. To create a new international governance system supporting sustainable development would, at minimum, require the agreement of the major industrialized countries whose economic activities do the most harm to the global environment and whose financial resources would be needed to overcome the development losses that might otherwise be suffered by the newly emerged manufacturing giants and the states waiting to follow them into the industrial world.

The United States, in particular, has recently tended to impede efforts to strengthen or deepen multilateral governance in almost all realms. The Bush administration has clearly signaled a retreat from multilateralism, as well as a profound disinterest in multilateral environmental governance and sustainable development. While domestic groups of academics and NGOs may support sustainable development reforms, the overall administration is uninterested. The EU [European Union] seems supportive of the idea of sustainable development, although it has not been able to pass a carbon tax or adopt measures which entail significant economic costs for its member states. G8 Summits have adopted declarations endorsing sustainable development, although they could be stronger. The Gleneagles Summit took the important step of inviting some of the leaders from key developing countries. The collective purpose of the industrialized countries is currently mobilized behind combating terrorism rather than promoting sustainable development, and there is some degree of institutional fatigue. The Netherlands and Scandinavia continue to support reforms. Domestic progressive elements within Canada and Italy may support multilateral institutional reform and sustainable development, but they are too small a coalition to sway the industrialized bloc. Germany and France are strong advocates of institutional reform and the establishment of a World Environmental Organization. Japan remains supportive in principle, but its primary interest in the UN reform agenda is that of the UN Security Council rather than over social and economic institutions.

The developing world remains suspicious of some of the policy goals pursued by the industrialized world, and is adamantly opposed to any reforms that would entail the movement of the headquarters of the principal international environmental institution, now in Nairobi, away from a developing country.

Towards constructive reform

Much progress has been made in the international environmental policy arena since Stockholm. The system remains fragile, however, and requires continuing support to bolster its many policy networks and to maintain the pressure on governments for sustained environmental protection. The current political situation does not seem conducive to far-reaching reform efforts. Indeed, the enemy of the good is the great. Given the strengths and weaknesses of the current environmental governance system centered around MEAs, and of limited political will within the next five years or so, I suggest that some streamlining of the international governance system may be the most politically tractable option for bolstering effectiveness of governance in the environmental and sustainable development arenas. For example, the Kyoto Protocol's first commitment period expires in 2012 and the negotiations on its follow-up will have to be concluded before 2012. The negotiations are likely to focus on climate change but may also provide a rare opportunity to review and streamline environmental governance.

Reform of the international governance structures needs to address the major functions of global governance while providing for the participation of all the principal actors involved at the global level. Financing remains problematic and further research is necessary on the international division of labor in terms of who performs which functions most effectively. For example, international organizations, MEA-related committees, and governments which have ratified MEAs have provided monitoring functions, but informally, this is also a role for scientists and grassroots NGOs. Rule-making, including sponsoring negotiations, is the function that national delegates to negotiation officially play, but NGOs can also participate in the process by providing principled positions (such as the precautionary principle). Business and industry also make rules by providing *de facto* standards.

According to current organizational thinking, decentralized information-rich systems are the best design for addressing highly complex and tightly interwoven problems.[27] Thus, international governance for sustainable development may be best served through a decentralized architecture coordinated by a sophisticated hub that is capable of quickly accessing usable information and transmitting it to the appropriate institutional nodes in the network. As discussed above, redundancy and efficiency turn out to be strengths in such decentralized systems. Redundancy amplifies the political influence of policy networks involved in governance, and also assures that the governance system persists even if one of the nodes suffers political setbacks. Redundancy in funding sources may also compensate for tentative shortfalls in financing from principal funding sources. Similarly, efficiency is a principle that obscures the symbiotic influences between the elements of the network. Decentralized systems do not cede full autonomy to states or markets: rather, they seek to engage states and markets with actors and policy networks that are sensitive to possible abuses of unfettered free markets.

MEAs should be placed in such a decentralized and densely networked system, and reform options for more effective environmental governance should be considered in such a context. The strengths of the MEA system, mostly the same as the very strengths of a decentralized system, should be preserved and further enhanced, while weaknesses should be resolved. When there is not sufficient political momentum for environmental governance reform to fully develop, seeds for reform should be cultivated where relevant so that when the right time arrives, the necessary growth can more easily take place.

The biggest weakness of the current governance system is lack of coordination. UNEP ought to play the central role in coordination, but UNEP's responsibilities have not been matched by adequate resources from the start. It is now widely recognized that UNEP can't perform all its assigned tasks, and some argue that it should rather concentrate on its science function and coordinate scientific activities throughout the UN system.[28] They propose that UNEP should oversee environmental monitoring, and provide the collected information to the international community through a variety of channels. If monitoring activities were clustered across environmental issues, it would be possible to gain economic efficiency and also to accelerate the flow of timely early warning information. In the context of MEAs, most environmental monitoring has taken place at the regional level, and given the current political environment and limited political will, accumulating experience at a smaller scale may facilitate bigger changes when the political environment changes. Some knowledge is also already collected regionally and not globally, as is the case in regard to regional seas. In this sense, institutions such as UNEP's regional offices may serve as a starting point for reform by creating regional hubs for monitoring, collecting, and disseminating environmental information.

At present, UNEP lacks the resources to perform all its governance functions effectively and to pressure states to pursue environmentally sustainable policies. However, it is also true that UNEP has long-standing experience with coordinating loose and decentralized networks around the world. Thus it may be capable of serving a coordinating role to ensure that the multiple elements of MEAs are coordinated, to anticipate any gaps, and to keep members of international policy networks in touch with one another. It could serve as an air-traffic controller for issues on the international environmental agenda, as well as for the multitude of associated ongoing studies and negotiations. The Secretary-General's High-level Panel on UN System Wide Coherence in the Areas of Development, Humanitarian Assistance, and the Environment recommended that "efficiencies and substantive coordination should be pursued by diverse treaty bodies to support effective implementation of major multilateral environmental agreements." It further recommends that "stronger efforts should be made to reduce costs and reporting burdens and to streamline implementation." Rather than serving as a coordinating body of MEAs, UNEP, or a reformed UNEP, it could more effectively serve as an air-traffic controller by sending signals for enhancing synergies and reducing disruption.

Centralization or co-location of MEA secretariats has the potential to reduce overall administrative costs, further increase coordination activities, and possibly increase the number of joint meetings. Increasing the number of simultaneous or concurrent meetings also has the potential to increase participation from developing countries, as mentioned earlier. This is in line with many recommendations on environmental governance reform, including the above-mentioned Secretary-General's High-Level Panel on UN System Wide Coherence, as it recommends that "greater coordination at headquarters should promote coherence at the country level, and greater coordination efforts at the country level should promote coherence at the international level."

The coordination of MEAs, or the creation of a sophisticated network hub for the MEA system, could be performed by UNEP if it is upgraded to a specialized agency, or by a reformed EMG or GMEF. But given the current situation regarding environmental and sustainable development issues and the lack of political will to reform, upgrading UNEP and providing it with "real authority as the 'environmental policy pillar' of the UN system, backed by normative and analytical capacity and with broad responsibility to review progress towards improving the global environment,"[29] seems difficult to achieve within the near future, although such a path should be pursued in the long run. As to reforming either EMG or GMEF, its purpose and mandates must first be clarified to make its institutional foundation firmer.

Environmental governance occurs through complex synergies between networks of actors involving various levels of international politics. Current governance arrangements remain a crazy quilt of overlapping activities, about which many governmental, academic, and NGO environmental analysts express misgivings. While the system is probably too complex to grasp easily, it should not be dismissed out of hand because a cursory view makes it appear incoherent. Gus Speth embraces the decentralized system, stressing its potential for innovation.[30] Needless to say, there are weaknesses in the current MEA system which will need to be addressed and unnecessary overlaps should be resolved. In order to identify where and how to reform, I suggest that more attention be paid to clarifying who the key actors are and which governance functions they perform best in addressing particular environmental threats. Only then can the institutional reforms required to create a successful MEA network system in a concrete manner become more apparent.

Notes

1. Ronald B. Mitchell, *International Environmental Agreements Website,* 2003. Available at http://www.uoregon.edu/~iea/ and described in Ronald B. Mitchell, "International Environmental Agreements: A Survey of Their Features, Formation, and Effects," *Annual Review of Environment and Resources* 28 (November 2003).

2. Mitchell 2003.

3. http://www.ecolex.org/indexen.php.

4. Adil Najam, Mihaela Papa, and Nadaa Taiyab, *Global Environmental Governance: A Reform Agenda* (IISD, 2006); Markus Knigge, Johannes Herweg, and David Huberman, *Geographical Aspects of International Environmental Governance: Illustrating Decentralization* (Berlin: Ecologic, 2005); and Peter Roch and Franz X. Perrez, "International Environmental Governance: The Strive Towards a Comprehensive, Coherent, Effective and Efficient International Environmental Regime," *Colorado Journal of Environmental Law and Policy* 16, no. 1 (2005).

5. Jan Pronk and Mahbub Ul Haq, *Sustainable Development: From Concept to Action,* The Ministry of Development Cooperation (Netherlands), UNDP and UNCED, 1992; Johan Holmberg, ed., *Making Development Sustainable* (Washington, DC: Island Press, 1992); and Joan Nelson and Stephanie J. Eglinton, "Global Goals, Contentious Means," *Policy Essay* No. 10 (Washington, DC: Overseas Development Council, 1995).

6. Vinod K. Aggarwal, *Institutional Designs for a Complex World* (Ithaca, NY: Cornell University Press, 1998); Elinor Ostrom, "Decentralization and Development: The New Panacea," in *Challenges to Democracy: Ideas, Involvement and Institution,* ed. Keith Dowding, James Hughes, and Helen Margetts (London: Palgrave Publishers, 2001), pp. 237–256; Christopher K. Ansell and Steven Weber, "Organizing International Politics," *International Political Science Review* (January 1999); and Peter M. Haas, Norichika Kanie, and Craig N. Murphy, "Conclusion: Institutional Design and Institutional Reform for Sustainable Development," in *Emerging Forces in Environmental Governance,* ed. Norichika Kanie and Peter M. Haas (Tokyo: UNU Press, 2004).

7. Najam et al. 2006.

8. Edith Brown Weiss, "International Environmental Issues and the Emergence of a New World Order," *Georgetown Law Journal* 81, no. 3 (1993): 675–710.

9. Najam et al. 2006; Knigge et al. 2005; and Roch and Perrez 2005.

10. Najam et al. 2006.

11. Sebastian Oberthur and Thomas Gehring, eds., *Institutional Interaction in Global Environmental Governance: Synergy and Conflict among International and EU Policies* (Cambridge, MA: MIT Press, 2006), p. 318.

12. Oberthur and Gehring 2006.

13. For example: Felix Dodds, "Reforming the International Institutions," in *Earth Summit 2002,* ed. Felix Dodds (London: Earthscan, 2000); Steve Charnovitz, "A World Environment Organization," *Columbia Journal of Environmental Law* 27, no. 2 (2002): 323–362; and Frank Biermann and Steffen Bauer, *A World Environment Organization: Solution or Threat for Effective International Environmental Governance?* (Aldershot, UK: Ashgate, 2005).

14. http://www.unemg.org/.

142 NORICHIKA KANIE

15. UN General Assembly Document A/53/463, Par. 11.

16. Najam et al. 2006.

17. Dodds 2000; Charnovitz 2002.

18. Daniel Esty, "The Case for a Global Environmental Organization," in *Managing the World Economy*, ed. Peter B. Kenen (Washington, DC: Institute for International Economics, 1994), pp. 287–310; Frank Biermann, "The Emerging Debate on the Need for a World Environment Organization," *Global Environmental Politics* (February 2001): 45–55; and Frank Biermann, "The Case for a World Environment Organization," *Environment* 42, no. 9 (2000): 22–31; German Advisory Council on Global Change (WBGU), *World in Transition 2* (London: Earthscan, 2001).

19. Daniel C. Esty and Maria H. Ivanova, eds., *Global Environmental Governance* (New Haven, CT: Yale School of Forestry & Environmental Studies, 2002); Peter M. Haas, "Pollution," in *Managing Global Issues*, ed. P. J. Simmons and Chantal de Jonge Oudraat (Washington, DC: Carnegie Endowment for International Peace, 2001), pp. 310–353; and Biermann, 2006, identified three types of WEO/GEO in the recent debate.

20. James G. Speth, "A Post-Rio Compact," *Foreign Policy* 88 (Fall 1992).

21. Mahbub Ul Haq, *Reflections on Human Development* (New York: Oxford University Press, 1995).

22. Governing Council of the United Nations Environment Programme, "Global Ministerial Environment Forum," S.S. VII/I. International Environmental Governance (UNEP/GC/21).

23. UNEP/IGM/5/2 and *Earth Negotiations Bulletin* 16, no. 20, IGM-NYC Final Summary, http://www.iisd.ca/linkages/unepgc/iegnyc/.

24. "Common but differentiated responsibility" is agreed as the Principle 7 of the Rio Declaration on Environment and Development (A/CONF.151/26) in 1992.

25. For example, Najam et al. 2006.

26. Biermann 2000, 2001; Esty 1994; Frank Biermann and Udo Simonis, "A World Environment and Development Organization," *SEF Policy Paper* 9 (1998); Geir Ulfstein, "The Proposed GEO and its Relationship to Existing MEAs," Paper presented at the International Conference on Synergies and Coordination between Multilateral Environmental Agreements, UNU, 14–16 July 1999. Also see *UNU/IAS Report International Sustainable Development Governance: The Question of Reform: Key Issues and Proposals*, UNU/IAS, August 2002.

27. Aggarwal 1998; Ansell and Weber 1999; Ostrom 2001; and Haas 2004.

28. Haas et al. 2004; see also UNEP Science Initiative http://science.unep.org.

29. The Report of the Secretary-General's High-Level Panel "Delivering as One" (A/61/583): 20–21.

30. James G. Speth, "A New Green Regime," *Environment* 44 (7) (2002): 16–25.

11

MOVING FORWARD BY LOOKING BACK: LEARNING FROM UNEP'S HISTORY

MARIA IVANOVA[*]

With a growing recognition that global problems demand global solutions, governments have created an increasingly complex network of international environmental treaties and organizations to deal with environmental challenges.[1] Yet, international environmental problems persist unabated and are even increasing in scale and scope, attesting that our first attempt at global environmental governance has been "an experiment that has largely failed."[2] Short-term economic considerations and sovereignty concerns have often overridden the political will to effectively combat environmental problems. The institutions created have been weak and "woefully inadequate to meet global environmental challenges."[3] Some analysts even argue that the system was deliberately designed to be ineffective.[4]

Careful analysis of archival materials, however, shows that the system for global environmental governance and the organization at its core—the United Nations Environment Programme (UNEP)—were not the product of malicious intent. UNEP was not purposefully established as a "weak, underfunded, overloaded, and remote organization."[5] Rather, it was created as the "anchor institution" for the global environment[6] to serve as the world's ecological conscience, to provide impartial monitoring and assessment, to serve as a global source of information on the environment, to "speed up international action on urgent environmental problems," and to "stimulate further international agreements of a regulatory character."[7] Most importantly, the mission of the new environment program was

    [*]   Originally published in Lydia Swart and Estelle Siegal Perry, *Global Environmental Governance: Perspectives on the Current Debate.* © 2007 Center for UN Reform Education. Reprinted with permission.

to ensure coherent collective environmental efforts by providing central leadership, assuring a comprehensive and integrated overview of environmental problems, and developing stronger linkages among environmental institutions and the constituencies they serve.[8] While UNEP's performance has been significantly affected by the early design choices, this has been the result of predictable but unintended consequences. This historical understanding opens a new line of analysis in the context of current UN environmental reform. If the system was not deliberately designed as ineffective, change in course becomes possible and even practical.

The analysis in this chapter shows the origins of the institutional design of the United Nations Environment Programme providing a factual account of key historical decisions that the architects of the global environmental governance system made in 1972 and straightens the record of global environmental governance. The analysis proceeds in two analytical steps. First, the political context within which the Stockholm Conference of 1972 took place is examined. Second, the article explains the decisions on the functions, form, and financing of the new intergovernmental body for the environment. It traces the historical roots and motivations behind these choices and shows the lack of evidence as to purposeful intent on the part of states to create a weak institution within the United Nations.

These historical dynamics carry implications for the contemporary international environmental governance reform process. As today's architects of reform seek to improve the complex system of global environmental governance, they face the task of rethinking how to restructure existing institutions and organizations for global collective action in the environmental field. In the context of current reform efforts, the North and the South are no longer at the two opposite ends of the spectrum. In February 2007, forty-six countries supported the upgrade of the United Nations Environment Programme to a United Nations Environment Organization (UNEO) and a "Friends of the UNEO" group was established comprised of developed and developing countries alike. Without solid understanding of past and present interests and positions of the actors in global environmental governance, critical choices are likely to be made based on faulty assumptions and might lead to unintended but serious consequences.

The Beginnings of
Global Environmental Governance

Environmental concerns were gaining domestic traction in the developed world through social movements in the 1960s. The effects of unbridled industrialization had manifested themselves across the United States and Europe in burning rivers, dying lakes, dead forests, and toxic chemicals that were being ingested by animals and humans. It was the efforts of a handful of individuals, however, that placed these concerns on the global political agenda.

In 1967, Inga Thorsson, Swedish negotiator and diplomat at the United Nations, set out to derail UN plans to convene the fourth international conference on the peaceful use of atomic energy. An ardent supporter of disarmament, she called for the termination of expensive UN conferences on nuclear energy as these mostly benefited the North's nuclear industry. Under her influence and the leadership of Sverker Åström, then Sweden's Permanent Representative at the United Nations, the Swedish delegation decided, without instructions from Stockholm, to challenge the latest UN atomic energy conference proposal when it was presented at the General Assembly.[9] As an alternative, Sweden's Deputy Permanent Representative Börje Billner proposed to the General Assembly on 13 December 1967 that a conference be held to "facilitate co-ordination and to focus the interest of Member countries on the extremely complex problems related to the human environment."[10] After multiple consultations with other delegations in the spring of 1968, the Swedish delegation in New York, led by Åström, convinced the Swedish government to launch a formal initiative.

In response, the General Assembly supported the convening of the first United Nations Conference on the Human Environment in 1972 and accepted the proposal of the Swedish government to host the event in its capital city, Stockholm. For the first time, environmental issues commanded attention at such a high level of international governance. The UN Secretariat, however, possessed neither the scientific nor the administrative capacities to deal with what came to be known as "the Swedish matter." Consequently, Philippe de Seynes, Under-Secretary-General for Economic and Social Affairs, frequently solicited expertise and advice from the Swedish delegation. Respect for Sweden as a neutral and progressive country that made substantive contributions to disarmament and development aid allowed the members of the Swedish delegation to lead the preparatory process, especially in the first two years.[11]

Much of the success of the Stockholm Conference was to a certain degree a product of its Secretary-General, Maurice Strong. A Canadian industrialist and businessman with an avid interest in international affairs, development, and UN matters, Maurice Strong was appointed Secretary-General of the Conference in 1970 because of his skills as a coordinator, collaborator, and convener. While not deeply familiar with the scientific aspects of environmental concerns, he understood the political and economic dimensions and had the capacity to convince leaders around the world that collective action was necessary. His extensive personal contacts and the respect he commanded in business and governmental arenas played a significant role in his ability to push for a progressive environmental agenda and galvanize the support of developed and developing countries alike.[12]

Developing countries' participation was not easily achieved. Having gained political independence only in the 1960s, much of these countries' concerns in the early 1970s focused on developing their economies as a way of ensuring autonomy and political sovereignty. The governments of many developing countries therefore viewed environmental initiatives from the North as preventing them from industrializing.[13] For them environmental concerns translated into the imposition of stringent standards and the institution of non-tariff barriers jeopardizing their export possibilities. Environmental regulations were expected to negatively influence the patterns of world trade, the international distribution of industry, the comparative costs of production, and thus the competitive position of developing countries. "Environmental concerns," it was argued, "were a neat excuse for the industrialized nations to pull the ladder up behind them."[14]

It took great energy and commitment from the Stockholm Conference team to convince leaders from developing countries that environmental issues could adversely impact economic development by lowering groundwater levels, causing soil erosion, increasing desertification, and depleting fisheries, and other similar problems. Some of the concerns were mitigated when, in 1971, many of the developing countries became involved in the drafting of "The Founex Report,"[15] which clarified the links between environment and development, and discredited the idea that these concepts were diametrically opposed. It helped to convince developing countries that environmental concerns were both more widespread and more relevant to their situation than they had appreciated. Moreover, the report affirmed that the environment should not be viewed as a barrier to development but as part of the process.[16]

While the tension between environment and development permeated the preparatory process for the Stockholm Conference, governments from the North were not deliberately attempting to stunt Southern development through environmental measures. Rather, they were responding to an unprecedented public awareness and pressure for environmental action from their domestic constituencies. In the United States, the late 1960s and early 1970s had marked a new era in policymaking. A strong national lobby for the environment emerged and asserted its voice through mass protests and the first Earth Day (held on April 22, 1970). It was this environmental constituency that propelled action from both President Richard Nixon and the US Congress, culminating in the passage of groundbreaking legislation that lay the foundation of US environmental policy.

In Europe, acid rain had not only brought environmental concerns to the fore of public attention but also demonstrated the need for international collective action. Lakes and forests in northern Europe were dying as a result of fossil fuel burning in the United Kingdom. Sulfur and nitrogen oxides were carried for hundreds of miles by northerly winds before depositing as rain, fog, and snow. Japan, the prodigy of economic growth, provided a stark picture of the costs of mindless industrialization. Japan had experienced firsthand that mercury, cadmium, and PCBs poisonings could cause death, neurological disorders, and fetus deformations. "We who had firmly believed since the war that greater production and higher GNP were the ways to happiness," Japan's environment minister told the Stockholm Conference plenary, "have been sorely disillusioned. The despoiling of nature by industry has led to a degradation of the spirit."[17] It was becoming evident that pollution knows no borders and that only through common efforts could significant solutions be realized.

Eventually, the Stockholm Conference attained an unprecedented level of agreement on the problems at hand and possible paths forward, including important underlying principles and necessary institutional arrangements. The level of cooperation that emerged between developed and developing countries was striking given the initial mistrust and suspicion. As Peter Stone, advisor to Maurice Strong on public information issues in the run-up to the Conference, observed in 1972, "Many governments began their participation in Stockholm with considerable reluctance founded on the suspicion that it was all a nine days' wonder, or a transient concern of the rich. But in the end, even the most reluctant took the Conference seriously."[18] The most tangible outcome of the Stockholm Conference was the creation of the United Nations Environment Programme, UNEP.

UNEP's Design: Form, Function, and Financing

While taken for granted today, UNEP's creation was less than certain in the 1970s. In his proposal to the General Assembly to hold a conference on the human environment, Sweden's ambassador to the United Nations stated that "no new institutional arrangements would result from the conference." But as the preparatory process progressed, it was increasingly clear that some type of institutional arrangement would be necessary to put the agreements into effect and to facilitate international cooperation. Thus governments agreed to create a new intergovernmental body as an "anchor institution" for the global environment. Following the Stockholm Conference, delegates from around the world gathered in New York at the UN General Assembly in the fall of 1972, to discuss, among other things, the institutional and financial framework for the environment. The decisions taken sealed the functions, form, financing, and location of what was to become UNEP [and] were taken in the Second Committee of the General Assembly responsible for economic and financial affairs.

Functions

While no international organization with an explicit and exclusively environmental mandate existed in the 1970s, the institutional landscape was not vacant. Many of the specialized agencies had "constitutional responsibilities in large areas of the human environment"[19] and were already undertaking a wide range of environmental activities. Long-standing international organizations were all charged with some aspect of environmental policy. The World Meteorological Organization (WMO), for example, was concerned with many aspects of air pollution and climatic change and operated a large number of monitoring stations and research programs; the Food and Agriculture Organization (FAO) was involved in a range of environmental concerns relating to land, water, forest resources, and fisheries;

the World Health Organization (WHO) was engaged in a major program of combating pollution of freshwater supplies and had broad responsibilities in the area of environmental impacts on human health; the International Atomic Energy Agency (IAEA) played a central role in the control of radioactive contamination of the environment. As recently as 1968, UNESCO had convened the Man and [the] Biosphere Conference and developed a comprehensive environmental portfolio with a focus on water, land, and scientific research. In addition to the specialized agencies, a number of other bodies within the United Nations were also heavily engaged in environmental work, including the regional economic commissions, the United Nations Development Programme (UNDP), the Department for Economic and Social Affairs, the UN Conference on Trade and Environment (UNCTAD), the UN Industrial Development Organization (UNIDO), and the financial agencies within the World Bank group. All of these organizations were reluctant to cede authority, and potentially financing, to a new agency.

Overlap, duplication, bureaucratic infighting, and jurisdictional turf battles among the agencies were a frequent occurrence but the potential for collaboration, synergy, and comprehensive actions reaching a large constituency was also within reach. If WHO and FAO, for example, both undertook operational programs aimed at water pollution, their activities did not by definition have to be duplicative or conflicting. One agency possesses access to doctors and public health officers, and the other to farmers and agricultural officials. Neither could reach the other's constituency as effectively and a new agency, it was believed, was not likely to "automatically command the loyalty and support of present agency constituencies and avoid the risks of duplication and inefficiency."[20] Yet, it was recognized that "even if all organizations in this bewildering array were effective and well managed, they would provide far too fragmented a structure for the conduct of international environmental affairs"[21] since environmental policy cuts across traditional functional areas as agriculture, health, labor, transport, and industrial development. Moreover, as Maurice Strong noted, environmental concerns were in fact "a cumulative result of a series of uncoordinated interventions in the environment and cannot be resolved by a series of *ad hoc* uncoordinated responses."[22]

While the institutional architecture for environmental governance in the early 1970s was obviously ill-suited for the scale and scope of the problems, a serious effort to reallocate environmental responsibilities among agencies or broader structural reform was deemed impossible given the legal autonomy of the agencies. "Under the circumstances," the Committee for International Environmental Programs convened by the US National Academy of Sciences wrote in 1971, "we recommend a new approach that goes beyond mere correction or adaptation of existing structures. It involves the creation of new, interrelated institutions designed to assure support from those societal resources—political, scientific, financial— whose cooperation is essential for effective management of global environmental problems."[23]

The new institutional arrangements for the global environment were to create a broad and comprehensive framework for environmental assessment, identification of alternatives, and determination of priorities. To this end, the new intergovernmental body that came to be called the United Nations Environment Programme was to serve as a center of leadership and initiative in international environmental matters and perform three core functions.

1. *Knowledge Acquisition and Assessment*—including monitoring of environmental quality, evaluation of the collected data, and forecasting of trends; scientific research; and information exchange with governments and other international organizations.
2. *Environmental Quality Management*—including setting goals and standards through a consultative, multilateral process; crafting of international agreements; and devising guidelines and policies for their implementation.
3. *International Supporting Actions*—or what we now term capacity building and development—including technical assistance, education and training, and public information. The new body was envisioned as normative and catalytic. It would thus not have operational functions—i.e., perform any activities on the ground—in order to avoid unnecessary competition with organizations already active in the field. Rather, it would maintain an overview of the activities of national governments, international organizations, and nongovernmental bodies identifying needed environmental programs and catalyzing action toward their realization. It would also serve as the center of information on global environmental trends. And, most importantly, it would administer the newly created Environment Fund proposed by the United States (see below) with the purpose to stimulate and support environmental activities within existing intergovernmental bodies and steer them on the path of sustainability.

These functions were officially mandated through General Assembly Resolution 2997 (XXII) of December 1972 establishing UNEP as the new intergovernmental body for the global environment. Its primary goal was to provide a center of gravity for environmental affairs within the UN system and pool, coordinate, and deploy existing expertise to solve pending environmental crises. Flexible and evolutionary, the new organization was anticipated to grow into its mandate as new issues emerged and as it proved it could successfully tackle them.

With a significant body of international environmental law developed since 1972 and environmental ministries established in almost every country, some analysts contend that UNEP needs to move into a more operational, or implementing, role.[24] Others, however, argue that its comparative advantage lies in the normative field and that operational activities should be performed by the sectorally focused specialized agencies.[25] However, despite the international efforts over the last thirty years, horizontal and trans-sectoral linkages among the specialized agencies are still lacking, environmental activities still amount to little more than rhetoric and competition for additional resources, and we are still "fighting fire with a thermometer."[26] The new patterns of organization that the founders of the system envisioned, "based on a multitude of centers of information and of energy and power, linked together within a system in which they can interact with each other,"[27] have yet to be created.

Institutional Form

UNEP's formal status within the UN system was the result of several dynamics and decisions. The most important one was the underlying principle of "form follows function." The catalytic and coordination functions envisioned for the new intergovernmental body demanded that it be placed in the United Nations so that it could exercise direct influence over the other agencies. A widely circulated article by George Kennan, which appeared in *Foreign Affairs* in April 1970, had argued that environmental concerns needed to be addressed by the countries that had caused them, and a new organization, outside the United Nations, would be most suitable for this purpose. A considerable outcry on the part of developing countries followed since they did not want to be excluded from a new institutional arrangement.[28] In the words of Indira Gandhi, India's Prime Minister at the time, "While each country must deal with that aspect of the problem which is most relevant to it, it is obvious that all countries must unite in an overall endeavor. There is no alternative to a cooperative approach on global scale to the entire spectrum of our problems."[29] At the time, the United States was going through a period of widespread dissatisfaction and erosion of confidence in the United Nations, yet it recognized that there was "in practice no effective alternative, whether governmental or non-governmental to working principally through that body to provide a global context for international cooperation on environmental matters."[30] During the preparatory process for Stockholm, it was therefore agreed that international environmental action and thus the agency responsible for it should be centered in the United Nations. This decision determined the range of institutional status options: (1) an autonomous Specialized Agency, (2) a unit within the UN Secretariat, or (3) a Program within the Economic and Social Council (ECOSOC).

While an early reaction to the new environmental awareness had been a call for a new UN Specialized Agency modeled after the existing ones, this option was dismissed during the preparatory process as unworkable for a number of reasons explained below. Specialized agencies are separate, autonomous intergovernmental organizations with governing bodies independent of the UN Secretariat and the General Assembly. They perform normative *and* operational functions in a specific issue area. Their governing bodies offer universal membership, i.e., any country can become an official member if it chooses. In 2006, for example, the World Health Assembly of the World Health Organization comprises 193 states; the membership of the World Meteorological Organization is 188 states, and that of the International Labor Organization, 175 states. Specialized Agency budgets consist of assessed, mandatory contributions levied on all members. The Specialized Agency institutional arrangement was considered counterproductive for the new environmental body for the following reasons.

First, as explained above, a large number of existing organizations were already performing environmental activities and creating a new Specialized Agency would only create unproductive competition among them. In this context, the new Specialized Agency "would be one among many." Moreover, the others would be older, with longer traditions and well-established relations with constituencies within national and international bureaucracies. A new Specialized Agency would therefore not be well-placed to exercise a leadership or coordinating function.

Second, a widespread dissatisfaction with UN agencies had taken hold in the 1970s especially in the United States. They were viewed as unnecessarily hierarchical, bureaucratic, and cumbersome, preventing the initiative, flexibility, and expertise deemed necessary in the emerging environmental field. The unwieldy administrative and governing arrangements could not be deployed quickly enough to emerging issues. In addition, the rigid customary staffing practices were counterproductive for recruitment of a secretariat with the necessary skills and qualifications.

Finally, many saw the environment as an integrative issue, one that could not and should not be relegated to one agency responsible for one sector. In fact, the establishment of a Specialized Agency for the environment was deemed counterproductive because its focus on the environment as another "sector" would marginalize it. As Maurice Strong put it, the core functions could "only be performed at the international level by a body which is not tied to any individual sectoral or operational responsibilities and is able to take an objective overall view of the technical and policy implications arising from a variety of multidisciplinary factors."[31]

On these grounds, the United States proposed the creation of a smaller unit, a Secretariat within the UN system to build on existing efforts both national and international and infuse the specialized agencies with an environmental ethic through information, persuasion, and direct funding. In the words of Christian A. Herter, Jr., Special Assistant for Environmental Affairs to the US Secretary of State, only a nimble, flexible unit was considered capable of building on existing capabilities and filling in the gaps to make the "global system effective."[32] To this end, the United States argued that "the intergovernmental body should be placed at the highest level in the United Nations [and] its functions should not be scattered through several administrative levels. It should enjoy the prestige and public visibility which its subject deserves." The United States also proposed that the unit be led by a high-ranking executive (High Commissioner, Under-Secretary-General, or Administrator) established at the highest possible level in the United Nations administrative structure to serve as the center of environmental activity. Placement of the office was to be determined in a way that would provide it with maximum prestige, strength, and freedom as well as ability to link and coordinate the environmental activities of United Nations agencies, governments, and nongovernmental organizations. The United States recognized that only an "active, resourceful, and creative leader" could ensure that environmental concerns receive the necessary priority. In fact, the US proposal advocated for an intergovernmental body to advise and support the executive rather than to receive his services. As negotiations proceeded throughout the preparatory process, an institutionally larger but somewhat weaker version of the unit the United States proposed began to take shape.

The UN Secretary-General's Report on the new intergovernmental organization suggested two alternatives for its placement: (1) within the United Nations as a subsidiary of the General Assembly pursuant to Article 22 of the Charter of the United Nations or (2) as a subsidiary of the Economic and Social Council (ECOSOC) pursuant to Article 68 of the Charter. The United States warned that "to place this body under ECOSOC would be to place it in serious jeopardy" and suggested that the new organization be a subsidiary of the General Assembly while reporting both to the General Assembly and to ECOSOC. The United Nations Environment Programme was ultimately established as a subsidiary body to both the General Assembly and to ECOSOC reporting to the General Assembly through ECOSOC. This entailed its status as a Programme rather than a Specialized Agency.

In the UN hierarchy, programs have the least independence and authority since they are subsidiary organs of the General Assembly. Programs are small and their membership, while geographically representative, is not universal. For example, thirty-six countries are members of the Executive Board of the UN Development Programme (UNDP), thirty-six countries are members of the Executive Board of the World Food Programme (WFP), and fifty-eight are members of the Governing Council of UNEP. As an integral part of the United Nations, however, they are overseen through the General Assembly and therefore *all* UN members have a say in their governance. Program budgets rely on voluntary financial contributions. Though the regular UN budget was originally expected to provide for the costs of staff and fundamental operations, these contributions have only been in the order of a few percent of a program's budget.

However, even though the budgets of programs consist of voluntary payments, they are not necessarily smaller than the mandatory budgets of specialized agencies. For example, UNDP's annual voluntary contributions budget of $3.2 billion is almost three times greater than WHO's annual assessed budget of $1.1 billion. UNEP's institutional status as a Program, therefore, cannot be simply assumed as a deliberate choice on the part of governments to incapacitate the new body. A product of a landmark event, the Stockholm Conference, the new organization was affected more by larger political dynamics than by narrowly calculated national self-interest. "Stockholm, like most conferences, showed less interest in an operationally manageable concept of the environment than in one broad enough to include the particular interests of every participant," wrote Gordon Harrison, an officer in charge of the Ford Foundation's program in Resources and Environment who supported the preparatory process for the Stockholm Conference and the maintenance of the Secretariat led by Maurice Strong during the transition process until UNEP's establishment. Harrison noted Strong's significant role in elaborating an organizational vision for an effective new agency: "Maurice Strong, by temperament a man who tends to expansive concepts, had no reason to think small about an agency that was in a real sense his personal creation and would clearly be his to lead."[33]

Noting that governments saw environmental problems as global and interrelated at their core and therefore demanded "comprehensive" and "integrated" solutions, Harrison explains the institutional choices about UNEP as follows:

> It was decided therefore to establish UNEP as a special secretariat in United Nations headquarters where, with an overview of all problems and all UN activities, it might make the UN as a whole environmentally responsible and constructive. UNEP's primary mission was to develop a *United Nations* environmental program that would be carried out by all relevant agencies. UNEP was not to take any independent environmental initiatives itself. It was not to do things. It was to make a program but let others carry it out. To provide the necessary incentives it was to have small sums of money with which to make grants. But in no case was it to buy an environmental program; it could if necessary buy an environmental component but it would rather use its money to divert operating agencies into environmental ways, to color their programs environmental. In short, UNEP was to be essentially an idea—or perhaps more accurately an aspiration—institutionalized. The founders chose for UNEP the only role that was both practical and potentially effective. *(emphasis in original)*

However, while not intended to diminish UNEP's authority, the decision to constitute it as a program rather than as a specialized agency has negatively impacted its clout and ability to fulfill its functions over the years. UNEP has not been able to establish the autonomy necessary to become a strong anchor institution for the global environment. While it has performed its catalytic function fairly well, it has failed to coordinate environmental activities throughout the UN system, partly as a result of its institutional status. Many UN bodies have refused to accept UNEP's mandate in regards to overall coordination of environmental activities as they see themselves as having "institutional seniority." As one UNEP official exclaimed, UNEP "just does not have a voice in front of the larger UN agencies." And as new institutions have sprung up across various levels of governance and many existing ones were endowed with substantial environmental mandates, UNEP could claim little authority over them. For example, the creation of the Commission on Sustainable Development and the Global Environment Facility in the early 1990s marginalized UNEP politically and eclipsed it financially. In addition, the increased emphasis on environmental work at the World Bank, while in itself commendable, also led to overlap with UNEP activities. In sum, UNEP has not succeeded in becoming the central forum for debate and deliberation in the environmental field, like the WTO for trade, the ILO for labor, or the WHO for health.

Financing Structure

At its inception in 1972, UNEP was provided with two sources of funding: an allocation from the UN regular budget and the Environment Fund consisting of unrestricted voluntary contributions. The UN regular budget was envisioned to cover the costs of "servicing the Governing Council" and a small secretariat required to provide "general policy guidance for the direction and management of environmental programs, [and] UNEP's role as a focal point for environmental action and coordination within the United Nations System."[34] Originally championed by the United States, the Environment Fund was established with $100 million to be budgeted over five years to "ensure that the Stockholm Conference proposals [would] have the necessary financial footing."[35] The sum of $100 million was intended only as a starting figure since it was recognized that the US Environmental Protection Agency spent five times this amount annually on administrative costs alone. The Environment Fund was envisioned for projects, studies, and "seeding," and was anticipated to increase with the growth of the environmental agenda. The United Nations was to report annually on the financial needs for its environmental agenda and the United States, the world's largest economy and biggest polluter, was prepared to play a leadership role and contribute the resources necessary to "ensure that vital international environmental efforts do not fall by the wayside from fiscal starvation."[36]

Both of these financial sources have proved inadequate—an oft-cited reason for lack of results in global environmental governance. The financing mechanisms for the environmental institutions, however, were not intentionally designed to be ineffective and inadequate. While meager by today's standards,[37] the voluntary Environment Fund was an innovation rather than an impediment at the time of its creation for three reasons. First, the Environment Fund was not designed as the specific financial mechanism for a new environmental body. Rather, the new intergovernmental body was designed as the institutional mechanism to administer the Environment Fund. The United States had suggested the establishment of the Fund before the form and functions of UNEP were determined. The initial vision in fact was for an Under-Secretary-General in New York to operate this Fund and coordinate the environmental activities of the UN system.

Second, the United States was in arrears in its assessed contributions and payments to the UN had just been cut by Congress by over twenty percent. The voluntary fund was to be administered by the President and thus not subject to the same Congressional oversight as assessed contributions. It was expected that such an arrangement would allow for an increase in funding over the years as new environmental needs appeared even if overall mandatory contributions to the United Nations were decreasing.

Third, had UNEP been given a budget dependent on assessed contributions, all Member States, including developing countries, would have been mandated to contribute, an unacceptable proposition in 1972 when environmental problems were mainly considered industrial pollution problems. Moreover, when a country fails to contribute its assessed contributions, it could be banished from participating in the organization. As the World Health Organization's Constitution mandates, "If a Member fails to meet its financial obligations to the Organization . . . the Health Assembly may . . . suspend the voting privileges . . . to which a Member is entitled." The US proposal recognized that industrialized countries held a responsibility to improve environmental conditions and should provide the bulk of the finances required. In his testimony to the Committee on Foreign Affairs at the US Congress, Christian A. Herter, Jr., explained:

> As the world's most industrialized nation, we are the greatest polluter. Thus, we cannot reasonably expect others to bear a disproportionate share of the costs in cleaning up the wastes that we generate. While it is difficult to express our pollution contribution in quantitative terms, nonetheless, with less than 6 percent of the world's population, we account for the use of more than one-third of the world's energy production. Roughly 93 percent of our currently installed electrical capacity is fossil fueled. We have almost half of the automobiles in use in the world, and we consume about one-fourth of the world's phosphate, potash, and nitrogenous fertilizers, almost half of its newsprint and synthetic rubber, and more than a fourth of its steel. The Council of Environmental Quality has estimated that we also dumped 48 million tons of wastes at sea in 1968. These few statistics are indicative of the relative global-pollution burden that we in the United States are creating. In conclusion, Mr. Chairman, I believe it has become manifestly clear that many environmental problems are global in character and only can be effectively dealt with internationally. Very little is known at present about their dimensions.[38]

Without the leadership of the United States, the Stockholm Conference commitments may indeed have gone unfunded. The Environment Fund proposal hinged in fact on a concept akin to assessed contributions. The largest consumers of energy, and thus the largest polluters, were to contribute on an escalating curve as suggested by the US Secretary of State's Advisory Committee on the Stockholm Conference. "A formula derived from each nation's consumption of energy," the committee contended, "could provide the basis for the suggested participation in the United Nations Voluntary Fund for the Environment. Or, it might provide the basis for a long-range system of funding, which could be a matter of assessment rather than voluntary participation."[39] This idea, however, was never implemented partly because of opposition by developing countries to the very creation of the Environment Fund.

Although developing countries recognized that the funds available to the international community for environmental research and action would be scarce in relation to the needs, they did not openly welcome the establishment of the Environment Fund. Three key concerns contributed to their lack of enthusiasm and outright suspicion about the new Fund. First, developing countries feared the diversion of development aid into environmental activities and created the "principle of additionality" to ensure that any financial resources for environmental activities would be in addition to existing financial flows marked for development purposes. The principle was affirmed in Resolution A/C.2/L.1236, which stated that "resources for environmental programs, both within and outside the United Nations system, be additional to the present level and projected growth of resources contemplated in the International Development Strategy." Second, developing countries opposed the proliferation and voluntary nature of financing mechanisms. The existence of numerous and, at times, competing funds impeded understanding of the overall financial situation, distorted priorities, and undermined the elaboration of a coherent development strategy. Third, developing countries also voiced the concern that "in recent years the developed countries had placed increasing emphasis on assistance channeled through voluntary contributions."[40] These funds were more readily available for purposes of interest to the donors themselves, such as the United Nations Fund for Population, while the availability and flow of resources for activities of primary interest to developing countries such as the United Nations Capital Development Fund had diminished.

Given the above concerns, it is not surprising that developing countries were suspicious rather than welcoming of the Environment Fund. Developed countries sought to alleviate these fears. Australia, for example, emphasized that it was contributing $265 million in grants to development assistance while it had pledged $2.5 million to the Environment Fund over five years. In the same year, Australia's contribution to UNDP had increased by twenty percent. The British net official aid was also increasing and contributions to the Environment Fund were less than 1/500th of the overall aid flow.

For many analysts, UNEP's limited financial resources are key in explaining UNEP's difficulties.[41] UNEP's annual budget of $215 million (including all contributions—Environment Fund, earmarked contributions, and all trust funds) is indeed miniscule compared to UNDP's $3.2 billion and the US Environmental Protection Agency's $7.6 billion. However, it is larger than the budget of the World Trade Organization. . . .

While the disparity in resources is striking, the nominal sum of the budget is just a symptom of the problem. The root cause of UNEP's problems is the organization's financial structure. About a dozen countries have regularly made annual contributions to the Environment Fund—the central financial mechanism at the discretion of UNEP's Secretariat—since its inception in 1973. In the past ten years, contributions to the Environment Fund have dropped thirty-six percent and have decreased in real terms since the 1970s and 1980s. Contributions to trust and earmarked funds directing UNEP into specific activities, on the other hand, have increased dramatically. The proportion of restricted financing now comprises more than two-thirds of UNEP's revenue.

This unreliable and highly discretionary financial arrangement allows for individual donors to dictate UNEP's priorities, which has resulted in a fragmentation of UNEP's activities and a lack of clear prioritization. Furthermore, UNEP's financial stability, ability to plan beyond the current budget cycle, and autonomy are compromised, thus instilling a risk-averse attitude within the organization's leadership.

Critical Choices and Consequences

In 1972, Peter Stone noted that "international organizations which are inefficient can be actually worse than nothing. Governments can use them to stifle projects. They can function like the 'stack' near airports where incoming planes fly round and round until permission to land is given. If something is 'stacked' in an inefficient organization for long enough it risks running out of fuel and has to fly off somewhere else or fall out of the sky."[44] Traditional wisdom claims that the system for global environmental governance was deliberately created as ineffective.

Through a historically grounded analysis, this chapter has shown that UNEP's potential for effectiveness was determined by political decisions in 1972 which were not purposefully taken to incapacitate the organization. The motives behind the decisions on the form, functions, and financing of the new international environment secretariat do not represent an interest in making the organization dysfunctional, nor a lack of interest in making it functional.

Nevertheless, the critical choices that were made have caused serious architectural flaws and subsequent policy failures in the global environmental governance system. The decisions to create a central organization for the environment, lacking universal membership in its governance, with the status of program rather than a specialized agency, without universal membership in its governance, and relying almost exclusively on voluntary funding, significantly constrained UNEP's ability to function effectively. While UNEP was explicitly charged with the functions of a normative organization in the environmental field, it was not endowed with the concomitant capacities and structural conditions that were needed. It is important to note, however, that the decisions determining these key structural conditions were not purposefully put in place to incapacitate the organization. Nevertheless, they led to inevitable, yet largely unforeseen, effects.

Although UNEP's functions are both relevant and necessary today, the organization does not currently possess the critical capacities needed to perform them properly. As we have seen, UNEP's authority has been severely constrained by its UN program status. It never gained the necessary clout possessed by its big sisters—the specialized agencies. Moreover, UNEP's governance structure, with a 58-member Governing Council and an 88-member Committee of Permanent Representatives comprised of the Ambassadors in Nairobi, has attended more to the needs and demands of the Member States than to the mission of the organization.

UNEP's financial structure of voluntary and earmarked contributions has enabled Member States to pursue their own agendas through UNEP rather than the common good. Finally, UNEP's physical distance from the UN agencies it was supposed to coordinate and the lack of adequate communications have made its coordination task difficult and even impossible and discouraged long-term commitment of high-quality senior policy staff. This in turn has led to a marginalization of the organization in world affairs, inability to fulfill many of its functions, and proliferation of alternative institutional structures in other physical locations. The result has been "a nightmare scenario . . . [a] crazy quilt pattern of environmental governance [that] is too complicated, and is getting worse each year."[45]

Today's reform architects again face the choices about UNEP's form, function, and financing, just like the organization's founding members did in 1972. As analysis of UNEP's performance[46] starkly illustrates, unless the key structural issues shackling UNEP are addressed, little progress in the UN's environmental domain is likely.

Notes

1. This chapter draws on an article by the author, "Designing the United Nations Environment Programme: A Story of Compromise and Confrontation," scheduled for publication in the journal *International Environmental Agreements: Politics, Economics and Law* 7, no. 3 (September 2007).

2. James G. Speth, *Red Sky at Morning: America and the Crisis of the Global Environment* (New Haven, CT: Yale University Press, 2004): 2.

3. Gary C. Bryner, "Global Interdependence," in *Environmental Governance Reconsidered: Challenges, Choices, and Opportunities*, ed. R. F. Durant, D. J. Fiorino, and R. O'Leary (Cambridge, MA, London, England: MIT Press, 2004): 69.

4. Adil Najam, "The Case Against GEO, WEO, or Whatever-else-EO," in *Global Environmental Institutions: Perspectives on Reform*, ed. D. Brack and J. Hyvarinen (London: Royal Institute of International Affairs, 2002a): 36.

5. Peter Haas, "When Does Power Listen to Truth? A Constructivist Approach to the Policy Process," in *UNEO—Towards an International Environment Organization: Approaches to a Sustainable Reform of Global Environmental Governance*, ed. A. Rechkemmer (Baden-Baden: Nomos Verlagsgesellschaft, 2005): 287–309.

6. For a more detailed discussion of the "anchor institution" terminology, see Maria Ivanova, *Can the Anchor Hold? Rethinking the United Nations Environment Programme for the 21st Century* (New Haven, CT: Yale School of Forestry & Environmental Studies, 2005).

7. US Congress. Committee on Foreign Affairs, Subcommittee on International Organizations and Movements, *Participation by the United States in the United Nations Environment Programme*, 93rd Congress, First Session (April 5 and 10, 1973): 4.

8. Environmental Studies Board, "Institutional Arrangements for International Environmental Cooperation: A Report to the Department of State by the Committee for International Environmental Programs" (Washington, DC: National Academy of Sciences, 1972).

9. Sverker Åström, *Ögonblick: Från Ett Halvsekel I Ud-Tjänst [Moment: From Half a Century of Foreign Affairs Duty]* (Stockholm: Lind & Co, 2003): 197; and Göran Bäckstrand,

Conversation at the State Committee for Science and Technology between the Soviet Union and Sweden, Moscow 1971.

10. Börjie Billner, Statement before the General Assembly, on December 13, 1967. On file with the author.

11. Åström 2003.

12. Åström 2003: 202.

13. Lorraine Elliott, *The Global Politics of the Environment* (New York: New York University Press, 1998); Peter Calvert and Susan Calvert, *The South, the North and the Environment* (New York: Pinter, 1999).

14. Wade Rowland, *The Plot to Save the World: The Life and Times of the Stockholm Conference on the Human Environment* (Toronto: Clarke, Irwin & Co, 1973): 47.

15. See http://www.southcentre.org/publications/conundrum/conundrum-04.htm. The Founex Report was the result of a meeting of a panel of scientists and development experts from developing countries in Founex, Switzerland, in June 1971.

16. Martin W. Holdgate, Mohammed Kassas, and Gilbert F. White, eds., *World Environment 1972–1982: A Report by the United Nations Environment Programme* (Dublin: Tycooly International, 1982): 579–586.

17. Cited in Rowland 1973: 78.

18. Peter Stone, *Did We Save the Earth at Stockholm?* (London: Earth Island, 1973): 16.

19. UN General Assembly, Consolidated Document on the UN System and the Human Environment, edited by A. C. o. Co-ordination, A/CONF.48/12, 1972.

20. Environmental Studies Board 1972: 21.

21. Environmental Studies Board 1972: 21.

22. United Nations Press Release, Statement by the Secretary-General of the UN Conference of the Human Environment, in *Second Session of the Preparatory Committee for the Conference*. Geneva: February 8, 1971.

23. Environmental Studies Board 1972: 23.

24. Adnan Amin, "UNEP—Reform Perspectives Two Years after Johannesburg," in *UNEO—Towards an International Environment Organization*, ed. A. Rechkemmer (Baden-Baden: Nomos Verlagsgesellschaft, 2005); Klaus Töpfer, "A Strengthened International Environmental Institution," in *UNEO—Towards an International Environmental Organization*, ed. A. Rechkemmer (Baden-Baden: Nomos Verlagsgesellschaft, 2005).

25. Mohamed El-Ashry, "Mainstreaming the Environment—Coherence Among International Governance Systems," Paper read at the International Environmental Governance Conference, Institute of Sustainable Development and International Relations, Paris, 2004; James G. Speth, "A Memorandum in Favor of a World Environment Organization," in *UNEO—Towards an International Environment Organization*, ed. A. Rechkemmer (Baden-Baden: Nomos Verlagsgesellschaft, 2005); and James G. Speth and Peter M. Haas, *Global Environmental Governance* (Washington, DC: Island Press, 2006).

26. Rowland 1973: 33.

27. Maurice Strong, "One Year After Stockholm: An Ecological Approach to Management," *Foreign Affairs* 51 (July 1973): 703.

28. United States, *Stockholm and Beyond: Report*, ed. Secretary of State's Advisory Committee on the 1972 United Nations Conference on the Human Environment (1972); Frank Biermann and Steffen Bauer, "Managers of Global Governance: Assessing and Explaining the Influence of Intergovernmental Bureaucracies," *Global Governance Working Paper No. 15*. (Amsterdam: The Global Governance Project, 2005).

29. Indira Gandhi, "Life Is One and the World Is One. Prime Minister Indira Gandhi Speaks to the Plenary," Speech at the Stockholm Conference on the Human Environment Reprinted in Environment (Stockholm: Centre for Economic and Social Information at the United Nations European Headquarters, Geneva, 1972).

30. Environmental Studies Board 1972: 17.

31. United Nations Press Release 1971.

32. US Congress, Committee on Foreign Affairs, Subcommittee on International Organizations and Movements, *Participation by the United States in the United Nations Environment Programme*, 93rd Congress, First Session (April 5 and 10, 1973).

33. Gordon Harrison, *Is There a United Nations Environment Programme? Special Investigation at the Request of the Ford Foundation* (Unpublished: On file with the author, 1977): 2.

34. UN General Assembly, Resolution 2997 (XXVII): Institutional and Financial Arrangements for International Environmental Cooperation, 1972.

35. United States 1972: 132.

36. United States 1972: 132.

37. The Environment Fund was about $144 million/year in 2004, UNEP (2004) Resource Mobilization, Environment Fund. Periodical Resource Mobilization, Environment Fund from: http://www.unep.org/rmu/en/Financing_environmentfund.htm.

38. US Congress 1973: 6.

39. United States 1972: 132.

40. UN General Assembly, 27th Session: Summary Record of the 1466th Meeting, ed. Second Committee: Official Record (1972a): 228.

41. Konrad von Moltke, "Why UNEP Matters," in *Green Globe Yearbook 1996* (Oxford: Oxford University Press, 1996); Adil Najam, "The Case Against a New International Environmental Organization," *Global Governance* 9, no. 3 (2003): 367–384.

44. Stone 1973: Epilogue.

45. Steve Charnovitz, "A World Environment Organization," *Columbia Journal of Environmental Law* 27, no. 2 (2002): 323–362.

46. For a systematic analysis of UNEP's performance, see Ivanova 2005.

12

A PARTICIPATORY
APPROACH TO
STRATEGIC PLANNING

R I C H A R D   E .   B I S S E L L[*]

There is a dismal history of international commissions—generally long-winded, obscenely expensive, producing reports with the conclusions decided from the beginning and destined to consume too many trees in publishing a list of platitudes. On occasion, history gets a rude shock. One report that belies such jaundiced prejudices of global observers is the report of the World Commission on Dams (WCD), *Dams and Development: A New Framework for Decision-Making*, released in November 2000.[1] WCD, comprising twelve commissioners, was created in 1998 to review the performance of large dams and make recommendations regarding future water and energy projects.

Consider the words of the commission's chair, Kader Asmal, in the first paragraph of the report: "If politics is the art of the possible, this document is a work of art." Rarely has a commission taken an intransigent international controversy further into politics rather than fulfilling the hopes of the initiators that the commission would find a nonpolitical answer. The commission rejected a purely nonpolitical role, instead opting for the conclusion that politics is inherent in macroscale decisions such as billion-dollar dam projects. The commission determined that it is essential to first establish a fair process, whereby a "rights and risk" approach will put the social and environmental dimensions of dams on a plane with traditional economic and engineering considerations. (A rights and risk approach is a new tool for participatory decisionmaking that recognizes all

[*]   *Environment* vol. 43, no. 7, pp. 37-40, September 2001. Reprinted with permission of the Helen Dwight Reid Educational Foundation. Published by Heldref Publications, 1319 Eighteenth St. N.W., Washington, D.C. 20036-1802. (c) 2001.

legitimate rights of stakeholders and requires a complete assessment of risks to provide a full and fair set of development choices.) In effect, the commission turned upside down the expectations of those who launched this effort—the World Bank and the World Conservation Union (IUCN)—by placing healthy politics at the center of a solution that gives due place to technical criteria that also are essential.

Given the terrible controversies over large dams in the past decade, people can be forgiven for having forgotten the history of water management, power issues, and dams in the twentieth century. In the last 100 years, 45,000 large dams (dams that are more than 15 meters in height) have been built, a record examined with great care by the commission's report. The "boom" in this technology—peaking from the 1930s to the 1950s—was followed by growing caution in the United States and northern Europe in the last two decades. It took many years of experience with dams before people realized that there was no "free lunch" to be had.

The report builds on the progress of recent decades by emphasizing the need for multidisciplinary analysis. In the not-too-distant past, dam construction and management was a preserve for civil engineers. In time, economists began to poach on the engineering preserve, demanding rates of return and other microeconomic standards. In some countries, there has been successful incorporation of people from other disciplines as well—including sociologists, environmentalists, anthropologists, and climatologists—who tended to take a role in dam debates as an assertion of veto rights. Too often the issue on the table was, "Should we build this dam and how high should it be?" rather than "Among the various alternatives, including this dam, how should we achieve the water, energy, development, and environmental goals set by responsible authorities?" There was no uniform standard among countries as these disciplines and questions were adopted.

In the widening gap between national standards, international financial institutions drew crossfire from all sides. The debate took on a particular virulence in the development banks—the one place where all countries met, whether rich or poor—to decide on major infrastructure investments. Developing, maintaining, and removing infrastructure involves enormous resources, and with the payoff occurring over many years, it was natural that developing countries with large hydroelectric potential would look to foreign financiers for the imported component costs—turbines, transmission systems, and engineering skills. Therefore, at one level, the World Bank and the regional development banks were inevitably drawn into the decisionmaking. There were other institutions, however, also stirring the pot. Export credit agencies where turbine manufacturers were located played a part, and bilateral-aid donor agencies often got involved except in rare cases (for example, when the U.S. Agency for International Development removed itself from the capital projects business in the early 1970s by transferring such projects to the World Bank). Finally, the nongovernmental environmental organizations could not resist the opportunity to push their agendas beyond national boundaries and join the debate as well.

The stage was set, therefore, for conflicts such as the Sardar Sarovar controversy in the Narmada Valley of India, a massive project likely to displace several hundred thousand people that ripped apart any semblance of international consensus on dams in the 1990s. The principal external financier of that project, the World Bank, was forced to withdraw in 1993 with the emergence of a profound split among the borrower, the government of India, and the Bank over what kind of conditions could be attached to a loan for construction of the dam. That controversy has been analyzed elsewhere on many occasions, but most importantly, it set the Bank on a course of attempting to clear up its rights and responsibilities with regard to borrowers.[2] The Bank first tried to find agreement on guidelines among its creditors and borrowers, even creating the Inspection Panel in 1994—a three-member, semi-independent body—to monitor and ensure compliance, inter alia, with dam-related policies.[3] Over the first five years of the Inspection Panel's existence, about half of all its project inspections related to the construction of dams in countries ranging from Nepal and India to Brazil, Paraguay, and Argentina.[4]

When it turned out that the effect of the Inspection Panel's presence was unlikely to dampen controversies, senior management of the Bank argued that they needed to either get out of the dam-building business altogether or find a new avenue for reconciliation with all of the stakeholders. Thus it was, in 1997, that the World Bank's Operations Evaluation Division (under the sage leadership of Robert Picciotto) proposed that IUCN host a "dialog" in Gland, Switzerland, bringing together the most outspoken opponents and supporters of dams. The dialog, as it turned out, was sufficiently cordial for the World Bank and IUCN to agree that they should explore the creation of an international commission to review the "development effectiveness" of dams (to be defined by the commission) and to make recommendations for future standards that could be applied globally.

There were skeptics on all sides of this proposal. Bank management had never before gone outside the Bank for policy guidance. Dam opponents had established a public position that *no* large dams were acceptable, limiting the scope for any kind of dialog that might lead to compromise. Dam builders and equipment suppliers had always left discussions with dam opponents to governments and the World Bank, finding the terms of the arguments rather distasteful. Utilities and government ministries of energy doubted the usefulness of dialog in stabilizing the long-term supply of power on which they depended. Despite all these doubts, there was one common element: Because of the ongoing war over each dam project, there was diminishing common ground and therefore less likelihood of persuading the parties of another view. Based on the slim thread of hope of each party that they could achieve more through dialog than confrontation, the planning for a World Commission on Dams went forward. Nevertheless, throughout the next three years, each stakeholder would, on more than one occasion, decide that the potential outcome was not worth the investment of time and political capital and threaten to withdraw. However, in the end, almost none withdrew.

The chair was chosen first: Kader Asmal, minister of water in South Africa, a veteran of the anti-apartheid movement and senior member of the African National Congress Executive Committee, known for bringing consensus out of the most intractable situations. The diverse commission was chosen, including the CEO of a major manufacturer of dam turbines, a leader of a militant protest group against dams in India's Narmada Valley, and a leading academic expert on the social and resettlement issues associated with dams.[5] The commissioners came from all regions of the world and covered most major fields of knowledge relevant to decisions on dams. Parallel to the choice of commissioners was an informal dialog among representatives of some forty to fifty organizations to ensure agreement on the mandate for the commission, the choice of staff and commissioners, the time frame, and the financing of the effort. Each decision had to reflect joint ownership of the commission and a strong sense of shared participation. By the spring of 1998, the commission held its first meeting in Washington, D.C., and began to establish the relationships that would enable them to produce a report by late 2000.[6]

The thirty months of labor that followed included a time-bound mandate and an expectation articulated by the chair that the commission probably would not fulfill 100 percent of its goals. Asmal argued that the commission had a choice: It could labor until it completely met its mandate, which might take decades, or it could use a specific amount of time to solve as much as it could and leave the remainder of the tasks to other bodies. He clearly chose the latter option, saying informally that if the commission could complete 80 percent of the job, it would be an enormous success. Indeed, it was argued that if the commission could establish 80 percent of a consensus, the momentum should be sufficient to carry the multistakeholder community towards eventual agreement. By leaving unclear just which issues might remain unsettled at the end of the day, Asmal's formulation served to create more negotiating room during the commission process itself, and he deliberately left all issues on the table throughout the several years of commission deliberations.

The commission went out of its way to create an inclusive process. Meetings were held on all continents, studies were commissioned from experts in any countries with large dams, and contributions were solicited from people and organizations of any orientation. The establishment of a Web site with voluminous information, including drafts of case studies, allowed participation by anyone with Internet access. On several occasions, the process was so open that organizations with established roles in the controversies felt bypassed and had to be persuaded that the openness was not an attempt to sideline them. The WCD experience on transparency and disclosure should be reviewed by anyone establishing a future commission on what can be achieved with current information technologies.

In pursuit of its first mandate—to review the development effectiveness of dams—the commission reviewed more than 1,000 dams to some degree and 125 dams in great detail. It undertook country studies in the two most controversial cases (India and China) and, most importantly, conducted river basin studies in several parts of the world. It also commissioned seventeen thematic reviews that examined the global inventory of 45,000 large dams in the context of specific attributes and policy issues. The thematic reviews involved evaluations of the social, environmental, and economic implications of dam projects, alternatives to dams, and governance and institutional processes. For instance, past plans for building dams included only the dam site and thus did not evaluate the effects of the dam on the rest of the river basin. The WCD staff developed an extensive review of river basins as a planning framework, drawing on the work of a generation of geographers, including the work of Gilbert F. White.[7] WCD proceeded to build a database from which the public could reach conclusions as readily as the commission and staff. The commission drew two lessons from its review of the development effectiveness of the world's large dams. The first lesson was predictable, that dams have brought significant benefits to publics throughout the world, and that a large cost, often unrecognized owing to its diffuse social and environmental impact, was also incurred. The second lesson was that the most successful dams historically shared three characteristics: They reflected a comprehensive approach to integrating social, environmental, and economic dimensions of development; they created greater levels of transparency and certainty for all involved; and they have resulted in increased levels of confidence in the ability of nations and communities to meet their future water and energy needs.

As previously mentioned, WCD accumulated a massive database on large dams in the process of meeting that first mandate. With the termination of the commission, the fate of that database is unclear. The research community needs to ensure its survival and maintenance. [Editors' note: The United Nations Environment Programme subsequently launched a follow-up Dams and Development Project initiative.]

The second mandate of WCD—to develop internationally acceptable criteria, guidelines, and standards, where appropriate, for the planning, design, appraisal, construction, operation, monitoring, and decommissioning of dams, was the main challenge for the commission members. The solution reached by WCD comprised three international norms: international recognition of human rights, the right to development, and the right to a healthy environment. In that context, WCD established seven policy principles for decisionmakers to follow: gain public agreement, conduct a comprehensive options assessment, address existing dams, sustain rivers and livelihoods, recognize entitlements and share benefits, ensure compliance, and share rivers for peace, development, and security.[8] At a minimum, the seven principles would serve as a valuable agenda from which any negotiation over a dam project might begin.

The impact of these seven principles issued unanimously by WCD has already been felt in the months since the report's release in November 2000. Many of the environmental nongovernmental organizations applauded the conclusions; WCD was cited as a legitimizing source by the Narmada Bachao Andolan (NBA)—a grassroots organization in the Narmada Valley of central India—in its press release about the Maheshwar hydroelectric project in India when a foreign financier pulled out.

On the other hand, the World Bank has experienced a major internal debate over the implications of the WCD report. The Bank's board of executive directors is visibly concerned about the "costs of compliance" with the WCD approach and is quite doubtful the Bank can afford the possible increase in design and compliance charges for dam projects. The private sector is reconfiguring its involvement; Asea Brown Boveri, Ltd. (ABB) has sold off its hydro turbine business to focus on other forms of energy-producing capital equipment. In the United States, the reviews of the Snake River dams in Idaho, as well as the Glen Canyon Dam in Arizona, should be conceptually reinforced by the WCD approach because the U.S. Bureau of Reclamation, which is involved in conducting the reviews, closely tracked the commission's process.

At the conceptual level, the WCD report should lead to more integrative, place-based analysis of projects, including alternatives. World Bank staff have already noted the practice in the Asian Development Bank of undertaking analyses of alternatives and impacts of proposed dams further "upstream" in the project design process. The need is not for mere assessment of a dam after deciding on the project but rather the consideration of alternative sources of power, water, and flood control. Indeed, a major contribution of WCD is to expand the contextual understanding for deciding whether to undertake a dam project; in effect, they have said that decisions must involve people from other disciplines besides just engineers and microeconomists. And if those involved in making decisions about whether to begin dam projects are going to include people from other fields, the central questions about rights and risks must be asked earlier in the process. For instance, by arguing that "displacement" is more than just physical loss of land, WCD implicitly endorses the World Bank's proposal to strengthen its policy on involuntary resettlement, an inevitable result of dam or other large infrastructure projects. Such projects also cause "livelihood displacement," because far more people lose their jobs than lose their land as a result of large dams.[9]

The report should also lead to greater focus on accountability for development decisions, a matter of concern to far more than the dam community. The decisionmaking that goes into building a dam is ultimately a political process as much as a technical issue, and therefore, a political body has to make the decisions about dams. Most environmental issues involve trade-offs between various public interests. The weighing of those trade-offs is not an exact science, and thus, WCD appropriately suggests that a body with political accountability has to make the decisions. Democracies know that to be true, but countries in transition are not sure whether to involve the public in decisions that may have major environmental impacts. WCD is clear: When in doubt, go public.

The commission model is a powerful one: Establish a clear mandate, work for two years, and go out of business. Its exemplar is international strategic planning rather than more international government. It keeps accountability in the appropriate places, locally, nationally, and internationally. It also establishes a means of periodically comparing experience among countries and regions on troubling issues. Finally, this particular commission did an especially outstanding job of keeping the various stakeholders onboard. That may be a function of the personalities rather than the structure, but for whatever reason, it showed that it can and should be done. Other highly contentious global issues could benefit from similar treatment.

Notes

1. World Commission on Dams (WCD), *Dams and Development: A New Framework for Decision-Making* (London and Sterling, VA: Earthscan, November 2000). This report is available in its entirety at http://www.dams.org.

2. B. Morse and T. R. Berger, *Sardar Sarovar: The Report of the Independent Review* (Ottawa: Resource Futures International, 1992).

3. I. F. I. Shihata, *The World Bank Inspection Panel* (Oxford University Press, published for the World Bank, 1994).

4. A. Umana, ed., *The World Bank Inspection Panel: The First Four Years* (1994–1998) (Washington, DC: World Bank for the Inspection Panel, 1998); and R. E. Bissell, "Recent Practice of the Inspection Panel of the World Bank," *American Journal of International Law* 91, no. 4 (1997): 741–744.

5. The commissioners who signed the report included Kader Asmal (South Africa), Lakshmi Chand Jain (India), Judy Henderson (Australia), Goran Lindahl (Sweden), Thayer Scudder (United States), Joji Carino (Philippines), Donald Blackmore (Australia), Medha Patkar (India), José Goldemberg (Brazil), Deborah Moore (United States), Jan Veltrop (United States), and Achim Steiner (Germany).

6. The author was asked by the World Conservation Union (IUCN) and the World Bank, the two initiators of the commission process, to coordinate the appointment of the chair and commission, to initiate the fundraising, to build consultative mechanisms involving all stakeholders, and after WCD's first meeting, to hand off the management of WCD to the secretariat in Cape Town.

7. G. F. White, "The River as a System: A Geographer's View of Promising Approaches," *Water International* 22, no. 2 (1997): 79–81; G. F. White, "Water Science and Technology: Some Lessons from the 20th Century," *Environment* (January/February 2000): 30–88; and I. Burton, R. W. Kates, and G. F. White, eds., *Selected Writings of Gilbert F. White* (Chicago: University of Chicago Press, 1986).

8. WCD, *Dams and Development*, xxxiv–xxxv.

9. Ibid., 102.

13

THE EVOLUTION
OF THE TRADE AND
ENVIRONMENT DEBATE
AT THE WTO

HUGO CAMERON[*]

The relationship between trade and environment has evolved over time. The inclusion of environmental issues on the negotiating agenda of the World Trade Organization (WTO) at the Doha Ministerial in 2001 moved this relationship into the spotlight. However, this is by no means a new relationship; indeed, as we will see below, this is a relationship that has gone through many phases and will continue to evolve in the future.

The Early Years

At a fundamental level, the production and exchange of goods and services relies on the environment in the form of natural resources. Trade in everything from shrimp to shampoo implies an environmental impact of some sort. The trade-environment relationship is, in fact, imbedded within the original text of the General Agreement on Tariffs and Trade (GATT), which was adopted in 1947 as the basis for the postwar global trading system. Among the exceptions to the GATT's core principles were provisions stating that nothing in the GATT would

[*] Reprinted from Adil Najam, Mark Halle and Ricardo Meléndez-Ortiz, eds., *Trade and Environment: A Resource Book*. © 2007 International Institute for Sustainable Development. www.iisd.org. Reprinted with permission.

prevent member countries from adopting or enforcing measures either "necessary to protect human, animal or plant life or health" or "relating to the conservation of exhaustible natural resources" (Article XX, paragraphs (b) and (g), respectively). However, Article XX also says that such measures cannot be disguised restrictions on trade applied for protectionist intent. This provision has since become a focal point for the trade and environment debate at the GATT and WTO.

Amidst growing environmental awareness that emerged in the late 1960s and the early 1970s, GATT members established a Group on Environmental Measures and International Trade (EMIT) in 1971. However, without a single request for it to be convened, the EMIT Group lay dormant for 20 years. Nevertheless, trade and environment lingered in the GATT hallways. At the 1972 UN Conference on the Human Environment in Stockholm, the GATT Secretariat presented a paper on the implications of environmental protection policies and how these could become obstacles to trade. Further, discussions during the Tokyo Round of the GATT (1973–79) over trade-related technical regulations and standards implemented for environmental purposes led to the adoption of the Agreement on Technical Barriers to Trade (TBT), or the "Standards Code," in 1979. The TBT Agreement called for transparency in the application of technical regulations and standards and marked the first reference to the environment in a GATT agreement.

While trade officials were factoring the environment into international trade agreements, trade measures were being used as a tool to advance global environmental goals. In 1975, the Convention on International Trade in Endangered Species of Wild Fauna and Flora (CITES) entered into force, mandating a system of trade bans and restrictions on traffic in endangered species. Trade restrictions subsequently formed key elements of other multilateral environmental agreements (MEAs), including those on trade in ozone-depleting substances (Montreal Protocol, 1987) and hazardous wastes (Basel Convention, 1989). By 2003, according to a paper released by the WTO Secretariat, there were no fewer than 14 MEAs with trade-related provisions, including a number of others with potential trade effects. The two streams of international interaction on environment and trade continued to evolve in parallel until they began coming into increasing contact with each other in the 1990s.

The 1990s: A Rocky Decade

The 1990s marked the coming of age of the trade-environment debate. In 1991, the European Free Trade Association (EFTA) finally prompted the EMIT Group to meet in order to study the trade and environment linkage and provide input to the 1992 Rio Earth Summit. Leaders at the Rio Summit recognized the substantive links between international trade and environment by agreeing to make policies in the two areas mutually supportive in favor of sustainable development. The entry into force and implementation of several major MEAs that included trade restrictions as enforcement measures was starting to draw the concern of the trade community. Meanwhile, Northern environmental groups were increasingly worried that GATT rules could chill or roll back domestic environmental legislation.

Two GATT panel decisions against the United States in the *Tuna-Dolphin* dispute cases confirmed the fears of environmentalists. These decisions also provoked major concern on the part of developing countries about the environment becoming a barrier to their exports, based on how they were produced or harvested. The first case was brought before the GATT by Mexico, which argued against a United States (U.S.) law imposed in 1990 that prohibited tuna imports from countries lacking appropriate dolphin conservation programs. Mexico believed that the U.S. legislation violated its GATT rights by prescribing extraterritorially how it should catch its exported tuna. The U.S. defended its action on the grounds that its neighbor was taking insufficient measures to prevent the accidental capture of dolphins by its tuna fishers. The GATT panel ruled in 1991 that the U.S. could not suspend Mexico's trading rights by prescribing unilaterally the process and production methods (PPMs) by which that country harvested tuna. The U.S. eventually lifted its embargo following an extensive domestic "dolphin safe" labeling campaign and negotiations with Mexico. A subsequent case brought against the U.S. tuna embargo by the European Union (EU) on behalf of the Netherlands Antilles in 1992 found that the U.S. *dolphin conservation policy* was GATT-consistent and could be applied extraterritorially. However, it broadly upheld the first panel decision by ruling that the *actual measure used* (i.e., the tuna embargo) was neither "necessary" (along the lines of Article XX) nor GATT-consistent. The *Tuna-Dolphin* cases brought into sharp focus how differing environmental norms between developed and developing countries could prove a source for conflict.

Partly as a result of the *Tuna-Dolphin* cases, trade and environment linkages were also being recognized at the regional level. For instance, in 1994 the U.S., Mexico and Canada signed the North American Free Trade Agreement (NAFTA), which included a side-accord on regional environmental cooperation. The side-agreement—and the tri-national organization it created—was intended to help ensure the effective implementation of existing environmental laws among signatories. Similar provisions subsequently found their way into bilateral trade agreements signed by the U.S. and Canada with other developing country trading partners, in order to guard against lower environmental standards as a source of comparative advantage. Environmental cooperation elements have since also been included in a number of regional trade arrangements.

The 1990s also saw the conclusion of the eight-year Uruguay Round negotiations and the creation of the WTO on January 1, 1995. By then, the trade body's ranks had swelled to 128 Members, over three-quarters of which were developing countries. In addition to including preambular language claiming sustainable development as an objective, the WTO agreements established a Committee on

Trade and Environment (CTE), included a new Agreement on the Application of Sanitary and Phytosanitary (SPS) Measures and instituted a strengthened dispute settlement mechanism. The CTE, a regular meeting of all WTO Members, was mandated to identify the relationship between trade and environmental measures and make appropriate recommendations on whether any modifications to WTO rules were required. While the Committee has provided a valuable forum to enhance understanding of the trade-environment relationship, it has struggled to fulfill its mandate, and many have accused it of being little more than a talking shop. The SPS Agreement elaborated on Article XX by setting out parameters for the application of measures to protect human, animal and plant life or health. The new dispute settlement mechanism rules, which made it virtually impossible for losing countries to overturn decisions by panels or the new Appellate Body (AB), were a major concern for environmental groups. They were worried that the WTO now had real teeth to force countries to dismantle environmental laws, should these come under challenge in the multilateral trading system.

A number of WTO disputes added further depth to the trade-environment debate, and underlined the difference in approach to the issue between developing and developed countries, notably the U.S. The 1998 *Shrimp-Turtle* dispute case, brought by four Asian countries against the U.S., proved a landmark in that it put into doubt the rationale that discrimination based on PPMs was not compatible with WTO rules. The WTO Appellate Body ultimately determined that while the disputed U.S. law prohibiting shrimp imports caught without the use of "turtle excluder devices" was justifiable under Article XX, it had been implemented in a discriminatory fashion. In other words, the Appellate Body did not require the U.S. to dismantle its law, but only change the way it was implemented. The decision was particularly disturbing to Thailand, India and a number of other developing countries, who were deeply concerned with the approach to interpretation of WTO law applied by the Appellate Body. They felt that the ruling permitted Members to discriminate against "like" products based on non-product-related PPMs, an issue that had not been negotiated in the Uruguay Round. From their perspective, the *Shrimp-Turtle* decision could be interpreted as allowing Members to take unilateral actions based on the way in which products are produced (i.e., the way in which shrimp are harvested), and that these actions could be justified under Article XX as long as they were not implemented in an arbitrary or discriminatory manner.

By the close of the 1990s, the field of trade and environment was receiving much more attention than at its start. Among other issues, eco-labeling, trade in genetically modified organisms (GMOs) and perverse subsidies in natural resource sectors were providing policy-makers with a host of new challenges. Supply chain issues were gaining prominence, and the use of private-sector green procurement schemes, for instance, by European grocery retailers, was leading to a reorganization of international production and of relations between exporters, distributors and consumers. Dramatic street protests by environmental and other groups at the WTO's failed Seattle Ministerial Conference in 1999 served to remind trade negotiators that the multilateral trading system needed to find a way to address how it dealt with the environment. However, developing countries remained wary, not least because they saw their own trade and environment concerns—such as green protectionism, the export of domestically prohibited goods and the equitable treatment of their biological resources—take a backseat to developed country trade and environment issues at the WTO.

Doha and Beyond

At the Doha Ministerial Conference in 2001, WTO Members decided to launch negotiations that, for the first time, would include trade and environment as part of the negotiating agenda. The negotiating issues agreed under Paragraph 31 of the Doha Ministerial Declaration were primarily those advocated by developed countries: the relationship between WTO rules and specific trade obligations in MEAs; observer status for MEA secretariats; and the liberalization of trade in environmental goods and services. This reflected the perception that accepting an environmental mandate remained a trade-off for developing countries, which have not been *demandeurs* in these areas.

Paragraphs 32, 33 and 51 make up Doha's "non-negotiating" trade and environment mandate. Paragraph 32 focuses the work of the CTE on three areas: the effect of environmental measures on market access; the relevant provisions of the Agreement on Trade-related Aspects of Intellectual Property Rights (TRIPS); and eco-labeling. Paragraph 33 outlines the importance of capacity building and encourages environmental impact assessments. Paragraph 51 instructs the CTE and the Committee on Trade and Development to "each act as a forum to identify and debate developmental and environmental aspects of the negotiations, in order to help achieve the objective of having sustainable development appropriately reflected."

Importantly, Paragraph 6 of the Preamble to the Doha Declaration makes a detailed case for the trade and environment linkage:

> We strongly reaffirm our commitment to the objective of sustainable development, as stated in the Preamble to the Marrakech Agreement. We are convinced that the aims of upholding and safeguarding an open and non-discriminatory multilateral trading system, and acting for the protection of the environment and the promotion of sustainable development can and must be mutually supportive. We take note of the efforts by Members to conduct national environmental assessments of trade policies on a voluntary basis. We recognize that under WTO rules no country should be prevented from taking measures for the protection of human, animal or plant life or health, or of the environment at the levels it considers appropriate, subject to the requirement that they are not applied in a manner which would constitute a means of arbitrary or unjustifiable discrimination between countries where the same conditions prevail, or a disguised restriction on international trade, and are otherwise

in accordance with the provisions of the WTO Agreements. We welcome the WTO's continued cooperation with UNEP and other inter-governmental environmental organizations.

The Doha Declaration also makes the linkage in other key areas. For example, on agriculture, the Declaration highlights "the need to protect the environment" as one of the non-trade concerns that should be taken into account in the negotiations. On intellectual property rights, the Doha Declaration instructs the TRIPS Council to examine the relationship between the TRIPS Agreement and the Convention on Biological Diversity (CBD), the protection of traditional knowledge and folklore. On fisheries, Paragraph 28 of the Declaration mandates Members to "clarify and improve WTO disciplines on fisheries subsidies, taking into account the importance of this sector to developing countries."

Less than a year after the launch of the Doha negotiations, leaders at the 2002 World Summit on Sustainable Development (WSSD) sent a clear message to WTO negotiators to step up their efforts to integrate sustainable development objectives into the trade round. Amongst other commitments, the Plan emphasized the phaseout of harmful fisheries and energy subsidies and discouraged the use of unilateral actions to deal with environmental challenges outside countries' jurisdictions.

Since Doha, Members have met several times in the CTE in Special Session to address the negotiating mandate. European countries have remained the most active supporters of the MEA-WTO relationship discussions. Some of the larger developing countries have engaged actively on different aspects of the mandate, for instance, by analyzing the potential benefits (and pitfalls) for their economies of further trade liberalization in environmental goods and services. However, modest progress has continued over this time and, slowly but surely, the trade and environment agenda has started digging in its roots within the corridors of the WTO.

Interests and Fault Lines

The major players in the debate on the trade-environment relationship have traditionally been European countries and the U.S. Developing countries have recently become more engaged, particularly around specific-issue areas, such as the relationship between the TRIPS Agreement and the CBD. North-South alliances around certain issues, such as fisheries subsidies, have also emerged. In addition, nongovernmental and intergovernmental bodies have made invaluable contributions to the field. . . .

The **European Union**, frequently supported by "like-minded" countries such as Switzerland and Norway, has been the central proponent of including environmental issues in trade discussions at the multilateral level. This position is informed, to a great extent, by the EU's support for multilateral environmental solutions and the influence of environmental groups. However, most other countries have remained suspicious of Europe's enthusiasm for environmental issues at the WTO, particularly its support for the precautionary principle in instances of scientific uncertainty. Developing countries, in particular, are wary of European efforts to push eco-labeling and the clarification of the MEA-WTO relationship. They view these efforts as an attempt by the EU to seek additional space to block imports in sensitive sectors and obtain trade-offs for concessions in other areas, such as agriculture.

The EU has made increasing efforts to integrate its trade strategy with the principles of sustainable development. In addition to conducting sustainability impact assessments (SIAs) of all its new trade arrangements, the EU has launched initiatives to help developing countries gain from sustainable trade. These include the promotion of trade in sustainably produced products, funding for technical assistance on trade and environment and an online "help desk" for developing country exporters to navigate Europe's often cumbersome import standards. However, many remain unconvinced and some developing countries have expressed concern that SIAs could enable hidden protectionism under the guise of environmental and social concerns.

The **United States** has a mixed track record on trade and environment. On the one hand, its support for PPM-based trade measures at the WTO, reform of fisheries subsidies rules and inclusion of environmental provisions in regional and bilateral trade arrangements points to an appreciation for balancing trade policy with effective implementation of environmental regulations. On the other hand, its refusal to "play by the rules" in key MEAs with trade-related elements—such as those on biodiversity, climate change and biosafety—has made its trading partners skeptical of its environmental intentions. At Doha, the U.S. was less enthusiastic than the EU about including trade and environment on the negotiating agenda. Indeed, the U.S. ensured that the negotiations would not open up more space for consideration of the precautionary principle in WTO rules, and has since sided with developing countries in advocating a limited interpretation of the MEA-WTO mandate.

Developing countries have engaged in trade and environment issues at the GATT at least since the 1980s. In 1982, a number of developing countries at the GATT expressed concern that products prohibited in developed countries due to environmental hazards, health or safety concerns—such as certain chemicals and pesticides—continued to be exported to them. With limited information on these products, developing countries made the case that they were unable to make informed decisions regarding their import. Domestically prohibited goods (DPGs) subsequently became a standing item on the agenda of the CTE, though the issue has received less attention since 2001 due to the focus of CTE discussions around the Doha issues.

While developing countries have been active contributors on trade and environment at the WTO, they have traditionally taken a defensive position. This is due primarily to concerns that trade-related environmental measures could be used as barriers to their exports. Developing countries have also strongly objected to any leeway in WTO rules for the use of unilateral or extraterritorial trade measures to enforce environmental norms. They argue that countries should be able to set their own environmental priorities, taking into account their level of development, and that they should not be subject to the domestic environmental standards set in other countries. At the same time, developing countries have advocated a range of issues that reflect Southern trade and environment interests. In addition to concerns surrounding trade in DPGs, many developing countries have sought to reconcile the TRIPS Agreement with the CBD. For their part, the least developed countries (LDCs) have emphasized the importance of financial resources for technical assistance to meet Northern environmental and health standards.

Developing countries have also joined North-South coalitions. These include the "Friends of Fish" which, in pushing for disciplines on fisheries subsidies, groups Argentina, Chile, Ecuador, Peru and the Philippines together with Australia, Iceland, New Zealand, Norway and the U.S. North-South cooperation has further emerged on environmental aspects of agriculture, with a wide coalition of developing and developed agriculture-exporting countries (the Cairns Group) denouncing the environmentally harmful effects of agricultural subsidies. Argentina, Chile and Uruguay have joined Australia, Canada and the U.S. in opposing restrictions on transboundary movements of GMOs under the CBD's Biosafety Protocol, while some African countries have voiced support for the EU's precautionary approach to GMO imports.

Developing countries agreed to the MEA-WTO linkage mandate from Doha, but only as part of a wider package that contained other trade-off issues, including reductions in agricultural subsidies. Since Doha, many developing countries have participated actively in the negotiations, for the most part preferring a narrow approach to the mandate to ensure talks do not result in further regulatory space for environmental provisions that could restrict their exports. Some developing countries are also cautiously exploring potential benefits from liberalization of trade in environmental goods and services.

Intergovernmental organizations have played a key role alongside WTO Members in the discussions on the trade-environment relationship. Secretariats from relevant MEAs have been regular invitees to the CTE and have participated in a limited fashion in the environment negotiations in the Doha Round. The United Nations Environment Programme (UNEP) has played a useful role in highlighting synergies and mutual supportiveness between MEAs and the WTO. UNEP has been an observer at the CTE since 1995 and, as host of the 1992 Rio Summit, was instrumental in elaborating the links between the trade and environment regimes. Together with the UN Conference on Trade and Development (UNCTAD), UNEP has engaged in extensive capacity building and research activities for developing countries on trade and environment.

Many **non-governmental groups** have emerged in both the North and South to follow the multifaceted issues around trade and environment. The number of these groups mushroomed in the mid-to-late 1990s, due in large part to the coming into force of the WTO and to the growing public interest in pursuing sustainable development. The fields of expertise of NGOs active in trade and environment are varied, and their impact can be substantial, especially through interaction with trade policy-makers. In particular, these groups have contributed significantly as monitors of the trade policy-making process, as knowledge providers, information disseminators and capacity builders.

Trends and Future Directions

Over the next five to ten years, the environment is likely to remain on the trade agenda, but in different ways than it is now. Once WTO Members come closer to mutually agreed terms around the relationship between WTO rules and MEAs, further space could open up to address areas of trade and environment concern to developing countries. China, India and Brazil—all members of the Group of Twenty (G20) of developing countries opposed to Northern agriculture subsidies—can be expected to bring their own trade-environment priorities to the table, including the environmental benefits of reductions in agricultural support. The question of GMOs is also likely to challenge the trade-environment relationship for years to come.

Changes in modes of international production, partly as a result of trade negotiations, are likely to shift issues of priority in trade and environment to more concrete areas, such as negotiating mutual recognition agreements for different product standards in different countries. Global supply chains and consumer preferences can also be expected to play an increasingly important role. Some developing countries, which can afford to, have already adopted their own domestic labeling and certification schemes in response to consumer preferences in the North. To continue meeting these challenges and to advance sustainable development, all countries will have to resist pressures to build protectionist fences and instead promote cooperation on green spaces. As neighbors in a globalized world economy, trade and environment cannot afford not to get along.

14

HAS FOREIGN AID
BEEN GREENED?

J. TIMMONS ROBERTS,
BRADLEY C. PARKS, MICHAEL J. TIERNEY,
AND ROBERT L. HICKS[*]

Since the first major international conference on environment and development in Stockholm, Sweden, in 1972, environmentalists, voters, and policymakers in the developed world have faced a vexing dilemma: with some of the richest stores of biodiversity, natural resources, and carbon located in developing countries, the greatest potential for damage to the global environment resides in places outside the sovereign control of the countries most able, financially speaking, to prevent it.

Developing countries have consistently taken the position that they cannot afford—and should not be asked—to divert large amounts of their own money to environmental protection. They argue that now-wealthy countries achieved high living standards through a resource-intensive industrialization process that often damaged the natural environment and only began to significantly invest in environmental protection at later stages of economic development.

International negotiators have repeatedly pointed to the transfer of financial resources from developed to developing countries as a possible way forward. Articles 2 and 12 of the Stockholm Declaration stated that "additional international technical and financial assistance" should be made available for environmental protection in developing countries. In the negotiations leading up to the Earth Summit in Rio de Janeiro in 1992, developed and developing nations struck a so-called Grand Bargain whereby wealthy countries agreed to underwrite the participation of less developed countries in global environmental accords. The 1991

[*] *Environment* Vol. 51, No. 1, Pp. 8-19, January/February 2009. Reprinted with Permission of the Helen Dwight Reid Educational Foundation. Published by Heldref Publications, 1319 Eighteenth St. N.W., Washington, D.C. 20036-1802. (C) 2001.

Beijing Ministerial Declaration on Environment and Development identified poverty as the primary cause of environmental degradation in the developing world and stated that "a special Green Fund should be established to provide adequate and additional financial assistance" to environmental projects in developing countries.[1]

During the Rio Earth Summit, wealthy countries vied in the international media to appear more "environmental" than their peers. The United States promised a 66 percent increase in environmental aid over its 1990 level; 12 members of the European Community promised a $4.3 billion environmental aid package; and Canada pledged $115 million. Japan tried to outbid everyone by offering $7.7 billion in environmental assistance over the next five years.[2] However, many developing countries feared that this new concern for environmental protection would supplant foreign aid for basic human needs and economic development.

Agenda 21, a 700-page sustainable development plan drawn up jointly by developed and developing countries in the lead-up to the Rio conference, was designed to break this impasse. It sought to bring poor countries into environmental agreements while simultaneously supporting their economic development. Chapter 33 of Agenda 21 stated that "the implementation of the huge sustainable development programs . . . [would] require the provision to developing countries of substantial new and additional financial resources." The cost of implementing *Agenda 21* was estimated at $561.5 billion a year, with developed countries bankrolling $141.9 billion (20 percent of the total cost) in low- or no-interest concessional assistance and developing countries footing the rest of the bill.[3] Of the assistance to developing countries, about $15 billion a year was supposed to be devoted to global environmental issues, with the rest targeting sustainable development programs like drinking water and sewage treatment in developing countries.[4]

Thirteen years later, in the summer of 2005, the leaders of the G8 countries—the United States, Germany, France, United Kingdom, Italy, Japan, Russia, and Canada—met at the Gleneagles golf resort in Scotland. British Prime Minister Tony Blair, who was serving as G8 president, set two priorities for the meeting: for members to agree to "make poverty history" by substantially increasing aid, especially for Africa, and to make more progress on addressing global climate change. Environmental aid was again highlighted to demonstrate developed countries' commitment to international environmental protection. Under the Gleneagles Plan of Action, the G8 made promises to help poor countries access clean energy technologies more readily. Yet after only three and a half years, it appears Gleneagles may be Rio all over again. Besides being almost an exact repetition of promises made in 1992, the Gleneagles declarations were very similar to those made at the first Earth Summit held in Stockholm 33 years before.

Despite repeated promises of aid to address critical global and local environmental problems, little systematic research exists on whether donors have honored their commitments. Claims of greening are often made by the World Bank and other big multilateral banks and by bilateral aid agencies like the U.S. Agency for International Development (USAID), U.K. Department for International

Development (DFID), or Deutsche Gesellschaft für Technische Zusammenarbeit (German Technical Cooperation). However, with very incomplete datasets and inconsistent categorization of projects, it has been impossible to answer the most basic questions about whether the aid prescribed at Rio is being administered appropriately.

In 2001, the Intergovernmental Panel on Climate Change reported that "data are simply not collected and analyzed in a manner that informs policy makers interested in the issue."[5] The European Commission noted in 2006 that their "statistical system does not enable an environmental analysis of aid flows" and "there is no generally accepted definition of an 'environmental project' or of the environmental component of an integrated development/environment project."[6] A decade earlier, the same point had been made by political scientists Barbara Connolly, Tamar L. Gutner, and Hildegard Berdarff: "Available data are highly distorted by the lack of any common definition of what is or is not 'environmental assistance.'"[7]

While scholars and policy analysts have produced a number of books and articles on the topic of environmental aid to developing countries, much of this research is based on qualitative case studies or small samples. Our collective knowledge remains limited largely due to the lack of comprehensive and reliable data on aid projects from bilateral and multilateral donors—data that are necessary for researchers to empirically evaluate competing hypotheses. As a result, we lack credible, cross-country evidence that can provide generalizable answers to some of the key questions that concern the academic, environmental, and policy communities:[8]

- Has aid been greened and, if so, by how much?
- Which donor governments spend the most on foreign assistance for the environment and why?
- Why do some donor governments delegate the allocation and implementation of environmental aid to multilateral agencies when they could simply allocate it themselves?
- Which countries receive the most environmental assistance and why?

To answer these questions, in 2003, researchers at the College of William and Mary and Brigham Young University launched the Project-Level Aid (PLAID) data collection initiative.[9] The first version of the PLAID database covers 1970–2000 and contains approximately 427,000 individual development projects funded by grants and loans from wealthy countries to poor countries.

Previous work on aid allocation has relied on the Organisation for Economic Co-operation and Development's (OECD) Creditor Reporting System database, where the aid categories assigned to each project are determined by the donor country or multilateral agency. However, there are serious problems with using these data to examine such questions. For example, the project coding was inconsistent, and some projects were categorized using criteria developed for other purposes. In addition, important donors were missing from the dataset.

The PLAID initiative filled existing gaps by adding development projects from donor agencies that do not report to the OECD. Each project in the PLAID database was then categorized according to its likely environmental impact by two PLAID researchers. (When there was disagreement between two researchers on the nature of a project, which happened infrequently, the project was referred to senior researchers for a final decision.) As shorthand, projects expected to have damaging environmental effects are referred to as "dirty."[10] Each project was assigned one of five values, from the most environmentally beneficial to the least: Environmental Strictly Defined, Environmental Broadly Defined, Neutral, Dirty Broadly Defined, and Dirty Strictly Defined.[11] [Editors' note: For a detailed definition of each category and the authors' classification strategy, see the original publication.] The projects coded as environmental are further divided into two categories: "green" projects, which are designed to address global environmental problems such as biodiversity loss and transboundary air pollution, and "brown" projects, which address local environmental problems such as land erosion, sewer systems, and water pollution. The coding scheme allowed the initiative to do what has never been done before: consistently evaluate projects across all 61 donors and over the two decades (the 1980s and 1990s) when the data was the most complete and reliable.[12]

Major Trends

During the first three decades of the post–World War II era, foreign aid played a central role in financing the heavy-duty infrastructure of development—roads, mines, dams, mechanization of agriculture, lumber mills, and colonization schemes. But in the mid-1980s, the political landscape changed significantly in many industrialized countries: a firestorm of protest exploded when environmentalists discovered the World Bank's role in funding environmental disasters in the Brazilian Amazon and Indonesia's . . . rain forest.[13] Conservation International and a network of nongovernmental organizations (NGOs) brought indigenous people and Brazilian rubber-tappers before the U.S. Congress to explain how the bank's actions were destroying their civilization and livelihoods and the forests that supported them.[14] The U.S. Senate threatened to withhold the bank's funding replenishments, and Congress went on to pass the Pelosi Amendment to the 1989 International Development and Finance Act, which required multilateral development banks to create environmental departments and conduct environmental impact assessments for any project with the potential to cause significant environmental damage.

Collecting and categorizing data on 427,000 projects suggests that aid has greened over these 20 years, but only partially, and certainly not to the level promised by donors at previous summits. The descriptive statistics reported in

Figures 1 and 2 suggest that most bilateral and multilateral aid agencies have responded to critiques by environmentalists and threats and sanctions from the legislatures that fund them. From 1980 to the end of the twentieth century, environmental aid increased substantially, from roughly $3 billion a year to about $10 billion a year (Figure 1). In all, $61.9 billion in environmental assistance flowed from donor governments to recipient countries during the 1980s and 1990s, out of $735.2 billion in total bilateral assistance, 8.4 percent of all bilateral aid over the two decades. Bilateral environmental assistance increased from a total of $5.8 billion for all donors in the first five years of the 1980s to $27.4 billion in the late 1990s. Multilateral agencies like the World Bank committed approximately $10 billion in environmental grants and loans in the early 1980s, nearly tripling that to $28 billion in the late 1990s.

Between 1982 and 1992, bilateral donors also scaled back their support for projects that were likely to damage the environment, from about 45 percent of bilateral aid in most of the 1980s to about 20 percent a year at the end of the 1990s.[15] Creating a ratio of dirty aid to environmental aid lends further support to the argument that there has been a major shift in the environmental composition of aid (see Figure 3). It also shows that bilateral aid agencies greened more quickly and thoroughly than multilateral agencies. At the beginning of the 1980s, dirty projects received roughly 10 times as much funding as pro-environment projects. But by the end of the 1990s, the ratio was about three to one. Case studies of USAID, DFID, and the Danish, German, and Japanese aid agencies shed light on the

Figure 14.1 *Total official environmental assistance, 1980–1999*

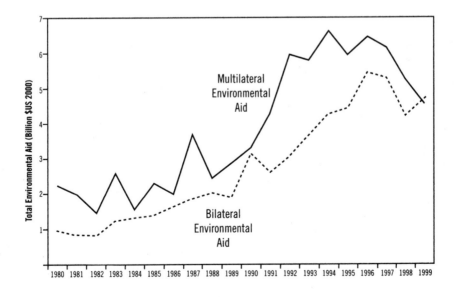

Figure 14.2 *Total official environmental, dirty, and environmentally neutral assistance, 1980–1999*

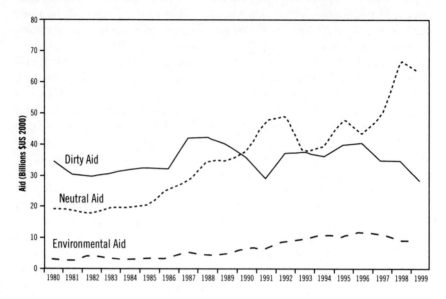

NOTE: The Project-Level Aid database from which these data were drawn designates any project expected to have damaging environmental effects as "dirty."

Figure 14.3 *Ratio of dirty aid to environmental aid, bilateral and multilateral donor agencies, 1980–1999*

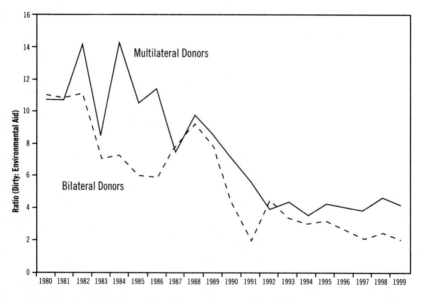

NOTE: The Project-Level Aid database from which these data were drawn designates any project expected to have damaging environmental effects as "dirty."

domestic political factors that encourage bilateral funders to green their aid portfolios.[16] The multilateral development banks also have greened substantially over these pivotal decades but continue to give about four times as much funding to dirty projects as environmental projects (Figure 3).[17] The data show that the ratio of dirty to clean projects stopped declining in 1992—the year of the Rio Earth Summit—through the end of the decade.[18]

An important but underappreciated trend has also surfaced: a massive increase in environmentally neutral projects—those that are on average neither environmental nor dirty. While some of these neutral projects have environmentally positive and negative elements, most are not directly related to environmental outcomes. For example, projects that fund judicial reform initiatives or that provide computer software to schoolchildren have no obvious impact on the natural environment. Neutral aid doubled from $20 billion a year in the early 1980s to about $40 billion by the early 1990s and increased to more than $60 billion in the late 1990s.

Were *Agenda 21* Promises Met?

Agenda 21 included specific recommendations about how much funding would be needed to address the major issues of the planet's health, including water and sanitation ($6.1 billion a year), desertification and land degradation ($18.2 billion a year), global climate change ($20 billion a year), and biodiversity loss ($1.75 billion a year). Were these prescribed funds delivered? PLAID environmental coding and keyword searching of project descriptions and titles facilitated the first systematic evaluation of this question. Of these four issues, water and sanitation projects appear to have attracted by far the most environmental funding, with climate change and biodiversity projects increasing substantially (in number and amount) only in the late 1990s (see Figure 4). The PLAID data collection effort suggests that the dire problems of desertification and soil erosion have been almost entirely neglected.

In the years following the publication of *Agenda 21* (1993–1999), the average annual amount of water aid rose to $5.6 billion—only $500 million short of the original estimated amount needed. By contrast, climate change received just $33.6 million—4 percent of the funding scientists prescribed in *Agenda 21* ($840 million a year)—and biodiversity protection received only $8.75 million—7 percent of the amount that was prescribed ($125 million a year). Funding to assist poor countries in combating desertification and other types of land degradation was the most neglected category throughout the 1980s and 1990s: despite continued warnings from the scientific community and staggering estimates of need, only $350 million per year, 2 percent of the funding prescribed at Rio, was delivered in the 1990s.

Figure 14.4 *Funding for environmental projects by sub-sector*

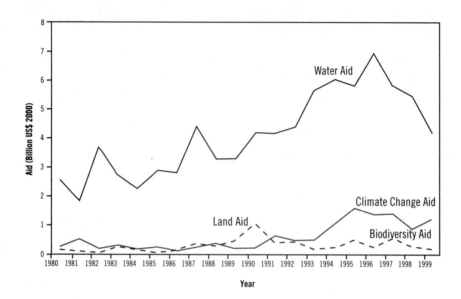

How Green Are Donors?

Which governments give the most environmental aid? In terms of total dollars sent abroad to protect the environment, the United States was first in the 1980s, giving a total of $3.8 billion. During the 1990s, that amount doubled, to just below $7.6 billion. However, the United States fell to third in total environmental aid during the second half of the 1990s, as Japan's environmental funding increased fivefold from $3 billion in the 1980s to nearly $15 billion in the 1990s.

Denmark has the distinction of having the greenest aid portfolio of any donor government, giving 13 percent of all its aid to projects categorized as environmental in the last five years of the 1980s and nearly 22 percent during the 1995–1999 period (see Table 1). In per capita terms, Denmark's environmental aid is unparalleled: in the late 1980s, they gave on average more than $180 per person (see Table 2). This amount was well over twice that of the next four donors, who gave between $70 and $85 per person. By 1999, 42 percent of Denmark's total aid portfolio was earmarked for pro-environment projects, nearly three times that of the next three countries: Germany, Austria, and Sweden (whose environmental funding ranged from 12 to 15 percent in 1999).

Table 14.1 *Environmental aid as a percentage of total bilateral aid portfolio*

Rank	Country	Percent of total bilateral aid (1980–1984)	(1995–1999)	Change in percent
1	Denmark	11.2	21.9	10.7
2	Germany	4.7	15.6	10.9
3	Finland	5.7	14.0	8.3
4	Japan	4.9	13.8	8.9
5	Austria	0.0	12.7	12.7
6	Netherlands	6.7	12.3	5.6
7	United States	5.3	11.2	5.9
8	Switzerland	4.3	10.1	5.8
9	France	3.4	10.1	6.7
10	United Kingdom	1.3	9.4	8.1
11	Australia	1.8	9.3	7.5
12	Norway	10.1	8.2	-1.9
13	Sweden	5.7	8.1	2.4
14	Spain	0.0	5.7	5.7
15	Italy	2.7	5.5	2.8
16	Canada	4.1	5.4	1.3
17	Belgium	1.5	3.9	2.4
18	New Zealand	6.6	3.7	-2.9
19	Portugal	0.0	0.4	0.4

Table 14.2 *Environmental aid per capita (1995–1999)*

Rank	Country	Environmental aid per capita (1995–1999)
1	Denmark	$181.26
2	Norway	$84.26
3	Germany	$81.86
4	Netherlands	$70.32
5	Japan	$70.22
6	Sweden	$50.13
7	Switzerland	$43.11
8	Finland	$30.95
9	Austria	$29.93
10	France	$24.46
11	Australia	$22.80
12	United Kingdom	$19.02
13	United States	$16.38
14	Canada	$11.53
15	Belgium	$9.32
16	Spain	$5.39
17	Italy	$3.46
18	New Zealand	$0.84
19	Portugal	$0.23
20	Luxembourg	$0.00

Comparing the period 1985–1989 to the period 1995–1999, Germany nearly tripled its environmental giving, from $2.3 billion to $6.7 billion, which meant a doubling of the proportion of its bilateral donations going to the environment, from 7.5 to more than 15 percent. New Zealand, meanwhile, was the only country to reduce the environmental share of its bilateral aid portfolio: channeling 6.6 percent of all bilateral aid to environmental projects in the early 1980s but only 3.7 percent in the late 1990s. Large increases in environmental aid spending over the last 20 years were also documented for the Netherlands, France, Sweden, Italy, the United Kingdom, Canada, and Denmark. Between 1990 and 1999, the top environmental donors scaled up from $2.9 billion to more than $5 billion a year.[19]

Several factors may help explain the greenness of donor portfolios: the level of national wealth; the prevalence of post-materialist values; the strength of domestic and international environmental policy preferences; the power of coalitions of environmental NGOs and environmental technology firms; dirty industry lobbying strength; and domestic political institutions (such as political party strength, corporatist decisionmaking structures, and the number of veto players and checks and balances). Testing this series of factors using multivariate statistical techniques found that the PLAID models better explain the drop in "dirty" aid than the rise in environmental aid. Wealthier countries and those scoring higher on post-materialist survey items seem to invest less in dirty projects but not necessarily more in environmental projects. Countries where environmental NGOs and environmental technology firms are both strong also appear to give less dirty aid and more aid focused on global environmental issues like biodiversity. Finally, as one might expect, countries with higher rates of environmental treaty ratification and compliance also tend to have larger environmental aid budgets.

Who Receives Environmental Aid?

On the recipient side, there are several unsurprising entries—Brazil, India, China, and Indonesia—on the top ten list of countries that received more than $2 billion in environmental aid during the 1990s (see Figure 5). Some of these countries have large stocks of natural capital that the international community would like to protect (Brazil's Amazon rain forest, for example); others have huge populations and economies that are major contributors to ozone depletion, climate change, and other international environmental threats (such as China and India). But there are also some surprising appearances on the list. For example, it is not immediately obvious why countries like Egypt or Turkey—which have not experienced well-known environmental crises and do not have globally critical biological resources—would receive more than $2 billion in environmental assistance.

In addition, there was considerable variation in the *type* of environmental assistance from one recipient country to the next. During the late 1990s, Egypt and

Figure 14.4 *Top environmental aid recipients, 1995–1999*

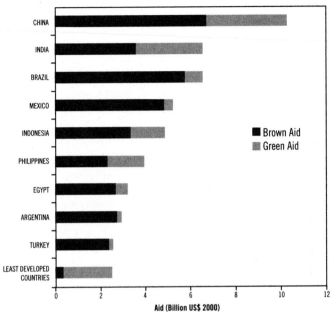

Turkey—two countries of significant geostrategic importance—received far more funding for locally focused (brown) aid than they did globally oriented (green) aid. However, the least developed countries in the world received far more green aid than brown aid. These descriptive statistics beg many questions about underlying donor motivations and the relative bargaining power of donors and recipients. For example, are major geopolitical players able to negotiate for a higher ratio of environmental aid that directly benefits their local populations, such as water and sewage projects?

Of particular interest to the PLAID research group was assessing whether environmental assistance is allocated differently than other types of foreign assistance. That is, is environmental aid channeled to military allies, geostrategic partners, and key trading partners, or are donors concerned with the environmental rate-of-return they receive on their aid investment? Here again, several factors may explain inter-recipient environmental aid allocation patterns, including global environmental significance; regional (environmental) significance; the severity of local environmental damage; the level of participation in international environmental agreements; the transparency and availability of environmental information; and the overall level of human need. Other questions arise as to whether donors favor recipient countries with sound economic policies, strong public institutions, and democratic credentials, and whether a recipient's political loyalty to a donor, existing commercial relationships with a donor, or former colonial ties have any impact on the amount of environmental aid it received.

Multivariate statistical techniques used to evaluate a series of such factors did find some evidence that environmental aid is allocated according to eco-functional criteria. In other words, some donors appear to be targeting countries where they think their environmental aid might have a better chance of actually ameliorating serious environmental problems. But many of the political, commercial, and historical factors that are identified in the broader literature on foreign aid allocation also appear to influence environmental aid. In fact, the overall impact of most eco-functional variables is small when compared with the more traditional determinants of foreign aid allocation, such as a recipient country's existing bilateral commercial relationship with a donor country and previous colonial ties to the donor country. This finding is important, as a growing body of evidence suggests that the way aid is allocated influences its ultimate effectiveness. Researchers and practitioners generally agree that aid allocated along political lines has a worse chance of leading to better development outcomes than aid allocated according to need and government commitment to good policy.[20]

Future Directions

With continued warnings of environmental crisis and repeated promises of action, many observers have become cynical about the prospects for significant cooperation on environmental issues among developed and developing countries. However, the evidence seems to show that the international community had it right back in Stockholm in 1972: development assistance, when allocated and implemented properly, can be an important tool for promoting international environmental cooperation and addressing local environmental issues in the world's poorest countries.

The overall picture that emerges from the PLAID database is that aid has partially greened but certainly not to the level promised by donors at previous summits. From 1980 to the end of the twentieth century, environmental aid increased substantially in absolute and relative terms; environmentally neutral aid increased by an even greater margin; and dirty aid declined in relative terms, while remaining virtually unchanged in absolute terms. Breaking down environmental aid into four major sectors revealed that water and sanitation projects attract the most environmental funding, with climate change and biodiversity project commitments increasing substantially (in numbers and amounts) only in the late 1990s. Financing for green projects—that is, those that deal with global public goods by addressing, for example, biodiversity or climate change—increased from just 1 percent of total aid during the whole of the 1980s to around 3 percent in the 1990s. Green aid's share of total environmental aid has grown; throughout much of the 1980s, it accounted for about 17 percent of environmental aid, and by the mid-to-late 1990s, this figure had reached about 27 percent.

The research presented here also draws attention to a simple but very important point about accountability: without independent categorization and evaluation of donor commitments at the project level, it is extremely difficult to monitor what donors are doing in the environmental sector. Influential political groups in many donor countries exert pressure on their governments to reduce aid for environmentally damaging projects and increase aid for environmental cleanup. Such pressure can create incentives for policymakers to overrepresent the amount of environmental aid they give so as to look and sound as green as possible.

The value of an independent, project-level aid database became evident in an evaluation of the United Kingdom's development agency. Comparing PLAID coding for what constitutes an environmental project with DFID's Policy Information Marker System for the same projects revealed a stark divergence of claims. DFID claimed that environmental projects accounted for 25 percent of its bilateral aid in the 1990s, while PLAID's analysis suggests the actual number is probably closer to 10 percent.

When these types of accounting differences are viewed within the context of the huge promises that donors have made to ramp up environmental spending at international summits, the need for a credible mechanism that independently monitors whether donors are honoring their commitments becomes obvious. What do these public commitments mean if there is no agreement or mechanism to track them? The PLAID database begins to address that problem.

The future will likely bring a growing focus on global climate change among major bilateral and multilateral donors. There is broad agreement that the key challenge to securing an effective global climate agreement among developed and developing countries will be to enlist the support and active participation of the latter. Many developing countries are highly vulnerable to the effects of global warming but see the need to fuel their economic growth with cheaper—and dirtier—sources of energy. As such, if developing countries are going to actively participate in a global agreement to curb greenhouse gas emissions, they will almost certainly need significant assistance making the transition from high-carbon to low-carbon energy technologies and adapting to the worst effects of climate change.[21] According to the latest UN Framework Convention on Climate Change estimates, by 2030, $100 billion a year will be needed to finance mitigation activities and $28–$67 billion a year to finance adaptation activities in the developing world. Even with major new sources of funding from the Clean Development Mechanism (CDM), the Adaptation Fund (financed by a 2 percent tax on CDM transactions), and the proposed Reducing Emissions from Deforestation and Degradation mechanism, there will still be a major role for official assistance, as market mechanisms will likely not channel money to all areas of need, and funding may be too slow or unpredictable.

Finally, in addition to the aid allocation issues dealt with here, the PLAID database provides an extremely valuable resource for those interested in evaluating the effectiveness of aid. The existing literature on aid effectiveness has focused on the relationship between total aid flows—including support for peacekeeping, land-mine clearance, free and fair elections, civil society, biodiversity protection, HIV/AIDS, anti–drug trafficking efforts, and refugees—and causally distant or unrelated outcomes, such as economic growth and infant mortality. However, there is a growing consensus that such research probably obscures more than it reveals.[22] Biodiversity aid is not designed to accelerate short-term economic growth, nor is renewable energy assistance intended to reduce infant mortality. Well-designed assessments of aid effectiveness should therefore evaluate the im-pact that specific types of aid have on more specific social, economic, political, and environmental outcomes. For example, with the PLAID database, researchers can now unbundle environmental aid into its constituent parts and study the re-lationships between biodiversity aid and species loss, climate adaptation assis-tance and human vulnerability to hydro-meteorological disasters, and land degradation aid and soil fertility.

Although the specific social and economic goals identified in *Agenda 21* (such as combating poverty, changing consumption patterns, and protecting and promot-ing human health) involve interconnected problems and target very different out-comes, aid's ability to contribute to these outcomes is best measured separately.

We hope that PLAID will inspire a new generation of research on the effec-tiveness of aid, including the impact of environmental aid on environmental protection. A broad range of stakeholders, including donor agencies, legislative overseers, advocacy groups, and beneficiaries in recipient countries, stands to benefit from such research.

Notes

1. "Beijing Ministerial Declaration on Environment and Development," adopted by 41 developing countries at the Ministerial Conference of Developing Countries on Environ-ment and Development, Beijing, 19 June 1991. See also H. Sjöberg, *Restructuring the Global Environment Facility*, Global Environment Facility (GEF) Working Paper 13 (Washington, DC: GEF, 1999), http://thegef.org/Outreach/outreach-Publications/WP13-Restructuring_the_GEF.pdf (accessed 6 November 2008).

2. R. Hicks, B. C. Parks, J. T. Roberts, and M. J. Tierney, *Greening Aid? Understanding the Environmental Impact of Development Assistance* (Oxford, UK: Oxford University Press, 2008), 124. Upon closer inspection of the aid increase promised by Japan, it appeared only to include an increase over existing levels of about $500 million per year. See P. Lewis, "Pact on Environment Near, But Hurdles on Aid Remain," *New York Times*, 12 June 1992.

3. United Nations Conference on Environment and Development (UNCED), *The Rio Declaration on Environment and Development*, Rio de Janeiro, 3–14 June 1992, Section 4, Chapter 33, http://www.unep.org/Documents.Multilingual/Default.asp?DocumentID=78&ArticleID=1163 (accessed 28 October 2008).

4. According to N. A. Robinson, ed., *Agenda 21 and UNCED Proceedings, Vol. 1 and 2* (New York: Oceana Publications, 1992), concessional financing under *Agenda 21* was more than $125 billion, of which $15 billion was to address global issues.

5. Intergovernmental Panel on Climate Change, *Climate Change 2001: A Synthesis Report* (Cambridge, UK: Cambridge University Press, 2001).

6. European Commission, *Environment Directorate-General of the European Commission*, 2006, http://ec.europa.eu/environment (accessed 15 June 2007).

7. B. Connolly, T. L. Gutner, and H. Berdarff, "Organizational Inertia and Environmental Assistance in Eastern Europe," in R. O. Keohane and M. A. Levy, *Institutions for Environmental Aid: Pitfalls and Promise*, 281–323 (Cambridge, MA: MIT Press, 1996), 286.

8. Cross-country patterns of environmental aid allocation have significant implications for the alleviation of local, regional, and global environmental problems. For example, if donors target recipient countries with sound policies and institutions and the potential to deliver significant environmental benefits, there is good reason to believe that such assistance will be put to more productive use.

9. The goal of the Project-Level Aid (PLAID) research project is to collect and standardize data on every individual development assistance project committed by official donors since 1970. The forthcoming PLAID 2.0, which updates the time series through 2006, includes more bilateral and multilateral donors and fills in gaps where new data have become available. To do so, the project has recently received generous support from the National Science Foundation (#SES-0454384), the William and Flora Hewlett Foundation, and the Bill and Melinda Gates Foundation. For more information about the PLAID database, see http://irtheoryandpractice.wm.edu/projects/plaid/ (accessed 10 December 2008).

10. The PLAID coding rules disregard the humanitarian dimensions of projects: a project's potentially positive overall impact on a recipient country's populations is analytically distinct from a project's environmental impact.

11. The environmental coding scheme is designed to capture the expected environmental impact of projects—not the actual environmental impact of projects. It is understood that some "environmental" projects may not deliver significant environmental benefits, and that donors can make course corrections during project implementation and modify "dirty" and "neutral" projects.

12. Because donor organizations have their own criteria for identifying and counting what is environmental aid (and these criteria often change over time within a given organization), it is difficult to make comparisons across donors or over time.

13. In addition to its problems in Brazil and Indonesia, the World Bank was also widely criticized for its involvement in huge dam projects that displaced millions of people and flooded sensitive lands. For example, see S. Schwartzman, *Bankrolling Disasters: International Development Banks and the Global Environment: A Citizen's Guide to the Multilateral Development Banks* (Washington, DC: Sierra Club, 1985).

14. I. A. Bowles and C. F. Kormos, "The American Campaign for Environmental Reforms at the World Bank," *The Fletcher Forum of World Affairs* 23, no. 1 (1999): 211–25; and D. L. Nielson and M. J. Tierney, "Delegation to International Organizations: Agency Theory and World Bank Environmental Reform," *International Organization* 57, no. 2 (2003): 241–76.

15. In inflation-adjusted, year 2000 dollars, environmentally damaging aid remained relatively unchanged at around $30 billion a year at the end of the 1990s.

16. Hicks, Parks, Roberts, and Tierney, note 2, chapter 5.

17. Multilateral environmental aid is a highly concentrated sector; 90 percent of such assistance comes from just five agencies: the World Bank, the Asian Development Bank, the Inter-American Development Bank, the European Union, and GEF. The World Bank alone

gave $38 billion in environmental aid over the 1980s and 1990s, in addition to the nearly $3 billion of GEF funding the bank administered.

18. A limitation of the PLAID study is that it did not address the "marbling," or mainstreaming, of environmental aid into larger projects. Several studies suggest that marbled environmental assistance represents a significant amount of total environmental assistance at the World Bank. For example, see Nielson and Tierney, note 12. However, research has found that that mainstreamed environmental funding at the World Bank has not increased significantly. In fact, between 2000 and 2006, mainstreamed environmental funding actually declined—from about 12 percent to 10 percent of each project. Yet during the same period, environment-themed bank publications have increased from 4 percent of all bank publications to approximately 32 percent of all bank publications. See R. M. Powers and M. J. Tierney, "A New Measure of Environmental Aid: Measuring Environmental Mainstreaming at the World Bank," paper prepared for the International Studies Association Conference, New York, 15–17 March 2009.

19. Beyond the bilateral funding, a similar amount was being pumped through multilateral agencies like the World Bank, the UN Development Programme, and the EU Technical Aid to the Commonwealth of Independent States fund.

20. P. Collier and D. Dollar, "Development Effectiveness: What Have We Learnt?" *Economic Journal* 114, no. 6 (2004): 244–71.

21. J. T. Roberts and B. C. Parks, *A Climate of Injustice: Global Inequality, North-South Politics, and Climate Policy* (Cambridge, MA: MIT Press, 2007).

22. For example, see M. Clemens, S. Radelet, and R. Bhavnani, "Counting Chickens When They Hatch: The Short-Term Effect of Aid on Growth," Center for Global Development Working Paper 44 (Washington, DC: Center for Global Development, 2004).

15

REPORT
AND FINDINGS ON
THE QINGHAI PROJECT:
EXECUTIVE SUMMARY

WORLD BANK INSPECTION PANEL[*]

Interpretation of the Bank's Policies and Procedures

. . . During the course of examining some twenty projects over the past five years, the Panel has encountered certain differences in views among staff on just how the Bank's operational policies and procedures should be applied. In this case, however, the Panel's interviews revealed an unusually and disturbingly wide range of divergent and, often, opposing views. These large differences pervade all ranks of the staff, from senior management to frontline professionals. And they apply to virtually all of the major decisions required by the policies. The implications of this for a reasonable application of the Bank's policies and procedures became a matter of serious concern to the Panel and ought to be of concern to the Bank generally since there is no way that the policies can be applied with reasonable consistency in the face of such wide divergences of opinion.

For example, a number of staff members felt that the Bank's Operational Directives and other policies were simply idealized policy statements and should be seen largely as a set of goals to be striven after. Others of equal or more senior rank disagreed with this view. They felt that this interpretation could render the

* Excerpted from World Bank Inspection Panel, *Inspection Panel's Report and Findings on the Qinghai Project: Executive Summary*, Washington, April 2000. © World Bank. Reprinted with permission.

policies virtually meaningless and certainly incapable of being employed as benchmarks against which to measure compliance.

In discussions about compliance, staff often pointed out that the policies allow for flexibility of interpretation. The decisions made on the specific matters were thus covered and in compliance. It was simply a matter of "judgment at Management's sole discretion." The Management Response itself makes several claims in this respect. Other staff argued, however, that the policies are clear enough to distinguish areas that are binding from areas where some reasonable flexibility in interpretation is called for. Read in their entirety, the Panel feels that the directives cannot possibly be taken to authorize a level of "interpretation" and "flexibility" that would permit those who must follow these directives to simply override the portions of the directives that are clearly binding. . . .

Interviews with some staff were punctuated by the refrain that "*in China things are done differently.*" This is echoed in the Management Response which states that: "*The level and quality of preparation and analysis for this Project were very much in line with Bank practice in applying social and environmental policies to projects in China in the context of its political and social systems.*" The Panel has carefully examined the policies and has failed to find any grounds for the view that precedents in a country, or a country's "social and political systems," can in any way determine what is required by the policies. . . .

The Qinghai Project in Space and Time

The Environmental Assessment does not distinguish between short-term impacts and those that will only occur at some time in the future. This raises serious questions about the time horizons over which the Project was evaluated.

Moreover, in examining the Project documentation, the Panel found a high level of ambiguity, uncertainty and inconsistency in the use of the term "project area." This confusion is compounded by the fact that the documentation is poorly supported by maps. (The Panel had eventually to prepare its own set of maps. . . .) As a result, it appears that significant numbers of people, including members of minority nationalities, have been left out of the environmental and social assessments required by Bank policy. . . .

In the Panel's view, given the letter and intent of [Operational Directives] 4.01 [on environmental assessment], 4.20 [on indigenous peoples] and 4.30 [on involuntary resettlement], the actual scale of the area to be impacted by the Qinghai Project, the ethnic composition of the Project's impacted populations, the boundaries of the "project area" were far too narrowly defined by Management. As a result, the assessments fail to address many of the most significant social and environmental impacts of the Project on the potentially affected populations, including those who are members of minority nationalities. The Panel finds that this is not in compliance with these ODs.

The Consultation and Survey Method

... Four points can be made concerning the survey in the Move-out area. First, the questionnaires are not confidential. (All four surveys required the respondent to put his or her name on the survey.) Second, from the internal evidence of the questionnaires themselves, they must have been filled out by someone other than the individual respondents. Third, the very limited source of information about the subject matter of the survey is striking; 93 percent of respondents indicated that they learned of the resettlement from "government propaganda." Fourth, an examination of the questions asked, and the context in which they were asked, indicates that opinions and information gathered are probably not reliable because respondents will probably think that this questionnaire could directly influence whether they get selected for the resettlement project.

... [I]n the Panel's view, the expressions of opinion it heard and the incidents it witnessed indicate the need for far greater efforts to obtain public consultation under adequate conditions before Management can be said to have met the requirements for public consultation in the Operational Directives. The mere fact that opinions expressed were so strikingly different, and especially the fact that there was a strong perception of risk from those expressing opposition to the Project during the Inspection Team's visit, indicates that methods of public consultation used for this Project have so far been inadequate.

The Consideration of Project Alternatives

If there is no alternative there can be no choice. The Bank's policies and procedures leave no room for doubt as to the need for a careful and systematic consideration of a number of different types of alternatives, including investment alternatives, alternative sites, alternative project designs, and alternative implementation plans. The purpose of considering these alternatives is to ensure that the option supported by the Bank will achieve the project's objectives most cost effectively, while meeting the Bank's safeguard policies.

One of the most noticeable and significant weaknesses of the assessments is that investment and project alternatives are neither identified nor systematically compared. For all practical purposes, the Environmental Assessment avoids consideration of alternatives. ... From the documentation, it is not possible to deduce whether the Qinghai Project as proposed is the best way for the Bank to meet the Project's objectives or to ensure that the Bank's safeguard policies are being respected.

Management failed to ensure that those responsible for the [environmental assessment] understood their brief to include an examination of alternatives to resettlement in both the Move-out and Move-in areas. Instead, the Panel found that they understood the main purpose of their studies to be to assist in the optimal resettlement of around 60,000 people from the Move-out area into the Balong-Xiangride irrigation area. . . . There is no systematic study of in situ alternatives to resettlement, or of alternative resettlement sites, or of alternative development plans for the national minorities affected within the Move-in area.

Why the Bank accepted Assessments conducted in such a circumscribed and limiting manner is unclear. Whatever the reasons, the Panel finds that the Assessments do not make any meaningful analysis of realistic project alternatives as required by Bank policy.

Environmental Assessment of the Qinghai Project

Management adopted a very limited definition of "environment" in the Project with the result that the Assessment fails to analyze the full range of Project effects. The Assessment also fails completely to place the Project in proper time frames. As noted above, the spatial boundaries of the Move-out and Move-in areas are defined narrowly, or not at all, with the result that whole communities and populations, whose lives will be impacted by the Project, have been left out of the Environmental and Social Assessments. . . .

In May/June 1999, following the outbreak of public concern, Management tried to compensate for this by requiring a study to evaluate the environmental and social impacts of the Voluntary Settlement Implementation Plan. This study (which is to recommend measures to enhance the environmental sustainability and the living conditions of the people in the Move-out counties) is to be undertaken not later than three years after the implementation of the Plan has commenced. Undertaking an environmental and social assessment three years after the commencement of resettlement is a bit late, not only in terms of the policies, but also in terms of any elemental understanding of the purposes of such assessments. Within the social arena, this is comparable to requiring that the safety of a proposed dam should be studied within three years after it has been built! . . .

The EA and other Project documents fail to consider the appropriateness of implanting large-scale irrigated agriculture in this Region. It does not examine its suitability or viability in comparison with the traditional forms of land use. . . . There appears simply to be an assumption that irrigated agriculture is "a good thing" without consideration of alternatives and relative costs. . . .

The Panel finds that the Environmental Assessment of the Qinghai Project is not in compliance with Bank policies as set out in [Operational Directive] 4.01.

Involuntary Resettlement

. . . [Operational Directive] 4.30 [on involuntary resettlement] applies to those people who are displaced or adversely affected by the Project. As noted repeatedly,

Management's narrow definition of the boundaries of the Project area resulted in many people and communities affected by the Project being left out of the assessments. This appears to be true of the population of persons who will be displaced by the Project, which is likely to be larger than that accounted for in Project documents. In the Panel's view, the Project is not in compliance with OD 4.30.

Paragraph 4 of OD 4.30 requires the development of a plan that will assist involuntarily resettled persons with their move and will provide fair compensation for their loss. . . . Adequate baseline data on pastoralism, including the data on land use and inheritance that would allow a proper assessment of the compensation offered, are unfortunately lacking for this Project. Although envisaged by the OD, it appears that this work was not done. Without the results of such work, it is difficult to assess the adequacy of the compensation offered, not only for the Panel but also, in the first instance, for Management. Indeed, it is difficult to understand how the OD's policy objectives can be achieved without this information.

PART FOUR

THE SUSTAINABILITY DEBATE

Effective responses to global environmental problems demand both international cooperation and institutional reform. As previous sections have indicated, these are substantial challenges. The prevailing structures and practices of the international system make attainment of these goals difficult, and they cannot be divorced from the larger political, economic, and cultural struggles that infuse world politics.

It would be a mistake, however, to study global environmental politics solely in terms of international treaties and institutional change. Perspectives on the essence of the global environmental problematique are another key variable, and one that has changed in important ways over time. Few would argue that ideas alone have the power to change history. But there is no doubt that paradigms—bundles of fundamental ideas and beliefs—shape the strategies and goals of actors in important ways. They influence how actors understand their interests, how policies are formulated, how resources are allocated, and which actors and institutions are empowered to make the critical decisions that affect global environmental quality.[1]

One powerful but controversial new paradigm that emerged in the build-up to the 1992 Rio de Janeiro Earth Summit is the idea of sustainability. As previously discussed, one of the central controversies at the Stockholm conference was the debate over whether economic growth and development are inherently destructive to the environment. This question revealed sharp cleavages between governments of the industrialized North and the developing South, as well as sharp divisions between growth-oriented governments in general and nongovernmental actors concerned about the negative consequences of continually expanding economic activity.

Concepts of sustainability and sustainable development appeal to many people because they hold out the promise of reconciling these divergent views. Sustainable development approaches are predicated on the premises that poverty and economic stagnation are themselves environmentally destructive and that all forms of economic organization and activity are not equal in their environmental impact. If these premises are true, then it might be possible to design environment-friendly forms of production and exchange that simultaneously facilitate economic development, alleviate the pressures of poverty, and minimize environmental damage. Such forms of production and exchange might be aimed at "development without growth"—that is, improvement in the quality of people's lives without an increase in the aggregate level of economic activity.[2] Or they might be tailored to forms of economic growth that are more acceptable ecologically. Whatever the path advocated, reconciling the tension between ecology and economy is the central goal of sustainable development.

The most frequently cited definition of sustainable development is found in *Our Common Future*, an influential report published by the World Commission on Environment and Development. In 1983 the United Nations General Assembly charged the commission—also known as the Brundtland Commission, after its chairperson, Norwegian prime minister Gro Harlem Brundtland—with devising a conceptual and practical "global agenda for change."[3] The commission, which included representatives from twenty-two nations on five continents, conducted a series of hearings around the world before preparing its final report and presenting it to the General Assembly in 1987. The report had an enormous influence on the global environmental debate and played a key role in shaping the content and format of the 1992 Earth Summit.

According to the Brundtland Commission, sustainable development is "development that meets the needs of the present without compromising the ability of future generations to meet their own needs."[4] To meet the goal of achieving sustainable development, the commission set forth a policy blueprint based on enhanced international cooperation, substantial changes in national policies, and a reoriented global economy. The report argues that the problem is not economic growth per se but the environmentally destructive character of many current activities and incentives. Economic growth remains vital, in the commission's view, given the substantial impact of poverty on the environment. Thus, the commission combined its recommendations for ecologically sound forms of production and exchange with a call for renewed global economic growth to solve the problems of Third World poverty.

Some observers saw the commission's advocacy of these positions as inherently contradictory. The continued commitment to a basically unreformed global economic system is, in this view, the biggest impediment to true sustainability, rather than a prerequisite for managing environmental problems more effectively. In an editorial originally published in the British environmental journal *The Ecologist*, Larry Lohmann questions whether the Brundtland Commission has provided an agenda for change or simply a justification of business as usual. In Lohmann's view, the Brundtland proposals merely put a green face on current practices while perpetuating unequal relationships of power and wealth—both within individual countries and between the overdeveloped North and underdeveloped South. Sustainable development, Lohmann asserts, is less threatening to powerful interests than other, more transformative approaches to environmental policy.[5]

Sharachchandra Lélé provides a different but in some ways equally critical assessment of the concept of sustainable development. A comprehensive review of the burgeoning literature on sustainability leads Lélé to conclude that the concept lacks a clear, widely accepted definition. There are many different conceptions of sustainable development, not all of which endorse the Brundtland Commission's formulation. Lélé argues that because of the many frequently contradictory uses of the term, sustainable development "is in real danger of becoming a cliché . . . a fashionable phrase that everyone pays homage to but nobody cares to define."

Like Lohmann, Lélé writes from the perspective of one who accepts the goal of meeting current needs without compromising the ability of future generations to meet their requirements. His quarrel is with several of the assumptions embedded in mainstream sustainable development thinking. These include a narrowly technical focus on the problem of poverty while ignoring its fundamentally sociopolitical roots; a neoclassical emphasis on economic growth as an end in itself, rather than a more precise specification of how to meet people's basic needs; and a lack of clarity about exactly what is to be sustained, for whom, and for how long. Definitions that begin instead with the ecological goal of sustaining the conditions for human life and well-being avoid some of these problems, in Lélé's view. But they suffer from an equally debilitating flaw: Too often they stress the ecological conditions required for ecological sustainability but overlook the complex array of social conditions that are also required.

Lélé also worries that mainstream notions of sustainable development place an undue burden of structural and value adjustment on the South so that current consumption practices in the North may continue. In his view, the problem of excessive Northern consumption poses fundamental challenges that are not being adequately addressed with the "managed-growth" model of sustainable development. The idea that the challenge lies primarily in the South is more a reflection of the power of some actors and institutions to set the global agenda than an accurate reflection of the true scope of the problem.

Lélé's concern for a global perspective on sustainability forces us to ask what sustainable societies might look like, and what the pathway for getting there might entail. Some influential actors and institutions prefer the Brundtland Commission's notion of growth-oriented sustainability, emphasizing efficiency in the context of open markets to improve existing systemic structures such as free trade and a modern industrial economy. This perspective takes an optimistic view on the possibilities for "ecological modernization," in which advanced industrial societies are seen as able to make significant environmental progress through reform in production systems, management practices, and market-based incentives, while remaining within the parameters of a globalizing capitalist economy.[6] Reflecting this vision, we present here a short essay on the "four capitals" of sustainability, by Ismail Serageldin, who served for several years as the World Bank's Vice President for Socially and Environmentally Sustainable Development, and coauthor Andrew Steer. Although preserving the emphasis on "capital" typical of a mainstream economic perspective, Serageldin and Steer's framework broadens the notion of capital to take into account environmental goods and services (natural capital), networks of social ties (social capital), and the possibilities of knowledge and learning (human capital). In doing so, the authors recognize an overly narrow emphasis within the World Bank (and much of economic development thinking and practice) on financial capital as the sole pillar of "development."

In contrast to this relatively optimistic scenario, some observers see a far deeper crisis of global unsustainability rooted in "the consumer society" and less amenable to technical and managerial solutions. Here, the primary culprit is not the undercapitalized status of the global South but the consumption habits of the smaller but wealthier populations in the North and, through international trade and the diffusion of consumerist lifestyles, the more affluent segments of society in the global South. Reporter Tom Knudson wrote a series of investigative reports for the *Sacramento Bee* on the consumption and conservation practices of California, which epitomizes the consumer society. The excerpt presented here focuses on a practice Knudson refers to as "shifting the pain": the tendency of Californians to protect their own environment through strict conservation laws, while simultaneously continuing their high-throughput lifestyles through international trade and the exploitation of resources from distant lands. Tellingly, the series as a whole was titled "State of Denial."

California's ecological shadow raises several questions that challenge mainstream consumer practices in industrial society: How much is enough?[7] Can the Earth survive a world where more is always assumed to be better? Are technical fixes enough, when the dominant trend is for influences as varied as Hollywood and the World Bank to market this acquisitive logic to developing countries as the proper model for their own development?

In conclusion, we might well ask whether the idea of sustainability can break the North-South stalemate on environment and development that emerged at the Stockholm conference. To some extent, it already has; there is no question that the power of the concept—and in particular, its vision of harmonizing environmental quality and economic well-being—has fundamentally altered the global debate. The next and more difficult step is to clarify whether and how that vision can be attained. Whether the debate on sustainability moves to this higher level hinges on our ability to meet several challenges. We must redirect our gaze to encompass the system as a whole and not just the South; we must clarify and reconcile the goals that underlie radically different visions of a sustainable society; and we must broaden our vision to engage the contested issues of power, wealth, and authority that underlie current environmental problems.

Thinking Critically

1. In your judgment, does "sustainable development" represent a powerful synthesis of the twin needs for environmental protection and economic development? Or is it a contradiction in terms? Is sustainability compatible with a wide array of definitions of "development" or does it narrowly limit what development can mean?

2. How do you think the members of the Brundtland Commission would respond to the criticisms voiced by Lohmann and Lélé?

3. Can there be a common framework for sustainability across the diverse societies of the global South? For the North as well as the South? Is a concept such as sustainability universal, or is it inherently contingent on culture?

4. Do Serageldin and Steer's "four capitals" provide a workable blueprint for building a more sustainable society? Is their list sufficient? Is capital formation and capital investment the right metaphor for the required processes of social change?

5. Are you an overconsumer? Is it accurate to say that California, or your community, is in a "state of denial"? Is it fair? How much control do you have over your consumption? What aspects of your life would have to change for you to change from overconsumer to sustainer? What are the barriers to the sort of change that Knudson's critique implicitly advocates?

Notes

1. For a view stressing the importance of paradigms in shaping global environmental futures, see Dennis C. Pirages, ed., *Building Sustainable Societies: A Blueprint for a Post-Industrial World* (Armonk, NY: M. E. Sharpe, 1996).

2. On the concept of development without growth, see Herman E. Daly and John B. Cobb Jr., *For the Common Good: Redirecting the Economy Toward Community, the Environment, and a Sustainable Future* (Boston: Beacon Press, 1989).

3. World Commission on Environment and Development (WCED), *Our Common Future* (New York: Oxford University Press, 1987), p. ix.

4. WCED, *Our Common Future*, p. 43.

5. A similar criticism has been made of the "global change" discourse that became increasingly influential in environmental circles beginning in the 1980s. See Frederick H. Buttel, Ann P. Hawkins, and Alison G. Power, "From Limits to Growth to Global Change," *Global Environmental Change* 1 (December 1990): 57–66.

6. On ecological modernization, see Arthur P. J. Mol, "Ecological Modernization and the Global Economy," *Global Environmental Politics* 2, no. 2 (May 2002): 92–115.

7. Alan Durning, *How Much Is Enough? The Consumer Society and the Future of the Earth* (Washington, DC: Worldwatch Institute, 1992).

16

TOWARDS
SUSTAINABLE
DEVELOPMENT*

WORLD COMMISSION
ON ENVIRONMENT
AND DEVELOPMENT

Sustainable development is development that meets the needs of the present without compromising the ability of future generations to meet their own needs. It contains within it two key concepts:

- the concept of "needs," in particular the essential needs of the world's poor, to which overriding priority should be given; and
- the idea of limitations imposed by the state of technology and social organization on the environment's ability to meet present and future needs.

Thus the goals of economic and social development must be defined in terms of sustainability in all countries—developed or developing, market-oriented or centrally planned. . . .

Development involves a progressive transformation of economy and society. A development path that is sustainable in a physical sense could theoretically be pursued even in a rigid social and political setting. But physical sustainability cannot be secured unless development policies pay attention to such considerations as changes in access to resources and in the distribution of costs and benefits. . . .

*   Excerpted from Chapter Two of World Commission on Environment and Development, *Our Common Future* (1987). Reprinted by permission of Oxford University Press.

The Concept of Sustainable Development

The satisfaction of human needs and aspirations is the major objective of development. The essential needs of vast numbers of people in developing countries—for food, clothing, shelter, jobs—are not being met, and beyond their basic needs these people have legitimate aspirations for an improved quality of life. A world in which poverty and inequity are endemic will always be prone to ecological and other crises. Sustainable development requires meeting the basic needs of all and extending to all the opportunity to satisfy their aspirations for a better life.

Living standards that go beyond the basic minimum are sustainable only if consumption standards everywhere have regard for long-term sustainability. Yet many of us live beyond the world's ecological means, for instance, in our patterns of energy use. Perceived needs are socially and culturally determined, and sustainable development requires the promotion of values that encourage consumption standards that are within the bounds of the ecological possible and to which all can reasonably aspire.

Meeting essential needs depends in part on achieving full growth potential, and sustainable development clearly requires economic growth in places where such needs are not being met. Elsewhere, it can be consistent with economic growth, provided the content of growth reflects the broad principles of sustainability and nonexploitation of others. But growth by itself is not enough. High levels of productive activity and widespread poverty can coexist, and can endanger the environment. Hence sustainable development requires that societies meet human needs both by increasing productive potential and by ensuring equitable opportunities for all.

An expansion in numbers can increase the pressure on resources and slow the rise in living standards in areas where deprivation is widespread. Though the issue is not merely one of population size but of the distribution of resources, sustainable development can only be pursued if demographic developments are in harmony with the changing productive potential of the ecosystem.

A society may in many ways compromise its ability to meet the essential needs of its people in the future—by overexploiting resources, for example. The direction of technological developments may solve some immediate problems but lead to even greater ones. . . . At a minimum, sustainable development must not endanger the natural systems that support life on Earth: the atmosphere, the waters, the soils, and the living beings.

Growth has no set limits in terms of population or resource use beyond which lies ecological disaster. Different limits hold for the use of energy, materials, water, and land. Many of these will manifest themselves in the form of rising costs and diminishing returns, rather than in the form of any sudden loss of a resource base. The accumulation of knowledge and the development of technology can enhance the carrying capacity of the resource base. But ultimate limits there are, and sustainability requires that long before these are reached, the world must ensure equitable access to the constrained resource and reorient technological efforts to relieve the pressure.

Economic growth and development obviously involve changes in the physical ecosystem. Every ecosystem everywhere cannot be preserved intact. . . . In general, renewable resources like forests and fish stocks need not be depleted provided the rate of use is within the limits of regeneration and natural growth. But most renewable resources are part of a complex and interlinked ecosystem, and maximum sustainable yield must be defined after taking into account system-wide effects of exploitation.

As for nonrenewable resources, like fossil fuels and minerals, their use reduces the stock available for future generations. But this does not mean that such resources should not be used. In general the rate of depletion should take into account the criticality of that resource, the availability of technologies for minimizing depletion, and the likelihood of substitutes being available. . . . Sustainable development requires that the rate of depletion of nonrenewable resources should foreclose as few future options as possible.

Development tends to simplify ecosystems and to reduce their diversity of species. . . . The loss of plant and animal species can greatly limit the options of future generations; so sustainable development requires the conservation of plant and animal species.

So-called free goods like air and water are also resources. . . . Sustainable development requires that the adverse impacts on the quality of air, water, and other natural elements are minimized so as to sustain the ecosystem's overall integrity.

In essence, sustainable development is a process of change in which the exploitation of resources, the direction of investments, the orientation of technological development, and institutional change are all in harmony and enhance both current and future potential to meet human needs and aspirations.

Equity and the Common Interest

. . . How are individuals in the real world to be persuaded or made to act in the common interest? The answer lies partly in education, institutional development, and law enforcement. But many problems of resource depletion and environmental stress arise from disparities in economic and political power. An industry may get away with unacceptable levels of air and water pollution because the people who bear the brunt of it are poor and unable to complain effectively. . . .

Ecological interactions do not respect the boundaries of individual ownership and political jurisdiction. . . . Traditional social systems recognized some aspects of this interdependence and enforced community control over agricultural practices and traditional rights relating to water, forests, and land. This enforcement of the "common interest" did not necessarily impede growth and expansion though it may have limited the acceptance and diffusion of technical innovations.

Local interdependence has, if anything, increased because of the technology used in modern agriculture and manufacturing. Yet with this surge of technical progress, the growing "enclosure" of common lands, the erosion of common rights in forests and other resources, and the spread of commerce and production for the market, the responsibilities for decision making are being taken away from both groups and individuals. This shift is still under way in many developing countries.

It is not that there is one set of villains and another of victims. All would be better off if each person took into account the effect of his or her acts upon others. But each is unwilling to assume that others will behave in this socially desirable fashion, and hence all continue to pursue narrow self-interest. Communities or governments can compensate for this isolation through laws, education, taxes, subsidies, and other methods. . . . Most important, effective participation in decisionmaking processes by local communities can help them articulate and effectively enforce their common interest. . . .

The enforcement of common interest often suffers because areas of political jurisdictions and areas of impact do not coincide. . . . No supranational authority exists to resolve such issues, and the common interest can only be articulated through international cooperation.

In the same way, the ability of a government to control its national economy is reduced by growing international economic interactions. . . . If economic power and the benefits of trade were more equally distributed, common interests would be generally recognized. But the gains from trade are unequally distributed, and patterns of trade in, say, sugar affect not merely a local sugar-producing sector, but the economies and ecologies of the many developing countries that depend heavily on this product.

The search for common interest would be less difficult if all development and environment problems had solutions that would leave everyone better off. This is seldom the case, and there are usually winners and losers. Many problems arise from inequalities in access to resources. . . . "Losers" in environment/development conflicts include those who suffer more than their fair share of the health, property, and ecosystem damage costs of pollution.

As a system approaches ecological limits, inequalities sharpen. Thus when a watershed deteriorates, poor farmers suffer more because they cannot afford the same anti-erosion measures as richer farmers. . . . Globally, wealthier nations are better placed financially and technologically to cope with the effects of possible climatic change.

Hence, our inability to promote the common interest in sustainable development is often a product of the relative neglect of economic and social justice within and amongst nations.

Strategic Imperatives

The world must quickly design strategies that will allow nations to move from their present, often destructive, processes of growth and development onto sustainable development paths. . . .

Critical objectives for environment and development policies that follow from the concept of sustainable development include:

- reviving growth;
- changing the quality of growth;
- meeting essential needs for jobs, food, energy, water, and sanitation;
- ensuring a sustainable level of population;
- conserving and enhancing the resource base;
- reorienting technology and managing risk; and
- merging environment and economics in decision making.

Reviving Growth

. . . Development that is sustainable has to address the problem of the large number of people who . . . are unable to satisfy even the most basic of their needs. Poverty reduces people's capacity to use resources in a sustainable manner; it intensifies pressure on the environment. . . . A necessary but not a sufficient condition for the elimination of absolute poverty is a relatively rapid rise in per capita incomes in the Third World. It is therefore essential that the stagnant or declining growth trends of . . . [the 1980s] be reversed.

While attainable growth rates will vary, a certain minimum is needed to have any impact on absolute poverty. It seems unlikely that, taking developing countries as a whole, these objectives can be accomplished with per capita income growth of under 3 percent. . . .

Growth must be revived in developing countries because that is where the links between economic growth, the alleviation of poverty, and environmental conditions operate most directly. Yet developing countries are part of an interdependent world economy; their prospects also depend on the levels and patterns of growth in industrialized nations. The medium-term prospects for industrial countries are for growth of 3–4 percent. . . . Such growth rates could be environmentally sustainable if industrialized nations can continue the recent shifts in the content of their growth towards less material- and energy-intensive activities and the improvement of their efficiency in using materials and energy.

As industrialized nations use less materials and energy, however, they will provide smaller markets for commodities and minerals from the developing nations. Yet if developing nations focus their efforts upon eliminating poverty and satisfying essential human needs, then domestic demand will increase for both agricultural products and manufactured goods and some services. Hence the very logic of sustainable development implies an internal stimulus to Third World growth. . . .

Changing the Quality of Growth

Sustainable development involves more than growth. It requires a change in the content of growth, to make it less material- and energy-intensive and more equitable in its impact. These changes are required in all countries as part of a package of measures to maintain the stock of ecological capital, to improve the distribution of income, and to reduce the degree of vulnerability to economic crises.

The process of economic development must be more soundly based upon the realities of the stock of capital that sustains it. . . . For example, income from forestry operations is conventionally measured in terms of the value of timber and other products extracted, minus the costs of extraction. The costs of regenerating the forest are not taken into account, unless money is actually spent on such work. Thus figuring profits from logging rarely takes full account of the losses in future revenue incurred through degradation of the forest. . . . In all countries, rich or poor, economic development must take full account in its measurements of growth of the improvement or deterioration in the stock of natural resources. . . .

Yet it is not enough to broaden the range of economic variables taken into account. Sustainability requires views of human needs and well-being that incorporate such noneconomic variables as education and health enjoyed for their own sake, clean air and water, and the protection of natural beauty. . . .

Economic and social development can and should be mutually reinforcing. Money spent on education and health can raise human productivity. Economic development can accelerate social development by providing opportunities for underprivileged groups or by spreading education more rapidly.

Meeting Essential Human Needs

The satisfaction of human needs and aspirations is so obviously an objective of productive activity that it may appear redundant to assert its central role in the concept of sustainable development. All too often poverty is such that people cannot satisfy their needs for survival and well-being even if goods and services are available. At the same time, the demands of those not in poverty may have major environmental consequences.

The principal development challenge is to meet the needs and aspirations of an expanding developing world population. The most basic of all needs is for a livelihood: that is, employment. Between 1985 and 2000 the labor force in developing countries will increase by nearly 900 million, and new livelihood opportunities will have to be generated for 60 million persons every year.[1] . . .

More food is required not merely to feed more people but to attack undernourishment. . . . Though the focus at present is necessarily on staple foods, the projections given above also highlight the need for a high rate of growth of protein availability. In Africa, the task is particularly challenging given the recent declining per capita food production and the current constraints on growth. In Asia and Latin America, the required growth rates in calorie and protein consumption seem to be more readily attainable. But increased food production should not be based on ecologically unsound production policies and compromise long-term prospects for food security.

Energy is another essential human need, one that cannot be universally met unless energy consumption patterns change. The most urgent problem is the requirements of poor Third World households, which depend mainly on fuelwood. By the turn of the century, 3 billion people may live in areas where wood is cut faster than it grows or where fuelwood is extremely scarce.[2] Corrective action would both reduce the drudgery of collecting wood over long distances and preserve the ecological base. . . .

The linked basic needs of housing, water supply, sanitation, and health care are also environmentally important. Deficiencies in these areas are often visible manifestations of environmental stress. In the Third World, the failure to meet these key needs is one of the major causes of many communicable diseases such as malaria, gastrointestinal infestations, cholera, and typhoid. . . .

Ensuring a Sustainable Level of Population

The sustainability of development is intimately linked to the dynamics of population growth. The issue, however, is not simply one of global population size. A child born in a country where levels of material and energy use are high places a greater burden on the Earth's resources than a child born in a poorer country. . . .

In industrial countries, the overall rate of population growth is under 1 percent, and several countries have reached or are approaching zero population growth. The total population of the industrialized world could increase from its current 1.2 billion to about 1.4 billion in the year 2025.[3]

The greater part of global population increase will take place in developing countries, where the 1985 population of 3.7 billion may increase to 6.8 billion by 2025.[4] The Third World does not have the option of migration to "new" lands, and the time available for adjustment is much less than industrial countries had. Hence the challenge now is to quickly lower population growth rates, especially in regions such as Africa, where these rates are increasing.

Birth rates declined in industrial countries largely because of economic and social development. Rising levels of income and urbanization and the changing role of women all played important roles. Similar processes are now at work in developing countries. These should be recognized and encouraged. Population policies should be integrated with other economic and social development programs—female education, health care, and the expansion of the livelihood base of the poor. . . .

Developing-country cities are growing much faster than the capacity of authorities to cope. Shortages of housing, water, sanitation, and mass transit are widespread. A growing proportion of city-dwellers live in slums and shanty-towns, many of them exposed to air and water pollution and to industrial and natural hazards. Further deterioration is likely, given that most urban growth will take place in the largest cities. Thus more manageable cities may be the principal gain from slower rates of population growth. . . .

Conserving and Enhancing the Resource Base

. . . Pressure on resources increases when people lack alternatives. Development policies must widen people's options for earning a sustainable livelihood, particularly for resource-poor households and in areas under ecological stress. . . .

The conservation of agricultural resources is an urgent task because in many parts of the world cultivation has already been extended to marginal lands, and fishery and forestry resources have been overexploited. These resources must be conserved and enhanced to meet the needs of growing populations. Land use in agriculture and forestry should be based on a scientific assessment of land capacity, and the annual depletion of topsoil, fish stock, or forest resources must not exceed the rate of regeneration.

The pressures on agricultural land from crop and livestock production can be partly relieved by increasing productivity. But shortsighted, short-term improvements in productivity can create different forms of ecological stress, such as the loss of genetic diversity in standing crops, salinization and alkalization of irrigated lands, nitrate pollution of groundwater, and pesticide residues in food. Ecologically more benign alternatives are available. Future increases in productivity, in both developed and developing countries, should be based on the better-controlled application of water and agrochemicals, as well as on more extensive use of organic manures and nonchemical means of pest control. These alternatives can be promoted only by an agricultural policy based on ecological realities. . . .

The ultimate limits to global development are perhaps determined by the availability of energy resources and by the biosphere's capacity to absorb the by-products of energy use.[5] These energy limits may be approached far sooner than the limits imposed by other material resources. First, there are the supply problems: the depletion of oil reserves, the high cost and environmental impact of coal mining, and the hazards of nuclear technology. Second, there are emission problems, most notably acid pollution and carbon dioxide buildup leading to global warming.

Some of these problems can be met by increased use of renewable energy sources. But the exploitation of renewable sources such as fuelwood and hydropower also entails ecological problems. Hence sustainability requires a clear focus on conserving and efficiently using energy.

Industrialized countries must recognize that their energy consumption is polluting the biosphere and eating into scarce fossil fuel supplies. Recent improvements in energy efficiency and a shift towards less energy-intensive sectors have helped limit consumption. But the process must be accelerated to reduce per capita consumption and encourage a shift to nonpolluting sources and technologies. The simple duplication in the developing world of industrial countries' energy use patterns is neither feasible nor desirable. . . .

The prevention and reduction of air and water pollution will remain a critical task of resource conservation. Air and water quality come under pressure from such activities as fertilizer and pesticide use, urban sewage, fossil fuel burning, the use of certain chemicals, and various other industrial activities. Each of these is expected to increase the pollution load on the biosphere substantially, particularly in developing countries. Cleaning up after the event is an expensive solution. Hence all countries need to anticipate and prevent these pollution problems. . . .

Reorienting Technology and Managing Risk

The fulfillment of all these tasks will require the reorientation of technology—the key link between humans and nature. First, the capacity for technological innovation needs to be greatly enhanced in developing countries. . . . Second, the orientation of technology development must be changed to pay greater attention to environmental factors.

The technologies of industrial countries are not always suited or easily adaptable to the socioeconomic and environmental conditions of developing countries. To compound the problem, the bulk of world research and development addresses few of the pressing issues facing these countries. . . . Not enough is being done to adapt recent innovations in materials technology, energy conservation, information technology, and biotechnology to the needs of developing countries. . . .

In all countries, the processes of generating alternative technologies, upgrading traditional ones, and selecting and adapting imported technologies should be informed by environmental resource concerns. Most technological research by commercial organizations is devoted to product and process innovations that have market value. Technologies are needed that produce "social goods," such as improved air quality or increased product life, or that resolve problems normally outside the cost calculus of individual enterprises, such as the external costs of pollution or waste disposal.

The role of public policy is to ensure, through incentives and disincentives, that commercial organizations find it worthwhile to take fuller account of environmental factors in the technologies they develop. . . .

Merging Environment and Economics in Decision Making

The common theme throughout this strategy for sustainable development is the need to integrate economic and ecological considerations in decision making.

They are, after all, integrated in the workings of the real world. This will require a change in attitudes and objectives and in institutional arrangements at every level.

Economic and ecological concerns are not necessarily in opposition. For example, policies that conserve the quality of agricultural land and protect forests improve the long-term prospects for agricultural development. . . . But the compatibility of environmental and economic objectives is often lost in the pursuit of individual or group gains, with little regard for the impacts on others, with a blind faith in science's ability to find solutions, and in ignorance of the distant consequences of today's decisions. Institutional rigidities add to this myopia. . . .

Intersectoral connections create patterns of economic and ecological interdependence rarely reflected in the ways in which policy is made. Sectoral organizations tend to pursue sectoral objectives and to treat their impacts on other sectors as side effects, taken into account only if compelled to do so. . . . Many of the environment and development problems that confront us have their roots in this sectoral fragmentation of responsibility. Sustainable development requires that such fragmentation be overcome.

Sustainability requires the enforcement of wider responsibilities for the impacts of decisions. This requires changes in the legal and institutional frameworks that will enforce the common interest. Some necessary changes in the legal framework start from the proposition that an environment adequate for health and well-being is essential for all human beings—including future generations. . . .

The law alone cannot enforce the common interest. It principally needs community knowledge and support, which entails greater public participation in the decisions that affect the environment. This is best secured by decentralizing the management of resources upon which local communities depend, and giving these communities an effective say over the use of these resources. . . .

Changes are also required in the attitudes and procedures of both public and private-sector enterprises. Moreover, environmental regulation must move beyond the usual menu of safety regulations, zoning laws, and pollution control enactments; environmental objectives must be built into taxation, prior approval procedures for investment and technology choice, foreign trade incentives, and all components of development policy.

The integration of economic and ecological factors into the law and into decisionmaking systems within countries has to be matched at the international level. The growth in fuel and material use dictates that direct physical linkages between ecosystems of different countries will increase. Economic interactions through trade, finance, investment, and travel will also grow and heighten economic and ecological interdependence. Hence in the future, even more so than now, sustainable development requires the unification of economics and ecology in international relations. . . .

Conclusion

In its broadest sense, the strategy for sustainable development aims to promote harmony among human beings and between humanity and nature. In the specific context of the development and environment crises of the 1980s, which current national and international political and economic institutions have not and perhaps cannot overcome, the pursuit of sustainable development requires:

- a political system that secures effective citizen participation in decision making,
- an economic system that is able to generate surpluses and technical knowledge on a self-reliant and sustained basis,
- a social system that provides for solutions for the tensions arising from disharmonious development,
- a production system that respects the obligation to preserve the ecological base for development,
- a technological system that can search continuously for new solutions,
- an international system that fosters sustainable patterns of trade and finance, and
- an administrative system that is flexible and has the capacity for self-correction.

These requirements are more in the nature of goals that should underlie national and international action on development. What matters is the sincerity with which these goals are pursued and the effectiveness with which departures from them are corrected.

Notes

1. Based on data from World Bank, *World Development Report 1984* (New York: Oxford University Press, 1984).

2. FAO, *Fuelwood Supplies in the Developing Countries*, Forestry Paper No. 42 (Rome: FAO, 1983).

3. Department of International Economic and Social Affairs, *World Population Prospects and Projections as Assessed in 1984* (New York: United Nations, 1986).

4. Ibid.

5. W. Häfele and W. Sassin, "Resources and Endowments, An Outline of Future Energy Systems," in P. W. Hemily and M. N. Ozdas (eds.), *Science and Future Choice* (Oxford: Clarendon Press, 1979).

17

WHOSE COMMON FUTURE?

LARRY LOHMANN[*]

Never underestimate the ability of modern elites to work out ways of coming through a crisis with their power intact.

From the days of the American populists through the Depression, postwar reconstruction, the end of colonialism and the age of "development," our contemporary leaders and their institutions have sought to turn pressures for change to their advantage. The New Deal, the Marshall Plan, Bretton Woods, multilateral lending—all in their turn have taken challenges to the system and transformed them into ways of defusing popular initiatives and developing the economic and political domains of the powerful.

Now comes the global environmental crisis. Once again those in high places are making solemn noises about "grave threats to our common security and the very survival of our planet." Once again their proposed solutions leave the main causes of the trouble untouched. As ordinary people try to reclaim local lands, forests and waters from the depredations of business and the state, and work to build democratic movements to preserve the planet's health, those in power continue to occupy themselves with damage control and the containment of threats to the way power is currently distributed and held. The difference is important to keep in mind when listening to the calls to arms from the new statesmen and women of "environmentalism."

---

[*] This article first appeared in the May/June 1990 issue of *The Ecologist* Volume 20, No. 3 www.theecologist.org. Reprinted with permission.

Political Management of the Crisis

Two of the most prominent of these, former Norwegian Prime Minister Gro Harlem Brundtland and Canadian businessman Maurice Strong, . . . Secretary-General of the 1992 United Nations Conference on Environment and Development (UNCED), were in Vancouver in March [1990] to reiterate the message that we all share a "common future" in environmental preservation and "sustainable development." Their speeches at the "Globe 90" conference and "green" trade fair gave valuable clues about how the more progressive global elites are organizing themselves for the political management of the environment crisis.

The first instinct of those in high places when faced with a problem is to avoid analyzing its causes if doing so would put the current power structure in an unfavorable light. In Vancouver, Brundtland averted her gaze from the destruction brought about through economic growth, technology transfer and capital flows from North to South and vice versa, and instead rounded up the usual suspects of "poverty," "population growth" and "underdevelopment," without exploring the origins of any of them. She spoke of global warming, a declining resource base, pollution, overexploitation of resources and a "crushing debt burden" for the South, but omitted mentioning who or what might be responsible. Environmental problems, she implied, were mainly to be found in the South. Admittedly the North had made some mistakes, she said, but luckily it knows the answers now and can prevent the South from making the same errors as it toddles along behind the North on the path to sustainable development.

Whose Security?

The stress of a crisis also tends to drive those in power to the use of vague code words that can rally other members of the elite. In Vancouver the word was "security." Brundtland and Strong warned of the "new (environmental) threats to our security" and dwelt on the ideas of a "global concept of security," a "safe future" and a new "security alliance" with an obsessiveness worthy of Richard Nixon.

What was all this talk of "security" about? In the rural societies where most of the world's people live, security generally means land, family, village and freedom from outside interference. Had the ex–Prime Minister of Norway and the Chairman of Strovest Holdings, Inc. suddenly become land reform activists and virulent opponents of the development projects and market economy expansion which uproot villagers from their farms, communities and livelihoods? Or were they perhaps hinting at another kind of security, the security that First World privilege wants against the economic and political chaos that would follow environmental collapse? In the atmosphere of Globe 90, where everyone was constantly assured that all humanity had "common security" interests, it was not

always easy to keep in mind the distinction between the first, which entails devo-
lution of power, and the second, which requires the reverse.

A third instinct of crisis managers in high places is to seek the "solution" that
requires the least change to the existing power structure. Here Brundtland and
Strong, as befits two contenders for the UN Secretary-Generalship, repeated a formula to be found partly in UN General Assembly documents relating to UNCED.
This is:

1. reverse the financial flows currently coursing from South to North, using
   debt relief, new lending and new infusions of aid possibly augmented by
   taxes on fossil fuels and transfers from military budgets;
2. transfer technology, particularly "green" technology, from North to
   South; and
3. boost economic growth, particularly in the South.

This scheme has obvious attractions for the world's powerful. For one thing, a re-
sumption of net North–South capital flows would provide a bonanza for Northern
export industries. Funds from the West and Japan would be sent on a quick round
trip through a few institutions in other parts of the world before being returned,
somewhat depleted by payoffs to elites along the way, to the coffers of Northern
firms. Third World income freed up by debt relief would add immensely to corporate profits. Buoyed up by a fresh flow of funds, Southern leaders would become
more receptive to the advice of Northern-dominated institutions and more dependent on Northern technology and aid. Injections of remedial technology, in addition, might well provide an incentive for the South to follow the strategy of dealing
with the effects rather than the causes of environmental degradation. That would
mean more money for both polluting and pollution-correcting industries.

The scheme also shores up the present industrial and financial system by suggesting that the solution to the environmental crisis lies within that system. . . . It
implies that environmental issues are technological and financial and not matters
of social equity and distribution of power—discussion of which would call much
of the system into question. The scheme invokes and reinforces the superstitions
that it is lack of capital that leads to environmental crisis; that capital flows are going to "expand the resource base," replace soil fertility and restore water tables and
tropical forests lost to commercial exploitation; that poverty will be somehow relieved rather than exacerbated by economic growth; and that capital flows "naturally" in large quantities from North to South.[1]

Weighing Up the Costs

Admittedly, the UNCED plan has costs for those in power. Bankers may not be
overjoyed at the prospect of debt relief, but since the alternatives seem to be either

continued insupportable and destabilizing South–North net financial transfers or the perpetuation of the process of servicing Third World debts with new loans, they may agree in the end. Northern countries will also have to spend massively on "green" technology now in order to be in a position to put pressure on the South to do the same later.[2] But this is not necessarily a bad thing for industry, which can "clean up" the mess it itself makes around the world, perhaps in the process creating new problems which will require further business solutions. As one of Globe 90's organizers put it, "a solution to most environmental issues is a business opportunity."[3] Another obstacle to the UNCED scheme is that it may stir resistance among its Southern "beneficiaries." . . .

Perhaps a bigger problem for the UNCED scheme is that it does not actually address the environmental crisis in either North or South. By tailoring solutions not to the problems but to the interests of those who created them, the plan is in fact likely to make things worse. . . . The UNCED plan will reinforce Southern dependence on environmentally destructive models of development imposed by the North and increase the power of Southern elites over their societies. It will promote technology most of which, like the tree-planting machine on display at Globe 90, has only a spurious claim to being "green" and which will have to be paid for eventually by cashing in resources. It does not examine the effects of importing large amounts of capital into the South and endorses the continuing devastating economization of the natural and social heritage of both North and South. It is, however, probably as far as elites can go at present without challenging their own position. As for the future, there is always the hope that, as the brochure of one Japanese organization present at Globe 90 put it, the problems of global warming, ozone depletion, acid rain, desertification and tropical forest destruction can someday be solved "through technological innovations."[4]

The "New" Alliance

A fourth tendency among elite crisis managers is to identify the executors of the solution with the existing power structure. . . .

The technical fixes of the UNCED agenda are to be promoted and implemented by a "new global partnership" or environmental quadruple alliance consisting of industry, government, scientists and nongovernmental organizations—"the most important security alliance we have ever entered into on this planet" according to Strong. . . .

Seasoned observers . . . may wonder what is supposed to distinguish the new environmental alliance from the familiar sort of elite ententes that helped land the world in its current environmental mess—the old-boy networks and clubs typified by the military-industrial complex, the World Bank's web of clients, consultants and contractors, the Trilateral Commission and so on.

Co-opting the NGOs

The answer is nongovernmental organizations (NGOs). . . . Why the interest in
NGOs? One reason is that they might be used to push business and government
in a slightly less destructive direction. Another is that official or corporate environmental initiatives need credibility. Establishment political strategists have not
failed to note the growing role of NGOs in recent popular movements from Latin
America to South and Southeast Asia and Eastern and Central Europe. . . . "New
alliance" leaders are thus courting and manipulating NGOs, particularly tame
NGO umbrella groups, groups with establishment links and groups with jet-set
ambitions, in the hope of being able to use their names to say that UNCED initiatives have the backing of environmentalists, youth, trade unions, women's groups,
the socially concerned and "all the nations and peoples of the world."

These maneuvers, however, cannot conceal the fact that grassroots NGO
"participation" in UNCED and other "new alliance" activities, to say nothing
of the participation of ordinary people, is a fraud. . . . It is governments who decide who is allowed to say what, just as it is governments who will be signing
agreements. . . . NGOs are expected to carry governments' message to the people
and help them stay in power.[5]

A Common Interest?

Outside official meetings, of course, it is business whose voice will inevitably
carry above that of all others in the "new alliance." If Globe 90 is any indication,
it is not likely to be a voice urging environmental and political sanity. Nor are
grassroots-oriented environmental activists likely to be excited about joining a
coalition carrying the industry agenda. . . .

Many environmentalists, nevertheless, will feel that joining the "new global alliance" can do no harm if it presents an opportunity for nudging business and
government in a more "green" direction. Such a conclusion is questionable. It is
one thing to pressure business and government into changing their ways with all
the means at one's disposal. It is quite another to pledge allegiance in advance to a
new elite coalition with a predetermined or unknown agenda which one will have
little power to change.

Any alliance which tells us that we *must* seek consensus, that no opposition is to
be brooked to Brundtland as Our Common Leader or that there is a perfect potential community of interest between, say, a UN bureaucrat and a Sri Lankan
subsistence fisherman is one that deserves suspicion at the outset. Consensus-
seeking is neither good nor necessary in itself—it may, after all, function merely
to conceal exploitation—but only when it is agreed by all parties after full discussion to be possible and fruitful.

This is not to denigrate the ambitious professionals associated with the UNCED, but merely to state a fact. To seek genuine solutions it is necessary to accept, respect and explore differences, to face causes, and to understand the workings of power. It may well be that parties with wildly divergent interests can come to agreements on the crisis confronting the planet. Come the millennium, we may all even be able to form one grand coalition. But until then, it is best to remember the lesson of history: that no matter how warmly it seems to have embraced the slogans of the rebels, the Empire always strikes back.

Notes

1. Payer, C., "Causes of the Debt Crisis," in B. Onimode (ed.), *The IMF, the World Bank and African Debt: The Social and Political Impact*, Zed, London, 1989, pp. 7–16.

2. "Action for Whose Common Future?" *Solidarity for Equality, Ecology and Development Newsletter* 1, 1989, Torggt. 34, N–1083 Oslo 1, Norway, pp. 6–7.

3. Wiebe, J. D., Vice-President, Globe 90, Executive Vice-President, Asia Pacific Foundation, in *Globe 90 Official Buyers' Guide and Trade Fair Directory*, p. 13.

4. Global Industrial and Social Progress Research Institute brochure, p. 3.

5. United Nations General Assembly, A/CONF 151/PC/2, 23 February 1990, p. 8.

18

SUSTAINABLE DEVELOPMENT: A CRITICAL REVIEW

SHARACHCHANDRA M. LÉLÉ*

Introduction

The last few years have seen a dramatic transformation in the environment-development debate. The question being asked is no longer "Do development and environmental concerns contradict each other?" but "How can sustainable development be achieved?" All of a sudden the phrase Sustainable Development (SD) has become pervasive. . . . It appears to have gained the broad-based support that earlier development concepts such as "ecodevelopment" lacked, and is poised to become the developmental paradigm of the 1990s.

But murmurs of disenchantment are also being heard. "What *is* SD?" is being asked increasingly frequently without, however, clear answers forthcoming. SD is in real danger of becoming a cliché like appropriate technology—a fashionable phrase that everyone pays homage to but nobody cares to define. . . . Agencies such as the World Bank, the Asian Development Bank and the Organization for Economic Cooperation and Development have been quick to adopt the new rhetoric. The absence of a clear theoretical and analytical framework, however, makes it difficult to determine whether the new policies will indeed foster an environmentally sound and socially meaningful form of development. . . .

---

*   Reprinted from *World Development* 19/6, Sharachchandra M. Lélé, "Sustainable Development: A Critical Review," pp. 607-621, Copyright 1991, with permission from Elsevier.

The persuasive power of SD (and hence the political strength of the SD movement) stems from the underlying claim that new insights into physical and social phenomena force one to concur with the operational conclusions of the SD platform almost regardless of one's fundamental ethical persuasions and priorities. I argue that while these new insights are important, the argument is not inexorable, and that the issues are more complex than is made out to be. Hence . . . many of the policy prescriptions being suggested in the name of SD stem from subjective (rather than consensual) ideas about goals and means, and worse, are often inadequate and even counterproductive. . . .

Interpreting Sustainable Development

The manner in which the phrase "sustainable development" is used and interpreted varies so much that while O'Riordan (1985) called SD a "contradiction in terms," Redclift suggests that it may be just "another development truism" (Redclift, 1987, p. 1). These interpretational problems, though ultimately conceptual, have some semantic roots. Most people use the phrase "sustainable development" interchangeably with "ecologically sustainable or environmentally sound development" (Tolba, 1984a). This interpretation is characterized by: (a) "sustainability" being understood as "ecological sustainability"; and (b) a conceptualization of SD as a process of change that has (ecological) sustainability added to its list of objectives.

In contrast, sustainable development is sometimes interpreted as "sustained growth," "sustained change" or simply "successful" development. Let us examine how these latter interpretations originate and why they are less useful than the former one. . . .

Contradictions and Trivialities

Taken literally, sustainable development would simply mean "development that can be continued—either indefinitely or for the implicit time period of concern." But what is development? Theorists and practitioners have both been grappling with the word and the concept for at least the past four decades. . . . Some equate development with GNP growth, others include any number of socially desirable phenomena in their conceptualization. The point to be noted is that development is *a process of directed change*. Definitions of development thus embody both (a) the objectives of this process, and (b) the means of achieving these objectives.

Unfortunately, a distinction between objectives and means is often not made in the development rhetoric. This has led to "sustainable development" frequently being interpreted as simply a process of change that can be continued forever. . . . This interpretation is either impossible or trivial. When development is taken to be synonymous with growth in material consumption—which it often is even today—SD would be "sustaining the growth in material consumption" (presumably indefinitely). But such an idea contradicts the general recognition that "*ultimate* limits [to usable resources] exist"[1] (WCED, p. 45, emphasis added). At best, it could be argued that growth in the per capita consumption of certain basic goods is necessary in certain regions of the world in the short term. To use "sustainable development" synonymously with "sustain[ing] growth performance" (Idachaba, 1987) or to cite the high rates of growth in agricultural production in South Asia as an example of SD is therefore a misleading usage, or at best a short-term and localized notion that goes against the long-term global perspective of SD.

One could finesse this contradiction by conceptualizing development as simply a process of socioeconomic change. But one cannot carry on a meaningful discussion unless one states what the objectives of such change are and why one should worry about continuing the process of change indefinitely. . . .

Sustainability

. . . The concept of sustainability originated in the context of renewable resources such as forests or fisheries, and has subsequently been adopted as a broad slogan by the environmental movement. Most proponents of sustainability therefore take it to mean "the existence of the ecological conditions necessary to support human life at a specified level of well-being through future generations," what I call *ecological sustainability*. . . .

Since ecological sustainability emphasizes the constraints and opportunities that nature presents to human activities, ecologists and physical scientists frequently dominate its discussion. But what they actually focus on are the ecological conditions for ecological sustainability—the biophysical "laws" or patterns that determine environmental responses to human activities and humans' ability to use the environment. The major contribution of the environment-development debate is, I believe, the realization that in addition to or in conjunction with these ecological conditions, there are social conditions that influence the ecological sustainability or unsustainability of the people-nature interaction. To give a stylized example, one could say that soil erosion undermining the agricultural basis for human society is a case of ecological (un)sustainability. It could be caused by farming on marginal lands without adequate soil conservation measures—the ecological cause. But the phenomenon of marginalization of peasants may have social roots, which would then be the social causes of ecological unsustainability. . . .

The Concept of Sustainable Development
Evolution of Objectives

The term sustainable development came into prominence in 1980, when the International Union for the Conservation of Nature and Natural Resources (IUCN) presented the World Conservation Strategy (WCS) with "the overall aim of achieving sustainable development through the conservation of living resources" (IUCN, 1980). Critics acknowledged that "By identifying Sustainable Development as the basic goal of society, the WCS was able to make a profound contribution toward reconciling the interests of the development community with those of the environmental movement" (Khosla, 1987). They pointed out, however, that the strategy restricted itself to living resources [and] focused primarily on the necessity of maintaining genetic diversity, habits and ecological processes. . . . It was . . . unable to deal adequately with sensitive or controversial issues—those relating to the international economic and political order, war and armament, population and urbanization (Khosla, 1987). . . .

The United Nations Environment Programme (UNEP) was at the forefront of the effort to articulate and popularize the concept. UNEP's concept of SD was said to encompass

1. help for the very poor, because they are left with no options but to destroy their environment;
2. the idea of self-reliant development, within natural resource constraints;
3. the idea of cost-effective development using nontraditional economic criteria;
4. the great issues of health control [*sic*], appropriate technology, food self-reliance, clean water and shelter for all; and
5. the notion that people-centered initiatives are needed (Tolba, 1984a).

This statement epitomizes the mixing of goals and means, or more precisely, of fundamental objectives and operational ones, that has burdened much of the SD literature. While providing food, water, good health and shelter have traditionally been the fundamental objectives of most development models (including UNEP's), it is not clear whether self-reliance, cost-effectiveness, appropriateness of technology and people-centeredness are additional objectives or the operational requirements for achieving the traditional ones. . . .

In contrast to the aforementioned, the currently popular definition of SD—the one adopted by the World Commission on Environment and Development (WCED)—is quite brief:

Sustainable development is development that meets the needs of the present without compromising the ability of future generations to meet their own needs (WCED, 1987; p. 43).

The constraint of "not compromising the ability of future generations to meet their needs" is (presumably) considered by the Commission to be equivalent to the requirement of some level of ecological and social sustainability.[2]

While the WCED's statement of the fundamental objectives of SD is brief, the Commission is much more elaborate about (what are essentially) the operational objectives of SD. It states that "the critical objectives which follow from the concept of SD" are:

1. reviving growth;
2. changing the quality of growth;
3. meeting essential needs for jobs, food, energy, water, and sanitation;
4. ensuring a sustainable level of population;
5. conserving and enhancing the resource base;
6. reorienting technology and managing risk;
7. merging environment and economics in decision making; and
8. reorienting international economic relations (WCED, 1987, p. 49).

Most organizations and agencies actively promoting the concept of SD subscribe to some or all of these objectives with, however, the notable addition of a ninth operational goal, viz.,

9. making development more participatory.[3]

This formulation can therefore be said to represent the mainstream of SD thinking. This "mainstream" includes international environmental agencies such as UNEP, IUCN and the World Wildlife Fund (WWF), developmental agencies including the World Bank, the US Agency for International Development, the Canadian and Swedish international development agencies, research and dissemination organizations such as the World Resources Institute, the International Institute for Environment and Development, the Worldwatch Institute (1984–88) and activist organizations and groups such as the Global Tomorrow Coalition. . . .

The Premises of SD

The perception in mainstream SD thinking of the environment-society link is based upon the following premises:

1. *Environmental degradation*:
   • Environmental degradation is already affecting millions in the Third World, and is likely to severely reduce human well-being all across the globe within the next few generations.

- Environmental degradation is very often caused by poverty, because the poor have no option but to exploit resources for short-term survival.
- The interlinked nature of most environmental problems is such that environmental degradation ultimately affects everybody, although poorer individuals/nations may suffer more and sooner than richer ones.

2. *Traditional development objectives*:
   - These are: providing basic needs and increasing the productivity of all resources (human, natural and economic) in developing countries, and maintaining the standard of living in the developed countries.
   - These objectives do not necessarily conflict with the objective of ecological sustainability. In fact, achieving sustainable patterns of resource use is necessary for achieving these objectives permanently.
   - It can be shown that, even for individual actors, environmentally sound methods are "profitable" in the long run, and often in the short run too.

3. *Process*:
   - The process of development must be participatory to succeed even in the short run.

Given these premises, the need for a process of development that achieves the traditional objectives, results in ecologically sustainable patterns of resource use and is implemented in a participatory manner is obvious.

Most of the SD literature is devoted to showing that this process is also feasible and can be made attractive to the actors involved. SD has become a bundle of neat fixes: technological changes that make industrial production processes less polluting and less resource intensive and yet more productive and profitable, economic policy changes that incorporate environmental considerations and yet achieve greater economic growth, procedural changes that use local nongovernmental organizations (NGOs) so as to ensure grassroots participation, agriculture that is less harmful, less resource intensive and yet more productive and so on. In short, SD is a "metafix" that will unite everybody from the profit-minded industrialist and risk-minimizing subsistence farmer to the equity-seeking social worker, the pollution-concerned or wildlife-loving First Worlder, the growth-maximizing policy maker, the goal-oriented bureaucrat and therefore, the vote-counting politician.

Weaknesses

The major impact of the SD movement is the rejection of the notion that environmental conservation necessarily constrains development or that development necessarily means environmental pollution—certainly not an insignificant gain. Where the SD movement has faltered is in its inability to develop a set of concepts, criteria and policies that are coherent or consistent—both externally (with physical and social reality) and internally (with each other). The mainstream formulation of SD suffers from significant weaknesses in:

- its characterization of the problems of poverty and environmental degradation;
- its conceptualization of the objectives of development, sustainability and participation; and
- the strategy it has adopted in the face of incomplete knowledge and uncertainty.

Poverty and Environmental Degradation: An Incomplete Characterization

The fundamental premise of mainstream SD thinking is the two-way link between poverty and environmental degradation. . . .

In fact, however, even a cursory examination of the vast amount of research that has been done on the links between social and environmental phenomena suggests that both poverty and environmental degradation have deep and complex causes. . . .

To say that mainstream SD thinking has completely ignored [this complexity] would be unfair. But . . . inadequate technical know-how and managerial capabilities, common property resource management, and pricing and subsidy policies have been the major themes addressed, and the solutions suggested have been essentially techno-economic ones. . . . Deeper sociopolitical changes (such as land reform) or changes in cultural values (such as overconsumption in the North) are either ignored or paid lip service. . . .

Conceptual Weaknesses

Removal of poverty (the traditional developmental objective), sustainability and participation are really the three fundamental objectives of the SD paradigm. Unfortunately, the manner in which these objectives are conceptualized and operationalized leaves much to be desired. On the one hand, economic growth is being adopted as a major operational objective that is consistent with both removal of poverty and sustainability. On the other hand, the concepts of sustainability and participation are poorly articulated, making it difficult to determine whether a particular development project actually promotes a particular form of sustainability, or what kind of participation will lead to what kind of social (and consequently, environmental) outcome.

The Role of Economic Growth. By the mid-1970s, it had seemed that the economic growth and trickle-down theory of development had been firmly rejected, and the "basic needs approach" (Streeten, 1979) had taken root in development circles. Yet economic growth continues to feature in today's debate on SD. In fact, "reviving [economic] growth" heads WCED's list of operational objectives quoted earlier. Two arguments are implicit in this adoption of economic growth as an operational objective. The first, a somewhat defensive one, is that there is no fundamental contradiction between economic growth and sustainability, because growth in economic activity may occur simultaneously with either an improvement or a deterioration in environmental quality. Thus, "governments concerned with long-term sustainability need not seek to limit growth in economic output so long as they stabilize aggregate natural resource consumption" (Goodland and Ledec, 1987). But one could turn this argument around and suggest that if economic growth is not correlated with environmental sustainability, there is no reason to have economic growth as an operational objective of SD.[4]

The second argument in favor of economic growth is more positive. The basic premise of SD is that poverty is largely responsible for environmental degradation. Therefore, removal of poverty (i.e., development) is necessary for environmental sustainability. This, it is argued, implies that economic growth is absolutely necessary for SD. The only thing that needs to be done is to "change the quality of [this] growth" (WCED, 1987, pp. 52–54) to ensure that it does not lead to environmental destruction. In drawing such an inference, however, there is the implicit belief that economic growth is necessary (if not sufficient) for the removal of poverty. But was it not the fact that economic growth per se could not ensure the removal of poverty that led to the adoption of the basic needs approach in the 1970s?

Thus, if economic growth by itself leads to neither environmental sustainability nor removal of poverty, it is clearly a "non-objective" for SD. The converse is a possibility worth exploring, viz., whether successful implementation of policies for poverty removal, long-term employment generation, environmental restoration and rural development will lead to growth in GNP, and, more important, to increases in investment, employment and income generation. This seems more than likely in developing countries, but not so certain in developed ones. In any case, economic growth may be the fallout of SD, but not its prime mover.

Sustainability. The World Conservation Strategy was probably the first attempt to carry the concept of sustainability beyond simple renewable resource systems. It suggested three ecological principles for ecological sustainability (see the nomenclature developed above), viz., "maintenance of essential ecological processes and life-support systems, the preservation of genetic diversity, and the sustainable utilization of species and resources" (IUCN, 1980). This definition, though a useful starting point, is clearly recursive as it invokes "sustainability" in resource use without defining it. Many subsequent attempts to discuss the notion are disturbingly muddled. There is a very real danger of the term becoming a meaningless cliché, unless a concerted effort is made to add precision and content to the discussion. . . .

Any discussion of sustainability must first answer the questions "What is to be sustained? For whom? How long?" The value of the concept (like that of SD), however, lies in its ability to generate an operational consensus between groups with fundamentally different answers to these questions, i.e., those concerned either about the survival of future human generations, or about the survival of wildlife, or human health, or the satisfaction of immediate subsistence needs (food, fuel, fodder) with a low degree of risk. It is therefore vital to identify those aspects of sustainability that do actually cater to such diverse interests, and those that involve trade-offs.

Differentiating between ecological and social sustainability could be a first step toward clarifying some of the discussion. Further, in the case of ecological sustainability, a distinction needs to be made between renewable resources, nonrenewable resources and environmental processes that are crucial to human life, as well as to life at large. The few researchers who have begun to explore the idea of ecological sustainability emphasize its multidimensional and complex nature. . . .

In the rush to derive ecological principles of (ecological) sustainability, we cannot afford to lose sight of the social conditions that determine which of these principles are socially acceptable, and to what extent. Sociologists, eco-Marxists and political ecologists are pointing out the crucial role of socioeconomic structures and institutions in the pattern and extent of environmental degradation globally. Neoclassical economists, whose theories have perhaps had the greatest influence in development policy making in the past and who therefore bear the responsibility for its social and environmental failures, however, have been very slow in modifying their theories and prescriptions. The SD movement will have to formulate a clear agenda for research in what is being called "ecological economics" and press for its adoption by the mainstream of economics in order to ensure the possibility of real changes in policy making.

Social sustainability is a more nebulous concept than ecological sustainability. Brown et al. (1987), in a somewhat techno-economic vein, state that sustainability implies "the existence and operation of an infrastructure (transportation and communication), services (health, education, and culture), and government (agreements, laws, and enforcement)." Tisdell (1988) talks about "the sustainability of political and social structures" and Norgaard (1988) argues for cultural sustainability, which includes value and belief systems. Detailed analyses of the concept, however, seem to be nonexistent.[5] Perhaps achieving desired social situations is itself so difficult that discussing their maintainability is not very useful;

perhaps goals are even more dynamic in a social context than in an ecological one, so that maintainability is not such an important attribute of social institutions/ structures. There is, however, no contradiction between the social and ecological sustainability; rather, they can complement and inform each other.

Participation. A notable feature of . . . some of the earlier SD literature was the emphasis placed on equity and social justice. . . . Subsequently, however, the mainstream appears to have quietly dropped these terms (suggesting at least a de-emphasizing of these objectives), and has instead focused on "local participation."

There are, however, three problems with this shift. First, by using the terms equity, participation and decentralization interchangeably, it is being suggested that participation and decentralization are equivalent, and that they can somehow substitute for equity and social justice. . . .

Second, the manner in which participation is being operationalized shows up the narrow-minded, quick-fix and deceptive approach adopted by the mainstream promoters of SD. . . . Mainstream SD literature blithely assumes and insists that "involvement of local NGOs" in project implementation will ensure project success (Maniates, 1990; he dubs this the "NGOization" of SD).

Third, there is an assumption that participation or at least equity and social justice will necessarily reinforce ecological sustainability. Attempts to test such assumptions rigorously have been rare. But preliminary results seem to suggest that equity in resource access may not lead to sustainable resource use unless new institutions for resource management are carefully built and nurtured. . . . This should not be misconstrued as an argument against the need for equity, but rather as a word of caution against the tendency to believe that social equity automatically ensures environmental sustainability (or vice versa). . . .

Concluding Remarks: Dilemmas and Agendas

The proponents of SD are faced with a dilemma that affects any program of political action and social change: the dilemma between the urge to take strong stands on fundamental concerns and the need to gain wide political acceptance and support. . . . SD is being packaged as the inevitable outcome of objective scientific analysis, virtually an historical necessity, that does not contradict the deep-rooted normative notion of development as economic growth. In other words, SD is an attempt to have one's cake and eat it too.

It may be argued that this is indeed possible, that the things that are wrong and need to be changed are quite obvious, and there are many ways of fixing them without significantly conflicting with either age-old power structures or the modern drive for a higher material standard of living. . . . If, by using the politically correct jargon of economic growth and development and by packaging SD in the manner mentioned above, it were possible to achieve even 50% success in implementing this bundle of "conceptually imprecise" policies, the net reduction achieved in environmental degradation and poverty would be unprecedented.

I believe, however, that (analogous to the arguments in SD) in the long run there is no contradiction between better articulation of the terms, concepts, analytical methods and policy-making principles, and gaining political strength and broad social acceptance—especially at the grassroots. In fact, such clarification and articulation is necessary if SD is to avoid either being dismissed as another development fad or being co-opted by forces opposed to changes in status quo. More specifically, proponents and analysts of SD need to:

A. clearly reject the attempts (and temptation) to focus on economic growth as [a] means to poverty removal and/or environmental sustainability;

B. recognize the internal inconsistencies and inadequacies in the theory and practice of neoclassical economics, particularly as it relates to environmental and distributional issues; in economic analyses, move away from arcane mathematical models toward exploring empirical questions such as limits to the substitution of capital for resources, impacts of different sustainability policies on different economic systems, etc.;

C. accept the existence of structural, technological and cultural causes of poverty and environmental degradation; develop methodologies for estimating relative importance of and interaction between these causes in specific situations; and explore political, institutional and educational solutions to them;

D. understand the multiple dimensions of sustainability, and attempt to develop measures, criteria and principles for them; and

E. explore what patterns and levels of source demand and use would be compatible with different forms or levels of ecological and social sustainability, and with different notions of equity and social justice.

There are, fortunately, some signs that a debate on these lines has now begun.

In a sense, if SD is to be really "sustained" as a development paradigm, two apparently divergent efforts are called for: making SD more precise in its conceptual underpinnings, while allowing more flexibility and diversity of approaches in developing strategies that might lead to a society living in harmony with the environment and with itself.

References

Brown, B. J., M. Hanson, D. Liverman, and R. Merideth, Jr., "Global Sustainability: Toward Definition," *Environmental Management*, Vol. 11, No. 6 (1987), pp. 713–719.

Brown, L. R., *Building a Sustainable Society* (New York: W. W. Norton, 1981).

Chambers, R., *Sustainable Livelihoods: An Opportunity for the World Commission on Environment and Development* (Brighton, UK: Institute of Development Studies, University of Sussex, 1986).

Daly, H., *Economics, Ecology, Ethics: Essays Toward a Steady-State Economy* (San Francisco: W. H. Freeman, 1980).

Goodland, R., and G. Ledec, "Neoclassical Economics and Principles of Sustainable Development," *Ecological Modelling*, Vol. 38 (1987), pp. 19–46.

Idachaba, F. S., "Sustainability Issues in Agriculture Development," in T. J. Davis and I. A. Schirmer (Eds.), *Sustainability Issues in Agricultural Development* (Washington, DC: World Bank, 1987), pp. 18–53.

IUCN, *World Conservation Strategy: Living Resource Conservation for Sustainable Development* (Gland, Switzerland: International Union for Conservation of Nature and Natural Resources, United Nations Environment Program and World Wildlife Fund, 1980).

Khosla, A., "Alternative Strategies in Achieving Sustainable Development," in P. Jacobs and D. A. Munro (Eds.), *Conservation with Equity: Strategies for Sustainable Development* (Cambridge, England: International Union for Conservation of Nature and Natural Resources, 1987), pp. 191–208.

Maniates, M., "Organizing for Rural Energy Development: Local Organizations, Improved Cookstoves, and the State in Gujarat, India," Ph.D. thesis (Berkeley: Energy & Resources Group, University of California, 1990).

Norgaard, R. B., "Sustainable Development: A Coevolutionary View," *Futures*, Vol. 20, No. 6 (1988), pp. 606–620.

———, "Three Dilemmas of Environmental Accounting," *Ecological Economics*, Vol. 1, No. 4 (1989), pp. 303–314.

O'Riordan, T., "Future Directions in Environmental Policy," *Journal of Environment and Planning*, Vol. 17 (1985), pp. 1431–1446.

Peskin, H. M., "National Income Accounts and the Environment," *Natural Resources Journal*, Vol. 21 (1981), pp. 511–537.

Redclift, M., *Sustainable Development: Exploring the Contradictions* (New York: Methuen, 1987).

Repetto, R., *World Enough and Time* (New Haven, CT: Yale University Press, 1986a).

Riddell, R., *Ecodevelopment* (New York: St. Martin's Press, 1981).

Sachs, I., *Environment and Development—A New Rationale for Domestic Policy Formulation and International Cooperation Strategies* (Ottawa: Environment Canada and Canadian International Development Agency, 1977).

Streeten, P., "Basic Needs: Premises and Promises," *Journal of Policy Modelling*, Vol. 1 (1979), pp. 136–146.

Tisdell, C., "Sustainable Development: Differing Perspectives of Ecologists and Economists, and Relevance to LDCs," *World Development*, Vol. 16, No. 3 (1988), pp. 373–384.

Tolba, M. K., "The Premises for Building a Sustainable Society. Address to the World Commission on Environment and Development," October 1984 (Nairobi: United Nations Environment Programme, 1984).

World Commission on Environment and Development, *Our Common Future* (New York: Oxford University Press, 1987).
Worldwatch Institute, *State of the World* (New York: Norton, various years).

Notes

1. More precisely, there are ultimate limits to the stocks of material resources, the flows of energy resources and (in the event of these being circumvented by a major breakthrough in fission/fusion technologies) to the environment's ability to absorb waste energy and other stresses. The limits-to-growth debate, while not conclusive as to specifics, appears to have effectively shifted the burden of proof about the absence of such fundamental limits onto the diehard "technological optimists" who deny the existence of such limits.

2. Of course, "meeting the needs" is a rather ambiguous phrase that may mean anything in practice. Substituting this phrase with "optimizing economic and other societal benefits" (Goodland and Ledec, 1987) or "managing all assets, natural resources and human resources, as well as financial and physical assets for increasing long-term wealth and well-being" (Repetto, 1986a, p. 15) does not define the objectives of development more precisely, although the importance attached to economic benefits or wealth is rather obvious.

3. It is tempting to conclude that this nine-point formulation of SD is identical with the concept of "ecodevelopment"—the original term coined by Maurice Strong of UNEP for environmentally sound development (see Sachs, 1977, and Riddell, 1981). Certainly the differences are less obvious than the similarities. Nevertheless, some changes are significant—such as the dropping of the emphasis on "local self-reliance" and the renewed emphasis on economic growth.

4. Economists have responded by suggesting that currently used indicators of economic growth (GNP in particular) could be modified so as to somehow "build in" this correlation (e.g., Peskin, 1981). To what extent this is possible and whether it will serve more than a marginal purpose are, however, open questions (Norgaard, 1989).

5. Three other "social" usages of sustainability need to be clarified. Sustainable economy (Daly, 1980) and sustainable society (Brown, 1981) are two of these. The focus there, however, is on the patterns and levels of resource use that might be ecologically sustainable while providing the goods and services necessary to maintain human well-being, and the social reorganization that might be required to make this possible. The third usage is Chambers' definition of "sustainable livelihoods" as "a level of wealth and of stocks and flows of food and cash which provide for physical and social well-being and security against becoming poorer" (Chambers, 1986). This can be thought of as a sophisticated version of "basic needs," in that security or risk-minimization is added to the list of needs. It is therefore relevant to any paradigm of development, rather than to SD in particular.

19

EXPANDING
THE CAPITAL STOCK

ISMAIL SERAGELDIN
AND ANDREW STEER[*]

Sustainable development means ensuring that future generations have as many opportunities as we have. Ensuring that this will be possible for the increased populations of the future requires increasing the world's stock of "capital." Four types of capital—which are often strong complements but weak substitutes for one another—need to be recognized.

Sustainable development is about development progress; it certainly is not a doctrine of "no-growth" environmental protectionism. But it is about a particular form of progress. Specifically, sustainable development places the focus on two groups of disenfranchised people: the poor of today and the generations of tomorrow. Its goals are to increase opportunities, improve livelihoods, and reduce the risk of disease or impoverishment for the 1 billion people who live below the line of acute poverty and the 2 billion who live not much above it, for the 1.7 billion who lack even basic sanitation services, the 1.4 billion who breathe badly polluted air, the hundreds of millions of farmers who are threatened by soil depletion or natural disturbance, and the 2.5 billion who yet cannot enjoy the benefits of modern energy.

Meeting the need of productive jobs, education, health, and infrastructure requires gains in productivity, pro-poor targeting of programs, and an expansion of the capital stock. But sustainable development also requires that such progress be sustained; today's progress must not be achieved at the expense of tomorrow's citizens. This is a more difficult concept to grapple with. Here again, it is helpful to

    * Originally published in Ismail Serageldin and Andrew Steer, eds., *Making Development Sustainable: From Concepts to Action* (Washington: World Bank, 1994). © World Bank. Reprinted with permission.

focus on the need to preserve—and given the expected future growth of population, to expand—the capital stock to ensure the option of enjoying at least the same flow of income and services in the future as exists today.

Four Types of Capital

We need to recognize at least four categories of capital: human-made or "fabricated" capital (machines, factories, buildings, and infrastructure), natural capital (as discussed in many works of environmental economics), human capital (investments in education, health, and nutrition of individuals), and social capital (the institutional and cultural bases for a society to function).

Human-made capital. Most economic analysis focuses on the first category, human-made capital, which is also the most measurable. Consistent with our tendency to "treasure what we measure," more efforts have gone into ensuring a rising stock of this type of capital than any other. For this reason discussions of sustainable development rightly tend to focus on the other forms of capital since it is there that remedial analysis and action are needed.

Natural capital. This is the stock of environmentally provided assets (such as soil, subsoil minerals, forests, atmosphere, water, wetlands) that provide a flow of useful renewable and nonrenewable goods and services, which may be marketed or unmarketed. As we have moved from an "empty world" to a "full world," these environmentally provided assets have become increasingly scarce; thus it is appropriate that attention should shift from concern about the adequacy of human-made capital to concern about the adequacy and effective use of natural capital. The services derived from natural capital can be greatly expanded when such capital is cultivated—that is, combined with human-made and human capital, as in agriculture. However, care must be taken that increased yields derived from increasing applications of other factors do not mask an underlying deterioration of the basic natural capital stock. There is growing evidence that this may be happening in many parts of the world, for example, in arable agriculture and forestry, where continued increments of complementary inputs are ensuring ever-increasing yields while vital ecological and physical services are being eroded. Substitution of nonnatural capital for natural capital is possible in the short to medium term but eventually is limited. Thresholds can be crossed, after which yields will decline, often sharply, regardless of how many other inputs are supplied. Deepening our understanding of sustainability in such situations of cultivated natural capital is a high priority.

Human capital. In the past three decades very considerable progress has been made in recognizing the importance of human capital formation; investment in people is now seen to be a very high return investment, especially in developing societies. The entire mainstream paradigm of development has been expanded to include investment in human resources as an essential, possibly the most essential, ingredient of development strategy.[1]

Investments in health and education and nutrition are increasingly central parts of national investment strategies. Nevertheless, we still have difficulties, methodologically, to define the monetary value of such investments, even if ingenious proxies, such as the discounted differential income stream, are used. However, even the most conservative measures in such proxies lead to an overwhelming positive value to such investments.

Less clear is the link between such investments and the shifting economic realities of an aging population profile in the industrialized countries and the persistence of unemployment and underemployment in many societies, both industrialized and developing. The negative and corrosive impacts of such phenomena on the social fabric and well-being of society as a whole, not only the individuals concerned, deserve more research and policy attention.

Social capital. The last observation leads directly to the fourth form of capital. Without a degree of common identification with the forms of governance and of cultural expression and social behavior that make a society more than the sum of a collection of individuals, it is impossible to imagine a functioning social or economic order. The myriad institutions that we take for granted as essential premises of a functioning society must be grounded in a common sense of belonging by its members, and the institutions must reflect a sense of legitimacy in their mediation of conflicts and competing claims. In short, if that social capital is inadequate, the resulting failures make it impossible to talk of either economic growth, environmental sustainability, or human well-being. Examples are all too painfully evident—from Somalia to Yugoslavia to Rwanda.

But what constitutes this social capital? It is a difficult question, and the definition is clearly different from and broader than that of individual human capital. It is based on inclusion, participation, and the promotion of an enabling environment. Yet it is more. The most ambitious work to date on this subject has been the effort to deal empirically with the link between good governance and development. This requires efforts at definition and measurement that face formidable methodological obstacles, but, happily, headway is being made.

In a landmark study presented in *Making Democracy Work: Civic Traditions in Modern Italy*, Professor Robert D. Putnam of Harvard University and colleagues have made a convincing case that the existence of civic community is not only the precursor and guarantor of good governance but also the key to sustained socioeconomic development.[2]

Strong civic community is defined as a preponderance of voluntary horizontal associations, in contrast to hierarchical vertical associations, and the density of these voluntary horizontal institutions throughout the society. The Putnam study found a matrix of voluntary horizontal associations in prosperous, rapidly developing northern Italy while the less developed, less effective south of Italy is characterized by autocratic vertical institutions.

But which is the cause and which is effect? Does northern Italy have a dense network of horizontal institutions (choral societies, soccer clubs, parent-teacher associations) because it is rich and can afford them? Or is it rich because it has good, responsive government nurtured by long-standing citizen involvement in many such voluntary institutions? The evidence suggests the latter. The twenty-year study documents a strong causal link between civic traditions and the effectiveness of governments to promote sustained socioeconomic development. The Italian case has potentially vital relevance for a deeper understanding of how to promote environmentally sustainable development. Questions remain as to how to measure social capital, and as to whether and how it is possible to "invest" in such capital. Similarly, the causal impacts—for good or bad—of economic development on civil society still are not known. These areas of research need to be addressed.

Sustainability and the Capital Stock

How does the above view of capital stock enlighten our understanding of sustainability? It clearly enables us to set aside the simplistic view that sustainability requires leaving to the next generation exactly the same amount of composition of natural capital as we found ourselves, and to substitute a more promising concept of giving future generations the same, if not more, opportunities than we found ourselves. In other words, the stock of capital that we leave them, defined to include all four forms of capital, should be the same if not larger than what we found ourselves. This new paradigm immediately opens the door for substituting one form of capital for another. Arguably, it is the most worthwhile to reduce some natural capital, for example, reducing the amount of oil in the ground, to invest in increasing human capital, for example, educating girls. The question then becomes, in the language of development economists, of the degree to which we can

- measure each kind of capital;
- define the production function, in terms of the degree of substitutability and complementarity between the different kinds of capital, and how these may change in a dynamic context;

- define (in the absence of a common numeric) an "exchange rate" for the different kinds of capital, accepting that it, too, may be dynamic;
- define sustainability in terms of a context of thresholds within which the more efficient (highest return) activities could be selected, in such a way that individual investments and entire strategies could be meaningfully evaluated.

Such an approach ultimately may be comprehensive and rigorous, but it is a long way off. A good way to think about proceeding is in a series of short steps. We have already made great strides in incorporating human capital into conventional economic analysis, and we are starting to incorporate various aspects of natural capital. This is where we should invest our primary efforts now, significantly improving our understanding of the interlinkages between these three kinds of capital. Social capital will take longer to elaborate, and in the meantime can be left to the political processes in each country to arbitrate.

This brings us to the definition of sustainability in terms of the maintenance of these four types of capital while producing an increasing stream of benefits to individuals and society as a whole.

Sustainability has several levels—weak, sensible, strong, and absurdly strong—depending on how strictly one elects to hew to the concept of maintenance or nondeclining capital.[3]

Weak sustainability is maintaining total capital intact without regard to the composition of that capital among the four different kinds of capital. This would imply that the different kinds of capital are substitutes, at least within the boundaries of current levels of economic activity and resource endowment.

Sensible sustainability would require that in addition to maintaining the total level of capital intact, some concern should be given to the composition of that capital (among natural, human-made, human, and social). Thus, oil may be depleted so long as the receipts are invested in other capital, for example, human capital development, elsewhere, but, in addition, efforts should be made to define critical levels of each type of capital, beyond which concerns about substitutability could arise. These levels should be monitored to ensure that patterns of development do not promote a decimation of one kind of capital, regardless of what is being accumulated in other forms of capital. This degree of sustainability still assumes that human-made and natural capital are to a large extent substitutable but recognizes that they are also complementary. The full functioning of the system requires at least a mix of the different kinds of capital. Since we do not know exactly where the boundaries of these critical limits for each type of capital lie, it behooves the sensible person to err on the side of caution in depleting resources (especially natural capital) at too fast a rate.

Strong sustainability requires maintaining different subcomponents of capital intact separately. Thus, for natural capital, loss of forest in one area should be replaced by new forest of a similar type elsewhere, and receipts from depleting oil should be invested in sustainable energy production. This assumes that natural and man-made capital are not really substitutes but complements in most production functions and that even within capital types, there is limited substitutability. Thus, a sawmill (human-made capital) is worthless without the complementary natural capital of a forest.

Absurdly strong sustainability would never deplete anything. Nonrenewable resources—absurdly—could not be used at all; for renewables, only net annual growth rates could be harvested, in the form of the overmature portion of the stock.

Pragmatism has to be our abiding concern in both the development of new measurements and methodologies and in the pursuit of policies and investments. Operationally, this translates into encouraging the growth of natural capital by reducing our level of current exploitation; by investing in projects to relieve pressure on natural capital stocks by expanding cultivated natural capital, such as tree plantations to relieve pressure on natural forests; and by increasing investment in human resources, particularly of the poor who are both the victims and the unwitting agents of economic degradation in many of the poorest societies on earth.

Methodologically, it is better to follow the wise advice of Nobel laureate Robert Solow, who advocated a series of imperfect steps to improve our current work rather than an interminable debate about the "perfect" formulation.[4] With this approach must come a major effort at improving our databases for the different kinds of capital, especially the physical stocks and flows of natural capital, and the interaction of these into coherent views of ecosystem integrity and resilience at the regional as well as the global level.

It is a tall order, and it will be a long journey before the concept of sustainability sketched here is operational in a meaningful sense. But the longest journey starts with a single step, and on this journey many steps have already been taken.

Notes

1. See World Bank, *World Development Report 1991: The Challenge of Development* (New York: Oxford University Press, 1991).

2. Robert D. Putnam (with Robert Leonardi and Raffaella Y. Nanetti), *Making Democracy Work: Civic Traditions in Modern Italy* (Princeton: Princeton University Press, 1993).

3. Ismail Serageldin, Herman Daly, and Robert Goodland, "The Concept of Environmental Sustainability," in *Principles of Sustainable Development*, ed. Wouter van Dieren (Amsterdam: Institute for Environment and Systems Analysis, 1994).

4. Robert M. Solow, "An Almost Practical Step Toward Sustainability." 40th Anniversary Lecture (Resources for the Future, Washington, DC, October 1992).

20

SHIFTING THE PAIN: WORLD'S RESOURCES FEED CALIFORNIA'S GROWING APPETITE

TOM KNUDSON*

Half a hemisphere separates the headwaters of the Amazon River and the frostbitten northern latitudes of Canada.

But the two landscapes have one thing in common.

You can see it along a muddy rain-forest road in Ecuador, in the silver glint of a pipeline snaking through the grass. North of Edmonton, Alberta, a different sight catches your eye: an old-growth forest of spruce, pine and aspen shredded by a dusty maze of logging roads.

That oil pipeline and those logging roads are linked, via quiet rivers of commerce, to the largest concentration of consumers in North America, to a culture that proudly protects its own coastline and forests from exploitation while using more gasoline, wood and paper than any other state in America: California.

With 34 million people and the world's fifth-largest economy, California has long consumed more than it produces. But today, its passion for protecting natural resources at home while importing them in record quantities from afar is backfiring on the world's environment.

It is exporting the pain of producing natural resources—polluted water, pipeline accidents, piecemeal forests and human conflicts—to the far corners of the planet, to places out of sight and out of mind. California is the state of denial.

"There is a disconnect going on," said William Libby, a professor emeritus of forestry at the University of California, Berkeley, who lectures and consults on forest issues around the globe.

"We consume like mad. And we preserve like mad."

Since the days of John Muir—the California naturalist whose writings and ramblings helped kindle the conservation movement just over a century ago—concern for the environment has been a cornerstone of California life.

And seldom has conservation touched California so deeply as during the past 10 years. Since 1992, environmental rules have eliminated or sharply reduced logging on 10 million acres of national forest land in the state—an area 13 times larger than Yosemite National Park. In the Mojave and Great Basin deserts, 3.5 million acres were declared wilderness in 1994—an expanse half again the size of Yellowstone National Park.

And while that conservation legacy will enrich Californians—and California ecosystems—for generations to come, its reach also extends far beyond the Golden State.

Libby was one of the first to notice, while on sabbatical in New Zealand in 1992. As the volume of wood cut from California forests dropped due to regulations to protect spotted owls, the demand for logs in New Zealand soared—making loggers there happy.

"Prices were insane," Libby said. "The New Zealanders wanted me to get them a dead spotted owl so they could stuff it, put it in the lobby and genuflect to it."

He soon discovered logging was on the rise in other places, too, and has since published several articles that link preservation of California forests with species extinctions elsewhere.

"We Californians are really not very good conservationists—we're very good preservationists," he said. "Conservation means you use resources well and responsibly. Preservation means you are rich enough to set aside things you want and buy them from someone else."

A half-century ago, California was self-sufficient in wood. Today, the state imports 80 percent of what it uses. Follow some of that wood back to its source and you find yourself in the northern boreal forest, where Canada allows trees to be cut in ways not permitted in California.

On average, nine of every ten acres logged in Canada are clear-cut—the contentious practice of leveling large patches of the forest. And more than two-thirds of Canadian logging takes place in stands that have never been nicked by a chain saw—virgin forests that in California would be regarded as sanctuaries.

"Many Americans believe Canada is this incredible wilderness, but it's not true," said Richard Thomas, an Edmonton consultant and author of a 1998 provincial study critical of logging practices in Alberta. "We are very much like a Third World country when it comes to our resources. We just let other countries have at it."

Six thousand miles south, a wave of development for another resource crucial to California—crude oil—is inflicting similarly serious wounds across Ecuador's

Amazon. Rain forests that were home to kaleidoscopic displays of plant and animal life in the 1970s and '80s now are showcases of pollution and poverty.

Every day, an average of 235,000 barrels of oil is pumped from the region for export to world markets. The largest portion—65,000 to 85,000 barrels a day—is shipped to refineries in Los Angeles and San Francisco.

The discovery of more reserves in the Amazon is setting off a new wave of controversy and threatening the cultural survival of seminomadic rain-forest tribes. Still, the country's new president, Lucio Gutiérrez, assured financiers in New York earlier this year that he supports more drilling because Ecuador is deeply in debt and needs foreign investment.

"The historical challenges for my government are very clear," Gutiérrez said at the time.

California's hunger for the planet's natural resources need not stir up trouble, if a system were in place to prevent it. You can find such a safeguard in the storm-tossed North Pacific, where Canadian fishermen, working under a federal plan that gives them an ownership stake in fish, are harvesting millions of pounds of rockfish every year for California without hurting the environment.

"Everybody is quite conscientious," said Jim Harris, a Canadian trawler. "We've got a fishery that is going to be here for the duration."

The clash of conservation and consumption in California may be large, but it is not unique in this country.

"We're the largest consuming nation basically of everything," said James Bowyer, a professor at the University of Minnesota who specializes in conservation policy and natural resource consumption.

"Yet we find every reason in the world why we shouldn't mine steel, why we shouldn't drill for oil," Bowyer said. "It's ironic because we are transferring the impacts to someplace else. And then we are telling ourselves what we are doing is good for the environment.

"And not only are we transferring those impacts, we are magnifying them by turning to nations that don't have the stringent environmental controls that we do."

No government agency maps the global impact of California consumers. But a small Oakland think tank, Redefining Progress, has assembled estimates of the mountain of resources, from wood to fossil fuel, freshwater to seafood, consumed by 146 nations—and some California counties—a yardstick it calls an "ecological footprint."

The United States, a world leader in the conservation of natural resources, has a larger footprint (24 acres per person) than all nations except the United Arab Emirates (with 25 acres). Do the math and you find America's 291 million people draw upon a 7 billion–acre chunk of the planet—an area roughly three times the size of the United States.

An assessment for Marin County—the pricey, conservation-minded San Francisco suburb—found citizens there eat, drink, spend and drive their way through even more of the planet's natural wealth: 27 acres per person a year—the largest ecological footprint ever calculated.

The group's footprints have attracted attention from scientists and policy-makers around the world. And although some people criticize the methods as imprecise, none denies the basic premise.

"The idea is right," said Libby, the forestry professor.

Last year, Libby found some Californians are not eager to hear about the global consequences of conservation and consumption.

At a conference on Sierra Nevada forest management, held in Nevada City, Libby asked the 250 people attending how many of them lived in houses made of wood.

Almost everyone did. Then he asked how many had houses built with alternatives such as used tires and straw bales. Only two or three people responded.

A few moments later, Libby recalled, he asked, "How many people are comfortable with species going extinct somewhere else because we're not going to cut any wood on the Tahoe National Forest?"

At that point, Libby said, "Somebody in the audience shouted: 'We don't like your question.'"

PART FIVE

FROM ECOLOGICAL CONFLICT TO ENVIRONMENTAL SECURITY?

As seen in the previous section, the concept of sustainability has emerged as a powerful paradigm shaping the interpretations, goals, and behavior of a broad range of actors on the global environmental stage. But the global environmental debate of the past four decades has engaged not only economic issues of welfare, production, and livelihood but also political questions of international conflict, violence, and geopolitics. It is not surprising that paradigms focused on the conflictual dimensions of environmental problems also have emerged.

One attempt to grapple with these intensely political themes is the paradigm of "environmental security." Like sustainability, environmental security offers a potentially powerful but also controversial way to think about the social dimensions of environmental problems. The environmental security paradigm rests on a series of claims: that environmental change is an important source of social conflict; that many societies face graver dangers from environmental change than from traditional military threats; and that security policies must be redefined to take account of these new realities.

The essay by Colin Kahl addresses the connection between environmental change and violent conflict. Scholars concerned with an environment-conflict link initially focused their attention largely on problems of increasing natural resource scarcity. A growing body of research suggested that scarcity of renewable resources—principally water, fish stocks, forests, and fertile land—could contribute to social instability, civil strife, and violent conflict, particularly when coupled with population growth and inequitable division of resources.[1] More recently, scholars have focused on the violence potential of resource abundance, which may create incentives for actors to capture "lootable" resources, to extend the duration of conflict in order to profit from war economies, or to promote distorted patterns of economic development that yield weak and brittle governments.[2] Kahl suggests that both scarcity and abundance may trigger violent conflict, particularly in the context of weak, illegitimate, or predatory political institutions. These mechanisms may be bottom-up grievance-based pathways or top-down conflict entrepreneurs' exploiting real or at times perceived scarcities between groups.

To illustrate the types of linkages that may occur between environmental degradation, access to natural resources, and violent conflict, we include an excerpt from a United Nations Environment

Programme (UNEP) report on Sudan. Beginning with the conflicts of the 1990s surrounding the dissolution of Yugoslavia, UNEP has played an increasing role in evaluating the state of the environment in societies emerging from periods of war. Working in consultation with the Sudanese government and a range of domestic and international civil-society groups, UNEP produced an unprecedentedly detailed look at the state of Sudan's environment, the environmental toll of war, and the ways in which resource issues fit into the country's multiple conflicts. The excerpt reproduced here indicates that, while not the prime trigger of violence, environmental conditions and concerns over natural resource access were very much at the center of both the goals and the strategies of parties to the conflicts that have torn Sudan in recent decades (including but by no means limited to the well-known situation in Darfur). Resource degradation and scarcity sharpened existing tensions between groups; and the resulting conflicts have taken a severe toll on the resources and ecosystems that people require for stable livelihoods. Tellingly, the Sudan case illustrates both the "scarcity" (pressures on rangelands and forests) and "abundance" (competition over petroleum and water resources) mechanisms alluded to by Kahl.

Given such conflict potential, proponents of environmental security have argued that there is an urgent, compelling need to "redefine" the concept of security.[3] Thus, environmental security is more than just an effort to reconceptualize threats or document empirical patterns of environmental degradation and violence. It is also a political agenda aimed at mobilizing the state and society toward a new set of goals and at redirecting resources and energies away from exclusively military concerns. Some proponents argue that only by framing the environmental problematique in security terms can the necessary level of governmental attention and social mobilization be ensured.[4] Others argue that security institutions could contribute directly to environmental protection, given their financial resources, monitoring and intelligence-gathering capabilities, and scientific and technological expertise.[5]

Thus, although the origins of the environmental security paradigm can be traced at least to the early post–World War II period,[6] it is surely no accident that the idea of rethinking security policy in ecological terms flourished in the post–Cold War era. Policymakers, military institutions, and entire societies have begun to reconsider the character of the threats they face. Many proponents of environmental security are driven by the belief that the end of the Cold War opened a window of opportunity for fundamental changes in security policies and a reordering of social priorities.

Among the many controversies surrounding the paradigm of environmental security, two are central. First, is there enough evidence to support the claim that ecological change is, or will be, a major new source of conflict? Although a growing body of research points to specific cases in which environmental change seems to have played a role in promoting or exacerbating social conflict, many questions remain. Why does environmental stress produce such conflict in some cases but not in others? Is it possible that environmental problems are a symptom of conflict-prone social systems rather than a root cause of conflict? Observers who pose these questions are indicating their doubt that environmental change is an important, independent source of conflict. A second set of questions involves the more nebulous concept of security. Are the advantages of linking environmental problems to security concerns worth the risk of militarizing a society's responses to environmental problems?

The essay by Daniel Deudney raises both sets of questions. Deudney is skeptical that environmental change precipitates acute conflict, at least in the form of war; he argues that environmental problems have little in common with the traditional security problem of interstate violence.[7] Deudney is also wary of evoking the powerful concept of security to mobilize society: "For environmentalists to dress their programs in the blood-soaked garments of the war system betrays their core values and creates confusion about the real tasks at hand." Others have voiced stronger criticisms, suggesting that the powerful association between the concept of security and the use of military force creates the danger of turning environmental problems into sources of military tension and conflict.[8] These critics share Deudney's view that the conflictual mind-set and the military tools of security institutions are poorly suited to the global environmental problematique.

The environmental security debate is further complicated by the way in which it intersects the North-South axis in world politics. The focus of ecological conflict research tends to be on the economically less-developed regions of the planet; most analysts emphasize these regions when identifying likely sites of future environmentally induced conflicts. There are many reasons for this focus on the South: its limited financial and technological resources, high population growth rates, preexisting political instability, and day-to-day struggles for survival that engulf large segments of the population.

However, even if it is plausible to claim that the South will be the site of conflicts with significant environmental dimensions, this concern cannot be divorced from the broader pattern of North-South relations. Many Southern governments and activists have viewed the

North's concern for "security" in the South, environmental or other-wise, with skepticism if not outright suspicion. They see the rhetoric of environmental security as an excuse to continue the North's long-standing practice of military and economic intervention, while also providing a way for the North to deny its own overwhelming respon-sibility for the deteriorating state of the planet. In a world where many people feel their security threatened by other people, calls for changes in security policies may seem like a way to break the cycle of violence, suspicion, and zero-sum thinking; but given the purposes that security policies have served in the past, such calls also raise deep suspicions about ulterior motives.

There is also the danger that environment-conflict linkages tell only part of the story. If tensions over environment and natural resources can trigger conflict, may they not also trigger cooperation? If actors recognize the conflict potential, might they not work to enhance ca-pacities for peaceful dispute resolution? Arguably this has been the case with regard to water, a resource around which there are many social tensions—but also many initiatives for cooperation, institution building, and shared resource governance. It would be a mistake to view only the conflictual side of social responses. As Kader Asmal, a South African government official who chaired the World Commis-sion on Dams (WCD—see Chapter 12 by Bissell in this volume), has argued, for all the gloom-and-doom talk from politicians and journal-ists about water scarcity triggering "water wars" in the near future, the historical record around water has overwhelmingly been one of cooperation and negotiation, not conflict and violence:

> With all due respect to my friends, *have* battles been fought over water? Is water scarcity a *casus belli*? Does it in fact divide nations? My own answer is no, no and no. I recognize the obvious value to sensational Water War rhetoric. Alarmists awaken people to the underlying reality of water scarcity, and rally troops to be-come more progressive and interdependent. By contrast, to challenge or dispute that rhetoric is to risk making us passive or smug about the status quo, or delay badly needed innovations or co-operation against stress.
>
> And yet I do challenge "Water War" rhetoric. For there is no hard evidence to back it up.[9]

In weighing both the conflictual and cooperative potential of eco-logical interdependence, it is also important not to limit our analysis to the level of interstate, intergovernmental relations. Balakrishnan Rajagopal provides a dramatic portrayal of the violence against peo-ple and communities that often accompanies natural resource devel-opment, in the absence of human rights guarantees and a voice for local, affected communities. He points to a different kind of violence problem: the "structural violence" of forced displacement of tens of millions of people around the world, to make way for large dams, agricultural colonization schemes, and other large-scale resource development projects. This suggests that the environmental security frame must be broadened to encompass human security concerns, rather than simply the question of interstate or intergroup violent conflict.

Social science may lack the tools to tell us exactly when and where environmental problems may produce violence. Nevertheless, the capacity of environmental change to disrupt people's lives, erode standards of living, and threaten established interests tells us that the possibility of widespread violent conflict must be taken seriously. Research that helps us understand when and where such conflict is likely to occur could be an important tool for avoiding conflict, building international confidence, and resolving nonviolent conflict. We conclude the section with a look back at the historical roots of the environmental security paradigm by Geoffrey Dabelko, which illustrates the difficulties of placing environmental security concerns on the international agenda and keeping them there. Looking to the future, he points hopefully toward the emergence of a new generation of more careful analytic scholarship and growing recognition of the peacebuilding potential inherent in environmental relationships, as opposed to a narrower view of the environment as simply a potential trigger for conflict. His piece highlights the strong origins of environmental security ideas from outside the United States, contrary to a common perception that the United States (and specifically its military) is the dominant and original proponent.

The paradigm of environmental security remains controversial because it links plausible claims about conflict to the symbolically powerful and highly charged concept of security. At best, linking environment and security could be a way to build trust among nations and make security a cooperative, global endeavor, while at the same time steering resources and public energy toward resolving environmental problems.[10] At worst, tying environmental concerns to militarized approaches to social conflict could itself be a recipe for greater violence in the future.

Thinking Critically

1. Can you think of examples that run counter to the Kahl argument—that is, cases where the conditions for environmentally induced violent conflict seem to exist but violence does not occur?

What social institutions or other conditions are likely to influence whether violence occurs? Is the connection between environment and conflict solely a problem for the developing world?

2. In what ways does the UNEP analysis of environment and conflict in Sudan illustrate Kahl's arguments? Are there connections between environment and violence in this case that are not discussed by Kahl?

3. Which seems more likely: the "greening" of security policy or the militarization of environmental policy? Are Deudney's concerns about the mismatched tools of traditional security institutions well founded? Can we generalize across countries in answering this question?

4. Might environmental cooperation also cause environmental conflict? Can international cooperation cause the sort of violence discussed by Rajagopal? If countries in a shared river basin agree to build a dam instead of fighting over the water, is that "environmental peacebuilding" or merely shifting violence from interstate affairs onto local communities in the basin? Is it possible to develop strategies that work for peace on both levels at once?

Notes

1. See, for example, Thomas Homer-Dixon, "Environmental Scarcities and Violent Conflict: Evidence from Cases," *International Security* 19, no. 1 (1994): 5–40.

2. For an overview of this literature, see Michael L. Ross, "What Do We Know About Natural Resources and Civil War?" *Journal of Peace Research* 41, no. 3 (May 2004): 337–356.

3. See, for example, Lester Brown, "Redefining National Security," *Worldwatch Paper* no. 14 (Washington, DC: Worldwatch Institute, 1977); Jessica Tuchman Mathews, "Redefining Security," *Foreign Affairs* 67 (1989): 162–177; Norman Myers, "Environment and Security," *Foreign Policy* 74 (Spring 1989): 23–41.

4. Former vice president Al Gore discusses this theme in his book on the global environment, *Earth in the Balance: Ecology and the Human Spirit* (New York: Houghton Mifflin, 1992).

5. Kent Hughes Butts, "Why the Military Is Good for the Environment," in Jyrki Käkönen, ed., *Green Security or Militarized Environment* (Aldershot, UK: Dartmouth Publishing, 1994). For a discussion of how the U.S. government has operationalized environmental security ideas in a variety of ways, see Geoffrey D. Dabelko and P. J. Simmons, "Environment and Security: Core Ideas and U.S. Government Initiatives," *SAIS Review* 17 (Winter–Spring 1997): 127–146. See also all issues of the Environmental Change and Security Project Report, published by the Washington-based Woodrow Wilson International Center for Scholars.

6. Early examples include Fairfield Osborn, *Our Plundered Planet* (Boston: Little, Brown, 1953), and Harrison Brown, *The Challenge of Man's Future* (New York: Viking, 1954).

7. For a similar critique regarding the role of the environment in causing conflict, see Marc A. Levy, "Is the Environment a National Security Issue?" *International Security* 20,

no. 2 (Fall 1995): 35–62; Thomas F. Homer-Dixon and Marc A. Levy, "Correspondence: Environment and Security," *International Security* 20, no. 3 (Winter 1995–1996): 189–194.

8. See, for example, Ken Conca, "In the Name of Sustainability: Peace Studies and Environmental Discourse," *Peace and Change* 19, no. 2 (April 1994): 91–113.

9. Kader Asmal, Speech to the 10th Stockholm Water Symposium, Stockholm, Sweden, August 14, 2000.

10. See, for example, Ken Conca and Geoffrey D. Dabelko, eds., *Environmental Peacemaking* (Washington, DC, and Baltimore: Woodrow Wilson Center Press and Johns Hopkins University Press, 2002).

21

DEMOGRAPHY, ENVIRONMENT, AND CIVIL STRIFE

COLIN H. KAHL[*]

At both the global and local levels, natural resource depletion and environmental degradation result from the interactions among extreme wealth, population pressures, and extreme poverty. The material-intensive and pollution-laden consumption habits and production activities of high-income countries are responsible for most of the world's greenhouse gases, solid and hazardous waste, and other environmental pollution. High-income countries also generate a disproportionate amount of the global demand for fossil fuels, nonfuel minerals, grain, meat, fish, tropical hardwoods, and products from endangered species.[1]

Poverty and inequality within developing countries, especially those with rapidly growing populations, also place burdens on the environment. Impoverished individuals frequently live in the most fragile ecological areas and are often driven to overexploit croplands, pastures, forests, fisheries, and water resources in order to eke out a living. Many have been forced to migrate to marginal areas due to overcrowding on better land. In the past fifty years, the number of people living on fragile land in developing countries has doubled to 1.3 billion, and rural population growth remains higher than average in countries with 30 percent or more of their population living on fragile land. Fragile ecological areas, which represent 73 percent of the Earth's land surface, have a very limited ability to sustain high population densities and are particularly vulnerable to degradation, erosion, flooding, fires, landslides, and climatic change.[2]

The relationship between the environment and poverty runs both ways. Poverty can contribute to environmental degradation, which in turn worsens poverty, and so on. Today, nearly half the world's population lives on less than

* Originally published in Lael Brainard and Derek Chollet, eds., "*Too Poor for Peace? Global Poverty, Conflict and Security in the 21st Century.* Washington: Brookings Institution Press, pp. 60-72. © Brookings Institution. Reprinted with permission.

$2 a day, and more than 1 billion people eke out a living on less than $1 a day. The absolute number of people living on less than $1 a day has actually fallen from 1.5 to 1.1 billion over the past twenty years, even as the world's population has expanded by 1.6 billion, but most of these gains have occurred in just two countries: China and India. In many other parts of the developing world, poverty remains a seemingly intractable problem. And in some regions, especially sub-Saharan Africa, the absolute number of extremely impoverished individuals has more than doubled since the early 1980s. Today, more than 1.3 billion people depend on agriculture, forests, and fisheries for their livelihoods. This represents around half of total global employment. Consequently, when the local environment is degraded and resource competition becomes more acute, it can have significant implications for the economic survival of entire communities.[3]

Numerous signs suggest that the combined effects of unsustainable consumption, population growth, and extreme poverty are taking their toll on the environment. To take one example, the World Wildlife Fund (WWF) has recently calculated humanity's "ecological footprint" by comparing renewable resource consumption to an estimate of nature's biological productive capacity. A country's ecological footprint represents the total area (measured in standardized global hectares of biologically productive land and water) required to produce the renewable resources consumed and to assimilate the wastes generated by human activities. All told, the global footprint in 1999 amounted to 13.7 billion biologically productive hectares, exceeding the 11.4 billion hectares estimated to exist by about 20 percent. Moreover, in the decades ahead as economic globalization accelerates, the human population continues to expand (with the fastest rates of growth occurring in the world's least developed nations), and the effects of human-induced climate change become more pronounced, the strain on the natural environment is likely to worsen.[4]

What are the implications of these trends for international security? Though there is scant evidence that population and environmental pressure produce armed clashes *between* countries (with the partial exceptions of conflicts over oil and water), a growing body of scholarship has linked these factors to violence *within* countries. Some see demographically and environmentally induced scarcity as a major source of civil strife, while others argue that a local abundance of valuable natural resources produces greater dangers.

The Demography–Environment–Civil Strife Connection

Since the early 1990s, a number of academics and international security specialists have argued that demographic and environmental pressures pose significant threats to political stability in developing countries. Initially, this discussion was dominated by neo-Malthusians, but more recently a number of scholars working within the tradition of neoclassical economics have entered the fray.

Deprivation and Failed States

Neo-Malthusians argue that rapid population growth, environmental degradation, resource depletion, and unequal resource access combine to exacerbate poverty and income inequality in many of the world's least developed countries. The resulting rise in absolute and relative deprivation translates into grievances, increasing the risks of rebellion and societal conflict.[5]

More recent work in this tradition acknowledges that deprivation by itself is rarely sufficient to produce large-scale organized violence, because the poor often lack the capabilities to rebel, especially in the context of a strong state. Therefore, neo-Malthusians contend that population and environmental pressures are most likely to contribute to internal wars when demographic and environmental pressures also weaken state authority, thereby opening "political space" for violence to occur.[6]

Demographic and environmental stress can undermine state authority in a number of ways. As population and environmental challenges mount, so will the demands placed on the state from suffering segments of the economy and marginalized individuals. Demands may include calls for costly development projects, such as hydroelectric dams, canals, and irrigation systems; subsidies for fertilizer and other agricultural inputs; and urban demands for employment, housing, schools, sanitation, energy, and lower food prices. These demands increase fiscal strains and thus erode a state's administrative capacity by requiring budgetary trade-offs. A state's legitimacy may also be cast in doubt if individuals and groups come to blame the government for their plight. Population growth, environmental degradation, and resource depletion can also undermine overall economic productivity, thereby reducing the revenue available to local and central governments at the very time that rising demands require greater expenditures.[7] Research suggests that these dynamics have historically contributed to civil strife in the state of Chiapas in Mexico, El Salvador, the Philippines, Somalia, and elsewhere.[8]

In addition to increasing the risks of violent rebellion from below, state weakness and rising social grievances emanating from demographic and environmental stress can sometimes encourage political elites themselves to instigate civil strife in an effort to cling to power. Ethnic clashes in Kenya in the early 1990s illustrate this pathway to violence. During the 1980s, population growth averaging 3.4 percent a year combined with soil erosion, desertification, and unequal land access to create an extreme scarcity of arable land, escalating economic marginalization in rural areas, and substantial rural-to-urban migration. As the population of Nairobi and Kenya's other urban centers soared, and related social and economic problems worsened, pressure mounted on President Daniel arap Moi's regime to forsake the KANU [Kenya African National Union] Party's monopoly on rule and allow multiparty elections. In response to this threat, Moi and many of his close associates set out to discredit the democratization process and consolidate their control over the valuable and fertile Rift Valley by orchestrating a series of tribal clashes that left 1,500 dead and hundreds of thousands homeless. To implement this strategy, KANU elites capitalized on and manipulated a set of demographically, environmentally, and historically rooted land grievances between pastoral groups and farming communities.[9] Similar dynamics have contributed to violent conflicts in Darfur (Sudan), Rwanda, and Zimbabwe.[10]

Honey Pots and the Resource Curse

Neoclassical economists advance a set of claims that, on the surface at least, appear to turn neo-Malthusian arguments on their head. Resource abundance, rather than scarcity, is argued to be the bigger threat to political instability.

One claim centers on so-called honey pot effects. According to this view, abundant supplies of valuable local resources create incentives for rebel groups to form and fight to capture them. This can spawn attempts by regional warlords and rebel organizations to cleave off resource-rich territories or violently hijack the state. Once seized, control over valuable natural resources fuels conflict escalation by allowing the parties to purchase weaponry and mobilize potential recruits.[11] Recent conflicts fueled by diamonds and other precious minerals in Sierra Leone and the Democratic Republic of the Congo demonstrate the honey pot effect in action.

Some neoclassical economists argue that natural resource abundance also produces weak states via a set of developmental pathologies known collectively as the resource curse. Economically, abundant natural resources are said to contribute to economic stagnation over the long run through a number of crowding-out effects sometimes referred to as "Dutch disease." When capital and labor focus on booming natural resource sectors, they are drawn away from other sectors of the economy, increasing their production costs. These economic distortions slow the maturity of non-resource-tradable sectors, harm their competitiveness, and thereby inhibit the kinds of economic diversification, especially an early period of labor-intensive manufacturing, that many neoclassical economists suggest is vital for long-term growth. It is also argued that overreliance on exports of minimally processed natural resources makes countries vulnerable to declining terms of trade and the highly volatile nature of international commodities markets. In the absence of a diverse array of exports, especially of manufactured goods that tend to have more stable prices, resource-rich countries are prone to dramatic economic shocks when prices for primary commodities inevitably crash.[12]

Beyond the economic distortions created by local resource abundance, there is also a political dimension to the resource curse. The most common political argument focuses on problems associated with "rentier states"; these states, which accrue a significant amount of revenue from natural resource exports they directly control, are prone to developing corrupt, narrowly based authoritarian or quasi-democratic governing institutions. When states capture enormous rents from natural resources, they face far fewer incentives to bargain away greater economic and political accountability to the populace in exchange for broader rights of taxation. Instead, natural resource wealth can be used to maintain rule through patronage networks and outright coercion. The institutional makeup of rentier states therefore reduces the prospects for broad-based, benevolent economic and political reform, weakening the state over the long term and generating substantial societal grievances.[13] These conditions are ripe for violent revolt.[14]

There appears to be strong cross-national evidence for the developmental problems associated with the resource curse. Statistical analyses suggest that countries that are highly dependent on primary commodity exports have, on average, lower rates of economic growth and more unequal distributions of income.[15] Underdevelopment and poor governance, in turn, can generate grievances and open political space for organized violence. For example, many oil-exporting countries, including Algeria, Angola, Ecuador, Indonesia, Iraq, and Nigeria, have historically been prone to authoritarianism, corruption, periodic social protests, and violence.[16] Recently, some have also expressed fears that Dutch disease and rentier-state pathologies could pose significant threats to the future stability of post-Saddam Iraq. If an equitable system is not established to manage and distribute the country's oil wealth among its various regions and religious and ethnic communities, these forces could have a corrupting influence on future political institutions, put any new government's legitimacy at risk, and spur bloody competition between Shiites, Sunnis, Kurds, and Turkmen.

Evaluating the Debate

Neo-Malthusians and neoclassical economists seem to advance polar-opposite views. The former see too few natural resources as the problem, while the latter see too many resources as the curse. Thus, while neo-Malthusians would be concerned about the potentially destabilizing effects of demographic, economic, and environmental trends, especially in the world's least developed countries, neoclassical economists might argue that rising demographic and environmental pressures will create incentives for countries to diversify their economies away from natural resource dependence, ultimately making them more prosperous and stable. Upon deeper reflection, however, the arguments advanced are not as incompatible as they first appear.

Scarcity Versus Abundance

Natural resource scarcity and abundance as conceptualized by neo-Malthusians and neoclassical economists are not opposites; they can, and often do, both exist at the same time at different levels of analysis. The vast majority of troublesome resources discussed by neoclassical economists (oil, gemstones, valuable metals, timber, etc.) are abundant locally but scarce globally, something neo-Malthusians are careful to point out.[17] Indeed, it is the global scarcity of these resources that makes them so valuable and thus such huge prizes to seize through violence.

Furthermore, abundance of one resource can produce scarcity of another. The extraction and production activities centered on locally abundant (and usually nonrenewable) resources can lead to environmental degradation and scarcities of *other* (usually renewable) resources, and the synergy may lead to violent conflict. In Nigeria, for example, revenue streams from the oil-rich Niger Delta have historically filled the coffers of a small minority and propped up a series of repressive regimes. Throughout the 1990s, inequities, environmental degradation, pollution, and health problems stemming from the oil industry generated substantial grievances among local communities in the Niger Delta, including the Ogoni people. In the mid-1990s, the military dictatorship in Nigeria responded to Ogoni protests with repression and the instigation of interethnic violence.[18]

Finally, abundance and scarcity combine to pose development challenges for resource-dependent countries. In many respects, neo-Malthusians and neoclassical economists speak past each other because they ignore the notions of time and sequence that are implicit in their analyses. To see how both types of logic may operate and actually reinforce one another, consider three idealized temporal stages in a country whose economy is dependent on local supplies of natural resources: (1) initial abundance; (2) emerging scarcity; and (3) the time at which exploitation of the scarce local resource is no longer economically viable, forcing diversification and a search for alternative supplies and substitutes. Neo-Malthusians and neoclassical economists should *both* agree that the second phase holds the highest risk of internal war.

The logic of the honey pot effect, for example, applies much more during a time of emerging scarcity. After all, when natural resources are consumed or degraded at unsustainable rates, their value increases and rival social groups confront greater incentives to seize them. The renewal of civil war in Sudan in 1983 provides a clear example here. By the end of the 1970s, environmental stress in northern Sudan, stemming in large part from mechanized farming, increased the value of water, land, and oil resources in the south. Northern elites, acting in support of allied northern mechanized farm owners, pushed south to capture these resources. This posed an enormous threat to the economic and physical survival of southerners, encouraging them to restart the war against the north. As the war raged on, oil exports became central to the north's ability to finance its campaign, encouraging it to seize and exploit oil deposits deeper and deeper into the south.[19]

Moreover, if development is viewed as a sequence of temporal stages, a good case can also be made that the developmental pathologies of the resource curse and those emerging from rapid population growth, environmental degradation, and resource scarcity can all occur and interact with one another within the same country over time. During stage 1, when resources are abundant, a country may become highly dependent on these resources and elements of Dutch disease and rentier-state politics may take hold. Then, during stage 2, demographic and environmental pressures may produce growing scarcities and undermine economic and political stability *precisely because* the country developed such a strong dependence on exporting natural resources in the first place. Finally, at stage 3, scarcity and economic crisis may force the government and the private sector to promote diversification as a means of resuscitating growth. This hypothetical sequence suggests that neoclassical theorists tend to focus on the logic involved in the leaps between these temporal stages without sufficiently recognizing the risks of transitional violence during the middle stage emphasized by neo-Malthusians.

By ignoring transitional dangers, neoclassical economists miss important contributors to civil strife. The experience of the world's poorest countries suggests that many are currently stuck in stage 2, where high dependence on natural resources, rapid population growth, environmental degradation, and emerging scarcity conspire to threaten political stability.

Different Resources, Different Risks

Different types of natural resources are likely to be implicated in different types of conflict. In fact, a close look at the conflict claims advanced by neo-Malthusians and neoclassical economists reveals that they are generally not talking about the same resources.

The broad grievance-based scenarios identified by neo-Malthusians are most likely when international demand, local population dynamics, unsustainable extraction practices, and unequal resource access interact to produce environmental degradation and emerging scarcities of *renewable* resources. Agriculture, forestry, and fishing contribute much more to employment than capital-intensive nonrenewable resource sectors. Moreover, access to arable land (or inexpensive food) and freshwater is vital to extremely poor individuals throughout the developing world. Degradation, depletion, and/or maldistributions of these resources can therefore directly implicate the survival of large numbers of people in rural areas in ways that nonrenewables usually do not. Of course, in some instances, the extraction of nonrenewable resources causes degradation, depletion, or unequal distributions of renewable ones, but even here it is the impact on the surrounding renewable resource base that is likely to have the widest direct effect on the quality of life and related grievances.

Nonrenewable resources are much more likely to be implicated in the conflict scenarios outlined by neoclassical economists. Nonrenewable resources are likely to be central to violent conflicts in which natural resources themselves are the main prize to be captured, as opposed to conflicts emanating from the more diffuse social and economic effects of environmental degradation and renewable resource scarcity. According to the honey pot logic, the incentive and capability to capture nonrenewable resources is especially high because mineral resources tend to be much more valuable per unit of volume, geographically concentrated, and easily tradable than most renewable resources. These features make nonrenewable resources considerably more "lootable."[20] It should come as no surprise, therefore, that the vast majority of honey pot–driven conflicts revolve around oil, diamonds, and other valuable minerals.

The economic and political components of the resource curse also apply much more to countries dependent on the export of nonrenewable resources. Here, several characteristics distinguish mineral-dependent economies and polities from countries dependent on renewables (again, with the partial exception of timber). Mineral-exporting countries tend to be economically dependent on a single resource. Consequently, their economies tend to be especially sensitive to price volatility.[21] Furthermore, mining countries are typically dependent on resources that generate extraordinary rents. This is especially true of oil, but is also the case with other minerals.

States in the developing world also exercise sole ownership rights over subsoil assets and, often, public forestlands. This means that the export revenue from these resources is not mediated through domestic private actors but instead accrues directly to the state and allied firms. This differs dramatically from the situation in most countries dependent on exports of agriculture because these resources tend to be privately owned (even if sometimes highly concentrated). Thus, because government officials have the ability to extract and control an unusually high income from nonrenewables, the pathologies of rentier-state politics are likely to be much more acute than in countries dependent on most renewable resources.[22]

The Importance of Political Institutions

Demographic and environmental pressures are rarely if ever sufficient to produce conflict; many countries experience these pressures yet avoid civil strife. Neo-Malthusians and neoclassical economists generally agree that demographically and environmentally induced civil wars are most likely in countries with weak governments and authoritarian political institutions.

As noted above, strong states are typically able to prevent, deter, or repress large-scale organized violence initiated by potential challengers. Strong states are also less vulnerable to conflicts initiated by state elites themselves because elites generally feel more secure and are able to advance their interests without risking society-wide warfare. Beyond the strength of the state, the character of a country's governing institutions also matters. Consolidated democracies are unlikely candidates for civil war and are less vulnerable to widespread upheaval during times of crisis. Democracies normally enjoy greater system legitimacy than authoritarian states and are better able to channel grievances into the normal political process. Democratic institutions also increase the transparency of political decisions and place constraints on executive authority, limiting the ability of state elites to instigate violence.[23]

Quantitative studies suggest that many consolidated authoritarian states also avoid civil war. Nevertheless, their stability typically relies on a high degree of coercive power and patronage, and these governments often generate substantial antistate grievances, especially among excluded social groups. Consequently, these states are vulnerable to rapid collapse and civil war during times of crisis or regime transition.[24]

All told, when the strength of the state and the character of its political institutions are taken into consideration, it becomes clear that some political contexts are especially vulnerable to demographically and environmentally induced violence. The natural resource–civil strife connection is likely to be particularly tight when population growth, environmental degradation, resource scarcity, and/or the pathologies of the resource curse contribute to state weakness and authoritarian institutions, or when demographically and environmentally induced grievances and honey pot effects occur in the context of states that are already weak and narrow or undergoing rapid regime transition.

Implications for the Future

During the next half century, the UN medium projection estimates that the world's population will increase from 6.5 billion in 2005 to 9.1 billion in 2050. Population growth is projected to slow across the board, but differential growth rates between rich and poor countries are expected to persist. Indeed, by 2050 the population of the high-income countries is expected to be in the midst of a twenty-year *decline*. In contrast, the population of the least developed countries is projected to more than double from 800 million in 2005 to 1.7 billion by 2050. In the rest of the developing world, the population is expected to increase from 4.5 to 6.1 billion over this period.[25]

Economic growth and consumption are also projected to increase in the decades ahead, spurred on by continued economic globalization. The World Bank projects growth in global income of 3 percent a year over the next fifty years, suggesting a fourfold rise in global gross domestic product (to a total of $140 trillion) by midcentury. Historically, higher income is associated with higher levels of consumption, although the relationship is usually nonlinear.[26]

Although it is impossible to predict the future of any complex system, let alone a future based on the intersection of several complex systems (demographic, economic, political, and environmental), some have offered possible scenarios. The WWF has projected humanity's ecological footprint forward from 2000 to 2050 by combining UN population growth estimates, Intergovernmental Panel on Climate Change estimates of future carbon dioxide emissions, and UN Food and Agriculture Organization estimates of trends in the consumption of agriculture products (crops, meat, and dairy), forest products (including fuelwood), and fish and seafood. According to this projection, a population of 9 billion in 2050 will require 1.8 to 2.2 Earth-sized planets to sustain its total consumption of crops, meat, fish, and wood, and to hold carbon dioxide levels constant in the atmosphere. Whether this scenario comes about obviously depends on future consumption habits and available technology. Rapid advances in technology that provide for significant improvements in resource efficiency, for example, could allow for long-term sustainability and continued advances in human welfare; however, without significant technological changes, the projected consumption would become unsustainable.[27]

Consumption will likely drive global patterns of resource depletion and pollution, but population growth and poverty will continue to have an important impact at the local level. Even as globalization raises the living standards of some countries and peoples, pockets of extreme poverty and yawning inequalities are likely to persist, placing their own strains on the environment. Current projections suggest that millions of people in the developing world will continue to rely on overcrowded and ecologically fragile lands where there is a real danger of becoming trapped in a vicious cycle of poverty and environmental decline. This is likely to generate substantial challenges for both human welfare and political stability.

Notes

1. World Bank, *World Development Report 2003: Sustainable Development in a Dynamic World* (Oxford University Press, 2003), 118; Worldwatch Institute, *Vital Signs 2003* (New York: W. W. Norton, 2003): 17; World Resources Institute, *World Resources 2000–2001* (Oxford: Elsevier Science, 2000), 26–27.

2. World Bank, *World Development Indicators* (Washington, 2003), 118; World Bank, *World Development Report 2003*, 7–8, 60–67; Worldwatch Institute, *Vital Signs 2003*, 17.

3. World Resources Institute, *World Resources* (Washington, 2005).

4. Mathis Wackernagel et al., "Tracking the Ecological Overshoot of the Human Economy," *Proceedings of the National Academy of Sciences* 99, no. 14 (2002): 9266–71; World Wildlife Fund, *Living Planet Report 2002* (Gland, Switzerland, 2002).

5. Norman Myers, *Ultimate Security: The Environmental Basis of Political Stability* (New York: W. W. Norton, 1993). Also see Jessica Tuchman Matthews, "Redefining Security," *Foreign Affairs*, Spring 1989, 162–77.

6. Jack A. Goldstone, *Revolution and Rebellion in the Early Modern World* (University of California Press, 1991); Jack A. Goldstone, "Population Growth and Revolutionary Crises," in *Theorizing Revolutions*, ed. John Foran (London: Routledge, 1997), 102–20; Jack A. Goldstone, "How Demographic Change Can Lead to Violent Conflict," *Journal of International Affairs* 56, no. 1 (2002): 3–24; Thomas F. Homer-Dixon, "On the Threshold: Environmental Changes as Causes of Acute Conflict," *International Security* 16, no. 2 (1991): 76–116; Thomas F. Homer-Dixon, "Environmental Scarcities and Violent Conflict: Evidence from Cases," *International Security* 19, no. 1 (1994): 4–40; Thomas F. Homer-Dixon, *Environment, Scarcity, and Violence* (Princeton University Press, 1999); Colin H. Kahl, *States, Scarcity, and Civil Strife in the Developing World* (Princeton University Press, 2006). Also see Robert D. Kaplan, "The Coming Anarchy," *Atlantic Monthly*, February 1994, 44–76.

7. Homer-Dixon, "Environmental Scarcities and Violent Conflict," 25–26; Kahl, *States, Scarcity, and Civil Strife*, 40–44.

8. Homer-Dixon, *Environment, Scarcity, and Violence*, 142–47; Kahl, *States, Scarcity, and Civil Strife*, chaps. 3, 6; Myers, *Ultimate Security*, 122–29.

9. Colin H. Kahl, "Population Growth, Environmental Degradation, and State-Sponsored Violence: The Case of Kenya, 1991–1993," *International Security* 23, no. 2 (1998): 80–119; Kahl, *States, Scarcity, and Civil Strife,* chap. 4.

10. Kahl, *States, Scarcity, and Civil Strife,* chap. 6.

11. Paul Collier and Anke Hoeffler, "Greed and Grievance in Civil War," World Bank, October 21, 2001; World Bank, *World Development Indicators* (Washington, 2003); Indra de Soysa, "The Resource Curse: Are Civil Wars Driven by Rapacity or Paucity?" in *Greed and Grievance: Economic Agendas in Civil Wars,* ed. Mats Berdal and David M. Malone (Boulder, Colo.: Lynne Rienner, 2000), 113–36; Indra de Soysa, "Paradise Is a Bazaar? Greed, Creed, and Governance in Civil War, 1989–99," *Journal of Peace Research* 39, no. 4 (2002): 395–416; Michael L. Ross, "What Do We Know About Natural Resources and Civil War?" *Journal of Peace Research* 41, no. 3 (2004): 337–56; Michael L. Ross, "How Do Natural Resources Influence Civil War? Evidence from Thirteen Cases," *International Organization* 58, no. 1 (2004): 35–67.

12. Michael L. Ross, "The Political Economy of the Resource Curse," *World Politics* 51, no. 2 (1999): 320–21; Jeffrey D. Sachs and Andrew M. Warner, "The Big Push, Natural Resource Booms, and Growth," *Journal of Development Economics* 59 (1999): 43–76.

13. Richard M. Auty, *Patterns of Development: Resources, Policy and Economic Growth* (London: Edward Arnold, 1995); Terry Lynn Karl, *The Paradox of Plenty: Oil Booms and Petro-States* (University of California Press, 1997).

14. de Soysa, "Paradise Is a Bazaar? 120–22; Michael Renner, *The Anatomy of Resource Wars,* Worldwatch Paper 162 (Washington: Worldwatch Institute, 2002), 14–18.

15. Jeffrey D. Sachs and Andrew M. Warner, *Natural Resource Abundance and Economic Growth,* Development Discussion Paper 517a (Cambridge, Mass.: Harvard Institute for International Development, 1995).

16. Renner, *Anatomy of Resource Wars,* 32–35, 45–47.

17. Fred Pearce, "Blood Diamonds and Oil," *New Scientist,* June 29, 2002, 40.

18. Renner, *Anatomy of Resource Wars,* 45–47; Michael Watts, "Petro-Violence: Community, Extraction, and Political Ecology of a Mythic Commodity," in *Violent Environments,* ed. Nancy Lee Peluso and Michael Watts (Cornell University Press, 2001), 189–212.

19. Renner, *Anatomy of Resource Wars,* 10; Mohamed Suliman, *Civil War in Sudan: The Impact of Ecological Degradation,* Occasional Paper 4, Environment and Conflicts Project (Berne and Zurich: Swiss Peace Foundation and Center for Security Studies and Conflict Research, 1992); Mohamed Suliman, "Civil War in the Sudan: From Ethnic to Ecological Conflict," *The Ecologist* 23, no. 3 (1993): 104–9.

20. Philippe Le Billon, "The Political Ecology of War: Natural Resources and Armed Conflicts," *Political Geography* 20 (2001): 569–70.

21. Karl, *Paradox of Plenty,* 47–48.

22. Richard M. Auty, *Resource Abundance and Economic Development: Improving the Performance of Resource-Rich Countries,* Research for Action 44 (Helsinki: World Institute for Development Economics and Research, 1998), 1; Karl, *Paradox of Plenty,* 15, 48–49, 52, 56–57; Ross, "Political Economy of the Resource Curse," 311, 319–20.

23. Kahl, *States, Scarcity, and Civil Strife,* chap. 2.

24. Jack A. Goldstone et al., *State Failure Task Force Report: Phase III Findings* (McLean, Va.: Science Applications International Corporation, 2000), 14–16.

25. United Nations Population Division, *World Population Prospects: The 2004 Revision* (New York, 2005).

26. World Bank, *World Development Report 2003,* 4.

27. World Wildlife Fund, *Living Planet Report 2002,* 20.

22

SUDAN:
CONFLICT AND
THE ENVIRONMENT

UNITED NATIONS
ENVIRONMENT PROGRAMME

POST-CONFLICT AND
DISASTER MANAGEMENT BRANCH[*]

Introduction

Sudan has been wracked by civil war and regional strife for most of the past fifty years, and at the time of finalizing this report, in June 2007, a major conflict rages on in Darfur. At the same time, Sudan suffers from a number of severe environmental problems, both within and outside current and historical conflict-affected areas. UNEP's assessment has found that the connections between conflict and environment in Sudan are both complex and pervasive: while many of the conflicts have been initiated partly by tension over the use of shared natural resources, those same resources have often been damaged by conflict. . . .

[*]   Excerpted from United Nations Environment Programme, *Sudan: Post-Conflict Environmental Assessment.* (c) United Nations, 2007. Reproduced with permission.

Overview of conflicts in Sudan

A complex mosaic

Conflicts have directly affected over 60 percent of the country for the last fifty years, and hence greatly influenced its development. Understanding Sudan's complex mosaic of conflicts is an essential first step in establishing the linkages between conflict and environment in the region. This section accordingly provides a brief summary of the chronology and geography of the various confrontations, together with a short account of the tactics and weaponry used. A thorough review of social and political factors might be taken into consideration in a comprehensive conflict analysis, but is outside the scope of this environmental assessment.

Tribal and small-scale conflicts

Tribal and small-scale conflicts fought only with small arms have occurred continuously throughout the history of Sudan. No part of the country has been exempt from such clashes, but they have been concentrated in the south, west and east of the country for the last thirty years. Their causes are generally poorly recorded, but include disputes over cattle theft, access to water and grazing, and local politics. Many—though not all—of the large-scale conflicts in Sudan have a connection to tribal friction.

The major conflicts

The majority of large-scale conflicts in Sudan have been long-term (five years or more) confrontations between forces aligned with the central Sudanese government based in Khartoum and an array of antigovernment forces. The government side has comprised conventional army and air forces, and allied local militias. The opposition has consisted of local militias which—in the case of the Sudan People's Liberation Army (SPLA) in Southern Sudan—evolved into a united resistance army with a parallel governance and administration structure (the Sudan People's Liberation Movement or SPLM).

Major conflicts have at times extended over as much as 60 percent of the territory of Sudan, principally in the ten southern states, but also in the west (all three Darfur states), the centre (Blue Nile and Southern Kordofan states), the east (Kassala state) and the northeast (Red Sea state). In total, over 15 million people have been directly affected, not including the approximately 6 million people currently still impacted in Darfur. Total conflict-related casualties are unknown, but estimated by a range of sources to be in the range of 2 to 3 million.

Although the government forces' weaponry has included tanks and heavy artillery, most military confrontations have been fought mainly with light weapons such as AK-47 assault rifles. The opposition forces' armament has been generally light, with a small number of tanks and other heavy weapons. Only government forces have had airpower.

Landmines have been used widely in most major conflicts. Minefields have been abandoned without marking or extraction and are mostly unmapped. As a result, Sudan now suffers from a severe landmine legacy which continues to cause civilian casualties. It should be noted that there are no reports of extensive use of landmines in the ongoing war in Darfur.

There is no firm field or documented evidence of any unconventional weapons (chemical, nuclear or biological) ever being held or used in Sudan. Some local communities reported that drinking water wells had been poisoned in Darfur, but in the absence of detail and opportunity for inspection, UNEP did not investigate this issue further.

The history and current status of each of the major conflict areas is briefly described below.

Darfur

Fighting in Darfur has occurred intermittently for at least thirty years. Until 2003, it was mostly confined to a series of partly connected tribal and local conflicts. In early 2003, these hostilities escalated into a full-scale military confrontation in all three Darfur states, which also frequently spills into neighboring Chad and the Central African Republic.

The ongoing Darfur conflict is characterized by a "scorched earth" campaign carried out by militias over large areas, resulting in a significant number of civilian deaths, the widespread destruction of villages and forests, and the displacement of victims into camps for protection, food and water. Over 2 million people are currently displaced, and casualties are estimated by a range of sources to be between 200,000 and 500,000.

Southern Sudan

In the fifty years since Sudan's independence, the south has experienced only eleven years of peace. During most of the civil war, the central Sudanese government held a number of major towns and launched air attacks and dry-season ground offensives into the surrounding countryside. The opposition forces, the Sudan People's Liberation Army (SPLA) and their allies, fought guerrilla actions, besieged towns and conducted ground offensives in both wet and dry seasons. Most of the countryside, however, saw little or no military activity. Frontlines with prolonged, active fighting were confined to northern-central border regions and besieged towns. The fiercest fighting took place in the 1990s, with frontlines changing constantly and several towns being taken many times.

The conflict extended to areas in central Sudan, such as Abyei district, Blue Nile and the Nuba mountains in Southern Kordofan. Known as the "Three Areas," these regions retain a high level of political uncertainty today. Small-scale conflict due to the Ugandan militia the Lord's Resistance Army (LRA) has also occurred intermittently in the far south even after the signing of the Comprehensive Peace Agreement in January 2005, and some instability persists in other border regions, particularly in Upper Nile.

Nuba mountains

The Nuba mountains were an SPLA stronghold in the 1990s. The SPLA held the forested regions and steeper terrain, while the open ground and surrounding plains were largely occupied by government forces. The area saw extensive fighting and aerial bombardment.

Kassala state—Eastern front

The region bordering Eritrea in Kassala state was a stronghold of the Beja people, who were allied with the SPLA. Conflict flared up in the 1990s, but a separate peace agreement between the central government and eastern forces—known as the Eastern Sudan Peace Agreement—was concluded in October 2006.

Red Sea state—Eritrean conflict

The Tokar region in Red Sea state was affected by low-level conflict between Sudan and Eritrea and local allied groups for twelve years, beginning in 1992. Hostilities ceased completely only with the signing of the CPA in early 2005.

The ongoing LRA conflict

Traditionally based in northern Uganda, directly south of Sudan's Eastern Equatoria state, the Lord's Resistance Army (LRA) has fought against the Ugandan armed forces for over twenty years. In 2005 and 2006, the conflict spread to Southern Sudan and the Democratic Republic of Congo. As of June 2007, a cease-fire is in effect but peace negotiations have stalled and sporadic conflict is ongoing.

Analysis of the role of natural resources as a contributing cause of conflict in Sudan

It is acknowledged that there are many factors that contribute to conflict in Sudan that have little or no link to the environment or natural resources. These include political, religious, ethnic, tribal and clan divisions, economic factors, land tenure deficiencies and historical feuds. In addition, where environment and natural resource management issues are important, they are generally *contributing* factors only, not the sole cause for tension.

As noted previously, "nonenvironmental" factors have been excluded from detailed examination in this assessment to allow for a tighter focus on the environmental dimensions of conflict. Also excluded is any analysis of the subsequent behavior of the conflicting parties, except where it is directly relevant to the environment, as is the case for the targeted destruction of natural resources.

Four natural resources closely linked to conflict in Sudan

In Sudan, four categories of natural resources are particularly linked to conflict as contributing causes:

1. oil and gas reserves;
2. Nile waters;
3. hardwood timber; and
4. rangeland and rain-fed agricultural land (and associated water points).

Potential conflicts over oil, Nile waters and hardwood timber are national-scale issues. Tensions over rangeland and rain-fed agricultural land are primarily local, but have the potential to escalate and exacerbate other sources of conflict to the extent of becoming national-scale issues, as is presently the case in Darfur.

The linkages between these resources/land uses and conflict are discussed below; the fourth category is examined in more detail in a separate section, as it has strong ties to the ongoing conflict in Darfur. Note that groundwater (on a regional scale), wildlife, freshwater fisheries and all types of marine resources are excluded from this list of important contributing causes, as there is no evidence that they have been major factors in instigating conflict in Sudan to date.

Competition over oil and gas reserves

Though the major north-south conflict started well before oil was discovered in central Sudan, competition for ownership and shares in the benefits of the country's oil and gas reserves was a driving force for the conflict and remains a source of political tension today. This is, however, considered to be primarily an economic, political and social issue, and is hence not addressed in detail in this report.

Of more relevance to UNEP, in this context, are the environmental impacts of the oil industry and their potential to catalyze conflict in the future. Consultations in central and south Sudan revealed widespread and intense dissatisfaction with the oil industry's environmental performance, coupled with the above-mentioned general concerns about ownership and benefit-sharing. In summary, the population in the vicinity of the oilfields said they felt subjected to all of the downsides of the presence of the oil industry (including its environmental impacts) without receiving a share in the benefits. Experience from other countries, such as Nigeria, shows that the root causes for this type of resentment must be addressed in order to avoid long-term instability and conflict at the local level. Part of the solution is to improve the environmental performance of the industry. . . .

Conflict over water rights and benefits from the Nile

Competition for the benefits accrued from the use of surface water was also an important contributing factor of the civil war, as illustrated by the Jonglei canal project, which was a cause as well as a victim of the conflict that flared up in Southern Sudan in 1983. The significance of this issue has not declined over time and tensions over attempts to restart the project are still high.

However, a number of institutional safeguards are likely to prevent a reinstigation of conflict over water rights alone at the state and federal level. First, as a high-profile and easily identifiable issue, it receives significant attention from GONU and GOSS leadership, as well as international assistance in the form of programs like the Nile Basin Initiative. Second, major projects such as new dams or canals require both large investments and long periods of time, and this development process (in its modern form at least) has a range of built-in safeguards to identify and mitigate the risk of conflict. . . .

Timber and the war economy

While there is no indication that timber has been a major contributing cause of the instigation of conflict in Sudan, there is clear evidence that revenue from hardwood timber sales helped sustain the north-south civil war. Timber became part of the war economy, and there are now signs that this process is being repeated with charcoal in Darfur. Overall, however, the timber-conflict linkage in Sudan is considered to be mainly an environmental impact issue (rather than a conflict catalyst). . . .

Local conflicts over rangeland and rain-fed agricultural land

Local clashes over rangeland and rain-fed agricultural land have occurred throughout Sudan's recorded history. In the absence of demographic and environmental change, such conflicts would generally be considered a social, political or economic issue and not warrant an assessment purely on environmental grounds. However, environmental issues like desertification, land degradation and climate change are becoming major factors in these conflicts. This topic is addressed in more detail in the following section.

Environmental linkages to local conflicts over rangeland and rain-fed agricultural land

Introduction and limits to the observed linkages

It is important to note that while environmental problems affect rangeland and rain-fed agricultural land across virtually all of Sudan, they are clearly and strongly linked to conflict in a minority of cases and regions only. These linkages do exist, but their significance and geographic scale should not be exaggerated.

That said, there is substantial evidence of a strong link between the recent occurrence of local conflict and environmental degradation of rangeland and rain-fed agricultural land in the drier parts of Sudan.

The actors of conflict at the local level: three major competing and conflicting groups

The rural ethnic and livelihood structures of Sudan are so complex and area-specific that any summary of the issue of resource competition on a national scale is by definition a gross simplification. For instance, traditional pastoralist and agricultural societies in Sudan are not always clearly separated: in many areas, societies (families, clans and even whole tribes) practice a mixture of crop-growing and animal-rearing. Nonetheless, there are some relatively clear boundaries—defined as much by livelihoods as by any other factor—between different tribes, clans and ethnic groups.

For the purposes of this discussion, UNEP has classified the hundreds of distinct rural social units present in the current and historical conflict regions into three major groups, based on livelihood strategies:

1. predominantly sedentary crop-rearing societies/tribes;
2. predominantly nomadic (transhumant) livestock-rearing societies/tribes; and
3. owners of and workers on mechanized agricultural schemes.

All three groups depend on rainfall for their livelihood. The other major rural group is comprised of farmers using river and groundwater for irrigation. To date, however, irrigated agriculture has not been a major factor in local conflicts in Sudan.

Most of the recorded local conflicts are within and between the first two groups: pastoralists and agriculturalists fighting over access to land and water. The third group, the mechanized farming lobby, is generally not directly involved in conflict, but has played a very strong role in precipitating it in some states, through uncontrolled land taken from the other two groups. In the Nuba mountains and in Blue Nile state, combatants reported that the expansion of mechanized agricultural schemes onto their land had precipitated the fighting, which had then escalated and coalesced with the major north-south political conflict.

The historical background:
a tradition of local conflict and resolution

Violent conflict resulting partly from competition over agricultural and grazing land is a worldwide and age-old phenomenon. In Sudan—and particularly in Darfur and Kordofan—there is an extensive history of local clashes associated with this issue. A 2003 study on the causes of conflict in Darfur from 1930 to 2000, for example, indicates that competition for pastoral land and water has been a driving force behind the majority of local confrontations for the last 70 years.

Until 1970, there is also a well-documented history of local resolution for such conflicts, through established mediation and dispute resolution mechanisms. Since then, however, legal reforms have essentially destroyed many of these traditional structures and processes, and failed to provide a viable substitute. In addition, the last thirty years have seen an influx of small arms into the region, with the unfortunate result that local conflicts today are both much more violent and more difficult to contain and mediate.

Theories of natural resource scarcity
and application to local conflict in Sudan

Academic research and the discourse on the role of natural resource scarcity as a driver of conflict have developed significantly over the last decade. In light of the ongoing Darfur crisis, Sudan is a prime example of the importance, complexity and political sensitivity of this topic. The following analysis borrows heavily from the language and concepts used by leading researchers in this field.

As a basis for discussion, the environmentally significant factors that contribute to conflict related to rangeland and rain-fed agricultural land have been divided into four groups:

- supply: factors affecting the available resources;
- demand: factors affecting the demand for resources;
- land use: changes affecting the way remaining resources are shared; and
- institutional and development factors.

While all the purely environmental factors are "supply" issues, they have to be put into the context of "demand" and "institution-specific" factors.

Supply—an unreliable and dwindling resource

The noted environmental issues affecting agriculture in Sudan all result in a dwindling supply of natural resources:

- *Desertification, soil erosion and soil exhaustion* (depletion of nutrients and compaction) lower agricultural productivity and, in the worst cases, take land out of use for the long term. This has been well documented but poorly quantified in Sudan;
- *Deforestation*, particularly in the drylands, has resulted in a near permanent loss of resources including seasonal forage for pastoralists and natural fertilizer/soil recovery services for farmers. Deforestation rates in the areas studied by UNEP average 1.87 percent per annum;
- *Historical climate change* has reduced productivity in some areas due to a decline in rainfall. A major and long-term drop in precipitation (30 percent over eighty years) has been recorded in Northern Darfur, for example. The implications of such a decline on dry rangeland quality are obvious; and
- *Forecast climate change* is expected to further reduce productivity due to declining rainfall and increased variability, particularly in the Sahel belt. A drop in productivity of up to 70 percent is forecast for the most vulnerable areas.

Ever increasing demands on resources

The demand for natural resources in Sudan is uniformly increasing, due to the following factors:

- *Human population growth* is the underlying driver of increased demand for natural resources. Sudan has an overall growth rate of over 2.6 percent per annum, masking much higher localized rates. In central Darfur, for example, government statistics indicate a regional population (linear) growth rate of 12 percent per annum, from 3 persons/km² in 1956 to 18 persons/km² in 2003. These growth rates are indicative of large-scale in-migration, in this case mainly from the north and possibly due to environmental factors such as desertification; and

- *Livestock population and growth rates*; government officials and academics have tracked the population increase of livestock since the 1960s. In northern and central Sudan alone, it is estimated to have increased by over 400 percent between 1961 and 2004.

Land use changes—
a dwindling share of resources for pastoralists

The horizontal expansion of agriculture into areas that were previously either rangeland or forest has been a well-recognized trend for the last four decades. The northwards expansion of rain-fed agriculture into marginal areas historically only used for grazing has been particularly damaging. Three examples from the recent UNEP-ICRAF [World Agroforestry Center] study of land use changes illustrate a major reduction in rangeland areas due to expanding agriculture:

- In Ed Damazin, Blue Nile state, agricultural land (mainly mechanized) increased from 42 to 77 percent between 1972 and 1999, while rangeland effectively disappeared, dropping from 8.3 to 0.1 percent;
- In the El Obeid region of Northern Kordofan, rain-fed agricultural land increased by 57.6 percent between 1973 and 1999, while rangeland decreased by 33.8 percent and wooded pasture by 27 percent; and
- In the Um Chelluta region of Southern Darfur, rain-fed agricultural land increased by 138 percent between 1973 and 2000, while rangeland and closed woodland decreased by 56 and 32 percent, respectively.

In addition to the loss of grazing land, agricultural expansion has also blocked livestock migratory routes between many of the widely separated dry- and wet-season pastures, and between the herds and daily watering points. A further complication is that sedentary farmers are increasingly raising their own livestock, and are hence less willing to give grazing rights to nomads in transit.

Institutional factors—
failing to rectify the issues

. . . In summary, the rural environment has been impacted by a combination of ill-fated reform and development programs, as well as legal reforms and failures in environmental governance. One key issue is the difficulty of developing and applying a practical, just and stable system of rural land tenure in an ethnically complex society of intermingled sedentary farmers and transhumants/nomads. This has not been achieved in Sudan so far.

A lack of development and livelihood options

Outside of the main urban areas, Sudan remains very poor and underdeveloped. Rural populations consequently have very few options to solve these agricultural crises, as solutions like agricultural development, improvements in pasture and stock quality, and using working capital to cover short-term needs and alternative employment are simply not available.

The net result—disappearing livelihoods for dryland pastoralist societies

The clear trend that emerges when these various elements are pieced together is that of a *significant long-term increase in livestock density on rangelands that are reducing in total area, accessibility and quality.* In environmental terms, the observed net result is overgrazing and land degradation. In social terms, the reported consequence for pastoralist societies is an effectively permanent loss of livelihoods and entrenched poverty.

Pastoralist societies in Sudan have always been relatively vulnerable to losing their livelihoods due to erratic rainfall, but the above-noted combination of factors has propelled many pastoralists into a negative spiral of poverty, displacement and, in the worst cases, conflict. Their coping strategies, which have been well documented, include:

- Abandoning pastoralism as a livelihood in favor of sedentary agriculture, or displacement to cities;
- Increasing or varying the extent of annual herd movements where possible, with a general trend towards a permanently more southerly migration;
- Maximizing herd sizes as an insurance measure (assisted by the provision of water points and veterinary services);
- Changing herd composition, replacing camels by small animals, mainly sheep, in response to the curtailment of long-distance migration;
- Competing directly with other grazers for preferred areas of higher productivity (*entailing a conflict risk*);
- Moving and grazing livestock on cropland without consent (*entailing a conflict risk*); and
- Reducing competition by forcing other pastoralists and agriculturalists off previously shared land (*as a last resort—the proactive conflict scenario*). Variations of all of these strategies can be observed throughout Sudan, particularly in the drier regions.

Conclusions on the role of environmental issues in conflicts over rangeland and rain-fed agricultural land

Pastoralist societies have been at the center of local conflicts in Sudan throughout recorded history. The most significant problems have occurred and continue to occur in the drier central regions, which are also the regions with the largest live-stock populations, and under the most severe environmental stress.

As there are many factors in play—most of which are not related to the environment—land degradation does not appear to be the dominant causative factor in local conflicts. It is, however, a very important element, which is growing in significance and is a critical issue for the long-term resolution of the Darfur crisis. The key cause for concern is the *historical, ongoing and forecast shrinkage and degradation of remaining rangelands in the northern part of the Sahel belt.*

Much of the evidence for UNEP's analysis is anecdotal and qualitative; it has been gathered through desk study work, satellite images and interviews of rural societies across Sudan. The consistency and convergence of reports from a range of sources lend credibility to this analysis, although further research is clearly needed, with a particular emphasis on improved quantification of the highlighted issues and moving beyond analysis to search for viable long-term solutions.

A conference on the topic of environmental degradation and conflict in Darfur was held in Khartoum in 2004. The proceedings illustrated the depth of local understanding of the issue. Given the situation observed in 2007, however, UNEP must conclude that this high-quality awareness-raising exercise was unfortunately apparently not transformed into lasting action.

23

THE CASE AGAINST LINKING ENVIRONMENTAL DEGRADATION AND NATIONAL SECURITY

DANIEL DEUDNEY*

Introduction

. . . Environmental issues are likely to become an increasingly important dimension of political life at all levels—locally, inside states, as well as internationally. How institutions respond to these emerging constraints is likely to shape politics in a profound manner. Because state and interstate conflict are such central features of both world politics and geopolitical theory, there is a strong tendency for people to think about environmental problems in terms of national security and to assume that environmental conflicts will fit into the established patterns of interstate conflict.

The aim of this essay is to cast doubt upon this tendency to link environmental degradation and national security. Specifically, I make three claims. First, it is analytically misleading to think of environmental degradation as a national security threat, because the traditional focus of national security—interstate violence—has little in common with either environmental problems or solutions. Second, the effort to harness the emotive power of nationalism to help mobilize environmental awareness and action may prove counterproductive by undermining globalist political sensibility. And third, environmental degradation is not very likely to cause interstate wars.

* Originally published as Daniel Deudney, "The Case Against Linking Environmental Degradation and National Security," *Millennium* 19, no. 3. Copyright © 1990 by SAGE. Reprinted by permission of SAGE.

The Weak Analytical Links between Environmental Degradation and National Security

One striking feature of the growing discussion of environmental issues in the United States is the attempt by many liberals, progressives and environmentalists to employ language traditionally associated with violence and war to understand environmental problems and to motivate action. Lester Brown, Jessica Tuchman Matthews, Michael Renner and others have proposed "redefining national security" to encompass resource and environmental threats.[1] More broadly, Richard Ullman and others have proposed "redefining security" to encompass a wide array of threats, ranging from earthquakes to environmental degradation.[2] Hal Harvey has proposed the concept of "natural security,"[3] and US Senator Albert Gore has spoken extensively in favor of thinking of the environment as a national security issue.[4] During the renewed Cold War tensions of the late 1970s and early 1980s, such concepts were advanced to prevent an excessive focus on military threats. As the Cold War winds down, such links are increasingly popular among national security experts and organizations looking for new missions. . . .

Historically, conceptual ferment of this sort has often accompanied important changes in politics.[5] New phrases are coined and old terms are appropriated for new purposes. Epochal developments like the emergence of capitalism, the growth of democracy and the end of slavery were accompanied by shifting, borrowing and expanding political language. The wide-ranging contemporary conceptual ferment in the language used to understand and act upon environmental problems is therefore both a natural and an encouraging development.

But not all neologisms and linkages are equally plausible or useful. Until this recent flurry of reconceptualizing, the concept of "national security" (as opposed to national interest or well-being) has been centered upon *organized violence.*[6] As is obvious to common sense and as Hobbes argued with such force, security from violence is a primal human need, because loss of life prevents the enjoyment of all other goods. Of course, various resource factors, such as access to fuels and ores, were understood as contributing to states' capacities to wage war and achieve security from violence.

Before either "expanding" the concept of "national security" to encompass both environmental and violence threats, or "redefining" "national security" or "security" to refer mainly to environmental threats, it is worth examining just how much the national pursuit of security from violence has in common with environmental problems and their solutions.

Military violence and environmental degradation are linked directly in at least three major ways. First, the pursuit of national-security-from-violence through military means consumes resources (fiscal, organizational and leadership) that could be spent on environmental restoration. Since approximately one trillion US dollars is spent worldwide on military activities, substantial resources are involved. However, this relationship is not unique to environmental concerns, and unfortunately there is no guarantee that the world would spend money saved from military expenditures on environmental restoration. Nor is it clear that the world cannot afford environmental restoration without cutting military expenditures.

Second, war is directly destructive of the environment. In ancient times, the military destruction of olive groves in Mediterranean lands contributed to the long-lasting destruction of the lands' carrying capacities. More recently, the United States' bombardment and use of defoliants in Indochina caused significant environmental damage. Further, extensive use of nuclear weapons could have significant impacts on the global environment, including altered weather (i.e., "nuclear winter") and further depletion of the ozone layer. Awareness of these environmental effects has played an important role in mobilizing popular resistance to the arms race and in generally delegitimizing use of nuclear explosives as weapons.

Third, preparation for war causes pollution and consumes significant quantities of resources. In both the United States and the Soviet Union, significant quantities of radioactive waste have been produced as a by-product of the nuclear arms race, and several significant releases of radiation have occurred—perhaps most disastrously when a waste dump at a Soviet nuclear weapons facility exploded and burned, spreading radioactive materials over a large area near the Urals. Military activities have also produced significant quantities of toxic wastes.

In short, war and the preparation for war are clearly environmental threats and consume resources that could be used to ameliorate environmental degradation. In effect, these environmental impacts mean that the war system has costs beyond the intentional loss of life and destruction. Nevertheless, most of the world's environmental degradation is not caused by war and the preparation for war. Completely eliminating the direct environmental effects of the war system would leave most environmental degradation unaffected. Most of the causes and most of the cures of environmental degradation must be found outside the domain of the traditional national security system related to violence.

The war system is a definite but limited environmental threat, but in what ways is environmental degradation a threat to "national security"? Making such an identification can be useful if the two phenomena—security from violence and security from environmental threats—are similar. Unfortunately, they have little in common, making such linkages largely useless for analytical and conceptual purposes. Four major dissimilarities . . . deserve mention.

First, environmental degradation and violence are very different types of threats. Both violence and environmental degradation may kill people and may reduce human well-being, but not all threats to life and property are threats to security. Disease, old age, crime and accidents routinely destroy life and property, but we do not think of them as "national security" threats or even threats to "security." (Crime is a partial exception, but crime is a "security" threat at the individual level, because crime involves violence.) And when an earthquake or hurricane strikes with great force, we speak about "natural disasters" or designate "national disaster areas," but we do not speak about such events threatening "national security." If everything that causes a decline in human well-being is labeled a "security" threat, the term loses any analytical usefulness and becomes a loose synonym of "bad."

Second, the scope and source of threats to environmental well-being and national-security-from-violence are very different. There is nothing about the problem of environmental degradation which is particularly "national" in character. Since environmental threats are often oblivious of the borders of the nation-state, they rarely afflict just one nation-state. Nevertheless, this said, it would be misleading to call most environmental problems "international." Many perpetrators and victims are within the borders of one nation-state. Individuals, families, communities, other species and future generations are harmed. A complete collapse of the biosphere would surely destroy "nations" as well as everything else, but there is nothing distinctively national about either the causes, the harms or the solutions that warrants us giving such privileged billing to the "national" grouping.

A third misfit between environmental well-being and national-security-from-violence stems from the differing degrees of intention involved. Violent threats involve a high degree of intentional behavior. Organizations are mobilized, weapons procured and wars waged with relatively definite aims in mind. Environmental degradation, on the other hand, is largely unintentional, the side effects of many other activities. No one really sets out with the aim of harming the environment (with the so far limited exception of environmental modification for military purposes).

Fourth, organizations that provide protection from violence differ greatly from those in environmental protection. National-security-from-violence is conventionally pursued by organizations with three distinctive features. First, military organizations are secretive, extremely hierarchical and centralized, and normally deploy vastly expensive, highly specialized and advanced technologies. Second, citizens typically delegate the goal of achieving national security to remote and highly specialized organizations that are far removed from the experience of civil society. And third, the specialized professional group staffing these national security organizations are trained in the arts of killing and destroying.

In contrast, responding to the environmental problem requires almost exactly opposite approaches and organizations. Certain aspects of virtually all mundane activities—for example, house construction, farming techniques, sewage treatment, factory design and land use planning—must be reformed. The routine everyday behavior of practically everyone must be altered. This requires behavior modification in situ. The professional ethos of environmental restoration is husbandmanship—more respectful cultivation and protection of plants, animals and the land.

In short, national-security-from-violence and environmental habitability have little in common. Given these differences, the rising fashion of linking them risks creating a conceptual muddle rather than a paradigm or world view shift—a *de-definition* rather than a *re-definition* of security. If we begin to speak about all the forces and events that threaten life, property and well-being (on a large scale) as threats to our national security, we shall soon drain the term of any meaning. All large-scale evils will become threats to national security. To speak meaningfully about actual problems, we shall have to invent new words to fill the job previously performed by the old spoiled ones.

The Risks in Harnessing the Rhetorical and Emotional Appeals of National Security for Environmental Restoration

Confronted with these arguments, the advocate of treating environmental degradation as a national security problem might retort:

> Yes, some semantic innovation without much analytical basis is occurring, but it has a sound goal—to get people to react as urgently and effectively to the environmental problem as they have to the national-security-from-violence problem. If people took the environmental problem as seriously as, say, an attack by a foreign power, think of all that could be done to solve the problems!

In other words, the aim of these new links is not primarily descriptive, but polemical. It is not a claim about fact, but a rhetorical device designed to stimulate action. Like William James, these environmentalists hope to find a "moral equivalent to war" to channel the energies behind war into constructive directions. . . . [Editors' note: See the philosopher William James's classic 1906 essay, "The Moral Equivalent of War," based on a speech he gave at Stanford University.]

At first glance, the most attractive feature of linking fears about environmental threats with national security mentalities is the sense of urgency engendered, and the corresponding willingness to accept great personal sacrifice. If in fact the basic habitability of the planet is being undermined, then it stands to reason that some crisis mentality is needed. Unfortunately, it may be difficult to engender a sense of urgency and a willingness to sacrifice for extended periods of time. . . . A second apparently valuable similarity between the national security mentality and the environmental problem is the tendency to use worst-case scenarios as the basis for planning. However, the extreme conservatism of military organizations in responding to potential threats is not unique to them. The insurance industry is built around preparations for the worst possibilities, and many fields of engineering, such as aeronautical design and nuclear power plant regulation, routinely employ extremely conservative planning assumptions. These can serve as useful models for improved environmental policies.

Third, the conventional national security mentality and its organizations are deeply committed to zero-sum thinking. "Our" gain is "their" loss. Trust between national security organizations is extremely low. The prevailing assumption is that everyone is a potential enemy, and that agreements mean little unless congruent with immediate interests. If the Pentagon had been put in charge of negotiating an ozone layer protocol, we might still be stockpiling chlorofluorocarbons as a bargaining chip.

Fourth, conventional national security organizations have short time horizons. The pervasive tendency for national security organizations to discount the future and pursue very near-term objectives is a poor model for environmental problem solving.

Finally, and perhaps most importantly, is the fact that the "nation" is not an empty vessel or blank slate waiting to be filled or scripted, but is instead profoundly linked to war and "us vs. them" thinking. The tendency for people to identify themselves with various tribal and kin groupings is as old as humanity. In the last century and a half, however, this sentiment of nationalism, amplified and manipulated by mass media propaganda techniques, has been an integral part of totalitarianism and militarism. Nationalism means a sense of "us vs. them," of the insider vs. the outsider, of the compatriot vs. the alien. The stronger the nationalism, the stronger this cleavage, and the weaker the transnational bonds. Nationalism reinforces militarism, fosters prejudice and discrimination and feeds the quest for "sovereign" autonomy. . . .

Thus, thinking of national security as an environmental problem risks undercutting both the globalist and common fate understanding of the situation and the sense of world community that may be necessary to solve the problem. In short, it seems doubtful that the environment can be wrapped in national flags without undercutting the "whole earth" sensibility at the core of environmental awareness.

If pollution comes to be seen widely as a national security problem, there is also a danger that the citizens of one country will feel much more threatened by the pollution from other countries than by the pollution created by their fellow citizens. This could increase international tensions and make international accords more difficult to achieve, while diverting attention from internal cleanup. Citizens of the United States, for example, could become much more concerned about deforestation in Brazil than in reversing the centuries of North American deforestation. Taken to an absurd extreme—as national security threats sometimes are—seeing environmental degradation in a neighboring country as a national security threat could trigger various types of interventions, a new imperialism of the strong against the weak.

Instead of linking "national security" to the environmental problem, environmentalists should emphasize that the environmental crisis calls into question the national grouping and its privileged status in world politics. The environmental crisis is not a threat to national security, but it does challenge the utility of thinking in "national" terms. . . .

Environmental Degradation and Interstate War

Many people are drawn to calling environmental degradation a national security problem, in part because they expect this phenomenon to stimulate interstate conflict and even violence. States often fight over what they value, particularly if related to "security." If states begin to be much more concerned with resources and environmental degradation, particularly if they think environmental decay is a threat to their "national security," then states may well fight resource and pollution wars. . . . In general, I argue that interstate violence is not likely to result from environmental degradation, because of several deeply rooted features of the contemporary world order—both material and institutional—and because of the character of environmental and resource interests.

Few ideas seem more intuitively sound than the notion that states will begin fighting each other as the world runs out of usable natural resources. The popular metaphor of a lifeboat adrift at sea with declining supplies of clean water and rations suggests there will be fewer and fewer opportunities for positive-sum gains between actors. . . .

There are, however, three strong reasons for concluding that the familiar scenarios of resource war are of diminishing plausibility for the foreseeable future. First, the robust character of the world trade system means that states no longer experience resource dependency as a major threat to their military security and political autonomy. During the 1930s, the world trading system had collapsed, driving states to pursue autarkic economies. In contrast, the resource needs of contemporary states are routinely met without territorial control of the resource source, as Ronnie Lipschutz has recently shown.[7]

Second, the prospects for resource wars are diminished, since states find it increasingly difficult to exploit foreign resources through territorial conquest. Although the invention of nuclear explosives has made it easy and cheap to annihilate humans and infrastructure in extensive areas, the spread of small arms and national consciousness has made it very costly for an invader, even one equipped with advanced technology, to subdue a resisting population—as France discovered in Indochina and Algeria, the United States in Vietnam and the Soviet Union in Afghanistan. . . .

Third, the world is entering what H. E. Goeller and Alvin M. Weinberg have called the "age of substitutability," in which industrial civilization is increasingly capable of taking earth materials such as iron, aluminum, silicon and hydrocarbons (which are ubiquitous and plentiful) and fashioning them into virtually everything needed.[8] The most striking manifestation of this trend is that prices for virtually every raw material have been stagnant or falling for the last several decades, despite the continued growth in world output. In contrast to the expectations voiced by many during the 1970s—that resource scarcity would drive up commodity prices to the benefit of Third World raw material suppliers—prices have fallen, with disastrous consequences for Third World development.

In a second scenario, increased interstate violence results from internal turmoil caused by declining living standards. . . . Faced with declining living standards, groups at all levels of affluence can be expected to resist this trend by pushing the deprivation upon other groups. Class relations would be increasingly "zero-sum games," producing class war and revolutionary upheavals. Faced with these pressures, liberal democracy and free-market systems would increasingly be replaced by authoritarian systems capable of maintaining minimum order.[9]

The international system consequences of these domestic changes may be increased conflict and war. If authoritarian regimes are more war-prone because of their lack of democratic control and if revolutionary regimes are more war-prone because of their ideological fervor and lack of socialization into international norms and processes, then a world political system containing more such states is likely to be an increasingly violent one. The historical record from previous economic depressions supports the general proposition that widespread economic stagnation and unmet economic expectations contribute to international conflict.

Although initially compelling, this scenario has flaws as well. First, the pessimistic interpretation of the relationship between environmental sustainability and economic growth is arguably based on unsound economic theory. Wealth formation is not so much a product of cheap natural resource availability as of capital formation via savings and more efficient ways of producing. The fact that so many resource-poor countries, like Japan, are very wealthy, while many countries with more extensive resource endowments are poor, suggests that there is no clear and direct relationship between abundant resource availability and national wealth. Environmental constraints require an end to economic growth based on increasing raw material throughputs, rather than an end to growth in the output of goods and services.

Second, even if economic decline does occur, interstate conflict may be dampened, not stoked. . . . How societies respond to economic decline may in large measure depend upon the rate at which such declines occur. An offsetting factor here is the possibility that as people get poorer, they will be less willing to spend increasingly scarce resources for military capabilities. In this regard, the experience of economic depressions over the last two centuries may not be relevant, because such depressions were characterized by underutilized production capacity and falling resource prices. In the 1930s, increased military spending had a stimulative effect, but in a world in which economic growth had been retarded by environmental constraints, military spending would exacerbate the problem. . . .

Environmental degradation in a country or region could become so extreme that the basic social and economic fabric comes apart. Should some areas of the world suffer this fate, the impact of this outcome on international order may not, however, be very great. If a particular country, even a large one like Brazil, were tragically to disintegrate, among the first casualties would be the capacity of the industrial and governmental structure to wage and sustain interstate conventional war. As Bernard Brodie observed in the modern era, "the predisposing factors to military aggression are full bellies, not empty ones."[10] The poor and wretched of the earth may be able to deny an outside aggressor an easy conquest, but they are themselves a minimal threat to outside states. Offensive war today requires complex organizational skills, specialized industrial products and surplus wealth.

In today's world everything is connected, but not everything is tightly coupled. Regional disasters of great severity may occur, with scarcely a ripple in the rest of the world. After all, Idi Amin drew Uganda back into savage darkness, the Khmer Rouge murdered an estimated two million Cambodians and the Sahara has advanced across the Sahel without the economies and political systems of the rest of the world being much perturbed. Indeed, many of the world's citizens did not even notice.

A fourth possible route from environmental degradation to interstate conflict and violence involves pollution across state borders. It is easy to envision situations in which country A dumps an intolerable amount of pollution on a neighboring country B (which is upstream and upwind), causing country B to attempt to pressure and coerce country A into eliminating its offending pollution. We can envision such conflict of interest leading to armed conflict.

Fortunately for interstate peace, strongly asymmetrical and significant environmental degradation between neighboring countries is relatively rare. Probably more typical is the situation in which activities in country A harm parts of country A and country B, and in which activities in country B also harm parts of both countries. This creates complex sets of winners and losers, and thus establishes a complex array of potential intrastate and interstate coalitions. In general, the more such interactions are occurring, the less likely it is that a persistent, significant and highly asymmetrical pollution "exchange" will result. The very multitude of interdependency in the contemporary world, particularly among the industrialized countries, makes it unlikely that intense cleavages of environmental harm will match interstate borders, and at the same time not be compensated and complicated by other military, economic or cultural interactions. Resolving such conflicts will be a complex and messy affair, but the conflicts are unlikely to lead to war.

Finally, there are conflict potentials related to the global commons. Many countries contribute to environmental degradation, and many countries are harmed, but since the impacts are widely distributed, no one country has an incentive to act alone to solve the problem. Solutions require collective action, and with collective action comes the possibility of the "free rider." . . .

It is difficult to judge this scenario, because we lack examples of this phenomenon on a large scale. "Free-rider" problems may generate severe conflict, but it is doubtful that states would find military instruments useful for coercion and compliance. . . .

Conclusion

The degradation of the natural environment upon which human well-being depends is a challenge of far-reaching significance for human societies everywhere. But this challenge has little to do with the national-security-from-violence problem that continues to plague human political life. Not only is there little in common between the causes and solutions of these two problems, but the nationalist and militarist mindsets closely associated with "national security" thinking directly

conflict with the core of the environmentalist world view. Harnessing these senti-
ments for a "war on pollution" is a dangerous and probably self-defeating enterprise. And fortunately, the prospects for resource and pollution wars are not as
great as often conjured by environmentalists.

The pervasive recourse to national security paradigms to conceptualize the
environmental problem represents a profound and disturbing failure of imagi-
nation and political awareness. If the nation-state enjoys a more prominent status in world politics than its competence and accomplishments warrant, then it
makes little sense to emphasize the links between it and the emerging problem of
global habitability.[11] Nationalist sentiment and the war system have a long-
established logic and staying power that are likely to defy any rhetorically conjured "re-direction" toward benign ends. The movement to preserve the habitability of the planet for future generations must directly challenge the tribal power of
nationalism and the chronic militarization of public discourse. Environmental
degradation is not a threat to national security. Rather, environmentalism is a
threat to "national security" mindsets and institutions. For environmentalists to
dress their programs in the blood-soaked garments of the war system betrays
their core values and creates confusion about the real tasks at hand.

Notes

1. Lester Brown, *Redefining National Security* (Washington, DC: Worldwatch Paper, No.
14, October 1977); Jessica Tuchman Mathews, "Redefining Security," *Foreign Affairs* (Vol.
68, No. 2, 1989), pp. 162–77; Michael Renner, *National Security: The Economic and Environmental Dimensions* (Washington, DC: Worldwatch Paper, No. 89, May 1989); and Norman Myers, "Environmental Security," *Foreign Policy* (No. 74, 1989), pp. 23–41.

2. Richard Ullman, "Redefining Security," *International Security* (Vol. 8, No. 1, Summer
1983), pp. 129–53.

3. Hal Harvey, "Natural Security," *Nuclear Times* (March/April 1988), pp. 24–26.

4. Philip Shabecoff, "Senator Urges Military Resources to be Turned to Environmental
Battle," *The New York Times*, 29 June 1990, p. 1A.

5. Quentin Skinner, "Language and Political Change," and James Farr, "Understanding
Political Change Conceptually," in Terence Ball et al. (eds.), *Political Innovation and Conceptual Change* (Cambridge: Cambridge University Press, 1989).

6. For a particularly lucid and well-rounded discussion of security, the state and violence, see Barry Buzan, *People, States, and Fear: The National Security Problem in International Relations* (Chapel Hill, NC: University of North Carolina Press, 1983), particularly
pp. 1–93.

7. Ronnie D. Lipschutz, *When Nations Clash: Raw Materials, Ideology and Foreign Policy*
(New York: Ballinger, 1989).

8. H. E. Goeller and Alvin Weinberg, "The Age of Substitutability," *Science* (Vol. 201, 20
February 1967). For some recent evidence supporting this hypothesis, see Eric D. Larson,
Marc H. Ross and Robert H. Williams, "Beyond the Era of Materials," *Scientific American*
(Vol. 254, 1986), pp. 34–41.

9. For a discussion of authoritarian and conflictual consequences of environmentally
constrained economies, see William Ophuls, *Ecology and the Politics of Scarcity* (San Fran-

cisco, CA: Freeman, 1976), p. 152. See also Susan M. Leeson, "Philosophical Implications of the Ecological Crisis: The Authoritarian Challenge to Liberalism," *Polity* (Vol. 11, No. 3, Spring 1979); Ted Gurr, "On the Political Consequences of Scarcity and Economic Decline," *International Studies Quarterly* (No. 29, 1985), pp. 51–75; and Robert Heilbroner, *An Inquiry Into the Human Prospect* (New York: W. W. Norton, 1974).

10. Bernard Brodie, "The Impact of Technological Change on the International System," in David Sullivan and Martin Sattler (eds.), *Change and the Future of the International System* (New York: Columbia University Press, 1972), p. 14.

11. For a particularly lucid argument that the nation-state system is overdeveloped relative to its actual problem-solving capacities, see George Modelski, *Principles of World Politics* (New York: The Free Press, 1972).

24

THE VIOLENCE
OF DEVELOPMENT

BALAKRISHNAN RAJAGOPAL[*]

"Ethnic cleansing"—the forcible dislocation of a large number of people belong-ing to particular ethnic groups—is an outlawed practice. Individuals who are ac-cused of ethnic cleansing are subjected to indictment by international criminal tribunals, and even domestic courts are increasingly used in the West to prosecute those who commit mass violence abroad.

Yet most large forced dislocations of people do not occur in conditions of armed conflict or genocide but in routine, everyday evictions to make way for de-velopment projects. A recent report by the World Commission on Dams estimates that 40 million to 80 million people have been physically displaced by dams worldwide, a disproportionate number of them being indigenous peoples. In-deed, this "development cleansing" may well constitute ethnic cleansing in dis-guise, as the people dislocated so often turn out to be from minority ethnic and racial communities.

In the Philippines, almost all the large dam schemes are on the land of the country's 6 million to 7 million indigenous people. In India, 40 percent to 50 per-cent of those displaced by development projects—a total estimated at more than 33 million since 1947—are tribal people, who account for just 8 percent of the country's 1 billion population.

Still, international human rights monitors remain oblivious to the violence of development. A biased focus on international criminal justice—the pursuit of a Milosevic, for example—has blinded the world's conscience to mass crimes that are often as serious as those that occurred in Rwanda and the former Yugoslavia.

The millions of people forcibly dislocated from their lands are usually from among the poorest and most vulnerable sections of populations. Upon disloca-

* Originally published in *The Washington Post*, August 8, 2001. Reprinted with permission of the author.

tion, these communities are pushed into further poverty and violence. These conditions are themselves grave human rights violations, but they also lead to further violations—for example, by exacerbating conflicts between large communities that lose land and are resettled and the communities into which they move.

Forcible dislocation destroys the livelihoods of entire communities as large dams and inappropriate agricultural projects alter the land-use patterns that traditionally support farming, grazing and fishing. And the number of people forcibly dislocated is probably far larger than reported, as the displaced are systematically undercounted—for example, by as much as 47 percent in the case of the projects funded by the World Bank. In China's Western Poverty Reduction Project in Qinghai, the World Bank Complaints Panel found that entire towns of thousands of Tibetan and Mongol minorities were not counted as affected.

The United Nations has declared mass eviction to be a violation of the human right to housing. And because of growing conflicts over water and natural resources, the World Commission on Dams was established in 1998 by the World Bank, the International Conservation Union and others. But despite these efforts, human rights violations continue in the name of development.

For instance, a judgment by the Indian Supreme Court in October 2000 will allow the construction of a mega-dam on the Narmada River to go forward. This is deeply disappointing given the Indian judiciary's history as the protector of the rights of the underprivileged. It is also tragic because the project will lead to the displacement of more than 200,000 people and the elimination of the rich ecological resources in the Narmada Valley, one of India's most fertile.

The Narmada Valley dam project is the second largest in the world, after the Three Gorges dam project in China, which is known for its excessive human and environmental costs. The World Bank, which originally was to have funded the Narmada project, withdrew funding in 1993 after being criticized for violating its own internal regulations on resettlement and rehabilitation and environmental clearance. Every funder since then—Japanese and Germans included—has withdrawn after running into criticism, and the project is now being funded by Indian state governments, redirecting scarce funds from much-needed health and education projects.

A broad coalition opposing the dam, consisting of the people of the Narmada Valley as well as domestic and foreign intellectuals, social activists, journalists, judges and lawyers, has repeatedly pointed out technological alternatives for producing power and providing water, but these have been dismissed by the Indian Supreme Court.

On the other side is the developmental nationalism displayed by Indian Home Minister L. K. Advani, who says opponents of such projects are working at the behest of "foreign nations"—a response commonly given by governments that commit gross human rights abuses.

It is clear that international indifference toward the violence of development projects needs to end.

25

AN UNCOMMON PEACE: ENVIRONMENT, DEVELOPMENT, AND THE GLOBAL SECURITY AGENDA

GEOFFREY D. DABELKO[*]

In 1988, nuclear war was "undoubtedly the gravest" threat facing the environment, according to *Our Common Future,* commonly known as the Brundtland report.[1] The possible environmental consequences of thermonuclear war—radioactive contamination, nuclear winter, and genetic mutations—were widely feared during the Cold War, especially by citizens of the United States and Soviet Union, which the report called "prisoners of their own arms race."[2]

Thankfully, these nightmare scenarios did not come to pass.... However, in the 20 years since the report's publication, the specter of nuclear destruction has not yet been "removed from the face of the Earth,"[3] as the report called for, but has merely changed scale: the threat of the mushroom cloud has been replaced by the threat of the dirty bomb—a crude device that a terrorist cell could fashion out of pilfered nuclear material. Setting off such a bomb in a world city—a major hub in the global economy—could create more disruption than the paradigm-shifting attacks of September 11, 2001, although the radioactivity would impact far fewer people than the feared global nuclear winter of old.

Since the end of the Cold War in 1989, the security community's focus has shifted from the global clash of superpowers to fragmented groups of stateless

[*] *Environment* Vol. 50, No. 3, Pp. 32-45, May/June 2008. Reprinted with Permission of the Helen Dwight Reid Educational Foundation. Published by Heldref Publications, 1319 Eighteenth St. N.W., Washington, D.C. 20036-1802. (C) 2001.

actors fomenting civil war and terrorism. The end of the Cold War also opened greater political space for analyzing a range of diverse threats to both individuals and the world beyond using the traditional state-centered approach. The environment—along with the related challenges of health and poverty—has become a key area of focus within that new space.

Our understanding of the links between environment and security has evolved in the last 20 years to reflect these changing threat scenarios. Today, "environmental security" has become a popular phrase used to encompass everything from oil exploration to pollution controls to corn subsidies. The Brundtland report, in an underappreciated chapter entitled "Peace, Security, Development, and the Environment," set the agenda for understanding these multiple links between environment and security. . . .

Redefining Security in *Our Common Future*

Our Common Future, produced by the World Commission on Environment and Development (WCED), is best known for its definition of sustainable development.[5] Yet the so-called Brundtland Commission, named after its chair, former Norwegian Prime Minister Gro Harlem Brundtland, also called for a broader conception of security that included instability caused in part by environmental factors. Conflict, attendant military spending, and the ultimate threat of nuclear exchange were highlighted as direct and indirect impediments to achieving sustainable development. As was to become the habit of many subsequent environmental security advocates, *Our Common Future* called for fundamentally broadening security definitions to accommodate these wider threats while simultaneously employing environment and conflict arguments that fell comfortably within the traditional confines of security.[6]

In the introductory chapter, the commissioners stated, "The whole notion of security as traditionally understood—in terms of political and military threats to national sovereignty—must be expanded to include the growing impacts of environmental stress—locally, nationally, regionally, and globally."[7] While acknowledging these linkages were "poorly understood," the commission held that "a comprehensive approach to international and national security must transcend the traditional emphasis on military power and armed competition."[8] . . .

While by no means the first advocate for this expanded notion of security,[10] the Brundtland Commission was a key legitimizing voice. Its influence was felt in the United Nations Development Programme's (UNDP) "human security" frame, which gained traction in UN forums and was championed by select national leaders such as Canada's Foreign Minister Lloyd Axworthy.[11] Even as it called for altering the security paradigm, the Brundtland Commission made arguments firmly ensconced in a traditional statist security perspective. The report flagged "environmental stress as both a cause and an effect of political tension and military conflict" and recognized that "environmental stress is seldom the only cause of major conflicts within or among nations" but could be "an important part of the web of causality associated with any conflict and can in some cases be catalytic."[12]

The commissioners identified climate change, loss of arable land, fisheries, and water as factors likely to contribute to conflict and spur other security-related problems, such as migration and economic dislocation. It also highlighted poverty, inequality, and lost development opportunities as key factors in creating insecurity. However, these factors were not consistently addressed in the early research on environmental stress and conflict that followed in the early 1990s, possibly due to relatively low levels of developing-country participation in these research efforts. Had more researchers adopted the Brundtland Commission's broader lens, analyses of environment-conflict links might have better integrated more robust analysis of poverty concerns and the physically remote, yet highly relevant, role of international markets for natural resources.[13]

The Brundtland Commission also identified political capacity as an important element in environment-conflict links 10 years before it was hailed "the missing ingredient" by the field's researchers.[14] The commissioners stated that environmental stress could contribute to interstate or subnational conflict "when political processes are unable to handle the effects of environmental stress resulting, for example, from erosion and desertification."[15] *Our Common Future*'s focus on environment and conflict provided a legitimizing foundation for what, just a few years later, became an explosion of analytical work within and outside of governments.[16] During the 20 years that followed the release of *Our Common Future*, scholarly and policy interest in the linkages it highlighted has risen, fallen, and risen again.[17] . . .

No Room for Environmental Security on the Rio Agenda

The environment, peace, and security chapter of *Our Common Future* did not receive extensive formal treatment at the 1992 UN Conference on Environment and Development in Rio de Janeiro. The developing world did not endorse a global dialogue on environmental issues within the context of conflict and security, reacting negatively to formal environmental security proposals in UN forums.[20] The coalition of developing nations, the Group of 77, perceived the security frame as a Pandora's box that, once opened, could dilute their claims of absolute sovereign control over their resources. The United States was equally wary, fearing environmental issues might dilute and undermine military-focused security definitions in the midst of the Cold War. More practically, the environment, conflict, and security issues raised in *Our Common Future* did not easily lend themselves to resolution in a multilateral environmental treaty, the preferred mechanism at Rio and of the international environmental community in general.[21]

The Soviet Union attempted—and failed—to institutionalize environment and security links at the United Nations prior to the Rio conference. In October 1987, in the wake of the Chernobyl accident, Mikhail Gorbachev launched his "Murmansk Initiatives" in a speech in that northern city on the Kola Peninsula.[22] Calling for *glasnost* and greater cooperation (particularly among the Arctic states) in trade, environment, culture, and arms control, he proposed "ecological security" as a top global priority for both bilateral relationships and international institutions.[23] While aimed at environmental challenges, the Murmansk Initiatives were a de facto forum for moving beyond environmental goals to broader confidence-building efforts across the Cold War divide.

Gorbachev and then–Soviet Foreign Minister Eduard Shevardnadze, in speeches to the United Nations in 1988 and 1989, proposed creating ecological security institutions because, in Shevardnadze's words, "Overcoming the global threat to the environment and ensuring universal environmental security through prompt and effective action is an imperative of our times."[24] In early May 1989, Shevardnadze called for the creation of a "UN Center for Emergency Environmental Assistance," commonly referred to as the "Green Helmets," to be headed by a UN undersecretary-general.

The foreign minister asked all member states to discuss this idea, in which a group of environmental experts would comprise a rapid-response force, "at a time when countries are starting preparation for a UN-sponsored conference on environment and development planned for 1992."[25] He also called on the UN General Assembly to create a UN Environmental Security Council. These specific proposals were predicated on the more fundamental premise that security had to be redefined: "For the first time we have understood clearly what we just guessed: that the traditional view of national and universal security based primarily on military means of defense is now totally obsolete and must be urgently revised."[26] . . .

The reaction to the Murmansk Initiatives and the subsequent UN proposals was mixed. The U.S. government response was "reserved," perceiving the Soviet ideas as posturing and rhetoric designed to play to the developing-country galleries at the UN General Assembly.[27] Environment was not yet widely linked with security in U.S. diplomatic circles, with then–U.S. Senator Al Gore one of the few politicians regularly promoting the connection.[28] With the concurrent collapse of communism in Central and Eastern Europe, the rest of the world glimpsed the massive toxic legacy lurking behind the Iron Curtain, which damaged the credibility of Soviet environmental decisionmaking. Shevardnadze's 27 September 1988 call for the United States and others to transfer funds from military programs to environmental efforts echoed similar efforts in the 1970s and 1980s by the Soviets to slow or constrain NATO weapons development by promoting international environment regimes.[29]

The Green Helmets proposal was highly unpopular with developing countries and became a political nonstarter. Countries such as Brazil feared (and continue to fear) developed-country intervention seeking to stop exploitation of natural resources such as those in the Brazilian Amazon.[30] The sovereign right of nonintervention was employed as an argument against the Green Helmets proposal, cutting off UN General Assembly discussion of further ecological security proposals. This dynamic repeated itself 10 years later in the UN context when then–UN Environment Programme Executive Director Klaus Toepfer reintroduced the Green Helmets idea, which was once again quickly rejected by the Group of 77 countries due to sovereignty concerns.

Environmental Security Takes Root

This failure to achieve high-profile traction on environmental security linkages at the United Nations in the 1990s did not imply a commensurate lack of interest among certain individual nations and regional organizations. The end of the Cold War did not produce the expected peace dividends, as hostilities held in check by the superpower competition were unleashed and the number of conflicts actually spiked in the 1990s. For some, such as Al Gore, by then U.S. vice president, the rise in civil conflicts—such as those in Liberia, Somalia, Rwanda, and Haiti— indicated that governments should pay greater attention to the underlying demographic, environmental, and distributional origins of these conflicts. These concerns led to a raft of analytical and policy initiatives which were prominent in, but by no means limited to, the United States.[31]

While environmental advocates and security actors remained wary of each other's focus, means, and ends, both analysts and policymakers sought to understand these linkages. Journalist Robert Kaplan captured the policy community's attention (and fears) in his 1994 *Atlantic Monthly* article entitled "The Coming Anarchy."[32] Kaplan held up demographic and natural resource pressures as primary explanations for West Africa's failing states, drawing heavily on the work of peace researcher Thomas Homer-Dixon from the University of Toronto. Many critics thought Kaplan oversold the environment as the national security issue of the twenty-first century, and his claims that West Africa's fundamental challenges were widely applicable to other regions of the world provoked an analytical and policy backlash when environmental scarcity did not prove to be the ultimate threat in the post–Cold War era. Environmental security would not provide an all-encompassing alternative security paradigm. Nevertheless, the contributions of natural resource scarcity and abundance to conflict—as well as larger environmental challenges to traditional definitions of security—became institutionalized concerns for foreign, development, and security communities.

In 1994—a key year in our understanding of the links between environment, development, and security—the UNDP dedicated its annual *Human Development Report* to human security, suggesting that environmental security was one of seven areas that should constitute a new global security paradigm.[33] Japan, Canada, and a wide range of UN bodies now commonly use this frame, and small island states commonly invoke it to dramatize the threat to survival posed by climate change–induced sea-level rise. Although its critics bemoan its lack of precision,[34] human security was prominently deployed in nonenvironmental successes such as the establishment of the 1997 Convention to Ban Landmines and the International Criminal Court in 2002.

In the late 1990s, climate change and the 1997 Kyoto Protocol captured the attention of most of the global environmental community. Climate change had not featured prominently in the debates over whether the environment is a contributing cause of conflict, and it had not yet been framed as an existential global security threat. The heavy focus on the multilateral environmental treaty mechanism and the all-country negotiations to reach a global agreement was not well suited to addressing the intertwined and site-specific social, political, economic, and environmental challenges of climate change. Scholars were mired in a set of testy methodological logjams that have only begun to break up in recent years due to innovative qualitative and quantitative work. In the policy realm, program implementation suffered from the reluctance of donors to integrate conflict considerations into their antipoverty or livelihoods efforts. At the same time, many developing countries and donors remained suspicious of environmental issues, considering them luxury items for wealthy countries rather than life-and-death livelihood problems for the world's poor. However, by the early twenty-first century, many overcame their hesitation to integrate environment, development, and conflict efforts, as evidenced by greater willingness to analyze these natural resource linkages and address them with local, field-based programs.

The reaction to the September 11 attacks certainly set back efforts to address environment and security linkages. Just as the superpower confrontation of the Cold War provided little political space for a broader array of security concerns, the "war on terror" kicked other threats off policymakers' priority lists. . . . And the antipathy of U.S. President George W. Bush's administration to anything dubbed "environmental" set back efforts in international forums and pushed much of the official U.S. work on environmental security behind the scenes, or forced it to be relabeled as disaster relief. Yet interest in environment, peace, and security linkages continues to grow within the UN system, the bilateral development and security communities, and in countries experiencing conflict. As the "force-only" responses to the September 11 attacks have fallen short of achieving either military or human security objectives, policymakers and practitioners have been returning to more inclusive notions of security.[36] . . .

The Future of Environment, Peace, and Security

. . . The sheer diversity of environment-security links, as complex today as they were 20 years ago, will continue to frustrate those in the policy and analytical realms who want more analytical precision and a narrower lens for a term as broad as "environmental security." Yet the failure of one set of environment and security linkages to achieve dominance has guaranteed that no avenues have been prematurely closed off. The temptation to crown one set of linkages the top priority or the only legitimate definition of environmental security ignores the diversity of valid concerns that arise in different contexts and sets up a false all-or-nothing choice.

Efforts to broaden the definition of security are again gaining traction, boosted by the widespread concern with the potential impacts of climate change and the perception that using force as the only approach to conflict is counterproductive. A few prominent scientists even claim that climate change is a bigger threat than terrorism.[39] These environment and security links have helped break down the stereotype that environmental issues are the province of wealthy advocates interested in saving charismatic wildlife. Instead, policymakers and practitioners are increasingly viewing these natural resources as critical to the day-to-day livelihoods of literally billions of people. By awarding recent peace prizes to Al Gore and the Intergovernmental Panel on Climate Change, as well as environmental activist Wangari Maathai, the Nobel Committee has helped push environmental security back into the limelight, 20 years after the Brundtland Commission brought it to the fore. A few areas, discussed below, illustrate the field's budding progress and the great potential for meaningful analytical development and practical action.

Down on the Ground: Subnational Analysis

Although there has been a dramatic decline in the number of conflicts over the past decade, persistent ones—including those in the Democratic Republic of the Congo, Nigeria, the Philippines, the Horn of Africa, and Nepal—often have strong environmental components.[40] Whether it is the abundance of valuable resources such as oil, forests, or minerals, or the scarcity of resources such as land or water, these underlying factors are increasingly viewed as central to spurring, prolonging, ending, and resolving these conflicts.[41] Analyzing the multiple roles environmental factors play before, during, and after conflict supports a much more robust research and policy agenda than does focusing exclusively on the environment's potential to cause conflict. This wider lens also helps address the misperception that environment is *the* factor causing conflict; those who analyze environment, conflict, and security issues seek only to be included in the larger conflict discussion.

New analytical developments are bolstering policymakers and practitioners' interest in practical ways to break the links between environment and conflict. In particular, the increasing ability to analyze georeferenced environmental and conflict data at much more local levels will improve the historically limited quantitative evaluations of these linkages. Preliminary research funded by the National

Science Foundation, for example, has found statistically significant correlations between rainfall and civil conflict, strongly suggesting the value of robust analytical work.[42] And while violent conflict continues to garner the most attention, broadening the definition of "conflict" to include nonviolent or less organized violent conflict has increased the range of cases under discussion. For example, the social protests that have met water privatization megaprojects (such as large dams), international markets for natural resources, or conservation areas that limit community usage expand the range (and relevance) of environmental security analysis.[43]

Climate Change and Security

The recent rise of concern over climate change has both spurred—and been spurred by—climate-security connections. Prominent reports in the European Union, United States, United Kingdom, and Germany aimed at garnering more policy attention to climate change have emphasized its security linkages.[44] With a push from the United Kingdom, the UN Security Council devoted an April 2007 session to climate change, peace, and security, the first Security Council session on an environmental topic.[45] UN Secretary-General Ban Ki-moon subsequently linked UN efforts to battle climate change with its mission to address the underlying causes of conflict in Darfur, Sudan.[46] In March 2008, European Union High Representative for the Common Foreign and Security Policy Javier Solana presented to the European Council a short climate change and security paper responding to pressure (particularly from Germany) to raise the profile of climate-security connections. Mirroring some of the language used in prominent reports from German, British, and U.S. nongovernmental organizations, the brief called climate change a "threat multiplier which exacerbates existing trends, tensions and instability" that could "overburden states and regions which are already fragile and conflict prone," posing "political and security risks that directly affect European interests."[47]

The 2007 Nobel Peace Prize, awarded to Al Gore and the Intergovernmental Panel on Climate Change, most prominently linked climate change and security. In announcing the award, the Norwegian Nobel Committee called climate change both a fundamental threat to human well-being and a contributing factor to more traditional violent conflict. In 1987, the Brundtland Commission argued, "Slowing, or adapting to, global warming is becoming an essential task to reduce the risks of conflict."[48] In 2007, the Norwegian Nobel Committee echoed those words:

> Extensive climate changes may alter and threaten the living conditions of much of mankind. They may induce large-scale migration and lead to greater competition for the earth's resources. Such changes will place particularly heavy burdens on the

world's most vulnerable countries. There may be increased danger of violent conflicts and wars, within and between states.[49]

The heightened attention to climate change boosts the prospects for constructively addressing environment, development, and security linkages. The wide range of potential climate impacts is reenergizing broader debates over human security that suggest redefining security beyond purely militaristic terms. At the same time, the traditional security community's concern with climate change (and the social reactions it may produce, such as migration) has helped garner wider attention. For example, examining its implications for desertification, precipitation, and crops in vulnerable areas such as the Sahel may also help illuminate the preexisting but neglected connections between these environmental variables and social conflict. Ironically, climate change mitigation efforts, such as increasing the use of biofuels, are arguably creating new natural resource and conflict links, as more forests are cleared for palm oil plantations and food prices are rising as we choose to grow our fuel supplies. These "knock-on effects" present a new research agenda for environment, development, and conflict scholars and practitioners.

Environmental Peacemaking

. . . A growing number of conflict-prevention and post-conflict scholars and practitioners argue that natural resource management can be a key tool for helping prevent or end conflict and for building peace in a post-conflict setting.[50] The cooperation imperative spurred by environmental interdependence and the long-term need for iterated interaction can be used as the basis for confidence building rather than merely engendering conflict.[51]

The Nile Basin is an unlikely example of conflict prevention. Many of the countries in the volatile region are beset by high levels of civil conflict, and their widespread dependence on the Nile's waters have led many to flag this river basin as the most likely to experience international water wars.[52] Yet for the past nine years, the basin's riparian states—Burundi, the Democratic Republic of the Congo, Egypt, Eritrea, Ethiopia, Kenya, Rwanda, Sudan, Tanzania, and Uganda—have convened the ministerial-level Nile Basin Initiative (NBI) to develop a shared vision of sustainable use of those waters.[53] The initiative centers around eight "Shared Vision" projects—including the Regional Power Trade, Water Resources Management, and Efficient Water Use for Agriculture projects—meant to foster trust and encourage investment. While formally framed as a development enterprise,[54] these efforts also implicitly serve as a means to prevent conflict predicated on environmental interdependence.[55] However, the NBI process is not without its critics, and issues of transparency and wider stakeholder participation remain concerns.[56]

In times of active conflict, management of a shared natural resource across lines of conflict can serve as a communication lifeline when other aspects of the relationship remain highly volatile. The "Picnic Table Talks"—in which Israeli and Jordanian water managers met at a picnic table to jointly manage their water resources while their countries were formally at war—are a vivid example. These technical exchanges helped build trust and personal connections that contributed to achieving the larger peace treaty between the countries in 1994.[57] More recently, Friends of the Earth launched the Good Water Makes Good Neighbors Middle East initiative to promote cooperation among Israelis, Palestinians, and Jordanians on shared water problems.

In this fashion, environmental management serves as a way to develop confidence that may carry over to other aspects of a relationship. Transboundary protected areas or "peace parks" are also an emerging—if still controversial—means to capitalize on shared ecological boundaries to build trust between parties in conflict.[58]

Finally, assessing post-conflict environmental conditions can serve as a necessary first step to building a sustainable peace. The UN Environment Programme's Post-Conflict and Disaster Management Branch (PCDMB) is leading the way on this post-conflict stage with what it calls "environmental diplomacy."[59] PCDMB's objective scientific assessments of wartime environmental damage in countries as diverse as Bosnia, Sudan, Liberia, Iraq, and Afghanistan (and forthcoming, in Nigeria, Nepal, Rwanda, and the Democratic Republic of the Congo) have become a foundation for efforts to strengthen environmental management institutions in ways that contribute to reconciliation and capacity building across lines of conflict. These steps toward "environmental diplomacy," like most efforts to capitalize on environmental peacemaking, are modest, small-scale, and remain to be fully tried and tested. Yet this robust analysis may soon be possible, as other parts of the United Nations focused on development and conflict issues move to capitalize on the environmental confidence building that can be fostered by addressing natural resource and pollution connections to livelihoods in post-conflict settings. Bilateral aid agencies are also pursuing similar practical steps by incorporating natural resource management into their peacemaking toolboxes.

Many hurdles remain, beginning with the imposing bureaucratic and institutional impediments to collaboration facing environment, development, and security actors, who speak different languages, use different tools, and often have very different bottom-line goals. But pushed by on-the-ground realities, researchers and practitioners are trying to navigate these complex linkages and find ways to work together. Environmental peacemaking efforts have limited use for unwieldy multilateral environmental agreements, the UN's go-to tool, which are poorly matched to the day-to-day intersections of environment, peace, and security issues at the intrastate level. Instead, parties seeking to break the negative links between environment and conflict must focus on local, national, and regional instruments that can grapple more effectively with the integrated problems of poverty, environment, and conflict.

Twenty years after the release of the Brundtland Report, our common future still depends on the health of our environment. It is increasingly clear that our common peace may rely on it as well. Preparing for and waging war often destroys the environment and diverts resources better deployed for sustainability. And a devastated environment can spur new conflicts over resources. Climate change threatens to destabilize not only our atmosphere, but also nations. But it is also garnering the attention of the wide range of actors necessary to tackle these fundamental challenges. Even as we become more attentive to the ways in which the environment can contribute to conflict, we must remain open to opportunities for environmental peacemaking to help us secure our environment—and ourselves.

Notes

1. World Commission on Environment and Development (WCED), *Our Common Future* (New York: Oxford University Press, 1987), 290.

2. Ibid., page 304.

3. Ibid., page 304.

5. Portions of this and subsequent sections are drawn from G. D. Dabelko, "Tactical Victories and Strategic Losses: The Evolution of Environmental Security," PhD diss., Department of Government and Politics (College Park, MD: University of Maryland, 2003).

6. J. Mathews, "Redefining Security," *Foreign Affairs* 68, no. 2 (1989): 162–77; and N. Myers, "Environment and Security," *Foreign Policy* 74 (Spring 1989): 23–41.

7. WCED, note 1 above, page 19.

8. WCED, note 1 above, page 290.

10. L. Brown, "Redefining Security," Worldwatch paper no. 14 (Washington, DC: Worldwatch Institute, 1977).

11. UN Development Programme (UNDP), *Human Development Report 1994* (New York: Oxford University Press, 1994); R. Paris, "Human Security: Paradigm Shift or Hot Air?" *International Security* 26, no. 2 (2001): 87–102; and L. Axworthy, "Introduction," in R. McRae and D. Hubert, eds., *Human Security and the New Diplomacy: Protecting People, Promoting Peace* (Montreal: McGill–Queen's University Press, 2001): 3–13.

12. WCED, note 1 above, pages 290–91.

13. N. L. Peluso and M. Watts, eds., *Violent Environment* (Ithaca, NY: Cornell University Press, 2001); and J. Barnett, *The Meaning of Environmental Security: Ecological Politics and Policy in the New Security Era* (London: Zed Books, 2001).

14. T. F. Homer-Dixon, *The Ingenuity Gap* (New York: Alfred A. Knopf, 2000); G. D. Dabelko and R. Matthew, "Environment, Population, and Conflict: Suggesting a Few Steps Forward," *Environmental Change and Security Project Report* 6 (2000): 99–103; and S. D. VanDeveer and G. D. Dabelko, "It's Capacity, Stupid: International Assistance and National Implementation," *Global Environmental Politics* 1, no. 2 (2001): 18–29.

15. WCED, note 1 above, page 291.

16. T. F. Homer-Dixon, "On the Threshold: Environmental Changes as Causes of Acute Conflict," *International Security* 16, no. 2 (1991): 76–116; T. F. Homer-Dixon, "Environmental Scarcities and Violent Conflict: Evidence from Cases," *International Security* 19, no. 1 (1994): 5–40; T. F. Homer-Dixon, *Environment, Scarcity, and Violence* (Princeton, NJ: Princeton University Press, 1999); G. Baechler, *Violence through Environmental Discrimina-*

tion: Causes, Rwanda Arena, and Conflict Model (Dordrecht, The Netherlands: Kluwer Academic Publishers, 1989); N. P. Gleditsch, ed., *Conflict and the Environment* (Dordrecht, The Netherlands: Kluwer Publications, 1989); P. F. Diehl and N.P. Gleditsch, eds., *Environmental Conflict* (Boulder, CO: Westview Press, 2001); D. H. Deudney and R. Matthew, eds., *Contested Grounds: Security and Conflict in the New Environmental Politics* (Albany, NY: State University of New York Press, 1999); UN Environment Programme (UNEP), *Understanding Environment, Conflict, and Cooperation* (Nairobi: UNEP, 2003); and C. Kahl, States, *Scarcity and Civil Strife in the Developing World* (Princeton, NJ: Princeton University Press, 2006).

17. R. Matthew, B. McDonald, and M. Brklacich, "Analyzing Environment, Conflict, and Cooperation," in UNEP, ibid., pages 5–15; and G. D. Dabelko, "The Environmental Factor," *Wilson Quarterly* 23, no. 4 (1999): 14–19.

20. J. M. Trolldalen, *International Environmental Conflict Resolution: The Role of the United Nations* (Washington, DC: World Foundation for Environment and Development, 1992).

21. The 1976 Convention on the Prohibition of Military or Any Other Hostile Use of Environmental Modification Techniques (ENMOD) and subsequent international law aimed at reducing the intentional use of the environment as a tool of war are exceptions to the global level agreement in this area. See J. E. Austin and C. E. Bruch, *The Environmental Consequences of War: Legal, Economic, and Scientific Perspectives* (Cambridge: Cambridge University Press, 2000).

22. See D. Scrivener, *Gorbachev's Murmansk Speech: The Soviet Initiative and Western Response* (Oslo: The Norwegian Atlantic Committee, 1989), for a discussion of Gorbachev's 1987 Murmansk Initiatives and the Western response.

23. "Ecological security" as opposed to "environmental security" is a closer translation of the Russian *ekologicheskaia bezopastnost*. It appears to be used interchangeably with no special distinction between "ecological" and "environmental." Others do use the term "ecological security" to connote the balance between Homo sapiens and other species. See D. Pirages and T. M. DeGeest, *Ecological Security: An Evolutionary Perspective on Globalization* (Lanham, MD: Rowman & Littlefield Publishers, 2003).

24. "Soviet Union Proposes Center for Emergency Environmental Aid," Reuters, 5 May 1989.

25. "Shevardnadze Calls for Steps to Protect Environment," Information Telegraph Agency of Russia (ITAR-TASS), 3 May 1989.

26. E. Shevardnadze, Speech to the 43rd session of the UN General Assembly, 27 September 1988.

27. B. Jancar-Webster and V. I. Sokolov, "Environmental Security: Challenges for the United States and Russia," in S. Cross, I. A. Zevelev, V. A. Kremenyuk, and V. Gevorgian, eds., *Global Security Beyond the Millennium: American and Russian Perspectives* (New York: MacMillan, 1999), 131.

28. F. Lewis, "Environment Is Security," *New York Times* (24 May 1989).

29. This call for the transfer of funds is also found in Trolldalen, note 20 above.

30. T. G. da Costa, "Brazil's SIVAM: Will It Fulfill Its Human Security Promise?" *Environmental Change and Security Project Report* 7 (2001): 47–58.

31. Dabelko, note 5 above; G. D. Dabelko and P. J. Simmons, "Environment and Security: Core Ideas and U.S. Government Initiatives," *SAIS Review* 17, no. 1 (1997): 127–46; R. Floyd, "Typologies of Securitisation and Desecuritisation: The Case of US Environmental Security 1993–2006," PhD diss., University of Warwick, 2007; and D. C. Esty et al., *State*

Failure Task Force Report: Phase II Findings (McLean, VA: Science Applications International Corporation, 31 July 1998).

32. R. D. Kaplan, "The Coming Anarchy," *Atlantic Monthly* 273, no. 2 (February 1994): 45–76.

33. UNDP, note 11 above. The seven securities were economic, food, health, environmental, personal, community, and political.

34. Paris, note 11 above.

36. J. Wolfensohn, Speech at the Woodrow Wilson International Center for Scholars, Washington, DC, 6 March 2002.

39. U.K. Science Adviser Sir David King claimed, "[C]limate change is the most severe problem that we are facing today—more serious even than the threat of terrorism." D. A. King, "Climate Change Science: Adapt, Mitigate, or Ignore?" *Science* 303, no. 5655 (9 January 2004): 176.

40. Uppsala Conflict Data Program, *Uppsala Conflict Database*, http://www.pcr.uu.se/database/.

41. UNEP, *Sudan Post-Conflict Environmental Assessment* (Geneva: UNEP, 2007); U.S. Agency for International Development (USAID), *Forests and Conflict: A Toolkit for Intervention* (Washington, DC: USAID, 2005); and USAID, *Land and Conflict: A Toolkit for Intervention* (Washington, DC: USAID, 2005).

42. M. A. Levy, "Is the Environment a National Security Issue?" *International Security* 20, no. 2 (1995): 35–62; and M. Levy, C. Thorkelson, C. Vörösmarty, E. Douglas, and M. Humphreys, "Freshwater Availability Anomalies and Outbreak of Internal War: Results from a Global Spatial Time Series Analysis," paper presented at Human Security and Climate Change, Oslo, Norway (21–23 June 2005).

43. K. Conca, *Governing Water: Contentious Transnational Politics and Global Institution Building* (Cambridge, MA: MIT Press, 2005).

44. Military Advisory Board, *National Security and the Threat of Climate Change* (Washington, DC: CNA Corporation, 2007); German Advisory Council on Global Change, *World in Transition: Climate Change as a Security Risk* (London: Earthscan, 2007); J. W. Busby, *Climate Change and National Security: An Agenda for Action*, Council Special Report no. 32 (New York: Council on Foreign Relations Press, 2007); and K. M. Campbell et al., *The Age of Consequences: The Foreign Policy and National Security Implications of Global Climate Change* (Washington, DC: Center for Strategic and International Studies and Center for a New American Security, 2007).

45. See "Security Council Holds First-Ever Debate on Impact of Climate Change on Peace, Security, Hearing Over 50 Speakers," UN Security Council press release SC/9000, 17 April 2007, http://www.un.org/News/Press/docs/2007/sc9000.doc.htm.

46. K. Ban, "A Climate Culprit in Darfur," *Washington Post* (16 June 2007).

47. EU Commission and the Secretary-General/High Representative, *Climate Change and International Security* (Brussels, Belgium: Council of the European Union, 3 March 2008), 2.

48. WCED, note 1, page 294.

49. The text of the announcement of the 2007 Nobel Peace Prize winners is available at http://nobelpeaceprize.org/eng_lau_announce2007.html.

50. K. Conca and G. D. Dabelko, eds., *Environmental Peacemaking* (Washington, DC, and Baltimore, MD: Woodrow Wilson Press and Johns Hopkins University Press, 2002); and K. Conca, A. Carius, and G. D. Dabelko, "Building Peace Through Environmental

Cooperation," *State of the World 2005: Redefining Global Security* (Washington, DC: Worldwatch Institute, 2005); E. Weinthal, "From Environmental Peacekeeping to Environmental Peacemaking," *Environmental Change and Security Program Report* 10 (2004): 19–23; and A. Carius, "Environmental Peacebuilding: Conditions for Success," *Environmental Change and Security Program Report* 12 (2006–2007): 59–75.

51. K. Conca, "The Case for Environmental Peacemaking," in K. Conca and G. D. Dabelko, eds., *Environmental Peacemaking* (Washington, DC, and Baltimore, MD: Woodrow Wilson Press and Johns Hopkins University Press, 2002): 1–22.

52. For example, World Bank Vice President Ismail Serageldin claimed in 1995 that "the wars of the next century will be about water," and Egyptian President Anwar Sadat said in 1979, "The only matter that could take Egypt to war again is water." Egyptian Minister of State for Foreign Affairs Boutros Boutros-Ghali echoed this statement when he predicted in 1985, "The next war in the Middle East will be fought over water, not politics." See "Talking Point: Ask Boutros Boutros-Ghali," BBC News, 10 June 2003, http://news.bbc.co.uk/2/hi/talking_point/2951028.stm.

53. See Nile Basin Initiative.

54. C. W. Sadoff and D. Grey, "Beyond the River: The Benefits of Cooperation on International Rivers," *Water Policy* 4, no. 5 (2002): 389–404.

55. Anecdotally, policy efforts from a range of geographical settings (Central Asia, the Caucasus, and East Africa) suggest that making the conflict prevention or post-conflict reconciliation goals of environmental peacemaking implicit or unstated is advantageous. Stating the conflict prevention goals explicitly makes the environmental and security cooperation more difficult to achieve in some settings, suggesting practitioners must find a way to capitalize on the peacemaking gains without overtly framing the goal of such efforts as peace rather than environmental sustainability.

56. P. Kameri-Mbote, "Water Conflict and Cooperation: Lessons from the Nile Basin Initiative," Navigating Peace Initiative Policy Brief 4 (Washington, DC: Environmental Change & Security Program, Woodrow Wilson International Center for Scholars, 2007), available at http://www.wilsoncenter.org/topics/pubs/NavigatingPeaceIssuePKM.pdf.

57. See A. Wolf, *Hydropolitics along the Jordan River: The Impact of Scarce Water Resources on the Arab-Israeli Conflict* (Tokyo: United Nations University Press, 1995).

58. Peace parks are also highlighted as means to (re)open political boundaries and stimulate economic growth from tourism in post-conflict environments. Early peace park efforts in southern Africa in particular have been widely criticized for not sharing benefits with local people and actually creating new human-animal conflicts. For an overview of perspectives, see S. Ali, ed., *Peace Parks: Conservation and Conflict Resolution* (Cambridge, MA: MIT Press, 2007), 6.

59. For the UN Environment Programme's Post-Conflict and Disaster Management Branch, see http://postconflict.unep.ch/. See also, J. Karensen, "Environmental Needs in Post-Crisis Assessments and Recovery: Interview with David Jensen," in European Commission, *From Early Warning to Early Action? The Debate on the Enhancement of the EU's Crisis Response Capability Continues* (Brussels, Belgium: European Commission, 2008).

PART SIX

ECOLOGICAL
JUSTICE

Some of the main controversies surrounding the paradigms of sustainable development and environmental security involve questions of justice. Critics have raised concerns that these paradigms can blur questions of fairness, power, and distribution. Worse, environmental arguments might be used to justify measures that deepen social inequality, promote authoritarian measures, or otherwise concentrate power in the hands of elites. Thus, questions of justice are raised not only by the unequal effects of pollution and ecosystem destruction but also by the socially unequal effects of environmental policy responses.

Concerns about the relationship between environmental protection and social equity have been voiced since the Stockholm conference first placed the environment on the international agenda.[1] As the pace of environmental degradation has accelerated and policy responses to environmental problems have grown more complex and ambitious, the question of how various forms of environmental change affect different social groups has become increasingly central to environmental debates.

Today the link between ecology and justice is being articulated by a diverse array of voices: people of color in cities throughout the United States challenging the "environmental racism" of concentrating toxic facilities in minority communities; rural women in India protesting the impact of damming or deforestation on their lives and communities; green activists in Europe drawing links between militarism, patriarchy, and environmental destruction; Third World activists arguing that the North imposes both environmental problems and inappropriate solutions to those problems on the South; indigenous peoples organizing to reclaim their lands and their traditions as an alternative to the ecological onslaught of modernity.[2] In some cases, long-standing environmental and human rights groups have discovered one another and begun to work together, as in the "Defending Environmental Defenders" campaign, a three-year initiative (1999–2002) launched jointly by Amnesty International and the Sierra Club.[3]

Given this diversity, is it possible to identify a single paradigm of ecological justice based on a common set of core arguments? While there are many different visions of an ecologically just world, a number of common themes lie at the heart of the ecological justice paradigm: first, the close linkage between violence against nature and violence against human beings; second, the linkage between the power to control nature and the power to control people; third, the observation that not all people or groups are affected equally by environmental problems or by the responses to those problems; fourth, the pursuit of solutions that are both ecologically sound and socially just, because neither can endure in the absence of the other; and fifth, the need for a fundamental transformation of politics, economics, and society.

The eco-justice paradigm can be used to analyze questions of ecology and justice at many different social levels. The question of justice among nations, with a particular focus on North-South inequality, was a central dispute at the Stockholm conference in 1972 (see the selection by Castro in Part One). Twenty years later at the Rio Earth Summit the question had not been resolved. According to then Malaysian prime minister Mahathir Mohamad, addressing the Rio conference:

> We know that the 25 per cent of the world population who are rich consume 85 per cent of its wealth and produce 90 per cent of its waste. Mathematically speaking, if the rich reduce their wasteful consumption by 25 per cent, worldwide pollution will be reduced by 22.5 per cent. But if the poor 75 per cent reduce consumption totally and disappear from this earth altogether, the reduction in pollution will only be by 10 per cent.
>
> It is what the rich do that counts, not what the poor do, however much they do it. . . . The rich will not accept a progressive and meaningful cutback in their emissions of carbon dioxide and other greenhouse gases because it will be a cost to them and retard their progress. Yet they expect the poor people of the developing countries to stifle even their minute growth as if it will cost them nothing. . . . Malaysia will do what can reasonably be expected of it for the environment.[4]

Despite the optimism at Rio that "sustainable development" merged the conflicting concerns of the North and the South with regard to environment and development, distributional issues remain central to the North-South environmental debate. Mahathir Mohamad and others have stressed that the question of justice applies not only to who should pay the costs of environmental protection in poor societies but also who holds decisionmaking power and who bears historical responsibility for the planet's predicament.

One of the most important themes of the eco-justice paradigm, however, is the idea that global environmental justice is not simply a question of equity among nation-states. Power and risk are distributed unequally not only among nations but also within them, in social divisions based on race, class, gender, ethnicity, and region. Inequality of voice is an issue not only in interstate negotiations but also within societies, in the workings of intergovernmental organizations, and even in dealings among environmentalists and other non-state actors.

The experiences of indigenous peoples around the world illustrate these linkages among inequality, power, voice, and the environment at levels ranging from local to global. Here we present two letters published in 1989—during the height of the international furor over the destruction of tropical rain forests—by the Coordinating Body for the Indigenous Peoples' Organizations of the Amazon Basin (COICA). COICA argues that the future of the Amazon basin and the fate of its indigenous occupants are inherently linked. The rampant quest for modernization, colonization, territorial occupation, and economic development of the Amazon basin has damaged natural ecosystems and destroyed indigenous communities. The destruction has been driven by governments of the Amazon basin countries, which have largely excluded indigenous communities from decisionmaking about the region. Much of the destructive activity has been funded by external sources, including multinational corporations and multilateral development agencies such as the World Bank. Decisions about the fate of the Amazon forest and its people, whether made at the national or the international level, have excluded those who are most directly affected by such decisions.

COICA addressed the first letter to the multilateral development banks that fund so many projects and policies threatening indigenous peoples (see the material on the World Bank in Part Three). The second letter is addressed to the international environmental movement, which is also taken to task for its lack of attention to indigenous concerns. While acknowledging the efforts of environmentalists and the potential for common cause between the environmental and indigenous peoples' movements, the letter points out that governments, international organizations, and Northern environmental groups have struck bargains that leave out the people most directly and immediately affected. The members of COICA defend an alternative vision: Given the long history of sustainable interaction between indigenous peoples and the region's ecology, they argue, the best way to ensure an ecologically sound future is to restore and protect the land rights and lifestyles of indigenous peoples. Although many international environmental organizations have sought to build local partnerships in their work, controversy about their sensitivity to the plight and rights of local communities endures.[5]

The struggles of indigenous peoples bear much in common with the movement against "environmental racism" that grew rapidly in the United States during the 1990s.[6] This movement has both urban and rural components: the struggle of urban communities of color against the practice of locating toxic facilities in the inner city, and the struggle of rural communities to combat the health and safety risks of environmentally unsound agricultural practices (in particular the heavy use of toxic agricultural chemicals)—risks borne disproportionately by low-paid agricultural workers. In both the North American and the South American case the goal is not merely to change environmental outcomes but also to return greater decisionmaking power to the community. And in both cases the notion that current practices are inherently unjust has been an important weapon in the struggle.

A very different struggle engaging forest peoples, but with equally strong links to questions of ecological justice, played out in Liberia during a fourteen-year civil war. Forests became central elements in the conflict, in that illegal logging became a key source of revenue for the combatants—with devastating effects for local communities. Here we present a speech by Silas Kpanan'Ayoung Siakor, an activist who helped to document and expose the timber-arms-violence connection in Liberia's forests. Siakor's work was recognized in 2006 when he received the highly prestigious Goldman Environmental Prize, given annually to a handful of community activists around the world who work for environmental protection and social justice. In his acceptance speech, Siakor underscores that for his people the struggle is not simply about the trees, but rather about a community's way of life, its livelihoods, and its cultural practices.

The rights of agricultural communities around the world have emerged as another critical front in the struggle for eco-justice. Scientist and activist Vandana Shiva, whose work has centered on the resource-based livelihoods of women in rural parts of India, ties processes of globalization to the poverty and marginalization of local agricultural communities in her home country of India. Shiva stresses how trade integration and the "intellectual property rights" in local biodiversity claimed by transnational corporations have stripped local communities of traditional nature-based livelihoods and rights. Shiva pays particular attention to the role of rural women as both food producers and storehouses of communal ecological knowledge—a status rendered invisible by modern agro-business practices, to the detriment of local communities:

> The most efficient means of rendering the destruction of nature, local economies and small autonomous producers is by rendering their production invisible.
>
> Women who produce for their families and communities are treated as "nonproductive" and "economically" inactive. The devaluation of women's work, and of work done in sustainable economies, is the natural outcome of a system constructed by capitalist patriarchy. This is how globalization destroys local economies and destruction itself is counted as growth.

And women themselves are devalued. Because many women in the rural and indigenous communities work co-operatively with nature's processes, their work is often contradictory to the dominant market driven "development" and trade policies. And because work that satisfies needs and ensures sustenance is devalued in general, there is less nurturing of life and life support systems.[7]

Again, core themes of the eco-justice paradigm emerge in this analysis: unequal effects rooted in class and gender hierarchies, control of nature as control of people, and the importance of social justice as a foundation for sustainability.

Shiva's focus on the links among gender, ecology, and power are the concern of a body of thought known as ecofeminism. Karen Warren summarizes the central tenets of ecofeminist perspectives:

Ecological feminism is the position that there are important connections—historical, symbolic, theoretical—between the domination of women and the domination of nonhuman nature. . . . Any feminist theory with any environmental ethic which fails to take seriously the interconnected dominations of women and nature is simply inadequate.[8]

Some ecofeminists see an inherent difference in how men and women relate to and interact with nature, and explain environmentally destructive societies as a consequence of male dominance. Other ecofeminists have pointed out that gender is in many important ways a socially constructed set of roles and rules and not a biological fact. These "social" ecofeminists tend to see patriarchy and environmental destruction as stemming from a common source: the hierarchical concentration of power in society.[9]

Advocates of ecological justice have played a crucial role in pointing out that environmental problems often cause greater harm to the poor and powerless than to other groups. Another important theme is that the "solutions" to environmental problems also can be unjust, both locally and globally—and that such outcomes may not be solutions at all. This idea is evident in COICA's rejection of environment-development dialogues that exclude indigenous peoples. The essay by Nancy Peluso raises the same concerns in an even more provocative fashion. Peluso argues that international environmental organizations, detached from the reality of local resource struggles, have sometimes participated in environmental preservation efforts that demonize local people and bolster oppressive, authoritarian regimes. Using wildlife conservation efforts in Kenya as an example, Peluso argues that the result—"coercing conservation"—pits the environment against social justice considerations, precluding an outcome that is both socially and ecologically sustainable.

If justice is at risk in both environmental degradation and responses to it, then a human rights framework may provide a more just path to sustainability. We close this section with an excerpt from a report of the UN High Commissioner for Human Rights, which examines links between climate change and human rights. Historically, the relationship between human rights and the environment has been complex and, at times, uneasy. Many human rights activists have been uncomfortable expanding the definition of the term to include "socioeconomic" rights such as environmental quality alongside more traditional concepts of political rights and civil liberties; at the same time, many eco-justice advocates have viewed a human right to clean water or breathable air as simply a minimum standard for human existence, rather than the more ambitious aim of social equality. Nonetheless, as demonstrated in the report's many substantive connections between climate change and rights at risk, the rights framework can be a powerful device for linking justice and sustainability.

Together, the chapters in this part reject the Stockholm-era assertion that effective environmental protection requires increasingly authoritarian governance. In contrast, they argue that genuine sustainability and meaningful environmental security will require responses to environmental problems that are both ecologically effective and socially just.

Thinking Critically

1. After reading the essays in this section, are you persuaded that the environment is a social justice issue? Must there be social justice for there to be environmental protection? Are there difficult trade-offs to be made between these two values?

2. Do you accept the suggestion that some types of global environmental protection impose an unfair burden on the global South? Does this mean that the resistance of many governments of the South to particular forms of international environmental protection has the effect of promoting social justice? What might COICA have to say to a Third World head of state such as Mahathir Mohamad? How might he respond?

3. Are the views of globalization that are implied or presented by the authors in this section consistent with that of Adil Najam and colleagues in Part Two? How are they similar or different?

4. Contrast the picture of international environmental NGOs drawn by Peluso with the essay by Smitu Kothari in Part Two. Are Kothari's concerns about the challenges of North-South solidarity be-

ing borne out in this case? What sorts of adjustments in social movement coalitions are required to address these concerns?

5. Governments concerned with the problem of climate change have spent most of their time bargaining over which countries must cut their greenhouse gas emissions and by how much. Does a human rights analysis of the climate change problem suggest a different or expanded agenda for international negotiations? What additional responsibilities of nations, individually and collectively, are identified?

Notes

1. For a discussion of some of these issues prior to the Stockholm conference, see United Nations, *Development and Environment: Report and Working Papers of a Panel of Experts Convened by the Secretary General of the U.N. Conference on the Human Environment*, Founex, Switzerland, June 4–12, 1971.

2. For a discussion of the links between ecology and social justice, see Nicholas Low and Brendan Gleeson, *Justice, Society, and Nature* (New York: Routledge, 1998).

3. See Sierra Club and Amnesty International, *Environmentalists Under Fire: Ten Urgent Cases of Human Rights Abuses*, 2nd ed., January 2000.

4. Mahathir Mohamad, "Statement to the U.N. Conference on Environment and Development," *Environmental Policy and Law* 22, no. 4 (1992): 232.

5. Mac Chapin, "A Challenge to Conservationists," *Worldwatch*, November 2004.

6. On environmental racism, see Robert D. Bullard, *Dumping in Dixie: Race, Class, and Environmental Quality*, 2nd ed. (Boulder, CO: Westview Press, 1994); Luke W. Cole and Sheila R. Foster, *From the Ground Up: Environmental Racism and the Rise of the Environmental Justice Movement* (New York: New York University Press, 2000).

7. Vandana Shiva, "Poverty and Globalization," BBC Radio 4, Reith Lectures, broadcast Wednesday, May 10, 2000, 2000 hours GMT. London: British Broadcasting Corporation.

8. Karen Warren, "The Power and the Promise of Ecological Feminism," *Environmental Ethics* 12 (Summer 1990): 125–146, 125. See also Wendy Harcourt, ed., *Feminist Perspectives on Sustainable Development* (London: Zed Books, 1994); Carolyn Merchant, *Earthcare: Women and the Environment* (New York: Routledge, 1995).

9. Janet Biehl, *Rethinking Ecofeminist Politics* (Boston: South End Press, 1991).

26

TWO AGENDAS
ON AMAZON
DEVELOPMENT

COORDINATING BODY FOR THE
INDIGENOUS PEOPLES' ORGANIZATIONS
OF THE AMAZON BASIN (COICA)*

For Bilateral and Multilateral Funders

(This document is addressed to the World Bank, the Inter-American Development Bank, the US Agency International Development, and the European Economic Community.)

We, the Indigenous Peoples, have been an integral part of the Amazon Biosphere for millennia. We have used and cared for the resources of that biosphere
with a great deal of respect, because it is our home, and because we know that
our survival and that of our future generations depends on it. Our accumulated
knowledge about the ecology of our home, our models for living with the peculiarities of the Amazon Biosphere, our reverence and respect for the tropical
forest and its other inhabitants, both plant and animal, are the keys to guaranteeing the future of the Amazon Basin, not only for our peoples, but also for all
of humanity.

---

*   Originally published in *Cultural Survival Quarterly* 13,4 (1989): 75–78. © Cultural Survival
www.cs.org. Reprinted with permission.

What COICA Wants

1. The most effective defense of the Amazonian Biosphere is the recognition and defense of the territories of the region's Indigenous Peoples and the promotion of their models for living within that Biosphere and for managing its resources in a sustainable way. The international funders of Amazonian development should educate themselves about the Indigenous Peoples' relationship with their environment, and formulate new concepts of Amazonian development together with new criteria for supporting Amazonian development projects which would be compatible with the Indigenous Peoples' principles of respect and care for the world around them, as well as with their concern for the survival and well-being of their future generations.

2. The international funders must recognize the rights of Indigenous Peoples as those are being defined within the Working Group on Indigenous Peoples, established by the UN Human Rights Commission. These rights should form the basis of the institution's policy towards the Indigenous Peoples and their territories who live in those areas where the funder is supporting development work. The funders should consult directly with the organizations of the Indigenous Peoples throughout the process of establishing this policy and should distribute that policy widely among governments and the organizations of Indigenous Peoples.

3. There can be no development projects in indigenous areas without the informed consent of the Indigenous Peoples affected. The funders must make every effort, through field research conducted by personnel of the funding institution, to verify the existence of an indigenous population, or the possible negative impact on an indigenous population, in areas where they are considering the implementation of a project. If either is the case, the funder must openly recognize the existence of this population or the negative impact on them, and then should establish as a condition for further funding the project
    - that the government responsible for implementing the project also recognize the existence of the population and/or the negative impact;
    - that the affected population be informed of the plans and impact of the plans; and
    - that the affected population consent to the implementation of the plans.

These conditions should be monitored by both the funder and the organization which represents the affected population.

4. If the indigenous population has given its informed consent to the implementation of a development project within its territory, the project must

be designed in such a way that it respects the territories of the population as they define them, their economy and their social organization, according to the institutional policy as described in Point One. There should be special components of the project which lend support directly to the indigenous population for their own needs and for the development proposals which they may have. The organization which represents the affected population should participate in the design of the project.

5. The international funders should enter into a direct relation of collaboration and mutual respect with the organizations of Indigenous Peoples, through their representatives. This relation should establish the basis for:
   - *consultations* on all aspects of projects implemented in areas with an indigenous population or which have an impact on an indigenous population;
   - *participation* of representatives of Indigenous Peoples in the planning, implementation, and evaluation of projects;
   - *exchange* of information of mutual interest on plans, projects, activities, and needs of both. . . .

Indigenous Peoples' Alternatives
for Amazonian Development

An important task of the Coordinating Body is to present to the international community the alternatives which we Indigenous Peoples offer for living with the Amazonian Biosphere, caring for it and developing within it. This is one of our important contributions to a better life for humankind. The following represent, in general terms, our program for the defense of the Amazonian Biosphere.

1. The best defense of the Amazonian Biosphere is the defense of the territories recognized as homeland by Indigenous Peoples, and their promotion of our models for living within that biosphere and for managing its resources. This implies:
   - education for the national and international communities regarding the Indigenous Peoples' concept of the unity between people and territory, and regarding our models for managing and caring for our environment.
   - work with national governments, environmental organizations, and international institutions which fund Amazon development to develop new concepts and models for occupying and using the Amazon Basin in keeping with our long-term perspective (future generations), our respect for the interdependence between humankind and our environments, and our need to improve the well-being of the entire community; further work with the same institutions to translate these new concepts into concrete programs for developing and caring for the Amazon Basin and its inhabitants.

- work with national governments, environmental organizations, and international funders to reorganize the occupation of supposedly empty Amazonian territories by combining indigenous territories, with forest, wildlife, and extractive reserves in favor of the indigenous and other current inhabitants; by discouraging the "conquest and colonization" of our homeland; and by recuperating those vast areas devastated by state policies of conquest and colonization.
- research on the natural resources and traditional crops used by Indigenous Peoples, on the traditional systems for utilizing and conserving resources, and on models for the extraction of renewable resources.
- evaluation and systematization of the development projects implemented by Indigenous Peoples which attempt to combine the demands of the market with a respect for indigenous principles of development.

2. The defense of the Amazon Biosphere/indigenous territories must go hand in hand with the recognition of and respect for the territorial, political, cultural, economic, and human rights of the Indigenous Peoples. This implies:
   - continued participation and support for the UN process for establishing an international instrument recognizing the rights of Indigenous Peoples.
   - education for the national and international communities regarding the rights of Indigenous Peoples.
   - establishment of mechanisms at both the national and international level for defending the rights of Indigenous Peoples in cases of violations of or conflicts over those rights.

3. The right of self-determination for Indigenous Peoples within their environment/territory is fundamental for guaranteeing the well-being of the indigenous population and of the Amazonian Biosphere. This implies:
   - respect for our autonomous forms of community, ethnic, and regional government.
   - indigenous control over the economic activities within the indigenous territories, including the extraction of mineral reserves.
   - respect for indigenous customary law and the indigenous norms for social control.

4. Concrete Proposals for International Cooperation: For many decades now, most of our peoples have been experimenting with ways to participate in the encroaching market economies of our respective countries while trying to survive as peoples intimately linked to the Amazonian forest. We have done this despite the hostility shown us by the frontier society and despite the fact that, within the context of the market economy, we are desperately poor. For these reasons, we have organized ourselves in new ways and developed and managed a variety of small programs to

improve our health, education, and economy. . . . It is these small scale, locally controlled initiatives which should be the cornerstone of future Amazonian development. . . .

To the Community of Concerned Environmentalists

We, the Indigenous Peoples, have been an integral part of the Amazonian Biosphere for millennia. We use and care for the resources of that biosphere with respect, because it is our home, and because we know that our survival and that of our future generations depend on it. Our accumulated knowledge about the ecology of our forest home, our models for living within the Amazonian Biosphere, our reverence and respect for the tropical forest and its other inhabitants, both plant and animal, are the keys to guaranteeing the future of the Amazon Basin. A guarantee not only for our peoples, but also for all of humanity. Our experience, especially during the past 100 years, has taught us that when politicians and developers take charge of our Amazon, they are capable of destroying it because of their shortsightedness, their ignorance, and their greed.

We are pleased and encouraged to see the interest and concern expressed by the environmentalist community for the future of our homeland. We are gratified by the efforts you have made in your country to educate your peoples about our homeland and the threat it now faces as well as the efforts you have made in South America to defend the Amazonian rain forests and to encourage proper management of their resources. We greatly appreciate and fully support the efforts some of you are making to lobby the US Congress, the World Bank, USAID, and the Inter-American Development Bank on behalf of the Amazonian Biosphere and its inhabitants. We recognize that through these efforts, the community of environmentalists has become an important political actor in determining the future of the Amazon Basin.

We are keenly aware that you share with us a common perception of the dangers which face our homeland. While we may differ about the methods to be used, we do share a fundamental concern for encouraging the long-term conservation and the intelligent use of the Amazonian rain forest. We have the same conservation goals.

Our Concerns

We are concerned that you have left us, the Indigenous Peoples, out of your vision of the Amazonian Biosphere. The focus of concern of the environmental community has typically been the preservation of the tropical forest and its plant and animal inhabitants. You have shown little interest in its human inhabitants who are also part of that biosphere.

We are concerned about the "debt for nature swaps" which put your organizations in a position of negotiating with our governments for the future of our homelands. We know of specific examples of such swaps which have shown the most brazen disregard for the rights of the indigenous inhabitants and which are resulting in the ultimate destruction of the very forests which they were meant to preserve.

We are concerned that you have left us Indigenous Peoples and our organizations out of the political process which is determining the future of our homeland. While we appreciate your efforts on our behalf, we want to make it clear that we never delegated any power of representation to the environmentalist community nor to any individual or organization within that community.

We are concerned about the violence and ecological destruction of our homeland caused by the increasing production and trafficking of cocaine, most of which is consumed here in the US.

What We Want

We want you, the environmental community, to recognize that the most effective defense of the Amazonian Biosphere is the recognition of our ownership rights over our territories and the promotion of our models for living within that biosphere.

We want you, the environmental community, to recognize that we Indigenous Peoples are an important and integral part of the Amazonian Biosphere.

We want you, the environmental community, to recognize and promote our rights as Indigenous Peoples as we have been defining those rights within the UN Working Group for Indigenous Peoples.

We want to represent ourselves and our interests directly in all negotiations concerning the future of our Amazonian homeland.

What We Propose

We propose that you work directly with our organizations on all your programs and campaigns which affect our homelands.

We propose that you swap "debt for indigenous stewardship" which would allow your organizations to help return areas of the Amazonian rain forest to our care and control.

We propose establishing a permanent dialogue with you to develop and implement new models for using the rain forest based on the list of alternatives presented with this document.

We propose joining hands with those members of the worldwide environmentalist community who:

- recognize our historical role as caretakers of the Amazon Basin.
- support our efforts to reclaim and defend our traditional territories.
- accept our organizations as legitimate and equal partners.

We propose reaching out to other Amazonian peoples such as the rubber tappers, the Brazil-nut gatherers, and others whose livelihood depends on the nondestructive extractive activities, many of whom are of indigenous origin.

We propose that you consider allying yourselves with us, the Indigenous Peoples of the Amazon, in defense of our Amazonian homeland.

27

A VOICE FOR THE FOREST AND ITS PEOPLE*

Silas Kpanan'Ayoung Siakor

[Editors' note: Silas Kpanan'Ayoung Siakor, a Liberian activist, was awarded the Goldman Environmental Prize in 2006 for his work exposing illegal logging and arms smuggling during Liberia's civil war. The following biography of Siakor and account of his activities was compiled by the Goldman Environmental Foundation; it is followed by his acceptance speech on receiving the prize in 2006.]

Silas Kpanan'Ayoung Siakor, 36, exposed evidence that Liberia President Charles Taylor used the profits of unchecked, rampant logging to pay the costs of a brutal 14-year civil war that left 150,000 people dead. At great personal risk, Siakor collected extremely hard-to-get evidence of falsified logging records, illegal logging practices and associated human rights abuses. He passed the evidence to the United Nations Security Council, which then banned the export of Liberian timber, part of wider trade sanctions. . . .

"The evidence Silas Siakor collected at great personal risk was vital to putting sanctions in place and cutting the links between the logging industry and conflict," said Arthur Blundell, chairman of the U.N. Panel of Experts on Liberia.

Since Taylor was ousted in 2003, Siakor has been working with Liberia's new leadership to create sustainable timber policies and give the local forest communities a voice through the first Forest People's Congress, which he organized. He also is working with the $4 million Liberian Forest Initiative led by the U.S. State Department and the National Forest Service to support Liberia's forest reform efforts.

Siakor has urged the U.N. Security Council to maintain the sanctions until the corrupt logging companies that operated under the Taylor regime are removed, the forestry sector is reformed and a workable forest management plan is in place.

---

* Reprinted with permission of the Goldman Foundation and the author.

Demonstrating the power of the sanctions and the evidence Siakor exposed, the first presidential order issued by new President Ellen Johnson-Sirleaf canceled all of Liberia's forest concessions. Johnson-Sirleaf, the first democratically elected female president in Africa, vowed that new forest use agreements will not be issued until a range of forest reforms has been carried out.

Plundering Liberia's Natural Resources

Liberia's forests cover 11.8 million acres, an area twice the size of Vermont, and include the last remaining closed-canopy tropical rain forest in the Upper Guinea Forests of West Africa. They are home to nearly half of Africa's mammal species, including the pygmy hippopotamus, Liberian mongoose and West Africa's largest forest elephant population.

When he was president, Taylor raided the valuable hardwood forests by entering into secret agreements with a favored lumber company and awarding it the largest logging concessions in the country. The company's private militia committed egregious human rights abuses including rape, beatings and indiscriminate destruction of entire villages.

Siakor worked amid this chaotic and dangerous environment to steadily document and disseminate evidence that would end the plundering of one of Liberia's greatest natural resources. Siakor hired observers at three ports, collecting information on 80 percent of logging exports. The observers found that the actual exports greatly exceeded official reports—and that arms shipments were being unloaded at the ports by timber company workers.

Planning a Sustainable Future

Siakor, the director of the Sustainable Development Institute, is coordinating civil society's participation in the forest sector reform, as mandated by the U.N. Security Council. Siakor organizes workshops and written proposals that outline forest sector reform priorities, emphasizing transparency, civil society input and sustainable forest management. His work led the interim government to protect 3.7 million acres of forest.

Despite his outstanding achievements to date, Siakor is still fighting powerful forces that want to tap into Liberia's forests as a source of income. The U.N. Security Council is under intense pressure from China, the new Liberian government and others to lift the timber sanctions. [Editors' note: The Security Council removed sanctions on Liberian timber exports in June 2006, contingent on the passage of national legal reforms for the forestry sector.]

Goldman Environmental Prize Acceptance Speech of Silas Kpanan'Ayoung Siakor

Tonight, as I moved toward the podium, it dawned on me that a moment of reckoning had arrived for me. The challenges that go with stepping forward, coming out of the shadows to accept this prize, had appeared insurmountable for so long. But now I realized that the many allies who worked with me over the years at the international level and, more importantly, at the community level—people who took far greater risks than I—are at this moment stepping out into the spotlight to accept the challenge to carry on this struggle.

Our struggle to defend the environment is not about trees per se. It is a more divine calling to defend our culture, our identity, our very lives. We cannot stand by and allow multinational companies to destroy our forest. Because when they tear down the trees, they strip the land, they tear down our people and strip away their lives. We have to fight for what should be our basic human rights: clean air, safe drinking water, and the right to conduct our traditional cultural practices under the undisturbed canopy of our forests.

This prize comes at a critical time in Liberia. Having successfully worked to halt illegal logging, our challenge now is to get the new government to make better choices, to make new laws that protect the land and the people, and to hear the voices of the people who have lost so much. We've all lost so much, it is hard to even measure.

The shadows of powerful, elusive and negative forces, including multinational business interests, darken our horizon and threaten our reform process. But shadows they will remain.

We know the strength of the human spirit. We know we have to speak up. No more will we and our new partners, and no longer just allies, allow business as usual to flourish in our sacred forests. No more business as usual.

Our heartfelt thanks go to the Goldman family for this recognition. Words are not adequate to express the gratitude I feel tonight. I had actually planned that this was going to be my last comment on this podium, the expression of gratitude. But I just realized that I won't be doing justice to the many young people in this hall tonight who by their presence have come to show solidarity with our cause. To all of you young people in the hall tonight, I say to you: never shy away from the good fight. There is no better fight than to fight for the environment. Thank you.

28

COERCING
CONSERVATION

NANCY LEE PELUSO*

The flurry of ecological awareness and action in the late 1980s has led to a proliferation of international environmental agreements among nation-states. . . . Such agreements assume that each nation-state, including those which have only recently emerged from colonialism, has the capacity, the internal legitimacy, and the will to manage all resources falling within its territorial boundaries. The implication is that the nation-state should be able to control the behavior of all users of all resources located within the state's (self) declared jurisdiction, whatever the origin of the state's claim, whatever the nature of competition for those resources, and whatever the nature or origins of resistance to the state's resource control.[1]

These strategies have elicited the formal commitment of many Third World officials and policymakers who, not surprisingly, stand to benefit from their involvement in such initiatives. Some states or state interests, however, appropriate the conservation concerns of international environmental groups as a means of eliciting support for their own control over productive natural resources. Indeed, some tropical developing states use conservation ideology to justify coercion in the name of conservation, often by using violence. The state's mandate to defend threatened resources and its monopolization of legitimate violence combine to facilitate state apparatus-building and social control. "Legitimate" violence in the name of resource control also helps states control people, especially recalcitrant regional groups, marginal groups, or minority groups who challenge the state's authority.

The environmental community, perhaps inadvertently, justifies coercive-protective actions on the basis of moral high grounds which are difficult to dis-

*   Excerpted from "Coercing Conservation: The Politics of State Resource Control," in *The State and Social Power in Global Environmental Politics*, eds. Ronnie D. Lipschutz and Ken Conca (New York: Columbia University Press, 1993). (c) 1993 Columbia University Press. Reprinted with permission.

pute, such as the preservation of the world's biological heritage or our common security. Indeed, the recognition of the "urgent need" to defend at any cost endangered species, endangered habitats, or whole ecosystems is becoming a more frequent part of the discourse of conservation.[2] Those who abhor state violence against its people are in some cases willing to turn a blind eye to the practice of violence or the threat of violence when conservation for (global) common security is being protected.[3] . . . Nevertheless, when a state must resort to violent means of protecting its own or the global community's claims to natural resources, it is an indicator of a failed, incomplete, or nonexistent legitimacy to govern society. Moreover, the states in question may (and often do) apply the tools and equipment they use to establish their resource sovereignty beyond the conservation endpoints envisioned by international facilitators of conservation, and appropriate the moral ideology of global conservation to justify state systems of resource extraction and production. . . .

Clashes between Central States and Local Resource Users

It is in developing countries, many of which are still struggling to redress the legacies of colonialism and the difficulties of maintaining multiethnic nation-states, that the most difficult circumstances for conservation are found. The origins of their territorial integration lie in colonialism, and were enforced by colonial armies and arms. Though international colonial pressures may have largely died down in the wake of worldwide independence movements, world market linkages continue to influence the decisions of former colonies by increasing the returns of market activities to the national elites who control the trading links.[4] Despite their contempt for the colonial regimes that preceded them, many contemporary developing states have adopted colonial policies for land and resource control, sometimes making them even more coercive.[5] Moreover, to enforce control where state hegemony is tenuous—because of deep-seated rifts between social groups, regional disparities in resource distribution, or competing concepts of appropriate or rightful use of resources—in many Third World countries, state leaders are increasingly members of, controlled by, or strongly allied with the military.[6]

Power struggles between the state and society are played out constantly in the process of allocation, control, and accessing of resources. Both internal and external pressures on states cause them to manage resources using particular tactics to achieve conservation or (sustainable) production management objectives. A state or a faction of the state may coerce conservation under one or all of three circumstances: when the resources are extremely valuable, when the state's legitimate control of the resource is questioned or challenged by other resource users, and when coercion is considered either the last resort or the easiest means of establishing control over people and territory. . . .

The conservation agenda, which is generally depicted as being in the common interest of the entire global community, is seen by some as a justification for external intervention in what were previously the sole affairs of states.[7] From a local perspective, however, both states and international conservation groups may be seen as illegitimate controllers of local resources. . . .

International intervention or support does not guarantee the realization of environmental goals or state legitimacy, however. Replacing or strengthening power holders in order to control resources may encourage increasing local resistance or rebellion against state or international controls on local resources. State concerns with the economic value of resources may influence conservation groups to use economic terms to justify their protection and preservation strategies. Whether for intensive production or for preservation, valuation strategies for resource territories frequently disenfranchise local people who had long histories of local resource use and may have played significant, though unrecognized, roles in creating "wild" habitats. Not only does this often have the effect of undermining conservation; it also changes the way resources are perceived, defined, valued, allocated, and used. When these management strategies change who has access to and control over local resources, the use of violence becomes an expedient means of exerting state control, in the name of "conservation" or "legitimate domain."

In sum, externally based resource claimants (including the state itself) frequently redefine resources, the means by which they will be conserved or harvested, and the distribution of benefits from their protection. Such redefinitions often override, ignore, or collide with local or customary forms of resource management. When competition between external and local legitimation mechanisms is played out in the environmental arena, the result is social and political conflict, which causes environmental degradation and ultimately fails to achieve the goals of international conservation interests.

Nevertheless, the state may not "lose." Even if conservation goals are not achieved, the state may succeed in strengthening its capacity to govern via the use of force.[8] No one monitors this type of aggression or this outcome of international conservation strategy. The means of violence and the ideologies of state stewardship of global resources, obtained directly or indirectly from the international conservation community, may facilitate the state's imposition and enforcement of its right to govern. . . .

Kenya

The resources discussed in this section are the lands set aside for national parks and wildlife reserves and resources within those lands (wildlife, pasture, and water). The traditional users of these lands, the Maasai, Somalis, and pastoralists of other ethnic groups, have been excluded from access to these lands to various degrees over the past century. State claims to nearly two-thirds of traditional

Maasai lands were first made by the British colonial state at the turn of the twentieth century. In 1904 the Maasai, who used to occupy all the land from Mt. Kenya in the north to the border with (and into) what is today Tanzania, were resettled in two reserves. Several years later, those in the northern reserve were resettled again in an extension of the southern reserve. By 1912, they were confined to an area of approximately 38,000 square kilometers.[9] The British allocated some of the Maasai's traditional lands to European planters whose activities were believed by colonial officials to be "more productive."[10] Early on, however, the British did not subscribe to the theory that the Maasai could not coexist with wildlife. Thus, in 1906 they created the Southern Game Reserve—a wildlife reserve within the Maasai reserve because the Maasai were not believed to threaten wildlife, having coexisted with the region's wild game for thousands of years.[11]

It was not until the 1940s and 1950s that the colonial government gave in to pressures from game hunters and some conservation groups to set aside rangeland exclusively for wild game. At that same time, the state wanted to settle the Maasai in fixed places, which meant changing their traditional migratory cattle-raising practices. The Amboseli Basin, occupying some 3,200 km of both the Maasai Reserve and the Southern Game Reserve, was an important source of water during the dry season for the region's wildlife as well as the Maasai and their cattle. Dams and boreholes to provide water outside the Amboseli Basin were constructed to benefit the Maasai. As the number of Maasai cattle increased, as they continued to migrate to areas where wild game also sought drinking water, and as hunters threatened wildlife in a different manner, conservationist interests grew more concerned that the wildlife dependent on the Basin waters were being threatened. Along with big game hunters, they pressured the colonial government to create reserves where human use would be more restricted. The Southern Game Reserve was abolished in 1952 and four smaller reserves were created, including a new one outside the area of the old Southern Game Reserve, called Maasai Mara. In the 1950s, hunting was first outlawed within these reserves, although the government issued permits for hunting outside the reserves. In the early 1960s livestock grazing was also forbidden in an 80 km^2 area of the Amboseli reserve, which was a direct threat to Maasai lifestyles and livelihoods.[12]

The Maasai did not so easily give up their traditional patterns of migration to seasonal water supplies; nor were water development efforts sufficient to permit them to do so. When their principal means of livelihood was restricted by reserve authorities, the Maasai responded by killing rhinoceroses and elephants. A decade later, some allegedly began collaborating with ivory poachers. They also resisted further appropriation of their access rights by increasing their use of the area surrounding the livestock-free zone, and later demanded tenure rights to all these lands.[13]

Meanwhile, another development increased the state's direct interest in the protection of wild game and the reservation of parklands: the increase in wildlife-oriented tourism beginning in the 1960s. Some tourism revenues, including hunting fees, were given to various Maasai district councils as an incentive to win their acceptance of the reserves.[14] Fees and revenues grew through the 1960s and early 1970s, after Kenyan independence. Not all district councils, however, truly represented the interests of the people in the immediate vicinity of the reserves and parks. In Amboseli, for example, the Kajiado Council receiving park revenues was 150 km from the park boundaries. Thus some Maasai were benefitting from the Park's existence, but not necessarily those who had the most to lose from the Park's creation.

The value of wildlife tourism soon became clear to the central government. In 1974, the government designated 488 km² of the Amboseli Basin as a national park, while still negotiating with the Maasai. In 1977 this area was reduced to 390 km², which was gazetted as a park and would remain free of livestock. A de facto buffer zone was to be established around the core area of the park, and group ranches—a brand-new form of social organization for these Maasai—were established to further the government's intentions of sedentarizing the Maasai. In addition, the Maasai were expected to allow wildlife to graze on these ranches in exchange for a "wildlife utilization fee," which was supposed to compensate them for losses of water and grazing area to their own livestock.[15]

By 1989, tourism in Kenya was contributing about 20 percent of the nation's total foreign exchange.[16] By 1991, tourists were spending some 50 million dollars a year to view elephants and other wildlife.[17] In this way, as Knowles and Collett have pointed out, the creation of national parks to protect wildlife has not only separated the Maasai from their livestock production base and created a mythical nature devoid of humans for tourist consumption but also provided the government with the financial means to "develop" and "modernize" them.[18] Moreover, "National Parks and Game Reserves are never justified solely in terms of the economics of tourism: both the conservationists and national governments support the creation and maintenance of these areas with *moral arguments* based on the need to conserve wildlife and the intangible benefits that conservation confers on humanity."[19]

The plans for development of the Maasai in Amboseli have not worked as well as they have in Mara. Some blame the failure on the basic conflict in the lifestyles of the Maasai and their unwillingness to allow outsiders to make decisions about their lives and their uses of resources. Collett, for example, claims that the main reason the provision of water supplies outside the park has not achieved the government's development goals is the preference of the Maasai for a migratory, pastoralist lifestyle.[20] However, a recent report by the World Bank indicates that there were also significant technical problems:

> [The conflicts] may be attributed . . . to failure to implement the agreements, to the lack of an official written agreement outlining the management responsibilities of the different parties and policy changes. The water pumping system, financed by the New York Zoological Society and the World Bank, worked well for a few years and then began to fail due to technical and administrative problems which were not cor-

rected by the central Government which had built it. An inadequate water supply left the Maasai little option but to return to find water inside the Park. The problems were aggravated by a drought in 1984, in which the Maasai lost a substantial part of their livestock and received no assistance from the Park authorities. The wildlife utilization fees were paid regularly until about 1981, then the payments became sporadic without explanation to the Maasai. The agreement for group ranches to retain a portion of Park entry fees fell through, perhaps due to administrative changes. . . . Anticipated income from tourism did not increase as quickly as expected. . . . Construction of new lodges and viewpoint circuits on group ranch lands did not materialize as expected. Finally, the 1977 hunting ban eliminated anticipated income from safari hunting license fees.[21]

In the past few years, the basic conflicts over land and resource fights in Kenyan national parks and reserves have been reconstructed in terms of a government mandate to stop the poaching of wildlife, especially of elephants and rhinoceroses. Major international environmental organizations, including the World-wide Fund for Nature, the African Wildlife Foundation, World Conservation International (WCI), the International Union for the Conservation of Nature (IUCN), Conservation International, and the National Geographic Society, have publicized the poaching issue and its threat to global and African biodiversity. The efforts of these and other environmental groups led to the creation of the Convention on International Trade in Endangered Species (CITES). By 1991, 105 world nations had signed the CITES declaration to ban the raw ivory trade in their effort to protect elephants in Asia and Africa.[22]

A great deal, however, has been left out of the international discussion of the poaching issue, and neither the origins nor the implications of the proposed solutions to the poaching problem have received the critical analysis they merit. Two gaps in the conservation community's discussion are particularly glaring. The first is the lack of historical perspective on the political and ecological contexts within which parks were created to protect wildlife, and the resulting dismissal of local people in creating particular environments. The other is the failure to consider the political-economic implications of the provision of arms and other equipment intended (at least ostensibly) to protect wildlife.

In April 1989, Richard Leakey became the director of Kenya's Wildlife Service. Since then Leakey has made his mark by firing administrative and field staff believed to be involved in the illegal ivory or rhino horn trade, by giving raises to underpaid and overworked park rangers, and by arming these rangers with automatic rifles and helicopter gunships in order to wage war more effectively on the poachers invading Kenya's national parks. Wage war they have: within two years of his taking over, more than a hundred poachers had been killed, many of them with no chance for discussion or trial; the rangers are licensed, like military in a state of emergency, to shoot to kill.[23] The Wildlife Service has also reclaimed direct control over the Maasai Mara Reserve, where the combination of wildlife management with local participation and benefits had reportedly been more successful. The government claimed that the reserve had been inadequately maintained and was deteriorating, denying earlier reports that elephants and rhinoceros populations within this park had been increasing while antipoaching costs were virtually negligible.[24]

. . . In their campaigns to save animals, international conservation groups never specify who the poachers are, although some fingers are pointed and accusations made. A letter to members from the WWF, for example, says, "Some poachers, tribesmen displaced from traditional occupations by drought or civil war, use primitive methods to kill elephants and transport tusks. But most use high-powered weapons and even airplanes and various sorts of poisons."[25]

What tribe these "tribesmen" are from is not clarified, whether they are Maasai, or Kikuyu, or one of the smaller ethnic minorities within the country. Later in the letter, however, "Somali tribesmen" are directly implicated, as well as people from an apparently different social group, i.e., "Somali officials." In reference to ivory tusks sold or stockpiled within Somalia, the letter says, "These tusks were not legally confiscated. Instead, they probably were poached from Kenya's nearby Tsavo National Park by well-equipped Somali tribesmen, then smuggled out of Kenya with the complicity of Somali officials."[26] The Somali president himself also apparently wrote a letter guaranteeing his government's purchase of ivory tusks from neighboring countries.[27]

The WWF does not specifically accuse the Maasai of killing wildlife for ivory, but implies that their increasing populations are a major threat to the survival of the elephants and other wildlife. Nowhere in the letter to WWF members is it mentioned that the Maasai and other pastoral and hunter-gatherer groups co-existed with elephants and other savannah wildlife over thousands of years; or that people—as well as the elephants—play an important role in creating and maintaining the contemporary savannah habitat that supports them both. Rather, they imply that the presence of the Maasai is a new phenomenon to which elephants must adapt: "One broad cause of the decrease in elephant numbers is surely the advance of human populations into *their* habitat. . . . To some extent, elephants are able to adapt to the growing presence of pastoralists such as Kenya's Maasai."[28]

Chadwick, writing for *National Geographic*, reflects a more explicit "people versus wildlife" view, with only conservation researchers and supporters exempt:

> Tusks became a sort of underground currency, like drugs, spreading webs of corruption from remote villages to urban centers throughout the world. . . . The seventies saw the price of ivory skyrocket. Suddenly, to a herder or subsistence farmer, this was no longer an animal, but a walking fortune, worth more than a dozen years of honest toil. . . . Ivory was running above a hundred dollars a pound, and officials from poorly paid park rangers to high ranking wildlife ministers had joined the poaching network. . . . Poaching gangs, including bush-wise bandits called shifta from Somalia, armed with AK-47 assault rifles, were increasingly turning their guns on tourists. This has all but shut down Meru National Park in the north.[29]

What is wrong with this description is its "snapshot" of a contemporary situation, with the camera angled in such a way as to keep the background out of focus. Everyone in the picture is considered equally guilty, regardless of the roots of their involvement, their power to prevent its happening, their public stance, or the historical basis of their claims to being where they are in relation to the wildlife and the lands. Both the average reader and the writer of the article are unfamiliar with the social history of these "wildlife habitats" and this gap in understanding is neither missed nor deemed necessary. The story, after all, is about people against nature. The people for nature, the heroes, are not the local people who lived alongside wildlife for thousands of years before their lands were appropriated by colonial and contemporary state agencies and carved into parks. The implicit heroes are Western wildlife scientists, environmental activists, and the conservation armies who rout the poachers. The indigenous people are implicated because of their proximity to the parks and the logistics of outside poachers gaining access, although it is unlikely that any "peasant farmer" sees one hundred dollars for any pound of ivory he has had a hand in obtaining. Peasants in this view are also guilty of "encroachment" on the elephants' habitat—the areas from which they were excluded not many decades ago: "Ultimately, though, people, not poachers, and growth, not guns, pose the most serious long-term threat to the elephant's survival."[30]

Ironically, Chadwick hints at another motive underlying the involvement of certain state and would-be state actors in this conservation drama: "To currency-strapped governments and revolutionaries alike [ivory poaching] was a way to pay for more firearms and supplies. In the eighties Africa had nearly ten times the weapons present a decade earlier, which encouraged more poaching than ever."[31]

Hence the "need" for increasing the power of the "good" government officials, particularly those working in the parks. As the WWF letter explained, "Antipoaching forces have been traditionally paid poorly, had insufficient training and equipment, and were understaffed. Moreover, they rarely enlisted the aid of nearby villagers by offering them economic incentives."[32]

As a result, WWF and its partners (IUCN, TRAFFIC, and WCI) began providing "emergency assistance to key African wildlife departments," improving ranger incentives and providing antipoaching equipment and training. They claim that "the only long-term security for elephants in Africa lies in strengthening national capabilities in wildlife conservation and management." Moreover, to its credit, WWF and other groups are "working to ensure that protected areas benefit from the income generated through access fees."[33] Leakey also asked the African Wildlife Federation for assistance, which AWF has provided, including airplanes and vehicles for antipoaching patrols in Tsavo National Park. Though it is a relatively small operation, AWF occasionally takes a more direct role in coercive wildlife protection by "mounting extra patrols when an emergency arises."[34]

That these aircraft, radios, vehicles, night-goggles, and other antipoaching equipment might serve another purpose besides conservation has been a secondary consideration in view of the emergency status of the quest to protect these wildlife. And yet, in an article appearing in January 1989, three months before Leakey's takeover and the subsequent high-powered, highly publicized crackdown on poaching, reports from Kenya showed how the government was already using its mandate to protect and manage resources to assert its authority where local people had resisted state controls on their activities since the colonial period.[35]

Ostensibly to settle a dispute over grazing rights between Somali and Borana groups residing in the north, the government sent in police, army helicopters, military aircraft, and the paramilitary General Service Unit. Over 600 people were detained and "large numbers" were killed in the course of the current incident. The conflict is not a new one: a 1984 clash left 2,169 people dead, and in 1987 some 200–300 Home Guards, none of them Somali, were armed "to assist in policing grazing rights and local disputes."[36]

Many of these disputes date from the time that the Kora National Reserve was created, when Somali pastoralists were excluded from access to parklands for grazing. Whole communities of Somalis were resettled onto arid lands in Borana districts. In the course of their resettlement, they were deprived of pasture and water for their livestock. Seeking these resources in the vicinity of the reserve, they are harassed by the Kenyan security forces in the same manner as illegal Somalis engaged in the smuggling trade. The present government's harassment of both the settled and nomadic Somali in the region is couched in conservation rhetoric, but dates back to the region's efforts to secede from independent Kenya in 1967. The colonial government also had difficulty establishing its authority previously. In the course of the recent clash near the Kora reserve, it was reported that "under the state of emergency, security forces have powers to act without warrant and detain without specific reason . . . clean-up operations are commonplace."[37] Moreover, the officials involved in the political security operations now form an integral part of the antipoaching operations.

The political implications of this trend in conserving Kenyan wildlife are clear. Though equipment and funds may be allocated to protect nature, they can directly or indirectly be used by the state to serve its own political ends. In this way, the commitment to preservation of wildlife for tourism and research serves both the economic and political interests of the Kenyan government, while its actual effectiveness in doing so is questionable. . . .

Conclusion

The environmental community's tacit or explicit support of coercive conservation tactics has far-reaching consequences. First, local resistance to what are perceived as illegitimate state claims and controls over local resources is likely to heighten, and may lead to violent response, sabotage of resources, and degradation.[38] Second, and most important, the outside environmental community may be weakening local resource claimants who possess less firepower than the state. While some conservationists are also "arming" local nongovernment organizations with symbolic and financial support, their ultimate goal is as much or more to influence state policy as to empower local resource users. The ethics underlying the spread of Western conservation ideologies, without considering their inevitable transformation when accepted or appropriated by developing states, require close reexamination. . . .

[A] growing body of evidence show[s] that wherever the state directly claims, controls, or manages land-based resources, state organizations and individual state actors have strong vested interests in the commercial exploitation of resources. Their control over the territories within which the resources occur, and over the people living within them, is a major aspect of their strategic territorial control. Militaries, paramilitary organizations, and state agencies often create or exacerbate resource-based conflicts by their participation in protective activities, their involvement as actors, or their coercive tactics. . . . Just as some military leaders can be co-opted to work for the sake of conservation agendas, conservation groups' resources and ideologies can be co-opted for separate military agendas. Once coercive conservation tactics are accepted, such co-optation is nearly impossible to prevent.

Failing to venture beyond the concept of thinking globally and acting locally, the writers of international conservation initiatives often brush aside or simply ignore the political implications of empowering states to coercively control access to natural resources. The militarization of resource control—whether for protection or production—leads to damaging relations with the environment, not benign ones. Whatever their approach on the ground, these conservation groups seek ultimately to change state policy and practice. Unfortunately, coercive conservation also strengthens or extends the state's military capacity—not only with the weapons of enforcement but also with new "moral" justifications to legitimate coercion in enforcing a narrowly defined "global community's" environmental will.

Notes

1. Piers Blaikie, *The Political Economy of Soil Erosion in Developing Countries* (London: Longman, 1985); Nancy Lee Peluso, *Rich Forests, Poor People: Resource Control and Resistance in Java* (Berkeley, CA: University of California Press, 1992).

2. Daniel Deudney, "Case Against Linking Environmental Degradation and National Security," *Millennium: Journal of International Studies* 19, no. 3 (1990):461–476; Jeffrey A. McNeeley, Kenton R. Miller, Walter V. Reid, Russell A. Mittermeier, and Timothy B. Wemer, *Conserving the World's Biodiversity* (Washington, DC: Worldwide Fund For Nature, 1988).

3. Deudney, "Case Against Linking."

4. Eric Wolf, *Europe and the People Without History* (Berkeley, CA: University of California Press, 1982).

5. Michael Watts, *Silent Violence: Food, Famine, and Peasantry in Northern Algeria* (Berkeley, CA: University of California Press, 1983); Ramachandra Guha, *The Unquiet*

Woods: Ecological History and Peasant Resistance in the Indian Himalaya (Berkeley, CA: University of California Press, 1990); Peluso, *Rich Forests, Poor People.*

6. Charles Tilly, "War-Making and State-Making as Organized Crime," in Peter B. Evans, Dietrich Rueschemeyer, and Theda Skocpol, eds., *Bringing the State Back In* (Cambridge: Cambridge University Press, 1985).

7. World Commission on Environment and Development, *Our Common Future* (New York: Oxford University Press, 1987); Lester Brown et al., *State of the World 1990* (New York: W. W. Norton, 1990).

8. Tilly, "War-Making and State-Making"; Migdal, *Strong Societies.*

9. W. K. Lindsay, "Integrating Parks and Pastoralists: Some Lessons from Amboseli," in David Anderson and Richard Grove, eds., *Conservation in Africa: People, Policies, and Practice* (Cambridge: Cambridge University Press, 1987), pp. 152–155.

10. David Collett, "Pastoralists and Wildlife: Image and Reality in Kenya Maasailand," in Anderson and Grove, *Conservation in Africa*, p. 138.

11. Ibid.

12. Lindsay, "Integrating Parks," pp. 153–155.

13. David Western, "Amboseli National Park: Enlisting Landowners to Conserve," *Ambio* 11, no. 5:304; Lindsay, "Integrating Parks," p. 155.

14. Western, "Amboseli National Park," p. 305; Lindsay, "Integrating Parks," p. 154.

15. Lindsay, "Integrating Parks," pp. 156–157; Agnes Kiss, *Wildlife Conservation in Kenya* (Washington, DC: World Bank, 1990), p. 72.

16. Joan N. Knowles and D. P. Collett, "Nature as Myth, Symbol, and Action: Notes Towards an Historical Understanding of Development and Conservation in Kenyan Maasailand," *Africa* 59, no. 4 (1989):452.

17. Douglas H. Chadwick, "Elephants—Out of Time, Out of Space," *National Geographic* 179, no. 5 (1991):11, 17.

18. Knowles and Collett, "Nature as Myth," p. 452.

19. Collett, "Pastoralists and Wildlife," p. 129; emphasis added.

20. Ibid., p. 144.

21. Kiss, *Wildlife Conservation*, p. 72.

22. Chadwick, "Elephants," p. 14.

23. Ibid., pp. 26–31.

24. Kiss, *Wildlife Conservation*, pp. 71, 74.

25. World Wildlife Fund, "A Program to Save the African Elephant," *World Wildlife Fund Letter*, no. 2, 1989, p. 6.

26. Ibid., pp. 8–9.

27. Ibid., p. 9.

28. Ibid., pp. 4–5; emphasis added.

29. Chadwick, "Elephants," p. 24.

30. Ibid., p. 14.

31. Ibid., p. 24.

32. World Wildlife Fund, "A Program to Save the African Elephant," *World Wildlife Fund Letter*, no. 2, 1989, p. 7.

33. Ibid., p. 10.

34. African Wildlife Foundation, "1989 Was a Very Good Year: Annual Report," *Wildlife News* 25, no. 2:3–5.33.

35. "Kenya: Crackdown on Somalis," *Africa Confidential* 30, no. 1 (1989):6–7.

36. Ibid.

37. Ibid.

38. Blaikie, *The Political Economy of Soil Erosion*; Susanna Hecht and Alexander Cockburn, *The Fate of the Forest: Developers, Destroyers, and Defenders of the Rainforest* (New York: Verso, 1989); Guha, *Unquiet Woods*; Peluso, *Rich Forests, Poor People*.

29

THE RELATIONSHIP BETWEEN CLIMATE CHANGE AND HUMAN RIGHTS

OFFICE OF THE UNITED NATIONS HIGH
COMMISSIONER FOR HUMAN RIGHTS[*]

Climate change, environmental harm and human rights

16. An increase in global average temperatures of approximately 2° C will have major, and predominantly negative, effects on ecosystems across the globe, on the goods and services they provide. Already today, climate change is among the most important drivers of ecosystem changes, along with overexploitation of resources and pollution.[15] Moreover, global warming will exacerbate the harmful effects of environmental pollution, including higher levels of ground-level ozone in urban areas. In view of such effects, which have implications for a wide range of human rights, it is relevant to discuss the relationship between human rights and the environment.

17. Principle 1 of the 1972 Declaration of the United Nations Conference on the Human Environment (the Stockholm Declaration) states that there is "a fundamental right to freedom, equality and adequate conditions of life, in an environment of a quality that permits a life of dignity and well-being." The Stockholm

[*] Excerpted from United Nations General Assembly, *Annual Report of the United Nations High Commissioner for Human Rights and Reports of the Office of the High Commissioner and the Secretary-General. Report of the Office of the United Nations High Commissioner for Human Rights on the Relationship between Climate Change and Human Rights.* UN Doc A/HRC/10/6115 January 2009. (c) United Nations, 2009. Reproduced with permission.

Declaration reflects a general recognition of the interdependence and interrelatedness of human rights and the environment.[16]

18. While the universal human rights treaties do not refer to a specific right to a safe and healthy environment, the United Nations human rights treaty bodies all recognize the intrinsic link between the environment and the realization of a range of human rights, such as the right to life, to health, to food, to water, and to housing.[17] The Convention on the Rights of the Child provides that States parties shall take appropriate measures to combat disease and malnutrition "through the provision of adequate nutritious foods and clean drinking water, taking into consideration the dangers and risks of environmental pollution."[18]

19. Equally, the Committee on Economic, Social and Cultural Rights (CESCR) has clarified that the right to adequate food requires the adoption of "appropriate economic, environmental and social policies" and that the right to health extends to its underlying determinants, including a healthy environment.[19]

Effects on specific rights

20. Whereas global warming will potentially have implications for the full range of human rights, the following subsections provide examples of rights which seem to relate most directly to climate change–related impacts identified by IPCC [Intergovernmental Panel on Climate Change].

1. The right to life

21. The right to life is explicitly protected under the International Covenant on Civil and Political Rights and the Convention on the Rights of the Child.[20] The Human Rights Committee has described the right to life as the "supreme right," "basic to all human rights," and it is a right from which no derogation is permitted even in time of public emergency.[21] Moreover, the Committee has clarified that the right to life imposes an obligation on States to take positive measures for its protection, including taking measures to reduce infant mortality, malnutrition and epidemics.[22] The Convention on the Rights of the Child explicitly links the right to life to the obligation of States "to ensure to the maximum extent possible the survival and development of the child."[23] According to the Committee on the Rights of the Child, the right to survival and development must be implemented in a holistic manner, "through the enforcement of all the other provisions of the Convention, including rights to health, adequate nutrition, social security, an adequate standard of living, a healthy and safe environment. . . ."[24]

22. A number of observed and projected effects of climate change will pose direct and indirect threats to human lives. IPCC AR4 projects with high confidence

an increase in people suffering from death, disease and injury from heat waves, floods, storms, fires and droughts. Equally, climate change will affect the right to life through an increase in hunger and malnutrition and related disorders impacting on child growth and development, cardio-respiratory morbidity and mortality related to ground-level ozone.[25]

23. Climate change will exacerbate weather-related disasters which already have devastating effects on people and their enjoyment of the right to life, particularly in the developing world. For example, an estimated 262 million people were affected by climate disasters annually from 2000 to 2004, of whom over 98 percent live in developing countries.[26] Tropical cyclone hazards, affecting approximately 120 million people annually, killed an estimated 250,000 people from 1980 to 2000.[27]

24. Protection of the right to life, generally and in the context of climate change, is closely related to measures for the fulfillment of other rights, such as those related to food, water, health and housing. With regard to weather-related natural disasters, this close interconnectedness of rights is reflected in the Inter-Agency Standing Committee (IASC) operational guidelines on human rights and natural disasters.[28]

2. The right to adequate food

25. The right to food is explicitly mentioned under the International Covenant on Economic, Social and Cultural Rights, the Convention on the Rights of the Child and the Convention on the Rights of Persons with Disabilities and implied in general provisions on an adequate standard of living of the Convention on the Elimination of All Forms of Discrimination against Women and the International Convention on the Elimination of All Forms of Racial Discrimination.[29] In addition to a right to adequate food, the International Covenant on Economic, Social and Cultural Rights also enshrines "the fundamental right of everyone to be free from hunger."[30] Elements of the right to food include the availability of adequate food (including through the possibility of feeding oneself from natural resources) and accessible to all individuals under the jurisdiction of a State. Equally, States must ensure freedom from hunger and take necessary action to alleviate hunger, even in times of natural or other disasters.[31]

26. As a consequence of climate change, the potential for food production is projected initially to increase at mid to high latitudes with an increase in global average temperature in the range of 1–3° C. However, at lower latitudes crop productivity is projected to decrease, increasing the risk of hunger and food insecurity in the poorer regions of the world.[32] According to one estimate, an additional 600 million people will face malnutrition due to climate change,[33] with a particularly negative effect on sub-Saharan Africa.[34] Poor people living in developing countries are particularly vulnerable given their disproportionate dependency on climate-sensitive resources for their food and livelihoods.[35]

27. The Special Rapporteur on the right to food has documented how extreme climate events are increasingly threatening livelihoods and food security.[36] In responding to this threat, the realization of the right to adequate food requires that special attention be given to vulnerable and disadvantaged groups, including people living in disaster-prone areas and indigenous peoples whose livelihood may be threatened.[37]

3. The right to water

28. CESCR has defined the right to water as the right of everyone to sufficient, safe, acceptable, physically accessible and affordable water for personal and domestic uses, such as drinking, food preparation and personal and household hygiene.[38] The Convention on the Elimination of All Forms of Discrimination against Women and the Convention on the Rights of Persons with Disabilities explicitly refer to access to water services in provisions on an adequate standard of living, while the Convention on the Rights of the Child refers to the provision of "clean drinking water" as part of the measures States shall take to combat disease and malnutrition.[39]

29. Loss of glaciers and reductions in snow cover are projected to increase and to negatively affect water availability for more than one-sixth of the world's population supplied by meltwater from mountain ranges. Weather extremes, such as drought and flooding, will also impact on water supplies.[40] Climate change will thus exacerbate existing stresses on water resources and compound the problem of access to safe drinking water, currently denied to an estimated 1.1 billion people globally and a major cause of morbidity and disease.[41] In this regard, climate change interacts with a range of other causes of water stress, such as population growth, environmental degradation, poor water management, poverty and inequality.[42]

30. As various studies document, the negative effects of climate change on water supply and on the effective enjoyment of the right to water can be mitigated through the adoption of appropriate measures and policies.[43]

4. The right to health

31. The right to the highest attainable standard of physical and mental health (the right to health) is most comprehensively addressed in article 12 of the International Covenant on Economic, Social and Cultural Rights and referred to in five other core international human rights treaties.[44] This right implies the enjoyment of, and equal access to, appropriate health care and, more broadly, to goods, services and conditions which enable a person to live a healthy life. Underlying determinants of health include adequate food and nutrition, housing, safe drinking water and adequate sanitation, and a healthy environment.[45] Other key elements

are the availability, accessibility (both physically and economically) and quality of health and health-care facilities, goods and services.[46]

32. Climate change is projected to affect the health status of millions of people, including through increases in malnutrition, increased diseases and injury due to extreme weather events, and an increased burden of diarrheal, cardio-respiratory and infectious diseases.[47] Global warming may also affect the spread of malaria and other vector-borne diseases in some parts of the world.[48] Overall, the negative health effects will disproportionately be felt in sub-Saharan Africa, South Asia and the Middle East. Poor health and malnutrition increase vulnerability and reduce the capacity of individuals and groups to adapt to climate change.

33. Climate change constitutes a severe additional stress to health systems worldwide, prompting the Special Rapporteur on the right to health to warn that a failure of the international community to confront the health threats posed by global warming will endanger the lives of millions of people.[49] Most at risk are those individuals and communities with a low adaptive capacity. Conversely, addressing poor health is one central aspect of reducing vulnerability to the effects of climate change.

34. Non-climate-related factors, such as education, health care, [and] public health initiatives, are critical in determining how global warming will affect the health of populations.[50] Protecting the right to health in the face of climate change will require comprehensive measures, including mitigating the adverse impacts of global warming on underlying determinants of health and giving priority to protecting vulnerable individuals and communities.

5. The right to adequate housing

35. The right to adequate housing is enshrined in several core international human rights instruments and most comprehensively under the International Covenant on Economic, Social and Cultural Rights as an element of the right to an adequate standard of living.[51] The right to adequate housing has been defined as "the right to live somewhere in security, peace and dignity."[52] Core elements of this right include security of tenure, protection against forced evictions,[53] availability of services, materials, facilities and infrastructure, affordability, habitability, accessibility, location and cultural adequacy.[54]

36. Observed and projected climate change will affect the right to adequate housing in several ways. Sea level rise and storm surges will have a direct impact on many coastal settlements.[55] In the Arctic region and in low-lying island States such impacts have already led to the relocation of peoples and communities.[56] Settlements in low-lying mega-deltas are also particularly at risk, as evidenced by the millions of people and homes affected by flooding in recent years.

37. The erosion of livelihoods, partly caused by climate change, is a main "push" factor for increasing rural to urban migration. Many will move to urban slums and

informal settlements where they are often forced to build shelters in hazardous areas.[57] Already today, an estimated 1 billion people live in urban slums on fragile hillsides or flood-prone riverbanks and face acute vulnerability to extreme climate events.[58]

38. Human rights guarantees in the context of climate change include: (a) adequate protection of housing from weather hazards (habitability of housing); (b) access to housing away from hazardous zones; (c) access to shelter and disaster preparedness in cases of displacement caused by extreme weather events; (d) protection of communities that are relocated away from hazardous zones, including protection against forced evictions without appropriate forms of legal or other protection, including adequate consultation with affected persons.[59]

6. The right to self-determination

39. The right to self-determination is a fundamental principle of international law. Common article 1, paragraph 1, of the International Covenant on Economic, Social and Cultural Rights and the International Covenant on Civil and Political Rights establishes that "all peoples have the right of self-determination," by virtue of which "they freely determine their political status and freely pursue their economic, social and cultural development."[60] Important aspects of the right to self-determination include the right of a people not to be deprived of its own means of subsistence and the obligation of a State party to promote the realization of the right to self-determination, including for people living outside its territory.[61] While the right to self-determination is a collective right held by peoples rather than individuals, its realization is an essential condition for the effective enjoyment of individual human rights.

40. Sea level rise and extreme weather events related to climate change are threatening the habitability and, in the longer term, the territorial existence of a number of low-lying island States. Equally, changes in the climate threaten to deprive indigenous peoples of their traditional territories and sources of livelihood. Either of these impacts would have implications for the right to self-determination.

41. The inundation and disappearance of small island States would have implications for the right to self-determination, as well as for the full range of human rights for which individuals depend on the State for their protection. The disappearance of a State for climate change–related reasons would give rise to a range of legal questions, including concerning the status of people inhabiting such disappearing territories and the protection afforded to them under international law (discussed further below). While there is no clear precedence to follow, it is clear that insofar as climate change poses a threat to the right of peoples to self-determination, States have a duty to take positive action, individually and jointly, to address and avert this threat. Equally, States have an obligation to take action to avert climate change impacts which threaten the cultural and social identity of indigenous peoples.

Effects on specific groups

42. The effects of climate change will be felt most acutely by those segments of the population who are already in vulnerable situations due to factors such as poverty, gender, age, minority status and disability.[62] Under international human rights law, States are legally bound to address such vulnerabilities in accordance with the principle of equality and nondiscrimination.

43. Vulnerability and impact assessments in the context of climate change largely focus on impacts on economic sectors, such as health and water, rather than on the vulnerabilities of specific segments of the population.[63] Submissions to this report and other studies indicate awareness of the need for more detailed assessments at the country level and point to some of the factors which affect individuals and communities.

44. The present section focuses on factors determining vulnerability to climate change for women, children and indigenous peoples.

1. Women

45. Women are especially exposed to climate change–related risks due to existing gender discrimination, inequality and inhibiting gender roles. It is established that women, particularly elderly women and girls, are affected more severely and are more at risk during all phases of weather-related disasters: risk preparedness, warning communication and response, social and economic impacts, recovery and reconstruction.[64] The death rate of women is markedly higher than that of men during natural disasters (often linked to reasons such as: women are more likely to be looking after children, to be wearing clothes which inhibit movement and are less likely to be able to swim). This is particularly the case in disaster-affected societies in which the socioeconomic status of women is low.[65] Women are susceptible to gender-based violence during natural disasters and during migration, and girls are more likely to drop out of school when households come under additional stress. Rural women are particularly affected by effects on agriculture and deteriorating living conditions in rural areas. Vulnerability is exacerbated by factors such as unequal rights to property, exclusion from decision-making and difficulties in accessing information and financial services.[66]

46. Studies document how crucial for successful climate change adaptation the knowledge and capacities of women are. For example, there are numerous examples of how measures to empower women and to address discriminatory practices have increased the capacity of communities to cope with extreme weather events.[67]

47. International human rights standards and principles underline the need to adequately assess and address the gender-differentiated impacts of climate change. In the context of negotiations on the United Nations Framework Convention on Climate Change, States have highlighted gender-specific vulnerability

assessments as important elements in determining adaptation options.[68] Yet, there is a general lack of accurate data disaggregated by gender in this area.

2. Children

48. Studies show that climate change will exacerbate existing health risks and undermine support structures that protect children from harm.[69] Overall, the health burden of climate change will primarily be borne by children in the developing world.[70] For example, extreme weather events and increased water stress already constitute leading causes of malnutrition and infant and child mortality and morbidity. Likewise, increased stress on livelihoods will make it more difficult for children to attend school. Girls will be particularly affected as traditional household chores, such as collecting firewood and water, require more time and energy when supplies are scarce. Moreover, like women, children have a higher mortality rate as a result of weather-related disasters.

49. As today's children and young persons will shape the world of tomorrow, children are central actors in promoting behavior change required to mitigate the effects of global warming. Children's knowledge and awareness of climate change also influence wider households and community actions.[71] Education on environmental matters among children is crucial and various initiatives at national and international levels seek to engage children and young people as actors in the climate change agenda.[72]

50. The Convention on the Rights of the Child, which enjoys near universal ratification, obliges States to take action to ensure the realization of all rights in the Convention for all children in their jurisdiction, including measures to safeguard children's right to life, survival and development through, inter alia, addressing problems of environmental pollution and degradation. Importantly, children must be recognized as active participants and stewards of natural resources in the promotion and protection of a safe and healthy environment.[73]

3. Indigenous peoples

51. Climate change, together with pollution and environmental degradation, poses a serious threat to indigenous peoples, who often live in marginal lands and fragile ecosystems which are particularly sensitive to alterations in the physical environment.[74] Climate change–related impacts have already led to the relocation of Inuit communities in polar regions and affected their traditional livelihoods. Indigenous peoples inhabiting low-lying island States face similar pressures, threatening their cultural identity, which is closely linked to their traditional lands and livelihoods.[75]

52. Indigenous peoples have been voicing their concern about the impacts of climate change on their collective human rights and their rights as distinct peoples.[76]

In particular, indigenous peoples have stressed the importance of giving them a voice in policymaking on climate change at both national and international levels and of taking into account and building upon their traditional knowledge.[77] As a study cited by the IPCC in its Fourth Assessment Report observes, "Incorporating indigenous knowledge into climate change policies can lead to the development of effective adaptation strategies that are cost-effective, participatory and sustainable."[78]

53. The United Nations Declaration on the Rights of Indigenous Peoples sets out several rights and principles of relevance to threats posed by climate change.[79] Core international human rights treaties also provide for protection of indigenous peoples, in particular with regard to the right to self-determination and rights related to culture.[80] The rights of indigenous peoples are also enshrined in [International Labour Organization] Convention No. 169 (1989) concerning Indigenous and Tribal Peoples in Independent Countries.

54. Indigenous peoples have brought several cases before national courts and regional and international human rights bodies claiming violations of human rights related to environmental issues. In 2005, a group of Inuit in the Canadian and Alaskan Arctic presented a case before the Inter-American Commission on Human Rights seeking compensation for alleged violations of their human rights resulting from climate change caused by greenhouse gas emissions from the United States of America.[81] While the Inter-American Commission deemed the case inadmissible, it drew international attention to the threats posed by climate change to indigenous peoples.

Conclusions

92. Climate change–related impacts, as set out in the assessment reports of the Intergovernmental Panel on Climate Change, have a range of implications for the effective enjoyment of human rights. The effects on human rights can be of a direct nature, such as the threat extreme weather events may pose to the right to life, but will often have an indirect and gradual effect on human rights, such as increasing stress on health systems and vulnerabilities related to climate change–induced migration.

93. The effects of climate change are already being felt by individuals and communities around the world. Particularly vulnerable are those living on the "front line" of climate change, in places where even small climatic changes can have catastrophic consequences for lives and livelihoods. Vulnerability due to geography is often compounded by a low capacity to adapt, rendering many of the poorest countries and communities particularly vulnerable to the effects of climate change.

94. Within countries, existing vulnerabilities are exacerbated by the effects of climate change. Groups such as children, women, the elderly and persons with

disabilities are often particularly vulnerable to the adverse effects of climate change on the enjoyment of their human rights. The application of a human rights approach in preventing and responding to the effects of climate change serves to empower individuals and groups, who should be perceived as active agents of change and not as passive victims.

95. Often the effects of climate change on human rights are determined by non-climatic factors, including discrimination and unequal power relationships. This underlines the importance of addressing human rights threats posed by climate change through adequate policies and measures which are coherent with overall human rights objectives. Human rights standards and principles should inform and strengthen policy measures in the area of climate change.

96. The physical impacts of global warming cannot easily be classified as human rights violations, not least because climate change–related harm often cannot clearly be attributed to acts or omissions of specific States. Yet, addressing that harm remains a critical human rights concern and obligation under international law. Hence, legal protection remains relevant as a safeguard against climate change–related risks and infringements of human rights resulting from policies and measures taken at the national level to address climate change.

97. There is a need for more detailed studies and data collection at country level in order to assess the human rights impact of climate change–related phenomena and of policies and measures adopted to address climate change. In this regard, States could usefully provide information on measures to assess and address vulnerabilities and impacts related to climate change as they affect individuals and groups, in reporting to the United Nations human rights treaty monitoring bodies and the United Nations Framework Convention on Climate Change.

98. Further study is also needed of protection mechanisms for persons who may be considered to have been displaced within or across national borders due to climate change–related events and for those populations which may be permanently displaced as a consequence of inundation of low-lying areas and island States.

99. Global warming can only be dealt with through cooperation by all members of the international community. Equally, international assistance is required to ensure sustainable development pathways in developing countries and enable them to adapt to now unavoidable climate change. International human rights law complements the United Nations Framework Convention on Climate Change by underlining that international cooperation is not only expedient but also a human rights obligation and that its central objective is the realization of human rights.

Notes

15. See Millennium Ecosystems Assessment 2005, *Ecosystems and Human Well-being*, Synthesis, pp. 67 and 79.

16. A joint seminar on human rights and the environment organized by OHCHR and UNEP in 2002 also documented a growing recognition of the connection between human rights, environmental protection, and sustainable development (see E/CN.4/2002/WP.7).

17. ILO Convention No. 169 (1989) concerning Indigenous and Tribal Peoples in Independent Countries provides for special protection of the environment of the areas which indigenous peoples occupy or otherwise use. At the regional level, the African Charter on Human and Peoples' Rights and the San Salvador Protocol to the American Convention on Human Rights recognize the right to live in a healthy or satisfactory environment. Moreover, many national constitutions refer to a right to an environment of a certain quality.

18. Convention on the Rights of the Child (CRC), art. 24, para. 2 (c).

19. Committee on Economic, Social and Cultural Rights (CESCR), general comments No. 12 (1999) on the right to adequate food (art. 11), para. 4, and No. 14 (2000) on the right to the highest attainable standard of health (art. 12), para. 4.

20. International Covenant on Civil and Political Rights (ICCPR), art. 6; CRC, art. 6.

21. Human Rights Committee, general comments No. 6 (1982) on art. 6 (Right to life), para. 1, and No. 14 (1984) on art. 6 (Right to life), para. 1.

22. Human Rights Committee, general comment No. 6, para. 5. Likewise, the Committee has asked States to provide data on pregnancy and childbirth-related deaths and gender-disaggregated data on infant mortality rates when reporting on the status of implementation of the right to life (general comment No. 28 (2000) on art. 3 (The equality of rights between men and women), para. 10).

23. CRC, art. 6, para. 2.

24. Committee on the Rights of the Child, general comment No. 7 (2006) on implementing rights in early childhood, para. 10.

25. IPCC AR4 Working Group II (WGII) Report, p. 393.

26. United Nations Development Programme (UNDP), Human Development Report 2007/2008, *Fighting climate change: Human solidarity in a divided world*, p. 8.

27. IPCC AR4 Working Group II Report, p. 317.

28. Inter-Agency Standing Committee, *Protecting Persons Affected by Natural Disasters— IASC Operational Guidelines on Human Rights and Natural Disasters*, Brooking-Bern Project on Internal Displacement, 2006.

29. International Covenant on Economic, Social and Cultural Rights (ICESCR), art. 11; CRC, art. 24 (c); Convention on the Rights of Persons with Disabilities (CRPD), art. 25 (f) and art. 28, para. 1; Convention on the Elimination of All Forms of Discrimination against Women (CEDAW), art. 14, para. 2 (h); International Convention on the Elimination of All Forms of Racial Discrimination (ICERD), art. 5 (e).

30. ICESCR, art. 11, para. 2.

31. CESCR general comment No. 12 (1999) on the right to adequate food (art. 11), para. 6.

32. IPCC AR4 Synthesis Report, p. 48.

33. UNDP Human Development Report 2006, *Beyond scarcity: Power, poverty and the global water crisis.*

34. IPCC AR4 WGII Report, p. 275.

35. IPCC AR4 WGII, p. 359. United Nations Millennium Project 2005, *Halving Hunger: It Can Be Done*, Task Force on Hunger, p. 66. Furthermore, according to the Human Rights Council Special Rapporteur on the right to food, "half of the world's hungry people . . . depend for their survival on lands which are inherently poor and which may be becoming less fertile and less productive as a result of the impacts of repeated droughts, climate change and unsustainable land use" (A/HRC/7/5, para. 51).

36. See e.g. A/HRC/7/5, para. 51; A/HRC/7/5/Add.2, paras. 11 and 15.

37. See e.g. CESCR general comment No. 12 (1999) on the right to adequate food (art. 11), para. 28.

38. CESCR general comment No. 15 (2002) on the right to water (arts. 11 and 12), para. 2. While not explicitly mentioned in ICESCR, the right is seen to be implicit in arts. 11 (adequate standard of living) and 12 (health). General comment No. 15 provides further guidance on the normative contents of the right to water and related obligations of States.

39. See CEDAW, art. 14, para. 2 (h); CRPD, art. 28, para. 2 (a); CRC, art. 24, para. 2 (c).

40. IPCC AR4 Synthesis Report, pp. 48–49.

41. Millennium Ecosystems Assessment 2005, *Ecosystems and Human Well-being*, Synthesis, p. 52.

42. According to the UNDP Human Development Report 2006, the root causes of the current water crisis lie in poor water management, poverty, and inequality, rather than in an absolute shortage of physical supply.

43. IPCC AR4 WGII Report, p. 191. UNDP Human Development Report 2006.

44. CEDAW, arts. 12 and 14, para. 2 (b); ICERD, art. 5 (e) (iv); CRC, art. 24; CRPD, arts. 16, para. 4, 22, para. 2, and 25; International Convention on the Protection of the Rights of All Migrant Workers and Members of Their Families (ICRMW), arts. 43, para. 1 (e), 45, para. 1 (c), and 70. See also ICESCR arts. 7 (b) and 10.

45. CESCR general comment No. 12, para. 8.

46. See CESCR general comment No. 12, CEDAW general recommendation No. 24 (1999) on art. 12 of the Convention (women and health); CRC general comment No. 4 (2003) on Adolescent health and development in the context of the Convention on the Rights of the Child.

47. IPCC AR4 Synthesis, p. 48.

48. Uncertainty remains about the potential impact of climate change on malaria at local and global scales because of a lack of data and the interplay of other contributing nonclimatic factors such as socioeconomic development, immunity, and drug resistance (see IPCC WGII Report, p. 404).

49. A/62/214, para. 102.

50. IPCC AR4 WGII Report, p. 12.

51. ICESCR, art. 11. See also Universal Declaration of Human Rights, art. 25, para. 1; ICERD, art. 5 (e) (iii); CEDAW, art. 14, para. 2; CRC, art. 27, para. 3; ICRMW, art. 43, para. 1 (d); CRPD, arts. 9, para. 1 (a), and 28, paras. 1 and 2 (d).

52. CESCR general comment No. 12, para. 6.

53. See CESCR general comment No. 7 (1997) on the right to adequate housing (art. 11 (1) of the Covenant): Forced evictions.

54. CESCR general comment No. 12, para. 8.

55. IPCC AR4 WGII Report, p. 333.

56. IPCC AR4 WGII Report, p. 672.

57. A/63/275, paras. 31–38.

58. UNDP Human Development Report 2007/2008, *Fighting climate change: Human solidarity in a divided world*, p. 9.

59. In this regard the Guiding Principles on Internal Displacement (E/CN.4/1998/53/Add.2, annex) provide that "at the minimum, regardless of the circumstances, and without discrimination, competent authorities shall provide internally displaced persons with and ensure safe access to: . . . basic shelter and housing" (principle 18).

60. The right to self-determination is enshrined in Articles 1 and 55 of the Charter of the United Nations and also contained in the Declaration on the Right to Development, art. 1, para. 2, and the United Nations Declaration on the Rights of Indigenous Peoples, arts. 3 and 4.

61. Human Rights Committee, general comment No. 12 (1984) on art. 1 (Right to self-determination), para. 6. See also Committee on the Elimination of Racial Discrimination (CERD), general recommendation 21 (1996) on the right to self-determination.

62. See e.g. IPCC AR4 WGII Report, p. 374.

63. National communications, submitted according to arts. 4 and 12 of UNFCCC, make frequent references to the human impacts of climate change, but generally do so in an aggregate and general manner, mentioning, for example, that people living in poverty are particularly vulnerable.

64. IPCC AR4 WGII, p. 398. See also submission by the United Nations Development Fund for Women available at: http://www2.ohchr.org/english/issues/climatechange/index.htm.

65. E. Neumayer and T. Plümper, *The Gendered Nature of Natural Disasters: The Impact of Catastrophic Events on the Gender Gap in Life Expectancy, 1981–2002*, available at http://ssrn.com/abstract=874965. As the authors conclude, based on the study of disasters in 141 countries, "[a] systematic effect on the gender gap in life expectancy is only plausible if natural disasters exacerbate previously existing patterns of discrimination that render females more vulnerable to the fatal impact of disasters" (p. 27).

66. Y. Lambrou and R. Laub, "Gender perspectives on the conventions on biodiversity, climate change and desertification," *Food and Agriculture Organization of the United Nations (FAO), Gender and Population Division*, pp. 7–8.

67. See e.g. IPCC AR4 WGII Report, p. 398; International Strategy for Disaster Reduction, *Gender Perspectives: Integrating Disaster Risk Reduction into Climate Change Adaptation. Good Practices and Lessons Learned*, UN/ISDR 2008.

68. UNFCCC, *Climate Change: Impacts, Vulnerabilities and Adaptation in Developing Countries*, 2007, p. 16.

69. UNICEF Innocenti Research Centre, *Climate Change and Children: A Human Security Challenge*, New York and Florence, 2008; UNICEF UK, *Our Climate, Our Children, Our Responsibility: The Implications of Climate Change for the World's Children*, London, 2008.

70. World Bank, *Global Monitoring Report 2008-MDGs and the Environment: Agenda for Inclusive and Sustainable Development*, p. 211.

71. UNICEF UK (see footnote 69 above), p. 29.

72. For example, UNEP and UNICEF have developed an environmental resource pack for child-friendly schools designed to empower children (see footnote 69 above, UNICEF Innocenti Research Centre, p. 28).

73. See e.g. CRC, general comment No. 4 (2003) on adolescent health and development in the context of the Convention on the Rights of the Child.

74. M. Macchi and others, *Indigenous and Traditional Peoples and Climate Change*, International Union for Conservation of Nature, 2008.

75. See e.g. report of the Special Rapporteur on the situation of human rights and fundamental freedoms of indigenous peoples, A/HRC/4/32, para. 49.

76. In April 2008, the Permanent Forum for Indigenous Issues stated that climate change "is an urgent and immediate threat to human rights" (E/C.19/2008/13, para. 23).

77. E/C.19/2008/13, para. 4. The Permanent Forum also recommended that a mechanism be put in place for the participation of indigenous peoples in climate change negotiations under UNFCCC (ibid., para. 30).

78. IPCC AR4 WGII Report, p. 865 (citing Robinson and Herbert, 2001).

79. Key provisions include the right to effective mechanisms for prevention of, and redress for, actions which have the aim or effect of dispossessing them of their lands, territories or resources (art. 8); the principle of free, prior and informed consent (art. 19), the right to the conservation and protection of the environment and indigenous lands and territories (art. 29), the right to maintain, control, protect and develop their cultural heritage and traditional knowledge and cultural expressions (art. 31).

80. See the provisions on cultural rights in ICCPR, art. 27, and ICESCR, art. 15.

81. Available at: http://inuitcircumpolar.com/files/uploads/icc-files/FINALPetitionICC .pdf.

INDEX